My wife taught me how to touch type when I was blinded in 1981.
Little did either of us know at the time of learning that I would write
Up t'th'Manor, a series of books about my time at Manor House.

This book is dedicated with heartfelt sincerity to my
Grandsons, Aaron and Jordan.

This book has been written in the same manner as
if I were talking to you in my native Cheshire
dialect. It is not in perfect English and neither
is it with perfect grammar, so please 'listen'
to my story as you read it.

Bob Weaver

Other works by the same author:

Raspberry Jam and Pickles

*A selection of short stories
about life in the 1950s.*

ISBN 978-0-9955799-0-3

A Walk in the Dark

*A two act play about a group of
blind and partially sighted people
(set in 1984), at a Centre for the
blind in southern England.*

ISBN 978-0-9955799-1-0

Up t'th'Manor
(Book One)

ISBN 978-0-9955799-2-7

Up t'th'Manor
(Book Two)

ISBN 978-0-9955799-3-4

Up t'th'Manor.

by R J Weaver

What can I say about the funeral of my Father-in-law? It was a funeral, a very sad occasion. We were going to put a good man to rest. He was about to go on his last journey to Buglawton Churchyard, less than a mile from the very land he had farmed for a large part of his lifetime. And it was raining, bitterly cold sleeting rain, by far the worst sort of weather for attending a funeral. Janet didn't get too upset by it all. All three of the sisters were built of sterner stuff. Dad wouldn't have wanted to see his daughters crying over him, and they didn't.

It was a nice service, as far as funeral services go, and I did something that day that I had never done before and haven't yet done since. We joined the small gathering of mourners huddling beneath dripping multi-coloured umbrellas beside the grave and Janet and I picked up a handful each of the cold wet earth and dropped it into the hole onto his coffin. Then it was over... We had paid our respects to a good man.

Life goes on, as the saying goes, and life had to go on for us as well. Janet was asleep in my arms that night and for the first time since I had come home, I began to think of the going back. All I wanted in the world was to be with my wife and children and never leave them again. Going back would mean there would be another four weeks to go before I could come home for good. Should I stay home... Or what? The money that they were paying me was certainly useful, but I didn't seem to be any closer to forging myself a new career. I had learned a heck of a lot about my fellow man, and woman, but not a lot about anything that might lead to a job at the end of the course. Down at the Manor they hadn't given me a particular date to return. But my Janet, my ever-wise wife, reminded me that I had made an agreement with Ian Allwood of the Manpower Services Commission to complete this course, and if I didn't then there might well be penalties to pay. We decided to spend at least one more precious day together, then decide what to do, and with that thought on my mind I drifted into sleep.

Wednesday came, and went, and before we knew it, we were into Thursday. The phone call around lunchtime spoiled everything. It was Sandra, Head of Care Staff, phoning all the way from the Manor in Torquay.

Early the following morning with a heavy heart and so full of mixed feelings that it hurt, I left my family behind and joined my brother Stuart who was going to drive me to Macclesfield Station to begin my train journey South.

1

It was a rather lonely and relatively uneventful train-ride for most of my journey south, which gave me time to think and in that thinking there were reflections on the things done and the things yet to do. There was the wedding of Ann and Cyril this coming Saturday for starters, and then there was my other friend, Royston? How would he be coping? Will he be missing me? Will any of the many people I had met so far at the Manor be missing me? A lot of them had already gone home. Mavis, Brenda, Daniel…The Welsh twins… Wandering hands William, and many others… What was I going back to? I had no way of knowing.

I was still in an extremely thoughtful state of mind when the train arrived at and then left Bristol Temple Meads. A little later a female voice distracted me from looking out of the window. I looked up to see a woman of about thirty years of age with dark shoulder length hair and wearing a long maroon coloured coat, these details were just about all that I noticed before she nervously spoke again and said: -

"Er, excuse me, but may I sit here opposite you please?"

"Yes, yes, please do." I replied hastily.

"Thank you…" She sat down and put her luggage on the seat beside her, then, removing her gloves she reached across the small table to shake my hand and continued. "You are married? The ring, I see you are wearing a ring."

Shades of my association with Fiona back in the past at the Manor sprang immediately to mind and were quickly dispelled as I confidently answered: -

Yes, and happily married thanks, you don't have to be nervous with me… er?"

"Oh! Rebecca, Rebecca Knight."

"I'm Bob, Bob Weaver, pleased to meet you Rebecca…"

"Your glasses, forgive me, but the lenses? Is there a reason for them to be so thick?"

I couldn't help but smile as I looked at her and said: - "There's nowt like a bit of straightforward talk…"

"Oh, I am sorry, forgive me please?"

"That's alright, these are the result of an accident that I had a few years ago. I normally wear a contact lens and thinner glasses but I lost them... How I lost them is a long, long story... much too long."

"My sister is blind... it's the reason I asked about your glasses. Hers are thick, or rather, were, she can't see now, so thick or thin glasses are of no use to her. Are you alright on your own or have you a fellow traveller with you? To look after you I mean?"

I didn't quite know how to respond, so I said: - "Is it so obvious that I have an eyesight problem?"

"Sorry once more, forgive me... Are you? I mean, this train is going south... There is a place on the south coast... A centre for blind people, called Manor House... Annette, my sister is there and I am going to visit her for a few days. The people at this place seem to have managed to persuade her to resume piano playing again...What? What is it? Why are you looking at me like that?"

Annette, is your sister? What a small world this is. I've met her, that's where I'm heading for, The Manor, or Manor House as it is sometimes called, in Torquay. So! Annette is your sister; she is a remarkable pianist... Has she told you about the concert the residents are organising?"

"Yes... Oh how nice to know that you know her. Unfortunately, I won't be able to be there. I would like to be but I can't. Annette stopped playing the piano about a year ago, soon after she lost her sight, but this weekend should make up for me not being able to come to your concert... I am so proud of her, I really am... There is a man called Terry? at the blind centre? He's arranged for me to accompany Annette when she's going to play a piano at a special place on Sunday afternoon. She and I are renting a hotel room for a few days. You have something called 'long weekends' during the course of your stay, don't you? Well, Annette has one beginning today at three o'clock and I have taken a few days off to be with her... Pardon me Bob, I do tend to talk a lot... would you like me to fetch us both a hot drink from the buffet car?"

And so began a friendship, that was to last way beyond my Manor days.

It seemed that Sandra had been concerned enough to arrange an early start to my journey back to the Manor so that I wouldn't get caught out in the dark. And if she hadn't done that then I might not have got to know Rebecca and a bit more about another of the many residents at the Manor, Rebecca's sister Annette.

3

We arrived at Torquay Station at around twelve thirty. It was a nice day, cool, dry and a bit blustery, which was a whole lot different than the weather back in Congleton. Rebecca had suggested that we share the cost of a taxi to complete our journey, but as we came out onto the car-park there was a sharp 'peep, peep.' I turned to Rebecca and said: -

"I don't think we're going to need a taxi Rebecca. It looks as if we've got a lift."

This was Gillian Roberts the Mobility Officer. It turned out that she had been sent to pick me up and having explained who Rebecca was related to, Gill offered to give her a lift too.

I had just spent a pleasant hour or more with this bubbly personality of a woman, so just as I was helping her to carry her luggage into the Hotel in Lisbourne Square I had a thought to set her a teaser: -

"When you meet up with Annette, ask her how a deaf man named Royston listened to her when she was playing the piano one night a couple of weeks ago. I won't say any more than that, it might spoil the surprise. Well! Goodbye for now Rebecca, it really is good to have met you."

With a final wave, I turned and went back to Gill and onwards Up t'th'Manor.

CHAPTER TWO

We were met by Sandra as we entered the Manor and she immediately took us into her office and began: -

"Welcome back Robert, sit, please. You too Gillian… Now then I am afraid that you have missed lunch altogether but…"

"I had something to eat on the train; thanks."

"Oh good, good, that should help… Now then, please accept our condolences with regard to the loss of your father-in-law and can I say that we sincerely hope that you, your wife, and your children, are adequately coping with this bereavement?"

"Yes, I think so."

"Fine. Now, it is with a certain haste that I continue by saying, that this rather unfortunate setback has somewhat interrupted the schedule we had planned for you... As you may be aware, your termination date is to be the fourteenth of December and I am afraid we cannot possibly extend the date of your leaving any further because the Centre closes for Christmas a few days later. So... to be blunt, you now have some catching up to do. Things are rather topsy- turvy. You are here when really you ought to be going home today; as most of your group are for their second, long weekend. Gillian tells me that you have begun mobility instruction, please continue, for I, and indeed, many of us consider it to be of paramount importance for your wellbeing. Now, when I informed your friend Royston earlier; about your imminent arrival, he was quite beside himself. I understand that you have been assisting him in the construction of a coffee table. So, without further ado, I would like you to leave your luggage here and unless there is a more pressing engagement, like a visit to the toilet for instance? Then might I suggest that you make your way to the wood- working section where..."

"Crikey I'm hitting the ground running, aren't I? Sorry it's just one of those sayings from up North... It means..."

"We know what it means Bob." Said Gillian.

"Oh, right then... I would like to phone home and let me wife know that I have got here, if that's alright?"

"I shall be pleased to do that for you." Said Sandra. "Now, time is short I am afraid but if you would be so kind as to indulge me, and make your way to the woodworking department. Then, you may have some free time after the three o'clock break all to yourself, and as it goes dark, I want you to be in a position, and this is important... I would like for you to be in a more co-operative frame of mind to the skills that Gillian here has to offer you, than you have been to date... It is... One fifteen. So, if you would be so kind"

"Is Royston there now?" I asked.

"Of course!"

"Right, I'd better get a move on then. I'll pick me luggage up from here after tea, then shall I? Right."

5

Now that I had arrived at the Manor it was with renewed enthusiasm that I entered the small courtyard and then on into the woodworking department, and there he was. He had his unmistakable back to me and was talking in sign language to the man in the white coat directly in front of him. Gordon had seen me enter and nodded his head by way of an acknowledgement. I felt glad in a way that he didn't give the game away… or did I?... Anyway, I stopped behind Royston, this gentle giant of a man and reached up to tap him on the shoulder. I had to do this twice before he stopped what he was doing and began to turn around, but when he did. Well! This was where I got more than I bargained for. Royston moved his head slowly as he carefully adjusted his gaze down on me and almost immediately a sparkle of recognition lit up his face, and even though he was usually a bit predictable I honestly didn't expect to get what I got… A whopping great big bear-hug. My arms were pinned to my sides and he lifted me up off my feet and then dropped me back down again, and just to round off this unusual greeting he followed up with one of his friendly pats right in the middle of my back.

After a bit more excitement and deep throated noises, Royston began to calm down. I had noticed Gordon, and others that could, taking pleasure in watching the pair of us as we started to talk in the sign language, but Royston was going too fast for me to understand him, or was this because I had been away from him and his unique language for just over a week? I don't know, but it didn't seem to matter, I got the gist of most of what he was saying. Someone had done the right thing and told Royston the reason for my hasty departure of more than a week since and he had worked and patiently waited for me to return, but there was also something else that had been kept waiting for my return. Without further ado Royston reached down beneath the bench that we were standing in front of and lifted up a bundle wrapped in sackcloth. I watched as he carefully laid it on the workbench and gently unfolded the bundle, then Gordon came up from behind me and said: -

"Do you remember sanding these before you went home? Royston wouldn't let anyone else touch them. He told me that you would finish them for him. So, how do you feel about that then? Go on take hold of them … your friend and I, and a few others no doubt, but more particularly Royston here, he wanted you and only you to get those coffee table legs to a fine finish and I'll tell you this my man, you had better do a damned fine job of smoothing them. Now then. There is not a lot of time left for today, so might I suggest that you make a start."

For a few seconds I was feeling extremely humbled and more in silence than my friend was. I was feeling honoured, bewildered and bemused and yet, there

6

was no big ceremony with Royston, other than a whopping great bear hug that is. Looking up at Royston I noticed the easy-going bland expression on his face, but there was also a twinkle in his eyes and I found myself murmuring: -

"How much of me can he see?"

"Enough to notice that you are still here." Remonstrated Gordon, and then, in a calmer voice he said: - "Go on Robert, take these and make a start on them, for Royston, Royston and... yourself; go."

I had forgotten that Gordon was still standing nearby. I had forgotten about him and almost everything else except for this gentle giant of a man. Royston had saved this job for me and only me, but what would have happened if I hadn't come back? But I was back and glad to be. I did try to look up at him once more but didn't quite manage to do it. Royston was gently folding the bare wooden objects up in the sackcloth and then he handed it carefully and purposefully towards me. I took hold of that bundle, I took hold of it and stood there for a moment longer, I just couldn't look up, so I looked to my left instead. Lying innocently on the top of the workbench, was something else. At first glance it wasn't much to look at but I could see it for what it was going to be; for there was already the beginnings of a veneered pattern laid out in the centre of the bare plywood board that was to become a much admired and beautiful coffee table top. I then turned and started to walk down the length of the room and as I walked, I found it rather difficult to swallow.

I kept myself very busy for the next hour or so, more so because there was no way that I could dare to let Royston or myself down. The work wasn't hard, I had already done most of the difficult sanding, but that had been just over a week since, in the intervening time the grain in the wood had raised a little, as it is bound to do with bare wood. I gradually worked my way down from fine sandpaper to the finest which is called flour paper, always going with the grain of the wood and all the while that I was working, I couldn't help but marvel at the quality of those four tapered coffee table legs which had been hewn out of rough wood. Of course, it should go without saying that all of this dedication to craftsmanship, was in the main, all on the part of Royston, and perhaps, his tutor as well. Whereas I had wasted my time and talents in this department so far and couldn't yet see any possibility of that situation changing, but then, I wasn't all that bothered, it felt good to be in a position to help Royston in my own small way, so that he could achieve his ambitions. The inlaid top of the table they were working on at the other end of the room, was throughout, entirely the work of Royston's hands, with only the skilled guidance of Gordon on hand to help. I can't recall even touching that table top, not until it was completely finished and lacquered, and that was going to take a few more weeks yet. In the meantime, and also by the end of that memorable session, where everyone else in the room were all busy in various stages of creating their own craftwork, be it a Jewellery box, or Chessboard, or Coffee table or whatever, I had been busily sanding the legs of Royston's coffee table and there was none more pleased than me to be doing so.

It was quite a ceremonious occasion, and it was also a tatty bit of silk, which was probably one of his wife's old scarves that he carried with him. I had finished and watched as Gordon came down to the bottom end of the room.

As he drew near, I could see the brightly coloured silk that he was holding in his hand and had a pretty good idea then, of what it was he was about to do.

Royston stood beside him as one or two of the other residents came up behind in order to watch. I stepped back and watched the ritual in silence. Gordon didn't say anything, he just picked up one coffee table leg and placed the silk at the top and let it slide to the bottom, and then he did the same with a second, then a third and finally the fourth leg, and each time the silk glided gracefully from top to bottom. I felt pleased. Yes, even proud. There was a growing delight in Royston's face as he carefully edged closer in order to see better, and there was the poker straight face of Gordon. There was no way that he was giving anything away. Not just yet anyway. A few of the residents began talking but Gordon remained silent. I studied his face as did a few of the others who could see. Now, why was he hesitating? Hadn't we just witnessed the effortless gliding of silk on beautiful smooth wood? Why was he holding back from giving his verdict? When Gordon's judgment finally came, it was only, or so it seemed, by way of a bit of prompting from a tall, dark haired Londoner whose name was Malcolm Tipper. Malcolm was a likeable character and he finished his goading by way of saying.

"Cam on Gordun... Sigh the word."

Gordon placed the fourth leg on the top of the bench and then meticulously began folding the silk up in his hands before suddenly screwing it up and smiling at the same time as he shoved it into his pocket... and then declared.

"Yes... They'll do... Go on Robert, take them to the lacquering room right now please and get the first sealing coat on them... and that, gentlemen; ought to take us conveniently up to the finishing time."

We don't very often get a chance to really and seriously study events when we are at the beginning or even part way through a situation. It's usually only when we have finished a particular event in our lives, when time has cheated us, and slipped by. It is usually only then that we are able to look back and sometimes think. "I wish I had done this or that a bit differently. If only I had thought of so and so at the time, things might have been a lot better or different." Well! I was fortunate enough to be experiencing that extremely rare and confusing feeling a short while after leaving the woodwork department that Friday afternoon, and it was more than likely due to what had happened in there. It was also just as well that this enlightenment occurred just before fate stepped in in the form of Gill Roberts. But before my meeting with Gill Roberts there was to be a meeting up with a some more of my fellow residents.

The familiarity of the magic of the Manor came back to me as I stood and watched the main hall filling to capacity with residents from every direction, and then they began to file down the narrow corridor to the right of the wide staircase toward the dining room. Ann, Big Ann from Doncaster had not seen me but I had seen her in amongst the others and a minute later I was about to sit down opposite her.

It was good to renew acquaintances with my three dining room companions. Ann, Laurie and Adrian, and after they had got over the initial surprise at my return to the Manor, Ann then brought me up to date with the details of her wedding plans.

"Oh, here's our tea and biscuits, thanks love… Laurie, help Adrian while I explain about tomorrow to Bob… Now Bob, you've got to realise that we weren't sure when you might be coming back, or if you were coming back… so… Well, Cyril and I wanted you to be a witness at our wedding tomorrow… but Terry, you know, Intake tutor? Well, he's doing it now. I asked him, day before yesterday… Sorry and all. You don't mind, do you? Not being a witness?"

"Nah, it'll be good to see the two of you getting married Ann, I'll settle for that."

Ann was all smiles and bubbly now and went on to say that as she had no parents still alive, she had asked Laurie to give her away and he had agreed. I couldn't help but look to my left at that particular moment and wonder what part Adrian was going to play in this most wonderful occasion, and sadly, I also found myself wondering what part could he play? He didn't seem all that worried, especially not after Ann reminded Adrian, Laurie and myself that he was going to the guide dog training centre on the following Monday morning, in order to get accustomed to the guide dog which was going to be allocated to him, at long last.

There was another pleasant surprise to come that afternoon. I met up with Jean of the Care Staff and she explained that we of our Intake group had had a free assessment choice for one session each day that week and that the following week, those of our Intake group could all choose two of our own assessment classes. Just as long as they were not both the same and they didn't clash with the ones that were still considered to be important to each of us.

A short while later I was walking aimlessly and deep in thought along by the front of the Manor on my own and at the start of the free period which Sandra had said I could have.

Something strange had started to happen, something which had at last begun to set my mind on a track towards a conclusion, towards a change of events or circumstances. A finality. A glimmer of the ending if you like of the tortured feelings I had suffered from ever since the accident of 1981. In short. This was probably the easing of the aftermath of a tragedy, and the beginnings of what has turned out to be my destiny. This was the starting point, and to use a sporting analogy this was where almost everything began to come together so that I could at last see the goal post instead of all the players, but the biggest midfield problem by far, was my fear of the dark. I began to mutter to myself. "If I can only get over my fear of the dark, I'll be alright, I know I will."

There were a few other residents nearby but they didn't seem to have over-heard me talking to myself, so I carried on and soon fell back into absent-mindedness once more. Eventually I found myself back at my starting point, the Porch entrance to the Manor.

I had only been on what you might call 'walkabout' for a few minutes, but it had been enough to have made a very significant difference to me and my outlook on the world, and in particular, all of that world which revolved around the Manor, and I had missed out on so much. I was beginning to realise this now, and it was a realisation which was very soon about to be emphasised even more.

On entering the main hall; I was quite surprised by the amount of people in the place. Amongst the many were Jim, Mike and Peter, they were too busy talking to notice me, but then there were the suitcases. This was no ordinary gathering of residents who might be late in going to an assessment class.

10

Elizabeth Dakin hadn't seen me and neither had Shaun. How could they? they were both completely blind. Ralph was there, Ralph the jolly Welshman. He saw and even spoke to me as I drew near. I had no idea just how bad his sight was or what the particular complaint was that he suffered from. I had never asked. Regrettably, I was distracted away from having a proper talk to Ralph, because just then, I noticed Albert, my fellow Intake companion come through to the main hall from outside, carrying two heavy looking suitcases. I could hardly believe my eyes as I excused myself from Ralph and made my way over towards Albert. He wouldn't have this much luggage if he was only going home for the weekend. Curiosity made me want to ask him what was going on, and I did. He walked over to and put the cases down beside the oblong table and then he turned to me with a deep sigh and said.

"I am doing Bob, what you should have done weeks ago... I'm going home. I've finished. I've had all the assessment classes I need and they need... The only thing which will give me back something like good sight is a corneal transplant, and the only trade I know is bricklaying, there's nothing like that here, so they're letting me go... This isn't a sudden decision you know. The rest of our team knew at the beginning of this week, aye, even Royston knows. I couldn't let you know, could I? Didn't expect to see you again. I thought you'd learned a bit of sense at last, but no... Here you are... Anyroad! None of my business anymore. If ever it was. Soon I'll be shut of this place and I can make a start on sorting my compensation out, which is something you might have been ahead of me in doing... Well! I suppose this will have to be our goodbye... Here... I'm offering you my hand. Shake on it and I'll say no more but wish you all the best for the future. That done. I'd best go and say goodbye to Mike, Jim and Peter and then get my ticket out of this place."

Albert left his luggage behind and I watched him make his slow, unaided way towards the three others of our Intake group. If I had just understood Albert, I had very little time left to dwell on what he had said, for I now had to say my goodbye's to Elizabeth and to Shaun and also Ralph, Jim, Peter and Mike.

I went over towards the easy going, pleasant lady with the artificial eyes. Elizabeth was dressed in a long black woollen coat and her dark hair hung down her back, she was holding a long white cane in her hands and leaned on it slightly as she began to talk to the bearded man in front of her. That same bearded man who I knew to be one of the mobility officers, had just come across the hall from Shaun, who was now on his own next to the huge disused grey stone fireplace. I changed course and went over to Shaun and said who I was and that I was sorry to see him go. He didn't move his head or his body. He was almost completely surrounded by suitcases, the most important one of

11

which, he was holding in his arms. This was the black case containing his accordion. He did speak though. I looked down on the shiny bald head and listened to his soft Irish voice as he said.

"I'm not going for good. Some kind people will be arranging it for me to come back in time for the concert… whenever it is."

This pleased me and I told him so, but Shaun was a man of few words and he said no more than what he had said. I asked him what he meant by his last bit but he had gone thoughtfully silent. A few awkward seconds later I turned and looked back towards Elizabeth. She was now on her own; so, excusing myself from Shaun I went over to her. There may be time in the future for me to be able to have a longer conversation with Shaun, but as for Elizabeth. I somehow knew that this would be the last I would ever see of her.

She was sad to be leaving the Manor and told me so, once we had both got over the initial awkwardness. We talked for a short while, mainly about the way she had confided in me that early morning of so long ago in the Den. This had been when she had told me about her worsening eye condition a year or so previous, when she had already lost the sight in one eye and was about to permanently lose her sight in the other eye, because of a rare form of cancer. But, just like that time before when she had confided in me, here she was once more, putting on a brave face to hide her emotions, but not doing a very good job of it; I have to say. I didn't wish to see her break down. I knew she didn't really want to leave the Manor; Elizabeth had made a lot of friends while she had been here and it was going to be hard for her to let go of all that. I offered to give her my address so that we might keep in touch when all of this was over, but it surprised me when she turned her sightless eyes in the general direction of myself and said.

"Oh goodness no. No that wouldn't do. It will never work. No, I don't think for one moment that it would. I remember a woman called Mavis. She was here up until a few weeks ago. You might have known her?"

"Yes," I said quietly. "I knew Mavis..."

"Did you? Oh good!... Well. Just before she left, I offered to keep in touch with her and do you know what she told me? she told me that it would never work out and that there would always be more important things to do than to keep in touch with companions from the Manor. And do you know what? I believe that she was right. It is a sad fact. She really was correct in what she said, and now I am doing the same to everyone that I know. It really is the only way..."

Another small piece of the jigsaw of destiny was about to fall into place by way of what Elizabeth's parting words were about to tell.

She carried on talking after only a brief hesitation and waved her white cane towards where she had detected me to be, and said. "This cane has been a Godsend. I really don't know how I ever managed without one of these... I can't help but wonder why you are so hesitant to use one... Oh! Say it is none of my business, I am sorry... Where was I...? I've learned how to type. I have also learned a little about pottery and an awful lot about daily living skills over in the bungalow, but best of all, was learning how to use a cane... I've been talking to Shirley and we both think you should use one. This cane is the best thing that could have happened to me since I lost my eyesight. I am far more confident and once I find my way around the landmarks of my home town, I will be a lot more independent than I used to be and I won't be trapped between four walls like I used to be..."

Her voice had begun to quiver and shake as she and I realised that her time left was short. Elizabeth was trying her best to be brave, and dignified. She just wanted to quietly get away from the Manor with the least possible fuss. At first, I couldn't quite understand why there hadn't been at least a small crowd of people there in the hall to see her off. After all, she was a very popular woman and very much liked by a lot of people. But now I began to understand. Now was the time that I ought to offer her as un-emotional a farewell that I could manage to in order to save her feelings. This woman had already said her goodbyes and I was upsetting the only way in which she could cope with leaving this place, but even here, Elizabeth helped me, she helped both of us when she stepped forward and defied Manor rules by using her cane indoors and as she did so and left my side, her shaky voice came back to me as she quietly said.

"Go to the den Bob, and make yourself a brew..."

She had called me Bob. Whereas before, she had always called me Robert... This plucked at a few heart strings I don't mind admitting... I did go... but not before taking one last look at Elizabeth and at the half dozen or so residents dotted around the hall who were all about to leave the Manor, I still hadn't had a chance to talk to them but I somehow knew that Peter, Jim, and Mike, would be coming back, but they were out of focus to my eyes now. So, with a sad heart, I turned my back on them all and went to the den.

13

It was while I was in the den, about half an hour or so later, that another, very significant piece, of the jigsaw of destiny was about to be fitted into place.

I was visited in my solitude by a woman of medium height dressed all in black... even to her large and floppy black felt hat. But she was also carrying something white. This was Gill Roberts. Her opening words were.

"Aha! So, this is where you are."

I think it was from that moment on that my attitude towards mobility really began to change. After all that I had put this woman through. I must have really astonished her there and then by my new found willingness to begin to learn how to use one of those white canes. And so it was; that I went with her.

There were a few sad seconds, on my part, when we entered the main hall from the side of the stairs entrance. Looking around the empty hall I murmured sadly. "They've gone... Albert... Elizabeth, and Shaun and Ralph... Jim, Peter and Mike… They've all gone..."

"Come on." Said Gillian. "Don't go and lose your bounciness now. You just have to accept that people come and go, they're leaving the Manor every week. How do you think we go on when we've been doing this sort of work for years? Come along, don't go getting broody on me now. That's better..."

A few minutes later, we were outside the Manor in the gathering gloom of a chilly November evening; beneath a cloudy and darkening sky. Almost gone were the sad thoughts following the departure of some of my fellow residents as I found to my concern that I had to concentrate on what I was now doing.

The cane she had brought into the den with her was now in my hands and I can honestly say that nothing of our surroundings, not the onset of evening or what I was at long last doing worried or bothered me in the slightest. I was doing what I should have been doing a long while since but had never really had the courage or willingness to do. Almost unbeknown to me at the time, a pattern in a jigsaw was beginning to emerge. As I walked along the tarmac at the front of that ancient building and swung the white cane from side to side in the recognised fashion. I really did, and for the first time begin to find the task to be less of an embarrassment and even comfortable to accomplish. I knew I was safe here within the Manor grounds and because of the cane in my hand I felt even safer in the gathering darkness of night, albeit for a short while before darkness did fall and I then had to put a greater reliance in the astonishing abilities of the cane.

That little exercise didn't last all that long but it was enough. Gill seemed to be pleased when she left me back at the Porch entrance. She gave me a little confidence talk and then went off with the cane, but before she had walked a few paces; she hesitated, turned around and came back towards me to push the cane back into my hands, and then; with a swish of dark clothing she turned away once more and disappeared into the night.

What with arriving here and all that had happened so far. If I was thinking all of that had been rather frenetic, then the next few hours were going to prove to be even more so.

Not many seconds after the departure of Gillian; there was a faint sound of bells ringing that signalled the end of another day at the Manor and the start of the weekend. I remained in the porch watching my fellow residents as they came and then went through into main hall, and then, in the company of Big Ann and a few other people that I knew, we followed the stragglers.

After the evening meal there was something of a seemingly chaotic hour or so in the main hall, where; first of all, I had been thinking that Royston had gone home for the weekend, but no. Here he was, about to depart with his new friend Sid, along with half a dozen others who were going to a rifle shooting match.

A short while later, it was pleasing to see a group of seven men readying themselves for a night on the town. Within this group there was Jack and his shadow; Ian. And, Christopher Hills. Now here was something really good happening. Christopher. This partially sighted giant of a man with Spina Bifida; at last being accepted by the Manor residents. Three of the remaining four men were staff members and these were, Terry, the Intake tutor... Blind Brian from the engineering department and his workshop companion Steven... And then, the amazing reason for this gathering, Cyril Thompson. The opening of the large old oak door over on my left proved to be a slight distraction for me, as Les Freeman of Freeman's taxi service came in and said.

"Party of seven for a Stag night outing."

CHAPTER THREE

About an hour later, at around eight, I was sitting on a bench talking to Samantha and Denise and had just finished telling them about my return journey back here, when I noticed a small group of women beginning to gather beside the oblong table at the base of the stairs, then, Jenny and Beryl of the care staff came in through the big old oak doors; they had their coats on but didn't remove them. These two were not coming on duty, but going out with the now sizeable; and slightly noisy; group of women who were about to be joined by the star of the show. I explained what was going on.

"It looks as if this is going to be a hen party for Ann by the looks of it. Here she comes, she's on the balcony and, coming down the stairs now."

Ann was smartly dressed in dark trousers and a dark top, she gave me a smile and then they were off, off for a night on the town by the looks of it.

A short while later the girls, Denise and Samantha, went off to the Lounge while I went to phone home.

Just before the painful parting that night, there came the sounds of the grand piano being played. Putting the phone back I followed the beautiful sounds as they reverberated from the Lounge and through into the main hall. Sure enough, just as I had suspected; there was Annette, with an enthusiastic group around her.

Annette's piano playing was so unique it just had to be her, and just to add to the pleasure, standing beside the grand piano was her sister Rebecca. Sad thoughts of my loved one's back home were quickly dissolved as I and quite a few others listened to and then ended up talking for a while to Annette and her sister. Rebecca went on to say how welcome she had been made by everyone at the Manor. I mentioned something about it having been a bit of a chaotic day and the shy person of Annette turned her sightless eyes towards me and said: -

"You have had a dizzy day then Bob, at least, I mean, I mean that's what I call it, when I have one, it has been a bit like that for us today, hasn't it Becky? What with the change in the date and everything else… I, I wonder, if I dare mention about the piano, it is quite remarkable but it is ever so slightly out of tune and it would be encouraging for it to be in better order for the concert… Is Barry still with us?"

"No." I replied. "He went just before you finished playing. What change of date?"

"Oh, that is a shame, I just thought a request for it to be tuned; might be better coming from Barry, he is the maestro after all."

"Perhaps you might get a chance to talk to him tomorrow sis," Said Rebecca. "Come on big sister let's get you ready, you look tired and a taxi is coming for us in ten minutes."

"But?"

"But what?" Said Annette. "Oh! you mean the date change. The date change of the concert. It is rather fortuitous as it happens Bob, at least for Rebecca and I that is, because it means she can come after all, and on Sunday, instead of Saturday. The staff have some problems for Saturday, so, it was agreed to move the event to Sunday the twenty fifth instead."

The Lounge gradually emptied. Five minutes later I was on my own. I stayed for another ten minutes or so before finally deciding to go for it. 'It,' was the germ of what must seem here to have been a totally idiotic idea, but it was something, a thought perhaps.

The bay window area of the lounge was where I had deposited the white cane shortly before going in for tea that night. The cane was still there, now to collect my suitcase from the Care Staff office, and then.

I was standing in the porch entrance the cane was extended and I was about to step into the abyss of a really dark looking night. My heart and my confidence were both sinking fast but my heart wasn't racing as it might have been.

I was, for the moment, all alone. There was hardly any wind and everything was Friday night eerily silent. Just then the old oak door behind me creaked on its iron hinges shedding the light from behind onto the stone slabbed floor of the Porch.

Then began the tap tapping sound of a cane which merged with the person wielding it as he tilted is head on one side to look at me. Barry stopped what he had just started with his cane and said in astonishment.

"Well if it isn't Bob... And what do you know, if he hasn't gone and got himself a cane of his very own. About bloody time too... Now don't try and hide it. I've got bad eyes but I've seen it, I've seen it... Where're you heading for Bob? Down to the Lodge? If you are, I'll come with you. Come on, let's go down there together, I won't interfere. This is the second time I've done this journey tonight. Hey! Wasn't Annette good at the piano?"

And so it was, that I didn't have to complete that, not so terrifying journey to the Lodge that night on my own after all. Anyway, between us we covered the quarter mile journey to the Lodge side by side with me on the inside and he on the kerbside, where he insisted that he wanted to be. This was so that he could cheat, a bit.

Barry's 'cheating' consisted of, not moving the cane from side to side so as to detect what was in front of him, but running the cane along the edge of the path and hovering over the gutter so that he could follow the kerb instead of having to do as I was doing. There didn't seem much sense in this practice because every time we came to a street light, and there weren't all that many, but when we did and I found it easier to see what was going on, I couldn't help but notice the awkwardness with which Barry negotiated his way around those street lamps. I got an explanation from him at the last one, which was just a few yards away from the Lodge gates. But just before that, there was also the telephone junction box. This too was situated at the edge of the footpath just like the street lamps were, and yet this obstacle didn't seem to present as much of a problem to Barry as I thought it should have; because there was nothing to light it up. Had I been on the outside I might very well have had a few problems. But not Barry. He encountered it when I hadn't even been aware of its presence, he pushed me up against the high stone wall so that we could both get past the obstacle together, then we carried on. Of course, I had seen this dark green junction box many times on my daylight travels up and down Middle Lincombe Road, so I soon realised what the obstacle must have been. We stopped beneath the last street lamp though and I was curious enough by then to want to know why he struggled so much when there was a light above him to help. I asked the question, but I didn't get an immediate reply. He seemed to be thoughtfully silent for a few seconds before he began, by saying.

"By heck you've certainly changed a lot in a short space of time Bob... Gill Roberts must have worked bloody hard on you this afternoon. Unlike you, these street lights are a real pain for me. I can travel a hell of a lot better in pitch darkness. I know it may sound daft to you but I can, I don't like these street lights at all and they don't help me one bit... Light coming from above us, like this is, is at the wrong angle for the likes of me. In fact, I'll go as far as to say as it bloody well near blinds me. Bloody crackers isn't it? I mean, you seen to be better when you get near a street light and I am worse. Anyway, now do you understand?"

I was beginning to. With Barry's, statement I was only just beginning to really understand what he must be going through. We all had an eyesight problem of one sort or another, I had mine and he had his and so did Royston and all the others. I thought that I had understood Barry's and other people's problems with their eyes, but no. I hadn't understood at all. Not until now that is, and even here, I was only just beginning to. We didn't linger too long beneath that white street lamp. A short while later we were standing at the dimly lit front door of the Lodge and Barry was pressing the buttons which would allow us entrance.

In my room later that night, I carried the desk over to the bed and took out some paper and a pen and sat on the edge of the bed so as to write the following.

Friday 16th of November. It's just as if an enormous burden has been lifted from my shoulders. I came down to the Lodge tonight with Barry and I've done it with a cane and without hurting myself and I can't believe how I've done it, or even why. But really, I do know why. It was just like after the accident in 1981. I had to get better then. I had to fight against all of those injuries which were inflicted on me by a thoughtless God, or a careless guardian angel. Or more to the point. A stupid young executive in a black sports ear. An idiot in a hurry to get to a meeting he probably never got to. No, I had to do it. I had to get better. Not just for myself but more so for my family. But I have only been able to come so far and no further in all of this time, but now, now I have some help in getting further. I have just been using the symbol of the blind. I am not blind, but somehow. For use in the dark, using a white cane doesn't seem to bother me now.

CHAPTER FOUR

I awakened the following morning and daylight was streaming in through the window, reaching for my glasses my hand caught the edge of the writing table, then I realised that I had gone to sleep with my clothes on.

Downstairs there were a few people about and the time was just after eight o'clock. Plenty of time for a shower or a good bath. If there was a bathroom free... and, if there was some hot water left.

Ann wasn't at the breakfast table in the Manor that morning, and as far as I could tell; Cyril wasn't in there either. The dining room was sparsely occupied as was usual at weekends. Laurie was also absent, but Adrian was there. I had brought him with me from the main hall. He was quiet, but his attitude altered dramatically the moment we arrived at our table and I mentioned his forth-coming acquisition of a guide dog. I only said. "You're going to the guide dog training centre on Monday aren't you Adrian?"

His face lit up and his unseeing eyes seemed to sparkle with life as he began to stammer. "Y, yes dollar doll dollar's her name... I've been to, I am going, tomorrow, I'm going to get her and then... and, and then I might be going home but I don't know... my own dog... my dog. Will you help me when I get there?"

I said yes. It didn't seem to matter. I didn't think that anything would matter once Adrian got his hands around the dog he so badly needed. Whether it was me or anyone else with him, nothing else would interest him when he finally got the dog that he could call his own.

After breakfast I escorted Adrian out into the hall and this was where we met up with Royston. He seemed very pleased with himself and he had something to show me. What he ceremoniously handed to me was a small, four-inch square card with concentric black circles on it, and slap bang in the centre was a small, neat, hole. There were a few other holes around the edges but that hole in the centre was what he had wanted to show me. He stood proudly looking down at me and at the same time that I was congratulating him on his rifle shooting, I couldn't help but wonder. Just how the hell did he do it? A guy with all his problems and nothing seemed to get him down. He just got on with it all and achieved the best that hc could. I could only marvel at this gentle giant.

I was perhaps, just a bit to engrossed in making sure that Royston knew how delighted I was. So much so that I failed to see that Adrian had begun to wander off and it was only when he encountered the edge of the oblong table and let out a mournful cry, that my attention was drawn back to him once more. I then found that I didn't know what to do with him. Ann's wedding was to be held at Torbay Registry Office at two o'clock. Adrian was to be one of the principal guests, as were all of us on Ann's table. Should I look after Adrian until then? I didn't really mind, but rescue was shortly on hand in the shape of Beryl of the Care Staff.

The three of us, Royston, Adrian and myself, were sitting on a wooden bench near the lounge entrance, when I became aware of Beryl walking towards us. She leaned a perfumed body over me and spoke softly to Adrian. He got to his feet and silently went with her. This left me and Royston on our own.

Watching Adrian's departure, I signed and told Royston that Adrian was getting a guide dog on the following Monday. He in turn, told me that Albert had finished and gone home the previous day. I already knew this and while he was signing, my mind flashed back as I looked down the length of the hall and tried to visualise Elizabeth Dakin, Albert, Shaun, and all the others.

A short while later we were outside the entrance to the Manor and were about to help a couple of the members of staff to decorate a shiny dark blue car with pure white silk ribbons. One of the men was John from the dining room staff and the other was the ginger haired Mobility Officer, Andrew. It had been John who had come out of the dining room; seen us and then asked if we would like to help.

That pleasant task took about twenty minutes or so and as we stood back to admire our handiwork; with the sun shining brightly, a gentle breeze ruffled the V shaped white ribbon draped over the bonnet, and then came the familiar sting in the middle of my back, which caught me completely off guard. Then I noticed Royston do the same thing to John, whilst Andrew had just nimbly stepped to one side.

We were inside the main hall along with other residents, waiting for the gong to sound, and then, after lunch, we would be getting ready for the wedding. And yet there was still no sign of Cyril or Ann. The staff at the Manor were about to be doing them proud though. I caught a glimpse of the room where the wedding buffet was going to be held, which was through the door in the corner to the left of the lounge entrance, there were white coated staff in there busily filling white covered table tops with loads of food, and then one of the women came over and closed the door.

There must only have been about thirty or so residents at the Manor that day and it seemed as if all of us were going to the wedding because there was a heck of a lot of activity soon after lunch, as everyone made haste to get ready for the big occasion. My suit was down at the Lodge, so I quickly realised that I would have to make even more haste to get there and back in time. I left Royston with the instruction to go upstairs and get himself smartened up ready for Ann's wedding.

It didn't take long to get changed and to get back up to the Manor again, and just in time to see the Bride come down the wide stairs. Perfect timing. Ann was dressed in a dark blue; short skirted suit, with a dark blue hat and a white rose in her lapel. There were a couple of other women with her and they were dressed more or less the same, but their skirts were significantly longer. When Ann got to the bottom of the stairs she stopped for a brief moment and pulled her clothes down around her bulging buttocks and her chubby legs. The only thing which marred her appearance was the dark eyepatch over her left eye. Other than that, she was a real stunning beauty. I got a chance just then to talk to her and asked if everything was going as planned. She smiled and whispered.

"Yeh, fine, everything's fine…Wow, did I have a skinful last night. I could do with a hair of the dog right now, Phew…" And then, Ann straightened herself up and in a louder, excitable voice she said. "Well… Come on folks, this is mine and Cyril's big day."

One posh dark blue car with white ribbons dancing in the bright sunlight. Terry; our Intake tutor in the back with the Bride and John from the dining room staff wearing a smart black suit in the driving seat, in the lead position, with three more cars and two mini buses full of Manor people behind, all going down the drive in a convoy. I was with Royston and a lot of others in the white bus. Someone in a grey suit boarded the blue bus. That man looked to be about the same build as Cyril.

When we arrived at the very large and very grand old Colonial style building, we drove around to the back and pulled up inside a courtyard and we were led over towards some old and blackened weather-beaten yellow sandstone steps. The rest of the exterior of the rear of that building looked to be in much the same aged condition, but inside, told a completely different story.

22

We made our way along a wide corridor for some distance and came out onto a wide open, bright and airy space which echoed to our footsteps. Then we started to climb an extremely ornate marble staircase. Not only were the steps marble but the bannister rails and the supporting columns were as well. It was a sort of two-tone brown marble with black and white streaks in it. Everything was beautifully carved and I wanted to stop and admire it, but we were now in a hurry and I was already lagging behind.

At the top of the stairs there was a very wide red carpeted balcony; with the same sort of marble railing on one side overlooking the wide and echoing expanse below. There were quite a few corridors on this level and they all seemed to spread out in different directions. The one we wanted was near enough opposite the top of the stairs. I followed in the wake of all the others.

Cyril and Ann had, to the best of my knowledge met for the first time that day at the foot of the marble staircase, which was now behind me. I continued to look around at the ornate gracefulness of the interior of this beautiful building, and for once I hadn't got the responsibility of escort for anyone, because that had all been taken care of by the abundant Care Staff who were in attendance.

The blissfully happy couple were somewhere up ahead. I had caught a glimpse of them together arm in arm, and having seen that sight, I knew that everything was going to be alright for them. This was their day and nothing was spoiling it for them, not even the weather. And especially not this splendid building. I suppose, best of all though, was Laurie. His appearance certainly boosted the atmosphere of the occasion. Back at the Manor I thought that I had caught a glimpse of him, or someone very much like him getting into one of the cars. It had been the pure white hair which had been the giveaway, but that was all that I had seen. There was a treat in store for everyone now though.

We were all assembled at the top of the marble staircase and after the apparent hurry to get us up here I couldn't quite grasp why we were now waiting. We were tightly packed on that landing and not many of us could see what was going on. I looked around the side of Royston to look at the bride once more. Ann was in no hurry; she was savouring every moment of this special day. I had noticed her trying to have a look around as she had begun to ascend the marble staircase while all that Cyril could do at the time was to concentrate on putting one foot in front of the other; as Ann automatically guided him along. We were now at the top of the stairs and waiting, but waiting for what? Just then a Scottish voice called for attention, this was Laurie's familiar voice.

"Arre ye rready? Awee we goo."

I couldn't see him yet but I heard the gentle tuneless wailing of the bagpipes as Laurie pumped up the bellows and then began to play a faultless wedding march for Ann and for Cyril, and the blind and not so blind and all the rest of our group very hastily organised ourselves and started to walk towards the large opening ahead and the room beyond which awaited us. Samantha and Denise were close by. Terry, our Intake tutor, was now acting as escort for Royston as we slowly edged forwards through a huge doorway which could easily have accommodated a full-grown horse, and on the inside, on our left was the splendid sight of Laurie in full highland dress of a dark green tartan. I wonder, now; as then, just how many of our group from the Manor had experienced that same nerve tingling shudder as we walked past him. Terry left Royston with me and then he took the Bride and Groom and escorted them through into another room over on the far-left hand side, while we were left to sort ourselves out with the row upon row of seats laid out in readiness. The pipes faded to a gentle wailing and then went silent. After a few minutes some of the group began to get a bit curious, mainly because they thought the wedding ceremony was actually happening in the other room. I knew what was going on. I had been to a few of these registry weddings before and could remember that Ann and Cyril would be in there, presumably with the Registrar; who would be preparing them for the ceremony itself.

And then I saw Shirley. She was wearing a long white dress and if I didn't know any different, I might have thought that this was her wedding. Just then the door over on our left opened. Ann, Cyril and Terry came out, the room went silent as Ann cried out.

"Alright folks, that was just the prep talk that's all. Now we can get on with the real thing… Now then! Is everyone ready?"

Royston was on my left and Shirley was sitting on my right with the Londoner, Malcolm Tipper, between me and her and we were more or less in the centre of the seating arrangements.

It was at the end of the proceedings, after Ann and Cyril had confirmed their vows, when Ann took it upon herself to do something compulsive. As she turned to look and smile radiantly at all of us in the audience, she removed the rose from the lapel of her jacket, then she turned away and threw the rose over her shoulder, and who caught it? With a shriek of delight Shirley got to her feet clutching the rose in her hands and began to look around.

Malcolm turned to her and said. "Don't look at me love; I'm married!"

I looked up at Shirley and said. "Me too." Shirley sat down mockingly deflated, but smiling all the same...

Malcolm turned back to me and said: - "It won't last, marry in haste and repent at leisure is what my old Ma would say."

Oh, but their marriage did last. One thing that Ann and Cyril insisted on before they finally left the Manor; was to give us theirs and also to have the addresses of Laurie, Adrian and myself so that she could at least send us, and receive Christmas cards to keep in touch with each other. This arrangement went on for twenty-one years, until Cyril passed away, and then I somehow lost contact with Ann. 'Big Ann' Big Ann from Doncaster. But I digress.

...and then we filed outside the large room to gather on the balcony for a rather noisy, if not fairly well organised photography session. Soon, that also was over and this was around about an hour after our arrival. We began to find our way downstairs and out of the building and then, having climbed aboard our transport once more we headed for the wedding reception back at the Manor.

There were quite a few of us, more interested in the food than anything else when we arrived back at the Manor. We were allowed access to the room to the left of the entrance to the lounge, only after an enforced assembly in the main hall, where we endured a few speeches and a lecture, as well as a lot of jollification, and another photography session as well.

I spent a lot of my time in the buffet room just sitting in a corner and gorging myself on the plate full of food on my knee, and when I had done that I went over to the tables and helped myself to more. Only when I had eaten my fill and things began to calm down did I venture to involve myself in the ceremonies once more. Ann was in a buoyant mood, as was her husband. They were walking around the room talking to their guests and having a good time of it as well. Eventually, they came to a stop in front of me. I stood up, and this was when I noticed both of them wore gold rings. Ann said something to Cyril which prompted him to say the following: -

"I've come a long way I think, since this fellow found me in the gardens..."

He then reached out to shake my hand. Without another word the happy couple moved on to another guest, leaving me with a glass of fizzy mineral water in my hand and contemplating on that fine epitaph to a fine day, yes, Cyril had come a long way... and so had I.

25

Around about the time that we should have been going to the dining room for our evening meal, but we didn't, there was Royston and myself, along with quite a few others, all sitting in the lounge whilst trying to relax after the celebrations. Ann and Cyril had departed about fifteen minutes earlier. There was to be no marital bliss within the humble confines of the Manor that night for these two. They had gone and booked themselves into a nearby Hotel instead.

Malcolm was somewhere in the lounge. He broke through my sleepy thoughts as I heard him say.

"I've just thought of something. I wouldn't like to be in Cyril's shoes if Ann wants him to carry her over the threshold. I'll tell you what… he'll be too knackered for nuptial bliss or anything else if he tries that one, I mean, she's big, and he's only about half as… hey! I wonder how he'll…"

A woman's voice, nearby, stopped the Londoner in mid-sentence, this was Shirley. "Alright Malcolm. That is enough thank you."

I was slouching in one of the easy chairs. It was difficult for me to concentrate, all I wanted to do now was to sleep. I somehow managed to open a bleary eye and with a bit of an effort looked across the space to where Royston was sitting. He was squinting and gazing contentedly at all those around him, I shifted my gaze before his could meet mine and looked at Malcolm and one or two of the others nearby, then I looked back to a Diabetic man named Gareth again. I quickly became at least halfway alert because there seemed to be something odd about Gareth's behaviour. I had noticed that he had been quiet for most of the afternoon, but then, so had Adrian as well as a few others I knew. I might have been concerned for Gareth earlier on if it hadn't been for the fact that my assistance wasn't needed by anyone. There had been more than enough of the Staff, both at the wedding ceremony and afterwards to take care of all of those who needed help, so people like myself were allowed complete freedom to look after no one else but ourselves. Nevertheless, I couldn't help but wonder where Adrian might have got to. He had come into the lounge with us after downing more food at the wedding reception than I thought he was capable of eating. Begrudgingly, I pulled myself up in the chair to look around. I needn't have bothered, except for my own peace of mind. Adrian was fast asleep in a high-backed chair similar to mine just behind me. I was awake by now, which was probably just as well. I sat down again and looked back at Gareth. He was more restless than before, and even Royston seemed to sense that something was wrong, but Malcolm was quicker than any of us. He was already on his way towards the door and within the next few seconds I noticed Shirley becoming involved as she floated towards Gareth, or at least she seemed to be floating, in that long white dress of hers.

It didn't take Malcolm long to find someone, but even at that, he and Beryl from the Care Staff were too late to prevent Gareth from being sick.

A few seconds more and I was trying my very best not to look at the mess on the polished wooden planks of the floor. Beryl had been at the tables in the other room and had been serving us with food during the wedding reception. We had all left her and others to clean up after us when we came into the lounge, and now, here she was. She quickly whipped off her white apron and used it to clean Gareth. As she did so she began to scold him. Not harshly, but she was scolding him all the same. She was saying: -

"Of all the people...! Of all the people to go and make themselves sick, it has to be you that goes and does something this silly... I don't know, I really don't... You do realise what this means don't you? Come along, can you stand up? You'll have to, you know that don't you? Come on we'll have to get you up to your room. I may even have to call out a doctor. Oh! Which one of you men are fit enough to help me get Gareth upstairs?"

On our way out I glanced down at Adrian, he was dead to the world, fast asleep and dreaming about nothing better than his guide dog. (I hoped.)

Meanwhile, we had to get Gareth to his room for some little-known reason to me, other than it had something to do with his diabetes.

I didn't say anything as we climbed the wide stairs and then onto and around the balcony, but I couldn't help thinking to myself and wondering why we weren't taking Gareth to the Care Staff office, which was a lot closer and easier to get to from the Lounge, but here we were, near enough carrying this medium built thirty year old, all the way to his room, which was just a short distance past Mike's bedroom. Beryl was leading the way and opened the bedroom door ahead of us. As gently as we could, both Malcolm and I lay the moaning man down on top of the nearest one of three beds in that room, as indicated by Beryl. Fortunately the man had finished with his biliousness, and we watched as Beryl hastily rummaged in the bedside locker to take out a small shiny metal case and started to open it on the bed, then Malcolm and I were asked to leave by another member of staff, as she hastily entered the room.

Having been dismissed without actually being able to find out what was going on, we made our way back downstairs and headed for the lounge once more.

When we entered the lounge, I think we both got a surprise. The mess had been cleaned up and nearly everyone else were fast asleep in their chairs, even Royston was snoozing. I spoke softly to Malcolm. "That little upset hasn't upset many has it? What should we do now?"

"Join them." Said Malcolm quietly.

That night was the only night that I can remember when there weren't any sausages for supper, but what we had was far better than cold sausages, we had the leftovers from the wedding reception. There was absolutely nothing wrong with the food, despite some concern over the way it had made Gareth ill. It certainly didn't do me or Royston, or even Malcolm any harm.

A bit later that night I went to the alcove in the main hall to phone home and explain to Janet; my reason for phoning from the Manor, and what I had been doing, then afterwards, I went back to the lounge to join Royston for a few more games of cards. Gareth came and put in an appearance around about ten o'clock, this settled our minds to the fact that he was now, seemingly alright once more. Then, at about ten thirty, I went with Royston to the bottom of the stairs and left him to climb them on his own. I watched him go up and then watched him come back down again. He stopped on the bottom step and indicated that he wanted to say something to me. Lifting up my hand a fair bit higher than I usually had to do, Royston signed.

"ME AND SID ARE GOING TO NAVY BASE TOMORROW WILL YOU COME"

I pulled my hand away thinking he had finished signing, but he pulled it back and continued with a plea which was emphasised by the look on his face.

"PLEASE"

I hesitated only briefly before replying. "YES" Not realising that the Navy base he was referring to was the one at Plymouth and that it was going to cost me more than ten quid for the outing. Still, it was to be a worthwhile outing on the morrow. As for tonight, I still had to get to my bed at the Lodge.

28

There was no one for company that night. The dull ache was still there as I looked out at the darkness from the well-lit sanctuary of the Porch.

I had felt very reluctant at first, even hoping against hope that my companion of the previous evening, Barry, or someone else might make an appearance from the interior of the Manor, but no. Then there was another thought… If I stayed here a while longer a taxi might come up the long drive to bring back some late-night revellers, and then I could get the driver to take me down to the Lodge and I wouldn't even mind paying for the service… but then... It had been just after ten thirty when I had been told by Jean of the Care Staff to: -

"Now take that cane out of your trouser belt Robert, and go on down to the lodge. If you take your time about it, you can do it, I know you can."

That little prep talk was just before we left the quietness of the main hall. Jean had then accompanied me down the short passage and through the other door to where I was now standing; under the light and on the outside of the Porch entrance. Jean had then gone back to her duties while I was trying to pluck up my courage and also calculate just how long ago had she locked that big wooden door in the archway behind and to my right.

"Well! Here I go."

There were no vehicles, either coming up Middle Lincombe Road, or going down it that night, and there was no one else on the footpath. Just me and the cane. All around me was in darkness with only the white lights of the spaced-out streetlights to guide me. There was not even a Moon, just the gentle moaning of the wind on my lonely, slow journey… Oh! And then there was a sneeze… not mine, someone else's. It was when I was about halfway towards the Lodge. I stopped and called out, "Who's there?" but no one answered. Reasoning that it might be someone in their front garden behind the hedges on the other side of the road, I moved on, eventually arriving at the gates to the Lodge and made my way nervously but cautiously up the dark drive.

CHAPTER FIVE

Sunday 18th November. What a mixed up and busy day this one was going to turn out to be. I wasn't going to bother travelling all the way back to the Manor for breakfast. I even told Barry so, over an early morning cup of coffee.

There were a few other Lodge residents in the Den, which had surprised me a bit when I had arrived a few minutes earlier. Some were doing their washing at the far end, a few more were cooking what appeared to be quite substantial breakfasts for themselves. I caught the tantalising smell of bacon cooking on the stove as I said to Barry. "Nah, I anna going up yet awhile. When they've have finished with the cooker, I think I'll do myself a bit of bacon and egg and a nice slice of fried bread..."

"Oh, and what about Royston then?" Remarked Barry abruptly. "When you came in here last night you told me you were going out with him today... Have you forgotten?"

A few minutes later I was having to force myself to leave behind the mouthwatering prospect of a self-cooked breakfast at the Lodge, for a hasty journey and the always, not so appetising Sunday breakfast back at the Manor. But food was food and then. I couldn't keep Royston waiting, could I?

He was waiting. Both Royston and Sid were waiting in the Porch entrance to the Manor. Sid explained that there was a bus leaving the sea front at nine o'clock and we might just make it down to the harbour if we left at that moment in order to walk there. I couldn't help but let out a sigh, which, for the most part went unnoticed. Leaving like this meant that I was going to miss breakfast inside the Manor as well as what I had already missed down at the lodge. I was beginning to wish I had got up a lot earlier that morning. But then, just as we began to move off, there came the sound of a vehicle approaching and the white minibus came into view. Pulling up in front of us, Terry got out and said: -

"Good morning gentlemen... Is it today that you and Royston are going to Plymouth? And Bob also... This is good, between the two of you I am sure Royston will be alright..."

"Yes, sorry about this Terry." Interrupted Sid. "but if we don't get a move on, we might miss our bus down at the harbour."

"Get in and I'll drop you off. I just have to take this inside... won't be many seconds."

Royston was delighted. I had no sooner signed, to tell him of Terry's offer of a lift when he went carefully over to the minibus with a smile on his face and climbed into the passenger seat. This left Sid and myself to climb aboard behind him.

Terry came and got into the driver's seat beside Royston and then turned to us and said: - "Well someone's highly delighted to be getting a lift... you are from Cheshire Bob... Tell me. Do Cheshire cats grin as much as Royston is doing? Something tells me he's enjoying this day out already... Now, take good care of him like I asked... you both know his language, so feed him with it... What I mean is, don't isolate him from your conversations. Right! Let's get going."

We had just gone past the Manor gates when Terry started to tell us something of his busy day ahead. "Do you remember the Sunday outings to the Bell Inn Bob? You ought to, the times you and Royston went."

"Yes, it was great, it's an amazing place."

"It is going to be even more amazing today. Grace and her husband acquired a piano a few weeks ago. A piano, very kindly donated, by a former resident... Richard Hurst, now there was a character... a marvellous multi-talented musician, but rather eccentric and he could be moody. He wasn't a total up until the time of his leaving, about three months ago, but, alas, it won't be all that long before he is. Not a lot to be done I'm afraid. Anyway, one of our current residents will be making splendid use of his gift today. I'm picking her up after dropping the three of you off..."

"Try and get these two and yourself back before it goes too dark Sidney."

Those were Terry's parting words. We watched him drive off and then we went to wait for our bus.

Sid was a pleasant, barrel shaped man whose native County we were in. A Devon man through and through. He had been a Petty Officer in the Navy until an accident cost him his right eye. His one and only irritating habit was his constant comments on his glass eye. At least twice during our descent of that hill from the Manor to the Harbour, he either prodded his artificial eye with his finger nail or made some gruesome comment on it. I think, in some peculiar

31

way, he rather liked having an artificial eye. This was going to be an eventful outing.

There were two girls who were our only companions on that bus journey. They didn't like the way that Sid was playing with their emotions either. I had brought my cane with me but it was hidden from view, tucked inside my trouser belt beneath my jacket. Royston had a cane. His was red and white striped with a crook handle but it was folded and inside a plastic carrier bag which he had on his knee. I think he was just as embarrassed as I was when it came to handling this necessary item. I can't remember Sid ever sporting a white cane. To the best of my knowledge he didn't have, or appear to need mobility lessons, but then, looks can be deceiving.

The day was dry and reasonably sunny to start with but not that bright as to cause us all that many problems in getting about in the daylight. Hence, all of this led the two young girls who were our travelling companions to the apparent visual deception that we were just three normal blokes out for the day, and I hasten to add. We were normal. Except for the fact that we hadn't got one decent pair of eyes between the three of us. The two girls started giggling when Sid pointed out that the tall man sitting between us on that back seat was deaf and nearly blind. They didn't believe Sid and started to make fun of him. They soon stopped their goading though when Sid did his party trick with his finger nail. In fact, one of them screamed so loud that the bus driver very nearly pulled to an unscheduled halt. I thought that the girls would avoid us like the plague after that outburst but instead of keeping away they came closer and wanted to know more about us and where we were from. They very quickly seemed to develop a rather macabre fascination for our afflictions, which soon became a bit off putting for me. I think Sid got more than he had bargained for, and as for Royston? All he could do was to sit and look more and more perplexed. The girls calmed down a bit and they eventually got off the bus somewhere inland about halfway to our destination. I think we were all glad to see them go.

We got to the part of Plymouth that Sid wanted to show us, by way of a taxi from the bus depot and when we arrived at this particular part of town, we found that it wasn't all that far off lunchtime. I wanted to encourage Sid to look for a Café but I had begun to get the impression that there wasn't one. In fact! There didn't seem to be anything. We were in an area which was nothing short of total destruction. All around us, as far as I could see, there were nothing but ruins and partly demolished buildings and rubble strewn ground. The only reasonably clear areas were the roads and footpaths. I couldn't understand why Sid had brought us here to this desolate spot, and by the look on the face of the taxi driver I wouldn't have been surprised if he had been thinking the same; when he dropped us off in the middle of this weird place. Thankfully, I very soon discovered that Sid was familiar with the area and for that I was grateful, as much for myself as for Royston's sake, because Sid proved to be an extremely good and useful guide that day. I don't think we would have seen or done half of what we did if it hadn't been for Sid

I couldn't restrain myself for much longer before I glanced around once more and then turned to speak to Sid. "Why've we come here Sid? This place looks as if it's been hit by a bomb. What are all these ruins?"

"What were they you mean... This was once a flourishing part of Plymouth. One of the oldest in fact... They say it was poor sanitation... houses crammed together. Clear them all out, knock their homes down and you end up with all of this. I used to play here when I was a lad...This fait-accompli was on the cards then. I could tell you about my Grandparents...But enough of the history lesson for now. It looks like Royston's getting a bit impatient waiting for us to make a move. Let me tell him a bit about where we are and then we'll get on our way. I only wanted to see how far they'd got... Wish I hadn't bothered now. It's at least a year since I was last here."

A short while later Royston and I were following Sid as he led us through the derelict landscape. All three of us had to be careful. Most of the rubble was contained where the houses once stood but some of it had spilled onto the footpaths and some of the walls of the partly demolished properties didn't look all that safe. There were no signs to warn us not to be here, at least none that I could see.

We found a Café, eventually, in a slightly more built up area, although even here there were all the signs of neglect and dilapidation, which accompanies the 'forced exodus,' as Sid put it, of the local population. The Café was a small white building with a low beamed entrance and a bow fronted window with flaking white paint. It was the sort of building you might glance at, then walk on by, and not think it was a Café. We went inside, Royston had a few problems due to his height and the low sagging beams supporting the dark nicotine stained ceiling, but he was alright once I had sat him down at the nearest one of the five tables. I too had some problems to begin with, but this was due to the dim interior and the strange surroundings. As for Sid? well, he had been here a few times in the past but I don't think even he expected the area and this Café to be in the state it was in. We had come to this particular destination on an almost direct route from the derelict area where the taxi had dropped us off. The drop off point had been at a crossroads and all of the buildings on that same crossroads had been demolished, leaving a vast panorama of open space littered with the after effects of rubble clearing. We had found it easier to walk along the, devoid of all traffic road; as Sid headed in the general direction of an unusually strange smell, it seemed to be the smell of burning oil mixed in with the salty smell of the sea and it gradually got stronger and stronger until we had come at last to more of a built-up area, and this Café. Opposite the Café, on the other side of the road, was a high steel net fence with barbed wire running along the top, which seemed to stretch all the way into the far distance parallel with the litter strewn road. The only thing I had seen on the other side of the fence was a vast open space dotted with buildings and then a few grey shapes which I understood to be ships. Then there was the dark grey sea and sky beyond that.

A few of the buildings on the Café side of the road had been knocked down and there were even more red brick and whitewashed buildings in that long row which were derelict or boarded up. Near enough the entire visible area was in severe decline and desperately short of a human presence, but that Café interior told an entirely different story though. The food was excellent, and the coffee was good and strong. I don't normally like strong tasting coffee but that was good and I've not yet tasted better. We each paid our own way which had sensibly been decided and agreed on at the outset of our journey.

There were fishing nets and oilskin clothing as well as items too numerous to mention of a nautical theme, all of which adorned the low interior white-washed walls, or else hung from the sagging ceiling beams. The walls too seemed to be bulging under the weight, but in reality, it was the age of the place which caused the buckling. There were only two other diners. Two men in Navy uniform sitting near to the entrance. Their caps were on the polished dark table top and Sid had greeted them both with a highly respectful, "Good Morning Sir... Good Morning Sir." when we entered the place. I think Sid would have liked to salute them as well, but quickly changed his mind. I left them talking to each other while I took Royston to a suitable table near the bow fronted window; where it was a bit brighter.

The man who served us was a rugged, lean and leathery faced individual who gave the impression that he had served long hard years in the galley of many a tough old ship. I had just finished signing to Royston to tell him what was on the menu when our host came to take our order. He gave me a searching; curious sort of look when I let go of Royston's hand, and then I hastily explained where we were from and what I had been doing, before the man could get the wrong idea. The smile of understanding that lit up his dark leathery face was quite a relief.

We were about halfway through eating our meal of Plaice, Chips and Mushy peas, when the two navy men got up to leave, which made Sid get to his feet and almost stand to attention. I was observing and reflecting on Sid's actions when Royston reached for my hand and signed: -

"ARE WE GOING"

"I signed back a simple "NO" and told Sid to sit down.

We carried on eating the delicious meal and then we paid up and all three of us hesitated before heading off once more. The wind outside was now getting stronger. We had been made aware of this fact quite a few times during our meal, when the outer door would open and other rugged looking individuals came inside. They seemed to be mostly made up of the local and very much depleted residential part of the community and we three fair skinned residents from the Manor in Torquay must have looked very much out of place, but for all of that, we were made and felt extremely, and yet soberly welcome.

 I buttoned up my jacket once we were outside on the near deserted street and indicated to Royston to do the same with his jacket. Sid pulled the hood of his large light blue anorak over his head and we set off once more. Sid led the way for a while and at one point we crossed over the road and walked along parallel with the high steel fence. Then Sid decided to drop to the rear for a while and shortly after this he pulled us to a stop. We were just a little way away from of a group of uniformed men standing beside a small wooden hut near to and on the other side of the fence. They were guarding a gate entrance. Sid's voice was full of suppressed alarm when he beckoned me to stop where I was. My first thought was that he was about to play one of his practical jokes on us, and I was right. But he caught me out just the same.

"Hey Bob! You had better stop for a moment. That bulge beneath your jacket at the back might be mistaken for a stick of dynamite. They've had a lot of trouble with the IRA in these parts you know, and Royston as well. They're bound to ask what's he got in that carrier bag? And as for me? I could be hiding half a hundred-weight of explosives beneath this anorak. What about this bulge? Not my belly. This! It's only a camera. Just a simple ordinary camera but to these people it's very much like a weapon... What do you think the response from these men might be if I try and take so much as one simple photograph? Is he a spy! Or what? Going back to my size. I mean. I may not be as well-endowed as I appear to be. Think about it! Those men up ahead won't stand for any nonsense you know. They are the type who shoot first and ask questions later. What do you think we should do eh?"

"Cross over the road and get the hell out of here." I said nervously

Sid had got me pretty well wound up by now and he knew it. I looked at the innocent face of Royston, blithely waiting by and even leaning on the fence. I wanted to pull him away, and quick. But it seemed a shame to alarm him. There he was, patiently and silently waiting for the signal for us to move on. He seemed to be totally oblivious to the knowledge that we might get shot at any moment. But of course. It was only my over-reacting imagination and Sid's exuberant nature both working overtime, and confusing reality for a few moments.

Instead of crossing over the road as I had suggested we ought to do. I became even more anxious when Sid started to walk on the same side of the road towards the men and the even stronger smell of burning oil which I could now see was coming from the funnel of a dark grey ship. Sid had made sure that I would follow by way of taking Royston's arm and leading him along. I walked in the litter strewn gutter watching warily as we got ever closer. And then the veil of anxiety was suddenly and infuriatingly lifted from me; when Sid arrived within speaking distance from the group of armed men and called out to them through the fence. He was more than cheerful enough, which seemed to alleviate the risk of animosity. And the armed men, although on their guard seemed to accept him and us for what we were. All of Sid's talk had been nothing but a wind-up and I had fallen for it.

After a few pleasantries exchanged through the fence we set off once more and thankfully, as far as I was concerned, we left the armed Navy men behind. A few yards further on, Sid began to smile and laughed as he said.

"I've been coming here ever since I was a mere lad. I had you going there... You really fell for that one Bob."

After a while the wire fencing and the derelict area began to be left behind us as we approached a more habitable area where there were more buildings, and more people. A lot of them, I could tell, were tourists like us. The presence of uniformed or armed Navy personnel were now apparent only by their absence. We eventually made our way along a sloping path towards what looked like a lighthouse. but it wasn't all that tall, only about fifty foot. It had red and white painted bands around the inward sloping smooth, round walls. There did seem to be a light of some sort at the top but I couldn't focus clearly on it. Sid took a couple of pictures of me and Royston, with the tower in the background. He took a few more photographs when we reached other prominent landmarks along the coastline and quite a lot more when we reached the huge ship's

36

anchor perched on a large concrete slab overlooking the sea. The anchor was of the traditional twin pronged shape and was painted white. I have often mentioned that Royston is a tall man. Gentle giant and all that. But, once he had seen it and he then made his way enthusiastically up to this great iron anchor, even he seemed dwarfed by the huge size. In fact, one of the prongs swept out and upwards almost twice as high as Royston, and as for the central column. That seemed to have been higher than a house and no way could any one man wrap his arms around it and touch his fingers on the other side, yes… it was that big.

"H.M.S. Ark Royal…" This was the legend on the brass plate that Sid read out to us, and then he continued. "…The aircraft carrier, the first one. Chopped up now I should imagine, and turned into nothing but dog food cans and razor blades. A bit of a sad ending for something so great and noble... Here! stand still you two, this should be a good shot if I can get it all in."

Sid took a lot of pictures that day and he eventually gave me some. The one he took of Royston and myself standing beneath that fifty-ton lump of Navy nostalgia, was, by far, the best one though and is still one of my treasured possessions.

Any outing was a special outing for Royston, and this one was no exception. I had already realised that this outing was the reason why Royston hadn't gone home for a long weekend like the rest of our Intake had. Looking at my friend now, it seemed he had made the right choice. The day had become very windy and rather cold, but this hadn't bothered us all that much. I had been far too engrossed in all that Sid's local knowledge could bestow on us, and besides. Even though Sid seemed to be a lot more competent than I was in the sign language, we both shared, and were kept busy enough with the task of telling Royston as much as we could about what was going on.

The cliffs were not cliffs in that area. Not the ones I saw anyway. These were more like grassy hillocks which rolled down towards the sea, and on the way met up with several large areas of grey blue smooth rocks, which disappeared into the equally grey blue sea. Somewhere around about mid-afternoon though, Royston began complaining about his feet hurting. Our tour came to an abrupt end as we had to find somewhere for a rest instead. This rest area turned out to be another Café.

Royston soon adopted an easy going, couldn't care less attitude as he sat in the grubby little dark blue and white Café. With his shoes off and his feet up on the narrow window sill, there was little danger of him contaminating it with sweaty socks. The risk, as it seemed, came from the other direction. At least three of the small panes of glass in the window were either cracked or broken. There weren't many other people inside the Café, but then, I wasn't all that surprised. I half expected a man, or a woman, in a greasy apron and puffing away on a fag, to come through the door on the other side of this dismal and square room with a low ceiling. It wasn't a man, or a woman. It was a young, quiet natured girl who eventually came to serve us. She was smartly dressed, with her hair tied up and her cotton apron was pure white. Appearances, can, be deceptive. After half an hour or so of sitting and talking, eating cake and sipping two or three cups of good hot tea apiece, it was decided that we should be finding a toilet before heading back.

The toilets were cleaner than I had expected and smelled of the same pine disinfectant as that used in the Manor and at America lodge. The apparent lack of comforts of that Café had been so misleading that Sid and I no longer thought as we had done on our arrival. The feeling of guilt at judging the place too harshly made me leave a bigger tip than I could afford to leave. I think Sid felt the same way as I did. He took a close look at the coins in the saucer on the bare wooden table top and put some of his own in with it. We were helping Royston up on his feet as Sid looked at me and said, quietly.

"I've doubled yours. Looks as if they need it."

Royston's feet had recovered a little but they would have hurt even more by the time we got back to the Manor if Sid had had his humorous way. And just to make matters worse, the wind and the darkening skies had brought a drizzly rain with them. At first, I couldn't be sure if Sid was having me on or what, when he suggested that we should make our way back to the derelict area. Now, that was a long way off, and even without the dark clouds above, and the rain, I knew that it would be very near naturally dark by the time we arrived back at our starting point. I stumbled over my words in alarm at his proposal.

"What! You can't, you can't be serious. There'll be no streetlamps whatsoever in that area, and there's the rubble to contend with..."

We were standing outside the Café when I said this to Sid. The smile on his face was sufficient to tell me that I had been caught out once again. Looking at Royston I could tell that he was becoming anxious. Or was this my anxicty rubbing off on him? I couldn't easily shrug off the kind of fear of the dark that had built up inside me over the previous few years. Even in the presence of someone who supposedly knew the area. Anyway, after a rather anxious few minutes of walking, we found a taxi, which was not all that far from the Café we had just vacated.

The bus journey to Torquay seemed to be very long and slow. None of us seemed to want to talk so we just sat back, exhausted after such a lot of walking and we allowed the warmth of the interior and the bus itself to safely cocoon us on our journey back.

When we eventually arrived in the town of our destination, it was raining harder than the place we had left behind and it was unanimously decided that we should have a taxi from Torquay harbour back to the Manor. I don't know about Royston or Sid, but my share of the taxi fare just about cleaned me out.

We were just in time for the evening meal, or so we thought, and we quickly joined the thirty or so residents, waiting in the brightly lit main hall for the gong to announce teatime. However, we had got it the wrong way around. They weren't waiting to go in to the dining room. They had all just come out. Anyway. We all three agreed that we had had a good day out. We had missed our evening meal but what did that matter, we headed for the Den instead, where we could dry out and fill up.

After eating his share of a large can of baked beans on toast, Royston hadn't moved from the spot where he had sat down, and for nearly half an hour his severely restricted vision had carefully studied most of the other residents as they came into the room. I knew only too well why he was doing this. He was constantly looking for someone who knew his language, who he could speak to and tell them about his day out in Plymouth. And then! In walked Terry. Royston nearly fell off his chair and amidst the consternation I heard Terry saying: -

"Whoa! Steady on there don't get so excited…" Terry then looked at me and Sid and reached for Royston's hand whilst saying. "I've just heard that you are back, and safely I see. Thought I would look in on you before I set off home. Have you had a good day out the three of you?"

There was hardly any need for a reply from Sid or myself.

Apart from the sounds of a washing machine and two men and a woman talking at the other end of the room, the Den went quiet as Royston and Terry talked in sign language to each other. Sid and I watched in fascination.

As dedicated as he was to his job, home was where he should be. Terry had been out and about for all of that Sunday, as he was most Sunday's, but he should really not be here now. On the following day he would be having a fresh group of Intakes to deal with. I had wanted to ask how the pub outing and the piano recital with Annette and Rebecca had gone, but the opportunity didn't present itself. It was Sid who broke up the near silent conversation when he said: -

"Beats me how you do it Terry, or why… All this voluntary work I mean."

"Look around you Sidney… What you see is what I do and why I do it… Alas though. I really must go."

Then Terry stopped the sign language with a gesture I had seen before but still didn't quite understand. Royston sat back in his chair with such a contented look on his face and it was truly heart-warming to witness. Terry looked at Sid and then at me and said just three words before leaving us. "Well done lads."

Unfortunately, during the next ten minutes or so, no one of any significance came into the Den and the inevitable look of disappointment on Royston's face made me turn to Sid and say. "What we need is a few good games of cards."

"What I need," Responded Sid. "Is a couple of beers. I know Royston will be keen... How about you?"

"Pass."

"Come on Bob you can't give in that easily... Haven't we enjoyed each other's company all day? Get your coat on and come with us! I'll tell you what... A couple pints apiece of good strong ale will do us a world of good. Come on what do you say?"

"Nah... I'll pass for tonight Sid... Sorry..."

I didn't want to be convinced and have to go out with Sid and Royston that night. I didn't want to have to explain that I had got very little money left. Or that. If I went out at all, in the dark... It would be imperative that I should be able to keep my wits about me in case anything went wrong.

I was only just beginning to come to terms with my problems with the dark and I knew that a visit to the local and the journey back would not be one of the best ways to tackle those problems. After two or three minutes of unsuccessful persuasion I stood and watched with just a hint of remorse as my two companions of the day departed through the ever-open doorway of the Den.

A number of other residents were in the Den and three young men caught my attention. They were down at the Laundry end trying to work the machines. Two of them were blind and were dependent on the third young man to help them. I watched for a few moments and then decided that I ought to be heading back to America Lodge. There were some notes to make and there was also a pile of washing that had to be done, and no one was going to do that for me.

I was just coming out into the hall by the side of the stairs, when I noticed the back of a woman in a pure white and fluffy cardigan and a long flowing pink skirt. She was bending down and doing something with the ornate wooden frame of the brass gong. I soon realised who she was and was about to leave the scene, hopefully unnoticed. No such luck. Shirley turned around to see who had just come through the door, adjusted her glasses and saw me.

"Oh!" She cried out. "Oh, I was just coming to look for you. Your friend Royston... He and Sidney told me just now that you were in the den... I'm afraid I've just had a rather unfortunate brush with the dinner gong... It was rather clumsy of me but never mind. I, I... How would you like to come... Oh, this is rather awkward please forgive me for blabbering on... Meeting you like this I mean oh bother... there, done it...Oh I hope I haven't torn it, where was I? You see, no one else wants to come with me and I do so want to go... Did I say where? I, I have even ordered a taxi cab. It will be here in a little while... I am sorry... I realise that I am a little forceful at times and this must seem to be one of those times, but when I found out that you were here, I mean, I have been looking for you all day long and, and here you are. Please say you'll come with me Bob."

I didn't want to, but curiosity compelled me to want to find out, 'where?' I had had a busy day, out there with Sid and Royston, my legs ached and I was tired. Royston and Sid had gone to the pub now by all accounts. I could have gone with them, So, why should I wish to go out with Shirley. Just me and her? I am sure that her motives were pure. Even more so, now that I can look back. But it didn't half feel unusual at the time. I began to think up all sorts of reasons in an attempt to get out of going with her, but I was still curious to find out where the destination was and what we would be doing once we got there, but time was fast running out and she had counteracted me so far. She even beat me to it when I suddenly remembered my nightly ritual of phoning home.

41

"Do it now." She said. "Come along. Over to the alcove we shall go together and you can phone your home from there. If the taxi comes in the meantime... I can ask it to wait."

I couldn't help but smile at what she had just said. It wasn't what she meant to say but I could just picture Shirley standing outside the porch entrance, in front of the taxi and asking 'it' to wait. That smile was my downfall however, because no sooner had the thought entered my head, than she took this to be my sign of submission and then I was quickly whisked off through the gap at the base of the stairs and the oblong table. Then we went past the two young ladies sitting on the bench, and inside the alcove we went, both of us. I hardly had time to acknowledge the gentle smile and the wave from Samantha as we shot past her and Denise. At least Shirley had the decency to leave me alone while I talked to my wife and children back home.

I could hear her hovering about outside the alcove. For obvious reasons I couldn't quite hear what she was saying, or even who Shirley was talking to but I had a pretty good idea that it might be Samantha and Denise.

I could have gone out with the lads that night. I could have gone for a drink with Sid and Royston, but I had turned them down and here I was, about to find out that it was to be an outing to a Church and that it was to be a Christmas Carol concert that I would be participating in on that Sunday evening in the company of Shirley, Samantha and Denise. And... Malcolm Tipper. Just how she had convinced these two to come along I'll never know, but she had. And as for when she collared Malcolm? Well, what can be said. Except that I felt sorry for him.

In all innocence. Malcolm had just come from the lounge opposite the alcove, and was negotiating his way towards the stairs, when Shirley instantly shot off at an angle to intercept him.

A few minutes later, there were five of us, outside the Manor, in the dark, climbing aboard the taxi. I had to remove the cane from my trouser belt in order to get in, and as I did so I was given a curious look from Samantha. Her face and long fair hair were bathed in the soft light of the interior. The taxi driver closed the door on us and then we were all distracted from our personal thoughts for a few seconds because Shirley was giggling with excitement at having captured us in so short a space of time. She stopped, momentarily though as we were rolling down the drive away from the Manor, when Malcolm insisted, that Shirley should pay the taxi fare out and back.

42

"Only kidding Shirley… don't worry, any of you; consider this my treat."

I don't know whereabouts the Church was that we eventually ended up at. I do have a vague recollection though, that it was somewhere not too far from the town of Torquay itself. This was mainly because it didn't seem to take us all that long to get there.

On the way. Apart from wondering again, just how the heck Shirley managed to persuade us to go with her! Apart from that, I also found myself being sandwiched in the back of the taxi, between Samantha and the door. Denise and Malcolm were squashed up in the corner on my right. Shirley's face suddenly peered at us from the gloom of the interior of the taxi and from between the two front seats.

"It's a pre-Christmas Carol concert we're going to." She said. 'Aaand... It is being recorded as well. Now then! I am not all that sure, I mean, I can't be absolutely positive... but, I do believe it is being organised by the BBC no less. Yes! I do hope that you are all in good voice tonight. Do you know... I simply cannot understand why so many residents did not wish to come with us tonight. I tried so hard to get others to come, but they just couldn't or wouldn't. Never mind, you four are here, the others just do not know what they might be missing do they? I mean. Can you imagine. We may even hear ourselves on the radio or we may even be on the television at Christmastide. Oh, I am just so excited. Aren't you all?"

"Thrilled… Absolutely thrilled." Responded Malcolm. Completely undaunted, Shirley's face disappeared and she began talking excitedly to the driver. I turned as best I could and whispered to Samantha.

"Why did I agree to this?"

"Indeed." Said Samantha quietly.

I had quite naturally been thinking that the darkness would be a great hazard to me when we arrived at our destination, because that would be when I would have to get out of the taxi and face the old peril once more. In the dim interior in the back of the taxi I tried to make out the expressions on the faces of my travelling companions. Denise's was blindly bland and she sat as perfectly still as a moving vehicle would allow her to. Malcolm's face was a bit different; he was fidgeting uncomfortably with being squashed up against the far door. I tried to look at the face of Samantha, which should have been easier than looking at the other two, after all, she was sitting next to me, but on my right and too close for me to focus on her with my good left eye. The taxi was warm and constricting, and it was impossible to get comfortable. It was probably just as well that it proved to be a short journey, under these circumstances.

CHAPTER SIX

We arrived at the extremely well-lit Church and the floodlit area all around it, and also the many people as well. I began to relax as my initial fears of the dark and what I might have to do out there began to melt away. Even from inside the taxi I could tell that, although this wasn't going to be all that easy. It certainly wasn't going to be all that difficult either. I found myself speaking my thoughts. "All these people! Maybe one or two of them might help me get you all inside." Perhaps, I shouldn't have said it. I don't know, because just as Shirley got out of the front seat, Samantha reached for the door and shoved it open, saying.

"Go on. When we want your help, we'll ask for it. Go, before Shirl' starts."

Malcolm was getting out on the other side of the taxi, and almost immediately I could hear that Shirley, and someone else had arrived there as well. I heard her saying.

"Come on Malcolm. Do hurry. I don't know how much time we have to get inside. Can you others manage? I do hope that you can. Come along... Oh! Hello... Oh... Pardon? Oh yes, yes please. If you don't mind. Yes, Yes. We are all from Manor House in Torquay. How astute of you to notice. Oh, that would be so kind. Malcolm! This Gentleman has kindly offered to escort you into the church. Now isn't that kind of him. Thank you very much. I am a little worried to be perfectly honest. I am not the sort of person to make a fuss, but I don't mind telling you that I am having a little difficulty. There's someone else. Robert's his name. He's on the other side of this vehicle. He can't see all that well in the dark. Oh! and then there's Denise. I almost forgot about Denise, but I'm sure Samantha, yes, I'm sure Samantha can manage, is there someone who can help Robert?"

I didn't then and I still don't like admitting to my problems. Having listened to Shirley for the past few seconds I suddenly came to life. "I'm okay Shirley. I'm following Samantha and Denise."

I had a good idea that Samantha and Denise would be alright. I wasn't all that sure just how they might cope in the dark but they had always seemed to cope together; somehow. Shirley still had the floor, so to speak.

"Now then. Oh my! We seem to be quite a way from the entrance. Is that it over there. I do like those Christmassy bright lights don't you Malcolm? Oh, dear I am sorry... and there goes that taxi man. Oh, it is a bit cool and windy tonight isn't it? It is good you girls are wearing trousers... I will have to be careful or else I shall be doing a Marilynn Monroe tonight and I mustn't let that happen now must I? What will these men think of me?"

I wasn't all that sure about Malcolm but both he and I should, perhaps, have been interested, but whatever, I think we both had more important things on our minds for the time being, like getting from where we were to the inside of the church I heard Denise speak as she edged forwards on the arm of Samantha just ahead of me.

"Would you mind." She said quietly but assertively. "Come on Shirley get a move on Please?"

"Yes! Bloody well shut up and let's get on." Responded Malcolm.

Shirley seemed to stand her ground for a second and then I heard her say.

"Really Malcolm. Do you have to be so crude?"

"Yes. And even more so if you don't get a bloody move on?"

Someone was messing about behind me. I could feel a hand running down the back of my jacket and then I heard Shirley's voice cry out once more.

"Oh yes! Robert has been having mobility lessons, haven't you? Here's his cane in his back pocket. Why aren't you using your cane Robert? Did you girls know that Robert's having mobility lessons? I am too, but I'm afraid I haven't brought my cane with me... In the excitement you see, I forgot."

It was Denise's turn now. "That's typical."

Well, we made it. I was forced, against my will to part with the cane, and I didn't get anywhere near a proper chance to use it for myself, or by myself. But that too, was Shirley's fault. As I shall explain.

45

The biggest problem we from the Manor faced, was in negotiating around the parking and parked cars. Samantha and Denise were up front, as I have already said, and I was behind them. Shirley was now beside me, linking my arm, and having removed the cane from my back pocket she was now attempting to use it herself and encourage me to use it at the same time. Needless to say, this proved to be a distracting thing to do. Meanwhile, bringing up the rear was a quiet stranger, and Malcolm. Shirley's insecurities had soon become very clear to me when she attached herself to me like she did once we had encountered the first of the cars between us and our objective. I dutifully followed in the wake of the two young women and hoped against hope that they wouldn't make many mistakes and thankfully, they didn't. Goodness knows what the paintwork on those cars was like after Shirley had swung that cane back and forth like she did though.

We were outside the church at last and about to be welcomed inside. Under the bright lights at the steps of the curved entrance I could see the face at last of the man who had offered to help Malcolm. He was a tall, dark suited, elderly man in his late sixties with grey hair and dark interesting eyes, topped with bushy grey eyebrows. He smiled pleasantly at each of us and then went inside.

To this day, I cannot say with any degree of accuracy, just how bad Shirley's vision was. Or indeed. Just what her condition was either. I only know that she couldn't see all that well, close up. Sometimes, she didn't seem to be able to see things at a distance either, and in the dark? Hopeless. But I could never really tell. Mainly I suppose, because in the dark. I couldn't see or cope well enough to see how she coped. I could only sense it. As I had done on our short journey from the taxi to the church entrance.

Inside that brightly lit entrance porch, a lot of people were milling about in front and more people were coming in behind us. Samantha moved off and I followed, taking Shirley with me.

The interior consisted of white plastered walls and dark wood, lots of dark wood, carved and decorated in such an elaborate style that all I wanted to do was to get as close as I could in order to appreciate it in the best way that I could, to see and feel it, but I couldn't, I wasn't being allowed to, for the moment at least, because someone was there. A tall lady in a long red dress and long fair hair down to her waist was showing us into one of the many beautifully carved box-pews, and once inside, the door on my right was closed on us. I ran my hand over the smooth ancient and lovingly carved door posts, as I suspected many others had done in the past. Then, despite all the noise going on around us, I slowly became aware of a peaceful, pervading, all embracing atmosphere. It shouldn't have felt strange, but it did. I have been in many churches but this was an old and well used one. Looking around I began to realise that this was no once a week, Sunday morning Church. This was truly a community Church, warm and inviting. The walls and the vaulted timber roof high above were very interesting, and so were the people. But where were the BBC people? I hadn't noticed any trailing cables as I had expected to. When Shirley had first mentioned about the BBC, it had occurred to me that once we arrived at the Church and left the dark of night behind us, then we might very well have just as many problems on the inside if there was going to be a television crew and lots of cables and equipment, but there weren't any. I looked all around, and then at Shirley. She had her glasses off and absent mindedly staring directly ahead as she cleaned her glasses with her skirt. I leaned forward a little and looked at Samantha. She was sitting at the far end of the pew occupied by the five of us and she had just finished wiping her eye beneath the eyepatch with a white hanky, then she re-adjusted the pink eye-patch, I continued to watch as she lifted up her paralysed right arm with her left hand and placed it on her knee. Then, she saw me looking and she smiled at me and then turned her attention to Denise as Denise began to remove her coat for her. Malcolm was sitting between Shirley and Denise and he looked miserable. Then the noisy babble of many voices suddenly ceased, and the music began.

That first Hymn was not for joining in, although some did, as an organ began playing. 'Oh Come All Ye Faithful.' The lady in the long red dress came up the side aisle and stopped at our pew. I leaned towards her as she said.

"Do you think you can you manage with the order of service sheets you were given when you came in?"

I looked along the row at my colleagues and then back at the woman and said.

"Yes, we'll manage, thanks."

The whole event was truly enjoyable and superbly well organised. After a short while longer, I began to feel glad that I had been persuaded by Shirley to come here. I looked at her, Shirley. It was somewhere during the middle of 'Hark the Herald Angels Sing.' She looked so demure, so attractive and so full of vigour and vitality as she sang, unaided by hymn sheets, in a place where she belonged. Somewhere loud and Holy and yet very serene and tranquil. And she stood there beside me, singing her beautiful little heart out. She was

47

every inch a beautiful woman. Right down to her wonderful Soprano voice, and I had already forgotten her sometimes infuriating ways. She seemed to be completely unaware that I was watching her. And then I remembered where I was… I was in a house of God... And it was in a house of God where I had made a solemn promise to another beautiful woman over fifteen years earlier when I had married her. For one very brief moment my voice was louder than any of those around about me as I looked to the front and sang, appropriately.

"God and sinners reconciled."

They played all the old favourites that evening. 'Away in a Manger.' Once in Royal David's City' and the whole of, 'Oh come all ye faithful. There were the traditional stories and a candle-light procession around the interior of the church by the choir and Minister and the congregation were invited to follow in their wake and continue to sing. We five chose to stay where we were.

It was during the closing speech by the Minister, that I began to feel aware of the time and date of the event. There was nothing wrong with the time, or even the day. Sunday evening. But the date? The 18th of November? This Carol concert was over a month early for Christmas and if it was being recorded, where were the cameras? Where was the sound crew? Shirley must have been wrong. The Minister's voice continued to come to us from the pulpit, in the vague distance to my eyes, and it was only during the closing minutes of the service that I heard the Minister saying.

"… I would like to say a special thank you to BBC radio four and their excellent professionalism this evening... And very special thanks to you all. Thank You. Thank you for filling our Church this evening and for making this Carol concert the thrilling success it has been… You have all been in excellent voice. Thank you and God bless you all on your way home and in your homes this night and always."

Only then did I begin to realise what had really been going on behind the scenes. We waited while most of the congregation drifted away and then we were able to make our own exit, safely.

We were outside the Church, under a pool of light from the entrance when two ladies came and offered to take us back to the Manor. The coloured lady in the dark blue coat was speaking while the other, taller lady; set about the task of helping my colleagues.

Shirley began to get excited. "Oh, this is nice, we are having a lift back to our temporary home... Where is that lady going?"

Malcolm had been fairly quiet. He came back to join us and said: -

"Don't panic Shirley... That lady has only gone to get the transport sorted out. She told me it might take a few minutes and we could wait in the room behind the main door, wherever that might be."

It took a good ten minutes as it happened, before the lady did come back. For a short while we waited and watched the last of the congregation leaving, but there still must have been people inside tidying up, because after the last of the members of the public went down the outside steps, I noticed then the first of the men in brown cotton coats carrying electrical equipment.

Malcolm found the room where we could wait. He took full advantage of the quiet setting and said.

"As there's only us here, let me tell you a joke I picked up recently. Now then... Here goes. It's outside the Pearly Gates and Saint Peter is there as usual. There's Bob, Bob and, and let's say your friend Jim Grice, after all it was Jim who told me this joke, your friend Jim Grice it is then? Don't worry Shirley, this is a clean enough joke, the rest of you want to hear it don't you? of course you do, Anyway Bob and Jim. Jim and Bob. Only Jim's already there when Bob gets outside the gates of heaven. Saint Peter lets him step inside but no further. He looks at his ledger and says. Oh dear. Oh dear. You've not been all that good down there have you James? I think you're going to have to do a little penance before you can go any further inside heaven. Now then... What will it be? Says Saint Peter. I know, for your penance, you will be chained for the next five years to that scruffy ugly old woman huddled in the corner beside the pearly gates, you will be chained to her for the next five years for your wrong doings on earth. Jim doesn't like this one little bit. He sees Bob over against the other gate and he's chained to a real dolly bird... Oh, I'm losing it now... Who can we name as Bob's dolly bird?"

"Marilyn Monroe..." Chirped Shirley, then she put her hand to her mouth and sat down again.

I think we were all more surprised than she was by her sudden compulsive outburst. Malcolm instantly picked up on this and said: -

"Hey! That's good, I like it I like it. Now then. Where was I? Oh yes. Bob is beside the other pearly gate and he's chained to Marilyn Monroe. So, Jim turns to Saint Peter and he says. Hey! Come on Saint Pete. I don't reckon as this is fair. It's not fair at all. No disrespect and all that, but you are having me chained up to her over there and Bob chained up to Marilyn Monroe. How come he's got her and I've got that one? Never mind all that. Says Saint Peter. You just get on with your penance and let Marilyn Monroe get on with hers."

It took a few seconds for us to begin to understand and just as we did, in walked the two posh ladies.

Soon we were all outside once more and about to board a bus with its engine purring. The coloured lady was telling us that they had hired the coach to bring their Women's Institute group from Kingkerswell and they would be more than pleased to take us back. They didn't need to do it but I think we were all glad that they did take us back to the Manor in that coach, and what a coach it was. Large and luxurious. How the driver managed to turn around when he dropped the others off up at the Manor I don't know.

Malcolm and I were let off outside the gates to America Lodge and as we stepped down towards the footpath, we thanked the good people who had brought us here, and all in all, it was a pleasant ending to a very busy day. Malcolm punched in the code for us entry to the Lodge. Once we were inside, I went up to my room and knew no more until early the following morning.

CHAPTER SEVEN

Monday 19th November.

I was in the Den, the time was 6 o'clock. I had woken around about five, done the necessary and then come down here for a good hot brew and something to eat. The peace and solitude of early morning never ceased to amaze me and I enjoyed it for at least the next five or ten minutes.

I had just finished my drink when I heard the first sounds which heralded the lodge's awakening. The first to enter the den and which was a huge surprise for me, was my fellow Intake companion Mike Walsh. I quickly and eagerly greeted him but I was suddenly also curious as to why he was here, when he wasn't due back from his long weekend until later that day. Mike started to tell me the reason for his early return while I made him a mug of tea.

He had arrived back at America Lodge at around ten the previous evening with his brother; for two reasons, one was for his brother to take Mike's canoe back home and the other was as follows, in his own words: -

"Me woife wants me to get as much as oy can from this course and so do oye."

I was quick to pick up on the fact that Mike was a heck of a lot better in himself than he had been for quite a long while. It also turned out that he fancied a bit more than just a drink of tea. He took hold of the mug that I handed to him and as he looked in the general direction of my face he said: -

"Oye c'dow with a bycon and egg butty Bob. Loike t'dow it fer meself, but oy don't loike 'andling' ot fat. Not now loike, now as oy can't see no more. Down't s'ppose yow'd dow one for me would yah?"

"Glad to Mike." I said eagerly, as I went over to the fridge and rummaged inside. It was nearly empty. I cursed quietly as I moved a few items around looking for some bacon. I didn't want anything to dampen Mike's spirits that morning. I was lucky. At the back of the fridge on the top shelf there was a half pack of bacon, and the eggs were already there, three of them, inside the door. I found the frying pan and figured out the controls on the cooker and while I was doing all of this, I wasn't aware that Mike had come up behind me. He wasn't all that sure of himself until he found my location then he surprised me by saying: -

"Oy can't let yow dow this for me Bob, mowve over oy'll troy meself, yow just watch un make sure oy down't burn me."

The situation with Mike was definitely improving. It was good to see him more like his old self once more. I didn't know what had happened to make him like this, I didn't really care, I was just glad that he seemed to be facing up to life and its brutalities once more, and yet? A newly blind man attempting to cook his own breakfast has to be applauded for the sheer guts and tenacity involved in the tackling of hot oil and spitting bacon. But then. It also has to be one of life's cruellest ironies as well. I dithered about in the background. I would rather have done this for him than with him. The bacon was sizzling safely under the grill. But what of the oil in the pan on the stove? Then I remembered just in time, a trick I had learned; someone, somewhere must have taught me, when there had been a time when I hadn't been able to see quite as well as I could at that moment. I turned the heat off so that the oil wouldn't yet get hot, and explained to Mike.

"Hold on Mike. I've just thought of something. It's something I learned when I was a bit like you. If you want to know when a frying pan is hot enough to cook an egg, all you have to do is wet your fingers and put one or two drops of water in the oil before you start heating it up, then, as soon as it starts to make a noise, you will know that it is hot enough, and you can turn the heat off and cook your egg safely, but most importantly! without the oil getting too hot. Here, I'll get some water in a cup for you and you can try. It worked for me, still does in fact. Let's see if it works for you as well."

It did work, and I had a feather in my cap at long last, to make up for the times that I had let Mike down over the past few weeks. A few minutes later I was quietly satisfied and sitting on the opposite side of the table as I watched Mike contentedly eating his bacon and egg butty.

We were joined a short while later by a handful of residents all at once. There was Barry, and two younger men, I had seen them before in the bungalow, when Barry and these two, amongst others, had been rehearsing for the forthcoming concert. All three of them were talking music and as the event was now less than one week away, I think it would have been surprising if they had not been talking music. Mike and I got up and left the music lovers to their business.

A short while later, when the mass exodus to the Manor was about to get under way, I was standing with about ten or so others, outside the lodge, on a cool and misty November morning. I had just been looking up to the sky to try and determine what the weather was likely to do that day. Just then my attention was brought back down to earthly matters and I was reminded by the many white canes which had suddenly appeared, as if from nowhere, that I had left mine up in my room. Once again, I felt reluctant to go and get it. I felt a fraud handling that cane in broad daylight. But then? What of the dark later that day?

The main hall at the Manor was crowded, as usual, and nothing had changed or was likely to change in that respect. However. The seating arrangements within the dining room had changed, and would change more, before the day was over. They seemed to have a unique system at the Manor of not advising of changes until changes had been made. Or at least it seemed to be that way to me. Nothing had happened yet though.

I had come across Adrian in the main hall while we had been waiting for the breakfast gong to ring out. He wasn't saying very much. I think he was just glad to latch on to someone he knew. We joined the mad throng and went into the dining room together.

I was more than somewhat surprised as we approached our table to notice Beryl from the care staff. She was struggling to help a man in difficulties into the space which ought to have been occupied by Ann. I noticed Laurie moving and then got a clear sighting of the large wobbly man, the man who went down on the chair and almost knocked everything off the table top at the same time. This was Christopher, the cheerful Spastic. Beryl turned around and must have noticed the curious look on my face because she looked back at Christopher and then back at me as she took Adrian off me and helped him into his seat. Over and above the buzz of the dining room, Beryl grunted with all the effort and said.

"Change of plans. I'm sure you three won't mind having Christopher on your table for a while... Now then. Oh, you can get in now Robert. Laurie? Ah! wasn't it a lovely wedding on Saturday? My you looked splendid Laurie, and the bagpipe playing was out of this world, truly amazing. You should all be fine where you are, for now. Later on this morning you can move over to this side of the table if you like and sit with Robert, because Adrian won't be here will he. Adrian is leaving us for a week or so aren't you dear. And when he comes back. If all goes well that is. Well! he should have his own guide dog with him by then won't you Adrian? That's it. You've waited a long time for this day, haven't you? Oh, you do have such a lovely smile. That's much better. Now then? Oh yes! There was something else... We thought it only right and proper that Mr Cyril and Mrs Ann Thompson should be together from now on, so, when they come back later this morning, we shall have them together, just a few tables further down the room in fact... Now then. All seated? That's good. I'll get out of the way then shall I and leave you to your breakfasts. Cynthia's coming with some plates already. Now, Adrian! I shall be coming back for you immediately after you have had your breakfast. Sandra has your case in her office all ready for you... You're not nervous, are you? I don't know... I wonder sometimes... Oh! By the way. Something else. In case any of you don't know. Christopher here; is perfectly capable of looking after himself. He's just a bit clumsy with his movements, aren't you Christopher? Well! Bye for now."

I watched Beryl as she departed, and then I turned my attention back to the confusion on our table. Christopher was sitting opposite, where Ann used to sit. He was smiling a smile of greeting. He seemed keen to want to talk, he knew me and I suppose he only wanted to get to know us all a little bit better. I wanted to ask him not to try and talk, but I wasn't sure how to put it without causing problems. Laurie, tactfully saved me the situation when he turned to face Christopher and said.

"Yourre alright mon. Save the worrds 'till later. Ye'll be better eating yourre breakfast noo it's afront o'yee."

I was already missing Ann on our table. Christopher dutifully ate most of his breakfast in silence and only started to talk at one point which was just before the latest House Captain demanded our attention. Frank was his name. His opening speech and Christopher's questioning of the silence of Adrian sitting next to me, came to my ears at the same instant. I gestured to Christopher to be quiet while the House Captain did his speech and by way of an explanation, I also mentioned that Adrian didn't say much and that it was the way he liked to be. I pushed the plate of toast, which lay in the centre of the table towards Christopher and invited him to get stuck in. Then the House Captain demanded our attention for a second time.

"Thank God for that! What a noisy rabble you are today... Now then... I suppose this is where I start my duties is it? Frank Turner is the name. Frank by name and Frank by nature... Most of the time... I am sorry that I wasn't here on Friday or over the weekend in order to take up this position. Now, first things first. Rifle shooting tonight. Bus is full, no more room. If it stays as popular as this, then I am told that a second bus will be made available for those who wish to go next week. Oh! And a week from today will be the end of the year finals, which should be an entertaining event in itself. Oh yes! We seem to have a champion of our own. Royston is his name. I know he can't hear me, so can anyone tell me... How the hell does the man do it? Marvellous guy... He's just great. Right, ah yes... The old perennial problem seems to have returned I'm afraid. Yes, you all know the one I'm about to mention."

A loud chorus of voices joined in when Frank said: - "Someone's missing his aim." Quite a few changed the M for a P. Frank asked for calm once more and continued with.

"This has all been said before, so here goes. Will all you total gentlemen. Please sit down, when you go to the toilet... Moving swiftly on. The er! Ah yes. The notice board over in the Commerce building. Those of you who haven't yet checked where you are going to for this week. Please, will you be very careful when you go over to the Commerce building... We don't want any more stupid situations like we had last week. I was there. Like a pack of wolves, you were. It's little wonder that only one or two of you got slight injuries... Oh... Going back to the old problem... I've just been asked to inform you... That means all of us men, to sit down when we go to the toilet. It isn't any trouble and I'll tell you what. I will be the first one to set the example, Aaand, any of you totals can come and watch me if you like. Right. I think that just about wraps it up for now. Carry on. Be careful out there, and... Thank you for voting me to this job. I hope I don't let you down."

Beryl came. I helped Adrian out into the aisle and handed him over with the thought on my mind. Will I ever see this young man again after this moment? I watched him walk away on the arm of Beryl, then I got back into my seat and looked across at Laurie. Laurie was a deep and quiet man, but I could tell by the expression on his pale anaemic looking face that he was more than likely thinking the same as I had been thinking about Adrian. He ran his fingers through his pure white hair and raised his white bushy eyebrows and then looked away from me. Then Christopher said something which immediately distracted me and captured my attention. Deep throated and with difficulty, he said.

"You're with, with, me today in typing Bobbb. I looked yester, yesterday... first lesson... after… After Lunch..."

Chris wiped his mouth with a hanky and looked quizzically at me for a response. I shuddered at the prospect and asked. "Who's going to be in charge? Not Pauline I hope."

"We had Pau... Pauline laaast week… I like Pauline I do."

"I'm glad someone does." I said as cheerfully as I could. Then, getting to my feet I excused myself and headed off out of the room.

I hadn't seen Royston in the hall, or in the dining room, but before I could try and find him, I knew it would make sense to go over to the Commerce building by myself and look on the board to find out where we should both be for that week.

A couple of minutes later, I was hastily escaping from the drizzling rain by way of pushing on the glass doors to the entrance and stepped inside the Commerce building. About half a dozen other residents had already beaten me to it and were studying the timetable for the week ahead. I waited until one or two of them had finished and then stepped forward.

Perhaps I should have been interested in what the others of my Intake were doing that week, but it was awkward enough to try and remember where just the two of us were supposed to be without any added confusion. I did notice in scanning the board that Josie had a free period every day that week just the same as Jim had. Then I noticed that Royston and myself had a free period marked off for the last period of each day as well. Then I remembered that this was what we were entitled to. Having come this far in the course, we were now being allowed to pick one session each day where we could do whatever assessment lesson we liked, as long as it didn't conflict with any of the scheduled ones. For that week. Royston had; Woodworking, Mobility, then lunch, Crafts, and a free choice. While, I had; Woodworking, Braille, lunch, Typing, and a free choice. Little did I know, but my free choice, wasn't exactly going to be my own free choice.

I was back inside the main hall a short while later and had just managed to find Royston in the few minutes before our scheduled departure time. I had just finished telling him what the programme of events were to be for the week ahead. When who should come on the scene? but Gillian Roberts. And she looked extremely miserable. Miserable, or very annoyed about something. I quickly stepped back out of her way while she pushed in and signed a message on Royston's hand. His face immediately lit up and he began gesturing with an imaginary cane as he carefully focussed his eyes on Gillian and then smiled as he gave her the universal thumbs up sign. Then. Completely ignoring Royston. Gillian turned on me and with a sharp exclamation, she went on to say.

"Good! That's another one sorted out... And now for you. I saw you go over and also come away from the Commerce building just now, so I presume you know where you are supposed to be for this week? Yes? Did you also notice your allocation of a free choice as well? Sorry! But that isn't a free choice. The last lesson for the day you are to be with me, and... With the exception of tomorrow. Tuesday. You are coming with me every day this week on mobility exercises. Now then, is that understood? Clear? Capiche? Good! I don't want any nonsense. None whatsoever. You have got me at the wrong time of the month to mess me about, now you are going to co-operate. Aren't you? Thank You... Bye for now."

And then she was gone. Royston indicated and then asked me what was that all about? I signed back and briefly explained, and then two slightly puzzled men headed for our joint joy over in the woodworking department.

Soon we were on the inside of the woodwork department. I somehow knew that my part in the creation of Royston's coffee table was as good as over and it really was time that I got stuck into something positive of my own doing. Royston eagerly headed for the bench where he had worked so hard and patiently over the past few weeks. He had forgotten me now and probably everyone else as well. There was only the one thing on his mind.

It was rather shrewd of Gordon White, our tutor, to have done what he did for me that morning. I entered his office a few seconds after he had called me in there and quickly became aware of the sweet and yet damp and musty smell. I had encountered this before and looked around for the source. On the floor was a long bundle of rush, which was partly covered in a wet grey blanket. Gordon explained his taking a liberty in assuming. Quite accurately as it happened. That I would still be willing to learn the ancient art of rush-work.

Not many more minutes had gone by before I was sitting on a low stool, (with a rush-work top) and I was ready and about to begin taking instructions from a master craftsman.

Gordon gave a lot of his time to me during that session… more time than I felt I deserved, and by the end of it, I had remembered all that he had already taught me and begun to learn a lot more besides. I did as he had been instructing me and selected two straight and tapering pieces of Rush and then turned them top to tail. Having done this a few times so that he could show me how to check the quality, I was then allowed to pick up the bare wooden frame. This was about ten inches by roughly fifteen inches in size and tapered from front to back rather like a small version of a chair seat in itself and in fact, that's what I was about to do, make a small chair seat, but without the chair. First of all, I had to fasten my first two strands of Rush to one side rail of the frame with a single, untwisted, strand of Rush. Even this comparatively simple task had to be done in a certain, somewhat obscure way, and having tied one end of the two strands to the frame. I was then instructed to twist the two strands together and lay them over the wooden bar at the front of the frame. I then had to go under, back through and over the corner section to my left, which took me over the top of the strands I had just laid down. I then had to bring the two pieces of Rush. Still twisting them together, and bring them across to and over the opposite side of the frame, then, wrap it under the frame and up through and over the strands again and back around and on to the other corner of the frame, and so on, until I came back to where I had started from, and then I was beginning my second turn around the wooden frame. By this time however, I had run out of the raw material. Gordon had come back by then to show me how to tie on. To do this, it was explained that it was best to finish underneath the frame so that the knots could be tidily tucked away out of sight between the top and the bottom of the woven rush-work seat top, which was magically already beginning to take shape.

I had done about half of the work by the time the coffee time break came around. At long, long, last, I had managed to find something that I could enjoy doing, and all too soon it was time to go. I don't mind admitting, that it was a reluctant two men, in me and Royston, who were almost the last to leave the woodworking department. Gordon followed us out, locked up and came with us across the yard towards the Porch entrance to the Manor and there he left us, but not without first making me promise to continue learning this unique and ancient craft.

We were both late arrivals for the dining room. By the time we got there, most of the residents were already seated. Royston went off to his place and I went to mine.

That coffee break consisted of a confusing rearrangement of our usual seating pattern. Laurie was now sitting beside me, on my left, where Adrian had been, and now Laurie appeared to be a lot more annoyed than confused. The reason seemed to be sitting directly across from him. Ann and Cyril had returned but they were now sitting together on a table three down from ours but they were far too busy talking to the residents in their immediate vicinity to cope with, or even to bother with us. I looked back at the large bulk of Christopher as he clumsily began, what to most of us is the simple task of picking up a coffee cup. Only to him it wasn't.

I don't know how people like Christopher came to be called Spastics. That may or may not have been a thought in my mind at that moment in time, but I do remember wondering what might happen and the chaos it would cause if he dropped that cup of coffee. Thankfully, he didn't. And thankfully, he didn't begin any attempt at conversation either. He seemed too intent on getting that hot drink inside and not outside him in the limited time we were allocated for this break.

Being extra careful not to sound patronising, or even cynical, I congratulated Christopher for doing what he had managed to do, I wasn't sure how he may react but my remarks seemed to please him somehow. Meanwhile, Laurie hardly uttered a word during the entire break. He just grunted occasionally and eventually got to his feet and left the table in a similar manner, which left me on our table with Christopher. I finished my drink and got up to go. Chris called me back though and in a deep voice and partially strangled vocal cords, he said.

"You've got... typing... this afternoon... w, with me, hav...en't you Bobbb?"

"Yes." I replied soberly. "Yes, I'll have to do something about that shan't I? I mean, I mean, about Pauline, the tutor over in the typing room, I'll have to do something about my relationship with her... You weren't to know Chris, but I fell out with her a few weeks ago. I'll see you at lunchtime, hopefully I might have thought of a way out by then."

Where to next? I rummaged in the timetable in my mind and came up with... Braille...

I met up with Malcolm in the main hall. It turned out that Royston's next destination was to be a Mobility lesson, and not Braille, so I found him and took him to the Mobility office. And it turned out that Malcolm's session in the Braille room was about to be short lived.

We hadn't been in Wendy's department for much more than ten minutes when a knock came at the door and in came the ginger haired and bearded Mobility Andrew and he asked with a clear voice if he might be able to take Malcolm with him for a mobility lesson.

I managed to cover a lot of ground that morning and learned a bit more about that confusing language of dots on stiff brown paper. I had already begun to take more of an interest in all that was going on around me. It had started a couple of days earlier, the day after my arrival back here. I may or may not have been aware of it at the time. Was it due to the death of my father-in-law? Or just simply the fact that I had been home and come back again? Something had changed though. Was it me? Or was it everything around me that was slowly changing. I do know I was beginning to like it, strange though this feeling was. Perhaps this was why Wendy had begun that morning, to take more notice of me and my attempts at Braille.

I had a chance to speak to the new Mr and Mrs just before we went in for lunch. I had entered the lounge via the French windows when I noticed Ann and Cyril sitting in the right-hand corner behind the curtains. I soon found out that they still considered themselves to be on an extended honeymoon. It was pleasant to witness what I was witnessing There they were. Big Ann and little Cyril and she was like putty in his hands. She was obviously devoted to him and it was perfectly clear to the blindest of the blind that they were good for each other. I was immediately made very welcome in their midst as were a lot of others who were still coming in through the open French windows. It was also still raining out there, which meant that there were a lot of folk in a hurry to get inside. It was a sizable crowd which had now gathered and we listened to Ann as she explained to all of us, what their plans were for the future. Cyril had had his stay at the Manor extended because of his late start in getting to grips with the place. Alas, even that extension was now about to run out. He had one more week to do and then he was due to leave. Ann had started at the Manor the week after I had and, accordingly, she was due to finish the week after me, which should have been Christmas week, but this wasn't to be. Ann and Cyril had decided to leave on the following Monday morning. I was just one amongst many who were genuinely saddened by the news but it had to come sooner or later and it was inevitable really. The pair of them certainly didn't seem disturbed by the prospect, and as I found out, they were going to set up their new home and live at Cyril's house.

I ate my lunch in a hurry. There was somewhere I had to be, and I hadn't got all that long to get there and do it. I was just on the point of getting to my feet to excuse myself when I noticed Malcolm coming towards me.

"Where are you off to Bob?" he asked.

I told him that I hadn't got very long in order to go upstairs to the typing room and get a bit of practice in before the dreaded typing session, with the doubly dreaded tutor named Pauline.

"Good...!" Said Malcolm. "Very good indeed. That's just what I wanted to see you about. Jim asked me to look after you in Pauline's place, before he went home for the weekend, so, if you're going up to the residents typing room then I'm coming with you if you don't mind."

Malcolm wasn't going to give me an opportunity to mind. Besides, standing there discussing the issue wasn't going to improve anything, so, reluctantly, I allowed him and Christopher to follow me out of the dining room and onwards towards the main hall.

I had heard Malcolm calling out to one or two people as we left the dining room, but I hadn't taken all that much notice. I must have been thinking that he was just greeting them. It was as we were approaching the wide staircase from the side elevation and I turned to my right in front of the oblong table in order to ascend the stairs, that I became aware of the sizable group of residents who had attached themselves to me. I stopped on the first step and looked down at them as they came to an abrupt halt. I looked quickly at each of them. There was Malcolm, Christopher, Laurie, and Tom, the Astrologer, and then there was Barry, the forthcoming concert organiser.

"Where are you all going?" I hissed quietly.

"With you of course." Responded Tom, cheerfully. "We've still got a bet on which has hung over from the other week. Come on, get going, there's no time to waste."

All I wanted was to be left alone so that I could concentrate on improving my typing skills. But I wasn't going to be allowed even that simple privilege by the looks of this lot.

By this time a lot more residents had begun to emerge from the dining room and were gradually filling the hall. I took another look at the group following me and then turned around and headed up the stairs. I knew it would do me no good arguing and trying to get them to leave me on my own. They followed me as close as a shadow all the way to the residents typing room.

I was just beginning to realise that the impending anarchy of the last typing session hadn't yet subsided as much as I would have liked it to have done. I could hardly believe that the problem with Pauline had been simmering in the minds of my colleagues for so long. Tom answered my question as I began to open the door.

"Yes Bob... She's still just as bad... Come on, get in there. Let me see what you are capable of doing?"

61

I was looking around the room trying to remember and decide which might be the best manual typewriter to work on, but it wasn't an easy task with Tom and the others goading me. Barry didn't say much and neither did Christopher or Laurie. The remaining two, Tom and Malcolm, made more than enough fuss though, but I was wasting too much time... I would have to ignore these people and concentrate on what I knew I had to do if I was going to stand any chance of clearing my wife's name as the good tutor who had taught me how to touch type.

Before I could start to get too frustrated, I went and sat down at the nearest desk. They all crowded around me. Malcolm was giving something of a running commentary, while I was silently wishing that he wouldn't, but then I remembered that I wouldn't be on my own once we entered the typing room at the Commerce building. I would, more than likely, have Pauline looking over my shoulder, just as my colleagues were doing here and the other, forthcoming ordeal, couldn't be more than fifteen minutes away at the most.

"Well, come on Bob." Said Barry. "Shush you others. Come on let's sit down over here. He hasn't got all that long to practice and we are holding our best hope up. Do you want us to go and leave you on your own Bob?"

"Yes…No." I said quietly. "No…You might as well stay now you're here. It won't be that much different when we get over there will it?"

I looked down at the keyboard and it reminded me.

"There's no boxes over these like there are over those in the Commerce building, in Pauline's place. I can see this one."

"Aren't you the lucky one Bob." Said Tom, rather a bit too sourly for my liking. I didn't like that and I didn't like Christopher hovering about in the background either. He was far too quiet for my liking. I couldn't be sure what he might be thinking about or what his feelings were. Was he relying on me to break Pauline's spell as well?

"This is hopeless. I'll never do it."

"You lot stay where you are for a minute." Said Barry. "Come on Malcolm. You and me are the only ones that can see well enough. Let's see if we can find something to cover up that keyboard and get on before it's too late."

62

I sighed a very heavy sigh and said. "Don't bother Barry. I'd rather not do it, but I've a better idea."

I removed and placed my thick lensed glasses down on the desk to my left and I was now staring at the blurred creamy colour of the typewriter in front of me. My hands were nothing more than a pair of reddish pink blobs hovering over the completely indistinguishable keys... and then.

"Blast! I forgot to get some paper ready."

In fact, there were a number of things I should have done in readiness, before I removed my glasses. I couldn't see to do any of those things now. The only way that I could see in order to get myself some paper was for me to reach for my thick lensed glasses and put them on again. I automatically reached out to where I had only seconds before put them down. Malcolm beat me to it.

"I'll hang on to these Bob, keep them safe, you know. Anyroad, I'll get some paper for you. Me or Barry will. You just sit there and tell us what you can see. Thanks Barry. Here you are Bob. He's not going to tell us, is he? What he can see I mean."

"Bugger all!"

I forced myself to calm down and then said. "Give'em back to me Malcolm. I'll be able to concentrate a hell of a lot better with'em than without them, even if they're only in me trouser pocket. Come on, give'em back to me and let's get on before it's too late."

Malcolm gave in and I was feeling only fractionally better as I began to feel for the way to feed the paper in through the top of the bulky machine in front of me. I could hear some of the others speaking in hushed tones behind and to my left and I could also hear the strangely comforting sounds of Barry's voice as well. None of them were talking to me, but they were talking to each other. I concentrated on what I had to do and tried not to listen. Malcolm and Barry stood either side of me. Malcolm on my left and Barry on my right. I didn't mind this, even though it was slightly intimidating. I then tried to make the situation a little bit lighter by speaking my thoughts.

"Huh! You're asking me what I can see? and here you pair are... You haven't a decent pair of eyes between you."

63

By now the paper was ready and so was I. Well... as ready as I would ever be. I began to type, slowly at first. This was so that I could familiarise myself with the layout of the keyboard. I tried to ignore Tom; when he said.

"What does his friend Josie call him? 'Supersonic?' I can go faster than that myself."

"Right!" I said enthusiastically. This was the first bit of real enthusiasm I had felt since coming up here. There was a small surge of adrenalin as I made myself a bit more comfortable in the chair and readied myself to really start.

Just before I did begin, I couldn't help but express the one thought on my mind that had just occurred to me, and as it happened, I was soon wishing that I hadn't said the following.

"It's a ruddy pity Pauline isn't here to see this. Right! Give me a bit more elbowroom you two."

I spoke as I wrote.

"Bronco Lane had a pain so they sent for Waggon train.
Waggon train was no good so they sent for Robin Hood.
Robin Hood broke his bow so they sent for Ivanhoe.
Ivanhoe killed a man so they sent for big Cheyenne.
Big Cheyenne was having tea so they sent for Laramie.
Laramie lost their cargo so they sent for Wells Fargo.
Wells Fargo lost their hunter so they sent for Billy Bunter.
Billy Bunter was too large so they sent for I'm in charge... There! How's that?"

"Bloo-dy hell!" Said Tom quietly, and then "Come on. Let's get over there. If this doesn't sort her out then nothing will..."

"Get over where? and who do you wish to sort out may I ask!"

It was a vaguely familiar female voice which came from somewhere near the entrance to the room. I must have visibly cringed as I realised who this person was. And so, must some, if not all of the others. Barry confirmed my worst fears as he fell over his own words. "Oh! Er, Ha ha, er, Oh Hell! er, Pauline... It's Pauline folks. Oh and who's this as well? Hello Beryl... What brings you two here then?"

"Suspicions. Just suspicions that is all." Said Pauline. "and well-founded they are by the looks of things here."

I could hear footsteps on the bare wooden floor. Two sets of heels seemed to click ominously in unison. They were coming towards me from the rear and I felt like I wanted to crawl underneath this desk. I couldn't see them do it but I felt Barry and Malcolm melting away from me. I didn't know, or for the moment, even care where the others had all vanished to, and then I caught a faint smell of perfume as a long white blur passed in front of my eyes and I heard the paper being gently eased from the typewriter. I sank even lower in my chair at the same time that I was feeling in my pocket for my glasses.

"Oh! please do be quiet Thomas. I don't have to tell you I'm sure. That we find this, this conspiracy of sorts to be well and truly, not, to our liking... At all! Now then. Mister Weaver... First of all! I am rather afraid. Or so it seems, that I may have to congratulate you on your apparent speed. But was your speed just now... accurate, speed? We shall see... Hmm... Hmm... Alright... You may all go now. I must say that I am more than a little surprised to see you here Barry. I don't believe I have had the pleasure of teaching you how to type. Ah well! Off you all go then, with the rest of your fellow conspirators, yes, you as well Robert."

I had got my glasses on by now and could see to gather up my belongings. Everyone else had gone. I didn't look at Pauline or Beryl on my way out.

It was a very much subdued group of people who were making their sullen way over to the Commerce building. Not one word was spoken by any of us, the silence amongst us was causing my mind to work overtime. I was thinking all sorts of things, and in a way, I realised that I was trying to rationalise the situation and turn it about face and somehow salvage something useful, so that I wouldn't, and we all wouldn't end up being intimidated by Pauline once more.

We were outside now. Barry left us to go into the Crafts building and the rest of us made our way to the railings and the concrete steps beyond which cut a grey path down through the grass embankment. I was the first to go down the steps and when I reached the bottom I looked up at the others and I think it must have been the look of embarrassed shame on Malcolm's face which made my mind up for me. I couldn't let these people down, and equally, I couldn't and I must not let my wife down.

Whatever was about to happen when Pauline came was something I had to deal with and deal with fast. Or else she would have the upper hand again and we would all be defeated. I remember thinking that the whole thing was almost too ridiculous. What was really happening here was a battle of wills. Mine and Pauline's and anyone else who dared to enter her domain in the first place, with anything more than the vaguest most basic knowledge of typing. I took hold of Christopher's arm, he looked as if he was about to fall down. Laurie spoke for the first time since leaving the residents typing room back at the Manor.

"Heeere we goo!"

We entered the typing room. There were a few there already, they were busy on the typewriters. I helped Christopher to the destination that he seemed to know of and then I looked at Laurie and said quietly. "Don't worry. We didn't do anything wrong. Pauline will not beat me again. I shan't let her get me worked up like she did the last time I was in here… I can't believe this is happening anyway. This whole thing's almost too daft for words."

I opened the inner door to let Laurie through the wood and glass partition on our left and allowed him to find his own way to his desk. Laurie, I already knew from our dining room conversations was a good typist and after only a few weeks he had moved on to the electronic typewriters. I gave a casual glance at the other residents who were in that section and then I turned to go out in order to find myself one of those large bulky manual typewriters in the other part of the room, and this I would need to do rather quickly. If, I was going to be able to settle myself down a bit before... before... Well. Enough criticism.

I had just about managed to find the one and only empty space, right at the back of the room. Which, incidentally, suited me fine. I couldn't get any further away from Pauline's desk without putting myself on the other side of the wall and outside in the Manor gardens. Everyone else was busily working, even Christopher. He was sitting two rows in front and over to my left. I could see that Tom was trying to help him as best he could. This pleased me, it couldn't have been easy for blind Tom to cope with Christopher's ungainly movements, but he was managing to help him, somehow. I looked down at the crude wooden box over the keyboard and wondered for a moment or two, who had made it and dare I remove it. I looked up at the vertical glazing bars in the screen nearby on my right and they bent as I moved my head. The optical quality of the shape of my glasses had lent itself to providing me with a bit of dry humour. Looking down again. I contemplated the prospect of removing

66

both the wooden box and then my glasses. Surely, she couldn't object to me doing whatever exercises she gave me if I couldn't see the keyboard anyway? That box was a psychological hindrance to both me and goodness knows how many others. I knew I could type better and faster without it. "Better leave it where it is." I muttered these words quietly as I resigned myself to the daunting object, and reached into the drawer for some paper. No one talked, there was only the spasmodic sound of a dozen or more typewriters clicking away. I do remember thinking that Pauline was a long while in coming to the typing room.

She eventually did come and when she did, she entered a room where no one dared to stop what they were doing. Not even me. I kept my head down and tapped randomly at the keys beneath the wooden box and I just happened to look up in time to see her coming along the back wall towards me.

"Oh, Oh. here we go." I mumbled.

She came to a standstill beside me on my left, and at the sound of her voice, all the machines, mine and nearly everyone else's in that part of the room, came to sudden halt. All except for Christopher's. But his typewriter soon stopped as well and he began looking around him for a reason. One or two of the sighted people there threw caution to the winds and dared to turn around to look in my direction. But not for long.

"You don't have to stop what you were doing, none of you. Please carry on. Most of you know what you are supposed to be doing and those who don't... Well! I shall be with you presently. In the meantime, Robert..." She dropped her voice a little and continued. "I wonder, if you would do me the courtesy of typing out a little exercise which I would like to read to you. But first... You must let me know if I worry you by standing here. Am I bothering you?"

I was bracing myself for any harshness. I may have been ready for some criticism as well, but I was not anywhere near ready for this. This patronising attitude. Was she just being extra clever? Was she trying to unnerve me once more? What was it with this woman? What was it with me...? I nodded and then quickly shook my head. I couldn't let it happen again. I couldn't allow this, or even the recent happening up in the residents typing room back inside the Manor to put me off now. Too much depended on me getting this right. Whatever she had in store for me. I just had to get it right. I knew I had to.

The erratic clicking of typewriters began in earnest once more. I listened to the sounds for a few seconds longer and then turned to look up at Pauline's face, and quickly changed my mind. Instead. I thrust my hands inside the crude box and waited for her to begin.

"Ready then are we? This is a short poem by Alfred Lord Tennyson. I shall narrate it in pace with your typing...

When cats run home and light is come... new line...
and dew is cold upon the ground... comma... new line...
and the far... hyphen... off stream is dumb... new line...
and the whirring sail goes round... semi colon... new line...
alone and warming his five wits... comma... new line...
the white owl in the belfry sits... full stop... fresh paragraph

When merry milkmaids click the latch...comma...new line...
and rarely smells the new...hyphen...mown hay...comma...new line...
and the cock hath sung beneath the thatch...new line...
twice or thrice his round...hyphen...e...hyphen lay...semi colon...new line...
alone and warming his five wits...semi colon...new line...
the white owl in the belfry sits...full stop... And stop there Robert, for that is the end of the narration."

I had typed, as follows: -

When cats run home and night is come
and dew is cold upon the ground,
and the far- off stream is dumb
and the whirrin g sail goes round;
alone and warming his five wits,
the white owl in the belfty sits.

When merry milkmaids click the latch,
and rarely smells the new-mown hay,
and the cock hath dung beneath the thatch
twice orthrice his round-e-lay;
alone and warming his five wits;
the white owl in the belfry sits.

I stopped and withdrew my hands from beneath the crude wooden box and watched while she reached down and gently eased the paper from the rear of the machine.

Pauline didn't say anything to begin with, she was obviously studying the contents of the paper. I sat stiff backed in my chair and stared straight ahead. I could feel the anxiety building up inside me now. Now that I hadn't got an outlet and had to just sit there and wait for a verdict. I began to notice things. I noticed that Tom had given up with trying to help Christopher and he and a lot of the others seemed to be typing in an automatic fashion, whilst all the while they were trying to discover for themselves what was happening between me and Pauline, without actually stopping what they were supposed to be doing. I glanced over to my right to look through the glass screen into the other part of the room. The scene in there was much the same as the one in front of me. No one dared to stop what they were doing. I thought that I could feel her eyes burning into the back of my head. Then she decided to speak. She didn't criticise me. Instead, she folded the paper in half and gave it to me with the instruction to put it away somewhere safe. And then, then, she took me completely by surprise when she leaned forward into my field of vision and said.

"Tell me... Have you ever worked on an electronic typewriter?"

"M, me?" I stammered. "Yes, a friend lent me one just before I came down here, here to the Manor."

"Come with me please."

She said it so calmly that I immediately began to suspect the worst was about to happen between me and her. I got to my feet and followed Pauline along the back row and down the side aisle and along the front of the class. The room had suddenly gone silent. All the machines had alarmingly ceased to function. This was it. All that had happened up until now could have been misconstrued and if nothing else, have been put down to alarmism and nothing more than a difference of opinion between two people, but the way that the residents had stopped what they were supposed to be doing, in order to watch... and listen... said it all. This wasn't some wild fanciful notion. This was real. They had been relying on me to bring about a change of attitude. But really, I was only a pawn in their game of wits with Pauline. It was a game which seemed to have been going on a lot longer than from the time when I had come on the scene. I couldn't look at the silent people. I looked down instead. I looked at the black high heeled shoes and at the back of the legs beneath the knee length red skirt, then up at the back of the black cardigan and the dark short hair as I followed Pauline. I looked out of the windows on my left in passing, and I looked at her desk and the large clock above and behind it on the wall. I seemed to be looking anywhere and everywhere. Except at the people on my right who had expected me to help them to beat Pauline. Had I let them down? I must have. Where were we going? Into the other part of the room? Through to where Laurie and the other maturing students were? What the heck was she going to do with me now?

"Wait here by the door for a moment." Pauline said to me. Then she went through while I stood there like an idiot, and yet, despite the subdued attention seeking noises made by Malcolm and one or two others as well. I still didn't look up. Instead, I seized the opportunity to snatch a glimpse of the paper, which I was holding in my hand. I pulled my glasses down to the tip of my nose and held the paper up and hurriedly scanned the writing. So many mistakes! and they all seemed to leap out from the white paper and hit me hard in the face. Only then did I look up and silently admit to those who could see my face, that I had, indeed, let them and myself down. I hadn't typed what she had told me to type. I was nowhere near as good as I should have been. She had only gone in there to sort some other business out. When she comes out again, she will dismiss me and I'll have to leave the room, in disgrace…

She came and opened the glass and wooden door, looked directly at me and then silently beckoned me inside. I felt stunned. I didn't know what to do now.

I didn't look back. All I could do was to follow her. She led the way to a vacant small desk which had a low and compact black case on the top of it. There was also another smaller black object to the right-hand side and black wires from both hung down the back edge of the white topped desk. In this part of the room there were two rows of desks, against the screen and the wall, with a central aisle between. Each row had four desks in it, eight desks in all. I was about to sit down against the solid wall and second from the front. Behind me and to my left, was where Josie would be sitting, if she was here. Laurie was working studiously on the front row. I didn't dare say anything to him. Besides. I didn't even know what was going to happen. I simply did not realise that I had won. Yes! I had won. They had won as well, and none of us seemed to realise it. It was nothing but an empty battle as it happened, an inglorious victory, but I hadn't seen it as anything like that. I had been selected by the Generals, against my will, to go into battle on their behalf and not until towards the end of that assessment lesson in the typing room, did I fully begin to realise.

The small black box was a tape recorder and the larger box was an electronic typewriter. Underneath the desk, on the floor, was a foot control for the recorder. Without speaking a word, Pauline removed the covers from both and fed the tape recorder with a smaller version of an ordinary conventional tape and then she turned to look at me and at last she spoke and said.

"This tape contains a poem. I will show you how to operate this equipment and then I shall leave you to get on with it. Here is a set of headphones which you will need to use... There will be no undue pressure on you. But what I must say is this... When you feel you are ready and you have familiarised yourself with these machines. Then I shall expect you to write that poem, 'word perfect.' And if you do that much... well! We'll see, shall we? but note! I want it done before the end of this session... Do you think you can manage to do that? Oh! yes... I know what goes on around here my man. You don't have to look so surprised. You must not fool yourself either. Actually. I am not the ogre some people make me out to be, you included... Now... I trust that you others will let him get on with this exercise... Good."

And she did. A few minutes later she was walking out of the room, just as I was beginning to recover from the shock of it all, and to find that this typewriter was so sensitive that if you breathed too hard on the keyboard then it might just go into overdrive and print half a page of gobbeldy-gook in no time at all. And as for resting my fingers in the appropriate position on the keyboard. Like I had always done on the manual machines… Well. That was now entirely out of the question. I was having to learn another approach to this skill of typing. My fingers must have to hover over the correct keys and lightly press down when I was ready. Wow! This really was 'Touch typing'

I sat and listened to the whole of the tape recording, trying to get a feel for the controls and store the words to memory at the same time. It was Pauline's voice on the machine. Every word was clearly spoken but a little slower than normal, capital letters, hyphens and all punctuation marks were also mentioned as was the requirement to create a new line and new paragraph wherever necessary. All in all, a very concise, first ever, lesson, in dictation, via a machine that I had to control with my foot, while at the same time; move my fingers over a sensitive keyboard and watch the blurred letters appearing as a black line across the paper at the back of the machine in front of me.

Having completed a test piece which I set for myself, I stopped what I was doing and tried to relax. I really needed to absorb the amazing fact that had brought me into this room, and so quickly as well… but I didn't dare because time was moving on and I hadn't started the exercise proper yet.

Lifting up my head for a brief moment I looked at the back of Laurie and was about to say something about the huge privilege of being in here, but he seemed to be concentrating hard on what he was doing and then I glanced to my left and noticed Pauline looking at me from the other side of the glass screen. I didn't dare to look to see what the others were doing behind me.

I had another practice run and had a bit of difficulty in operating the controls to the tape deck with my foot. All the while though it was on my mind that time was limited. I rewound the tape once more and made a concentrated effort to get everything as co-ordinated as I possibly could. Then I began and wrote the following, which I was later allowed to keep.

Hope, by Emily Bronte.

Hope was but a timid friend;
she sat without the grated den,
watching how my fate would tend,
even as selfish-hearted men.

She was cruel in her fear;
through the bars, one dreary day,
I looked out to see her there,
and she turned her face away!

Like a false guard, false watch keeping,
Still, in strife, she whispered peace;
she would sing while I was weeping;
if I listened, she would cease.

False she was, and unrelenting;
when my last joys strewed the ground,
even sorrow saw, repenting,
those sad relics scattered round;

Hope, whose whisper would have given
balm to all my frenzied pain,
stretched her wings, and soared to heaven,
went, and ne'er returned again!

A few seconds later a bell rang out in the corridor outside the typing room and I realised that I had only just, made it.

CHAPTER EIGHT

The next session, for the remainder of that day was supposed to be my free session. One where I could choose to do or go where I liked. Just as long as it was somewhere within the Manor and had the relevant tutor's permission to attend their assessment class. However, I was due to have a Mobility lesson with Gill Roberts instead. She will be coming out of the Mobility office at the other end of the Hall any moment now and I knew that it would still be daylight by the time she came and we went outside to begin the lesson...Then Jack Townley came up from behind me and said.

"What at thee weetin'fer Bob?"

"Hello Jack. I'm waiting, against me better feelings, for a mobility lesson..."

It was good that Jack was there. I could talk to Jack; he was a sensible man. Turning around to face him properly I noticed that he was holding a white cane in one hand. I couldn't help but say. "You too eh?" He looked down at the object with his one good eye and then he looked back at me and said.

"This? Nay lad... Thisuns razzlarse's... I'm keepin'owd on it while ay's gone fer a pee... Ahm takin'im dine Lisbourne steps t'dee... Did it Satdee nayte with th'rate folk, ahm just gooin see as ay dunna'urt 'im self... Weere's thine? Thee cane?"

I told him that I had left it in the lounge earlier on and then I went on to say.

"I'm more than a bit mixed up over this mobility lark Jack. I still dunna know as I need it… I anna blind... makes me feel a bit daft sometimes."

"Tak them glasses off and theyat be blind enough... 'ow blind dust want bay afore tha larns."

Like I said, Jack was a sensible man.

The crowds in the hall were thinning out by now and going their various ways for the last session of the day. Ian came down just as a few, seemingly new faces were about to go up the wide stairs.

"New Intake." I said to Jack. "Here's Ian as well."

"Aye and yonder's th'lass theyst got fer th'next hour or more."

I glanced in the direction he was indicating but couldn't see her clearly enough yet. Besides, I was feeling intrigued enough to want to see a bit more of how Ian coped with his dark world. He came around the newel post at the bottom of the stairs and reached out to his right for the oblong table, so as to make his way towards Jack's guiding voice. I stepped back and let him come past and I couldn't help but notice and be pleased at the same time when I saw that he was smiling as he took hold of the cane which Jack was offering him.

The white cane and Ian? Ian and the white cane? They belonged together. How different it had all been, just a few short weeks earlier.

I watched them go on their way and also watched Gill Roberts coming ever closer to where I was. A voice cried out from the direction of the lounge. It was Malcolm's voice

"Hey Bob! I'm going to the crafts room, are you coming with us?"

Malcolm had said his piece about the incident in the typing room on our way in for afternoon tea, and what he had had to say then had been embarrassing enough. I wasn't of the opinion that I had done anything significantly clever in dealing with Pauline. I had won. That much was certain, but I wasn't feeling very pleased about it. Malcolm was though. I didn't want him to start again. Fortunately, Gillian saved the day.

"No, he is not going to the crafts room with you Malcolm, he is coming with me. Come along."

And go with her I did.

We went much further afield than I thought we would that day. I had assumed that the Mobility lesson would take place within the Manor grounds, in the daylight, but I was wrong. Once we were outside the Manor, Gill indicated for me to follow her towards the white minibus and soon, just the two of us were heading down the long drive and then along Middle Lincombe Road towards? destination unknown.

We travelled for a good ten minutes until we came to the top of a hill in an old part of town. There were old houses on our left and a low, dark brick wall on our right. On the top of the low wall were iron railings and beyond the railings was a playground. Gillian pulled up at the side of the road.

There were still quite a lot of schoolchildren in the area. Gillian seemed to be waiting for the stragglers to go, and when they and the last of the cars left the compound, she decided it was time to move. Up until now Gillian hadn't said more than a dozen or so words since we had left the Manor grounds, and most of those had been directed at other road users, so I had no real idea what it was that was about to happen. Or even why we had come to this place. She got out on the driver's side and I got out on the other, then we headed towards the main building.

I walked behind and wondered about the woman in front. She hadn't got her floppy black hat on that day. She was still dressed all in black though. From her collar to her cuffs and right down almost to her ankles. Even her shoes were black and as I looked upwards again, I saw the boyish style of her short black hair and the neat way it just about covered her small ears.

We arrived at the main door together and she was just about to lift the shiny brass latch when she turned to me and asked me how far I could see? I looked up to the steadily darkening sky and said: -

"About a quarter of a million miles, or thereabouts."

"What?"

"The moon, the moon up there, it's about a quarter of a million miles away. I can see that. It's hazy but I can see it."

"Oh, Come on. Let's have you inside."

She lifted the brass latch on the dark red door and I followed her inside the building. I still had no idea what we were going to do and with the mood she seemed to be in I couldn't really care. Whatever it was, I just hoped we could get it over with as soon as possible and then get back to the Manor where I could have my tea and then go and involve myself with other, more sociable people.

We stopped while Gillian spoke to a tall bald-headed man in a dark blue boiler suit. He was cleaning one of the classrooms near to the way we had come in. They both passed pleasantries for a short while. Then I dutifully followed Gillian along a maze of empty corridors in this old building, until we came to a door with glass in it. On the other side of the glass there seemed to be a longer corridor at right angles to the one where we were and this one was about forty-foot long by about eight or ten feet wide. There were windows on the right-

75

hand side and solid walls interspersed with classroom doors on the other. I didn't know what was at the far end of that long corridor beyond the door. But I was shortly going to find out. And in quite an alarming manner.

It was obvious that something had upset Gillian. But what? Was it that time of the month with her as she had indicated earlier on that day? Or was it something else. Was it me? I certainly had a knack of getting on the wrong side of the staff at the Manor. Maybe I had done, was doing, or not done, something. But something was wrong and I didn't feel like trying to find out what that something was. I stood and watched while she rummaged in her coat pockets. Then she turned and caused me complete bewilderment by asking me to remove my glasses so that she could blindfold me with the black mask in her hand. I refused to oblige, and in no uncertain terms either.

"What the hell's going on here?" I demanded to know. "You anna puttin' that thing on me... no bloody way!"

"Oh! Don't be so silly! I am not going to use this as it is, I shall put these tissues inside to protect your eyes for you. Come on now don't be awkward. I do this with most of my wards. I thought you must have heard of my doing this by now... No? Oh well! Never mind, but I'm afraid I must insist that you wear this blindfold. It is so that I can see for myself how you might cope. Come on now. Please do as I say and we can get this little exercise done and then we can go back."

I was in quite a dilemma. I couldn't bring myself to do what she wanted me to, but then. I didn't really want to antagonise her any more than she seemed to be already, and I couldn't just walk away and try to ignore her. Where could I go? I didn't know where we were, and it was going properly dark out there now, beyond the glass windows of this dimly lit corridor. I needed this woman to take me back to the Manor. There would come a time when I wouldn't need her when darkness fell but that time was not yet.

After a fair bit of deliberation on my part and a lot more persuading on her part. I was eventually, and very reluctantly, almost at the point of agreeing to do her bidding. She wanted me to be part of an entirely different environment. And I wasn't liking it. I wasn't liking it one little bit.

"Why do we have to do this?" I asked. "I mean. Why come all the way out here just so as you can blindfold me and expect me to do what you want me to do? Whatever that is? I can't even get you to understand, can I? that having taken my glasses off I can't see a damned thing of any use anyroad. Why are you insisting on that blindfold so much?

Her answers were sharp and plainly spoken. "Now look here... I told you this morning that I would not stand for any nonsense today. You made a promise to me that you would co-operate but you are not co-operating, you are just as stubborn as ever you were. If, if I really have to explain to you then I shall. I have brought you here because you have never been here before have you? So, you will not in the slightest way be familiar with any of these surroundings, will you? Now everyone knows that the most confusing situations for blind people arise out of being in unfamiliar locations. You can, well, most blind people can cope better when they know at least a few landmarks, that is why they can do so much better on their own patch. What I am trying to do with you, you stupidly awkward man, is to try and ascertain; just how you might cope in unfamiliar surroundings, without being able to see. I don't know for certain what it is you can or cannot see without your glasses, but I do know that even without your glasses, you are not a total. You can see something even if it is only shadows... All that I want to do is to block out your visual senses for a little while so I can find out the best way to help you. Is that really too much for me to expect?"

"Sorry."

"There's no need to apologise, but I accept anyway. Can we get on? Just stand still while I fasten this."

Cane in hand and the blindfold covering my eyes. I heard the door in front of me creak on its hinges and then I was being guided through. I wasn't being truly submissive, there was still the rebellious independent streak in me. If she had tried to destroy that, then she would have destroyed the man.

I had seen her point though and that was the only reason why I had decided to go along with her plans. I only wish that she had explained it on our way here or while we were in the minibus outside the school waiting for the children to come out, but she didn't.

It was a nasty experience all in all, because she wanted me to walk along that other corridor and there were all sorts of obstacles in my way. Gillian was ahead of me and she was either putting them in front of me deliberately or else they must have had a really peculiar system at that school. The first object I encountered clanged metallically against the tip of the cane I was swinging from side to side. I stopped and struck it again and then realised that it must be a fire extinguisher, but why was there a fire extinguisher in the middle of this seemingly wide corridor? I decided to go around it to my right. But then I realised with a bump to my shoulder that there was a solid wall on my right. "What am I doing over here?" I muttered. Then I tried to get back on course and I found myself going in the opposite direction to the intended one and I wasn't even aware that I had turned around, never mind how? The sound of Gillian's voice turned me but I wasn't walking now in the straight line that I thought I was. I soon found myself in an alcove of sorts and realised that it must be a doorway to one of the classrooms.

"I shall not say anything further for a few seconds." Said Gillian.

"Oh, thanks... Leaving me to sort this out for meself are you?"

I wasn't thinking rationally enough yet. I turned half a circle as I thought and moved forward a couple of paces. Then I walked a few more steps, swinging the cane from side to side in front of me. My intention was to find the opposite wall but it was either a very wide corridor or else I was going in the wrong direction again. Or maybe it was the right direction. I was getting confused now. Was I going up or down that corridor? Or was I going from side to side? I had no visual way of knowing and inside I began to worry. I stopped for a moment and reached up with my hand.

"No!" Said Gillian. "Leave it on. You are doing alright so far. If you take that off. I will not help you anymore. I mean it!"

She did as well. I could tell by the sound of her voice. But I could also tell by the sound of her voice that she was over on my right-hand side, just behind my shoulder. I straightened myself up. As I thought, so as to be in parallel with the line of the corridor. I was wrong again. I was nowhere near in line with the corridor. The cane struck something metallic again. I instantly thought that it was the same fire extinguisher, but it wasn't, this metal object sounded slightly different than the other one. I went to my left this time, to get past it, but my knee brushed against a radiator. Quickly realising what it was when I felt the heat against my leg I turned carefully around. A radiator had to be on a wall. which wall? It didn't matter. It was against a wall. That's all that mattered. I turned around with my back to the radiator and squared myself up in just the same manner as I had done at the base of my bed back in Stepping Hill eye Hospital, more than three years previous.

My eyes were covered then as well, but covered with bandages. It was around the third week of Hospitalisation. I had done nine days flat on my back and in the following days, eating, resting and getting aware of my surroundings. I had undergone preliminary walks around the ward with the nurses in order to try and get me back on my feet again. I had been assisted on my way to the toilet, and a few hours later I had wanted to go again. But there was no one there to help me. I had called out once more but there was no reply. Except from the man in the next bed and I knew he was bedfast. I was bursting to go and there was no one to help me. Or so I thought. I had got out of bed and had lined myself up at the foot of my bed. My head was spinning. My legs were wobbly and my hands were sweating whilst I readied myself for the eleven steps that I would have to take and which I had somehow had the sense to have counted previously. I had hesitatingly let go of the base rail of my bed and taken the first tentative step forward. I then heard Joe Devine's voice over on my right and on the opposite side of the ward, he was full of sleepy concern and I realised he had just woken up. He had called out for me to stay where I was while he came to help me, but a woman's voice interrupted him. This was the voice of the nurse, Helen, she was saying "No Joe. Leave him he'll be alright." Helen's coming, I thought. But Helen didn't come. She stayed in the distance and gently encouraged me to continue on my own. I wanted to give in and cry for help, but Joe was encouraging me now and there was someone else as well. Another nurse. This was Dorothy, Dorothy was the one who had held my hands when they had taken the one hundred and eighty-six stitches from my face and my eyelids just a few days previous. "Come on Robert." She said. "What's a short walk like this compared to what you went through the other day. Come on love. You can make it to wherever you want to go."

"You can make it to wherever you want to go." Those same words were ringing hauntingly in my ears from the depths of memory. Joe's voice too, and Helen's… but where was Gillian's voice of encouragement?

My mind came back to the present. I was somewhere in the depths of an old school. I was stupidly blindfolded with a cane in my hands and leaning against a hot radiator which seemed to be getting hotter. And there were no words of encouragement at all. None... Which way should I go? Right or left? Straight on would bring me to the opposite side of the corridor. Or would it? I began to swing the cane from side to side and then in an arc around my body, it connected against an obstacle on my left, near the end of the cane swing. This must be the fire extinguisher again? But no! What the hell was it doing halfway out into the corridor? And why wasn't there the metallic sound like before. I started to bend down and reach out with my left hand in order to find out what it was. Then I remembered what Sarah had said that night when she and Henry her guide dog, had brought me back from the Lodge, the night my glasses had been stolen. And I remembered what they had said in the daily living skills bungalow as well. "Go down within your own space." Gillian didn't say this though. She didn't say anything. I'm sure she would have though, if she had seen me doing it wrong. Anyway! I went down, within my own space, and when I was sitting on my heels. I reached out with my left-hand and found, a wastepaper basket.

I knew she was watching me, she had to be. She wouldn't be doing anything else, but, where was she? and why didn't she say anything? Then I started to realise…This was a period of discovery, finding out how I could cope if I was blind. But I wasn't blind! I was just damned well blinded by this stupid blind-fold. I stood up. Enough was enough. I turned to where I imagined her to be and said. "Okay. I've had enough of this. Can I take this off and can we go now?"

"Not yet." Said Gillian, soothingly, surprisingly soothingly. And I was facing the wrong way. I turned toward the sound of her voice and said.

"Why not? What more do you want me do?"

"Get yourself parallel to the wall. That's right, keep your hand on the wall. Now, remove your hand and concentrate as you come towards me... Just two more minutes and then you can take it off and we will go."

"Anything for a peaceful life." I muttered.

She spoke once more in order to give me a pinpoint direction, and then left the rest to me... me, and the cane in my hand.

I must have walked at least twenty paces before she spoke again and she asked me what was different about the area. I had to think hard, but it was the way her voice had carried to my ears more than anything else, which told me that the ceiling seemed to be lower here. My guess seemed to please her.

"Concentrate now Robert. This next is crucial... I now want you to carry on walking forward and be ready to instantly stop on my command."

Walking nervously, I was worrying what might be about to happen… A few more paces and she cried out. "Stop!" and grabbed hold of the back of my jacket at the same time.

How did she get behind me? I was feeling bewildered. I hadn't detected any obstacle in front of me. Not even a wall. But I wasn't supposed to detect something solid. I was supposed to detect 'Nothing!'

Gillian got me to take a few steps back and took the blindfold off me. I rubbed my eyes and then reached into my trouser pocket for my glasses and put them on, feeling immensely glad to be able to see once more, but I was also very shocked by what I saw. So much so that I inadvertently let out an exclamation that I shouldn't have. There was a flight of steps going down in front of me and I was standing near to the top of them. I hadn't sensed them and the cane in my hand had not detected them either. Her tone was serious as she got me to look at her as she said: -

"Perhaps now you will begin to understand what I am trying to do for you."

We stopped to pick up a group of residents who were waiting in the dark for us somewhere near to the harbour area of Torquay and we were all just in time for the evening meal when we arrived back at the Manor. All that is. Except for Gillian. The gong sounded in the main hall and the residents began moving towards the dining room when I noticed Gillian coming out of the mobility office door a few yards over on my left. She stopped and looked at me but said nothing. Then she put on her large floppy black felt hat she was so fond of wearing and then she turned up the brim and looked at me once more and smiled before she departed through the old oak door with a subtle swish of her long black coat.

A lot of people thought that Christopher was stupid, but this was mainly due to his physical afflictions. He was not stupid, not by a long shot. Once I or anyone else got to know him, we very soon discovered that he was quite a clever man. And those who didn't even try to get to know him, were dafter than they thought he was.

I was feeling glad that Monday night that Christopher had quickly realised that his troubled way of talking might cause a few health problems during meal-times. He was sitting opposite me, where Ann used to sit. I saw him throw back his large head as he began to deep throated say.

"I know there... there is a problem... You will have to excuse me please... I can't help myself... If I do not talk at m, m, meals... will that b, b, be alright?"

Laurie raised a white eyebrow as he looked across the angle of the table at me, and said. "Talk as much as ye like mon. Therr's oonly Bob across the wee."

81

After the evening meal of something tasting like beef stew, but with very little beef in it. I ended up out in the main hall again and sat on one of the wooden benches for a while and talked to Christopher. He told me about his blond haired, blue eyed girlfriend Gwendoline. He always had to say her name in full whenever he mentioned her, even though he struggled with the effort of doing so. Gwendoline seemed to be a nice person from his description of her and she also had the same kind of physical condition. They were planning to marry at some date in the near future but he wasn't exactly sure when. He went on to tell me that he wanted to learn how to type so that he could improve his job skills at a printing works. I was surprised that he was able to hold down a job at all. This was another enlightenment into the character of this crippled man.

A short while later we were interrupted in our conversations by the arrival of Royston and Sid. They sat with us and talked for the next few minutes while they waited for their transport to arrive. It was good that Royston and Sid were there. We reflected on our Sunday outing in Plymouth and as best we could we included Christopher in with the topic, then Royston signed that he was going to the quarter final rifle shooting that evening and that he had been selected to take a leading part in the event. I think Christopher might easily have been tempted to go with Royston and Sid that night if they had asked him, but they didn't. A couple of minutes later they were off, and about five minutes later Jean of the Care Staff came and took Christopher away to the office. I phoned home at nine o'clock and after that I managed to have a talk about the forth-coming Concert with Denise and Samantha when they came in from an evening outing at about half past nine. A short while later they went upstairs to bed.

I was in the lounge observing a few of the new arrivals. And then there was Peter and a few others of the more mature residents to watch, listen to and to talk to as well. Peter had arrived back from his long weekend about an hour earlier. Somehow, he had missed his train from London, so a relative had driven him here instead. I could only wonder if the remainder of our Intake had arrived. If they had, and they should have done by now, then they will be settling in down at the Lodge.

As the hour drew closer to bedtime, I watched in quiet fascination as the veterans slowly drifted out of the lounge a few at a time. I said goodnight to Peter and watched him go also. Then there were only a few of us left, which consisted mostly the new Intake. There was a young fair haired, very badly disfigured blind girl sitting on her own. She was about eighteen years old, and a short distance from her sat two forty something men, one blind the other not so. Both of the men were smartly dressed in dark suits and ties. Then there were the two women stood near the grand piano, who I could also tell, were new recruits to the Manor. One of them was tall and in her mid to late-twenties. She wore a dark dress and had short dark hair which was cut and shaped like a ball around her head and neatly trimmed in line with her chin. She wore dark, rather mysterious glasses as well, which couldn't hide, and indeed, betrayed the fact that she was completely blind. Her narrow mouth widened in a grin at something the other woman was saying to her. Then the other woman, who was about the same age looked across the room to where I was sitting and observing. I couldn't be sure if she was looking at me or not, or even if she could see me. She seemed to be giving me a sour look or it could have been something more innocent, but whatever! I began to get the distinct impression that I ought to be elsewhere. I looked away just as the door opened and in walked Jenny from the care staff to advise us that it was time for bed.

There was no need for me to leave just yet, with me being a Manor veteran and all that. Besides, I knew that it would take at least five more minutes for Jenny to round up the stragglers and pack them off upstairs before she could begin to put all the lights out. I watched the last blind resident as he silently found the exit and went out of the door, and slowly getting to my feet I went over to the bay window area to retrieve the cane. Then I stopped for a moment to look out through the partly open curtain at the darkness of night beyond the glass. I was alone now, alone with just my quietly spoken thoughts for company.

"It's dark out there but I'll be alright with this. Those steps back at that school didn't half spook me though. Aye, there's a lot to learn with this thing yet."

The hall was brightly lit and quiet. The few remaining residents were climbing the stairs. This must have been the very first time that I hadn't made any attempt to hide the white cane. Maybe it was because I knew, or at least had a good idea that the hall would be empty by now. Or, perhaps I had already psychologically begun to accept the cane for what it was. I don't know. I'm no psychologist... but I was soon going to meet up with someone who was.

I made my way across the emptiness of the hall and then I heard Jenny's voice on the balcony above and to my left. She was talking to someone up there and then I heard the voices of two men saying goodnight to her. Any moment now she would be making her way back around the balcony and come down the wide stairs over on my right and then she would ask me to leave and then she would lock the ancient oak doors behind me.

I wasn't feeling afraid. Apprehensive, but not really and truly afraid, as I stood beneath the arched curve of the stone porch entrance, staring out into the darkness of night. Then I heard the heavy iron bolt being shot home from the other side of the old oak door, I waited half expectantly for the porch light to be extinguished, but I knew that it really wouldn't be. The cane gave out a metallic echo as I tapped it on the stone slabs at my feet. I had done this to compress the four sections together and soon wished that I hadn't for fear of attracting attention. But then, who was there to attract at this time of the night?

"Come on Bob." I mumbled "Come on... time to get going..."

The night air was cold. There was a gentle rustle of wind in the tree-tops nearby, but the wind didn't reach to where I was. I had made my slow but careful way across the yard and had reached the first curve at the beginning of the long drive; down towards the main gates. If this had been daylight and I had deemed to look back as I was at that moment, it would be at this point that the Manor would begin to disappear from view. Looking in the opposite direction, the way I was supposed to be heading. I could see nothing. I looked upwards to the sky and I could see nothing there either, nothing at all. Ahead there was nothing but the foreboding blackness. I turned my head to my left and looked back in the direction of the Manor again. There were three lights in the distance. One, the larger one, I knew to be the yellow porch light. The other two, closer together lights I didn't know. They hadn't been there a second or two ago. I could only assume that they must be the lights from the Braille teachers flat which was perched above the Commerce building over to the right. But no, these lights were moving, and they were coming towards me. I knew then that it must be a car, or a vehicle of some description. Stepping back to put myself tighter up against the wall, I waited for it to come past me. It did and soon there was nothing more to show for the intrusion on the beginnings of my lonely journey to the Lodge, than two red lights fading into the distance. Looking back to where I had come from, I could only see one light now. The red lights and the sounds of the car had gone, it was just as if nothing had happened, except for the tell-tale acrid smell of burnt petrol fumes.

The old spectre hadn't shown its ugly head yet. I was feeling edgy, that's true to say, but I still wasn't truly afraid. I was in no big hurry. I tested the unseen ground around me and couldn't help but wonder once more at the uncanny abilities of holding and using a white cane. I felt a weird tingle travel down my spine. It wasn't a tingle of pleasure or anything like that. No, this was the tingling feeling of a challenge. I was actually stepping out beyond the barriers at long, long last. This was the last great hurdle in coming to terms with my disability. I knew that now. Swinging my body around to my right I headed off once more into the darkness.

The first street lamp was situated just beyond the main gateway and I reached that point safely enough then carried on my way without stopping. I passed the second street lamp and the third, and so on, and in between, in the dark spots between the street lamps, was where I constantly tested the ground in front of me by casually and deliberately swinging the cane in a wider arc to my right so that I could continue to be reassured by the clicking of the cane against the solid assurance of the base of that long, high and ancient stone wall.

Eventually I arrived at the dark and slightly intimidating entrance to the drive at America Lodge. It was dark in there on the other side of the Lodge gates… very dark, compared to where I was standing. I began to look around me and wonder why I was so reluctant to venture any further. I had come this far down from the Manor with no mishaps, none at all. So why didn't I want to carry on when I was so near to my goal? Turning my head to the left, I could see street lamps fading away into the distance, downhill in the direction of Torquay, and over on my right there was the white light of the last street lamp which I had passed beneath, and the parked car as well. I could see the faint and hazy white light of the street lamp but I couldn't see the car anymore. Could it really have been only a few minutes previous, that I had come past that light and that car?

Directly behind me was pitch black darkness. Ahead of me lay another area of darkness. And ahead further still, I could just make out the dim yellow lights from one of the windows of the Lodge. There was nowhere else to go except straight ahead up that dark drive, this was the most sensible direction to take, so what was I waiting for?

A man's voice startled me and made me instantly look over to my right, but I couldn't see anything of any use. There it was again and then there was the sound of a car door closing.

"You took your time in getting down here didn't you...? Said the voice. "Why have you stopped now?"

I was puzzling about where I had heard that voice before, but the recollection was slow in coming. Apart from the sound of his footsteps, he made no other sound until he came out of the darkness and stood in front of me, but I still couldn't make out his features. Then I remembered who he was at the same instant that he said his name. "Don't you remember me? Tim, Tim Dunce? I'm the Psychologist here, I have been watching you. By the time I left the main building I thought that you would have been more than halfway towards your destination…"

"Shows what you know about me then doesn't it." I remarked, a little hastily, and sourly as well. This intrusion was not very welcome. I was feeling further annoyed that this person had taken it upon himself to study me as he had apparently done so. If he had offered to help me to get here I wouldn't have felt so annoyed. It was almost as if he was using me in some way. I had done it now, so I didn't immediately alter the tone of my voice as I continued with.

"What do you want? Sorry, what do you want?"

"Nothing really... I saw that you had become extremely hesitant at this point and wondered what might be the matter. If I am interfering, I apologise... Actually though. As I am here, there was something I would like to ask of you. Would you mind? I really would like to know, what is your driving force? I am most intrigued... I must admit, I have not yet seen anyone displaying such potent and aggressive determination as I have seen in you over the previous three evenings. Although... I also hasten to say, I have only been here for a matter of a few short weeks myself, so it may just be pure conjecture on my part, or perhaps, just a little too early to tell, but you do fascinate me, you really do. You're not going to answer me are you. Never mind I didn't really expect you would... Now, is there something I can do here? Some way that I may help you perhaps? Why don't we go inside? perhaps you might feel more inclined to talk once we're safely indoors... Hmmm?"

I didn't want to carry on up that drive now, especially not in the same way that I had done on my way down from the Manor. Even though he had been spying on me... This business with the cane was too much of a personal thing with me as yet. I didn't want anyone else other than Gillian Roberts to be involved with the combination of cane and me. At least, not until I could bring myself to really accept it for what it was. It was no use standing there all night either. Did I really want to talk to this man who had been watching me? Observing me on my nightly excursions for goodness knows how many nights?

"I'll manage by meself thanks. You can go now. I'll be alright, I'm tired anyway. Goodnight!"

He didn't go though. He did initially. He said he would have to go and lock his car up and then he would make sure I got to my destination. I wasn't sure what else to do other than to become rude to the man. It was either that or else do what I did do. I used his momentary departure to the best effect.

The moment he began to walk away from me, I set off on the epic last leg of my journey that dark night in rather a hasty fashion. I got maybe three quarters of the way up the drive before he came up behind me and took hold of my arm for the rest of the way. It's true. I had been stumbling a bit, but I wasn't that unsteady for him to have to help me to the main door.

He was punching in the code just as a rather loud and seemingly large group of Lodge residents were coming up the drive behind us.

"Hold that doorrr!" Shouted one of the men, and they followed us inside.

The Den was packed. The washing machines were spinning down at the far end of the room. There was alcohol induced merriment from some of the residents as they prepared late suppers. Four men nearest the door were having a heated conversation on religious affairs. I noticed Mike sitting nearby at the head of the long row of tables. He was trying his best to keep out of everyone's way but failing miserably and because of his nearly completely blind condition he seemed to be having a bit of difficulty in locating the hot drink on the table top in front of him. I went to help him but changed my mind when I noticed the guy who had been spying on me lean over and place the mug nearer to Mike's wandering hands. Then Tim Dunce turned to me and said.

"It's a bit noisy and crowded in here. How would you like me to come up to your room? I'm sure we'll be able to talk much better up there than here."

"No! This'll do..." I said impatiently. Heads were already turning in our direction. Two men in a single bedroom, together! Guaranteed to set tongues wagging was that. Or maybe, I was just getting a bit overwrought with the whole situation and letting paranoia carry me away in its slimy grip.

Looking straight into the face of this man; this Occupational Psychologist I began to wonder what he was making of all of this and me. I couldn't take much more. I was already confused and this guy was confusing me even more. But he wouldn't take no for an answer. I knew we couldn't talk there in the Den. It really was far too noisy, and crowded as well. I turned to go out and hesitated for a moment as I looked across the way to the typing room door on the other side and a bit further down the dimly lit corridor. I went over, reasoning to myself that this was probably the best and closest room where he could try to analyse me, if he really had to. I put my hand towards the doorknob and froze for a second as I remembered that early morning of the first of November, a couple of weeks since. That was the day after Halloween and I was reminded of what had happened when I had last opened this door.

As I wrapped my fingers around the knob, the man behind me couldn't have known the reason for my hesitation, but he read the signals the wrong way and just for once; the situation was turned to my advantage. My hesitation caused Tim to say.

"Oh alright. Maybe some other time perhaps... Goodnight."

I watched him as he easily negotiated his way past a group of residents coming towards the Den entrance, and then he was gone, lost to my eyes ahead of the crowd now entering the Den. "Nowt wrong with his eyes." I muttered quietly to myself as I relaxed my grip on the door to the typing room. I didn't go in. I didn't go into the crowded Den either. Instead, I went up to bed.

CHAPTER NINE

Compared to how it had been the night before, the Den at five o'clock the following morning was as different as it was possible to be. I stood at the ever-open doorway entrance and surveyed the scene after I had reached around the corner to switch on the lights. It was windy out there, outside the lodge. I think this was what had woken me up half an hour earlier. The only sound was the tap tapping of a tree branch on the Den windows. I had an armful of washing with me which badly needed doing. I had already run out of underwear, and no one here was going to do my washing for me. The staff even made as many of the Totals as they could, do their own washing.

The machines at the far end of the room were as still and quiet as the corridors I had travelled along in order to get here, but they were not quiet for long. Ten minutes later I was beginning to wonder if it had been a good idea to do some washing at this hour of the morning. Another five minutes and I was anxiously trying to shut the door to the Den soon after the spin cycle kicked in. I managed to do it. The door was stiff on its hinges and I could tell that it had been a long while since anyone had attempted to do this. I sat down again and picked up the mug of coffee. I then looked up at the green ceiling and tried to work out what was above. This part of the Den; nearest the door, was directly below the corridor at the top of the stairs, which ran almost the entire length of the Lodge. This also meant that the washing machines on my right, at the far end of this oblong shaped room were directly beneath one of the bedrooms which were all on the right- hand side of the corridor above.

"Oh, sod it."

I got to my feet and went over to switch the machine off before it brought the wrath of some of the residents down on my back, but I was already too late.

The electric motor wound to a stop after being robbed of its energy source and a momentary silence descended, this was quickly replaced by a loud squeak. It wasn't an angry resident who pushed on the door and made the hinges squeal. It was an angry Ruth; the night care staff lady.

"Whatever in the world is going on in here at this time in the morning!" She exclaimed in a forced voice.

"Sorry." I said. "I should have realised... sorry."

"I should think so too. I'll tell you what, now that I'm here, you can just make me a cup of coffee for causing me to nearly have a heart attack. You bloody insomniacs will be the death of me I swear."

I made her a drink as requested and then we sat and talked about life and its ups and downs, and eventually, to where her career was going. And what would I be doing when I finally decide on my future career after all those secure years at the Post Office. They were gone now. I had no career. No real security any more. And talking to Ruth only highlighted this fact.

"So?" She said. "What would you like to do when you leave this place?"

"I don't know. Back home at the job centre, they didn't want to know me, they kept fobbing me off with excuses and that someone else would see to me. Someone did. Ian Allwood's his name. He's the man who got me to come here."

"I know him. I know Ian. He's introduced a lot of people to this place, particularly over the last two years or so."

This led Ruth off at a tangent as she began to explain about some of the people, she had known who Ian Allwood and others like him had introduced to the Manor.

A short while later around about half an hour from her hasty entrance, she was on her feet and about to leave the den. She turned to look back at me when she got to the doorway, and said. "You don't fancy having another go at the typing room door again, do you?"

I could hear her soft laughter as she turned and disappeared out of sight in the corridor.

The branches of a tree outside tapped intermittently against the dark glass, this and the soft howling of the wind, were again; the only sounds I could hear now. But it wasn't much more than ten minutes or so later that a few other insomniacs began to filter downstairs to the Den.

I stayed and watched and joined in conversations where I was allowed to and generally waited until I felt it prudent to be able to switch on the washing machine once more and finish off what I had started earlier on.

I was still there in the Den when the fire alarm bells rang out for fire practice at about half past seven, Ruth had given me a bit of advance warning of the fire drill but it soon became clear that a lot of the residents had been caught out.

We stood in a large group on the lawn outside the entrance to the Lodge, and as I looked around me for familiar faces I couldn't help but smile at one scene nearby as a group of four women and two men were guided onto the lawn, and they were dressed in billowing nightdresses and cardigans and coats and the two blind men were frantically clutching at the lapels of their dressing gowns, while at the same time they were doing their best to follow the leader and keep out of the cool wind as much as possible. The roll call didn't take more than a couple of minutes and then we were allowed to disperse. I searched the crowd for Mike, Jim and Josie and arranged for us to go up to the Manor together. I helped where I could, those who needed help, to get them back indoors and then I went up to my room to get ready for another day.

Mike was the, not so proud possessor, of a white cane that morning. He too had begun to have Mobility lessons. My cane was tucked away beneath my jacket. The day was bright and cool and a bit windy.

Josie and Jim were in the lead, we four were somewhere in the middle of a sizeable group walking up Middle Lincombe Road. I wasn't really experienced enough to be of any practical help to Mike, and most of all, I didn't want to do anything wrong. If I showed him how to use his cane as I was being taught how to use mine, it might be wrong, and it would only have confused him. I didn't want that. I was pleased to see that he had resumed some of his former confidence, for he was smartly dressed once again in the pale blue suit and tie with a white shirt and highly polished black shoes. The white cane he swung looked out of place though and the way he was swinging it from side to side didn't help either. The arc was far too wide, even I knew that, but I still didn't say anything. Mike hesitated briefly at one point to fold up the cane and then he let out a frustrated remark concerning that cane. (Unprintable here.) And finally, with the wind behind us, he grabbed hold of my arm and we carried on walking the remaining distance to the Manor, with me as his escort.

I stayed with Mike up to and until we arrived in the dining room, and it was good to be there with a man I had started this course with. In fact, by some strange set of circumstances. All the remaining members of our Intake were rather conveniently gathered together in the main hall that morning.

Mike and I had managed to find an empty bench in the hall near to the alcove where the phone is and we sat down to wait for the breakfast gong. It wasn't long before we were joined by Royston. He came down the wide stairs on his own and even though he did appear to be sleepy he soon aroused himself when his wandering gaze found us. Royston had come over to join us at about the same time that Peter was crossing the crowded hall from the lounge. I called out to him and he changed course. Then, Jim and Josie came and stood in amongst the crowd and I called out to them as well.

We reminisced for the next few minutes on various things and particularly on the colleagues we had lost, and those of us who remained. Mike asked the question.

"Who'll be the next to gow oye wonder?"

"Does it have to be someone?" Josie begged. "I mean, we've lost Brenda and Daniel and Albert. I don't want anyone else to go. I'd like it for the six of us to finish the course together so I would. Nigh don't let's have any more talk like that."

A few seconds later and the gong sounded out as loud as ever. Our party broke up as we joined in with the crowd all heading for the dining room. I escorted Mike to his table and then went over to the far side of the room to where my place was.

Laurie was there and so was Christopher. And there was also someone else. A woman... Dark haired with dark squinty eyes and about average build. She was sitting in Adrian's place, and if I wasn't very much mistaken, and I wasn't as it turned out, this seemed to be one of the new Intake and the same woman who had given me a scornful look the previous night in the lounge. I said good-morning all the same, and hoped that she wouldn't remember. She did though and I had to explain that I had only been casually observing her and the other new Intakes and not really being nosy. Anita was her name and I think I momentarily broke the ice as soon as I managed to find this out, by announcing, cheerfully. "Hey! We've just parted with an Ann and now we've got an Anita with us."

Breakfast was brought and we all busied ourselves. Anita seemed to be a pleasant enough person; on the surface, but then, she soon began to show her true colours.

Christopher's unusual eating habits were entirely due to his physical condition. I am no puritan and I would the first to admit that he had offended me a bit the previous day, when he had arrived at our table. But I knew he couldn't help being the way he was. I still wouldn't have liked it if he had tried to talk and eat at the same time. And I could have understood Anita's reaction if he had done, but he hadn't. All he did was sit there and put the food into his mouth and chew it in the best way that he could, with difficulty. I was alarmed when Anita threw down her knife and fork on the table and declared.

"Well really! Do we have to put up with such gross eating habits from that, that man?"

I looked across at Christopher. There was a piece of tomato skin hanging from his mouth. He had suddenly stopped chewing and seemed to be extremely offended. I wanted to say something. I even looked to my left and glowered as best I could at this unthinking insensitive woman sitting next to me. Then I looked diagonally across the table to Laurie. He had finished eating his sausages, egg and tomatoes and the anaemic eyes beneath that mop of pure white hair were magnetically drawing Anita to look across to him. Then he quietly spoke and said: -

"Yourre a guest at oour table lassie. The mon canna help it onc wee bit. If ye doon't like what ye see ye can just piss off and find somewherre else."

Anita got quickly to her feet and impatiently jostled the back of my chair to make me move and then she declared.

"Well, really! I have never been so offended. I did not come all the way here to this place to be treated like this."

It was a shame Anita got the treatment that she did. She didn't really deserve it, everything here was new to her, as it was to her colleagues. As it had been to all of us. I stood in the aisle, having let her out and watched her faltering pace as she quickly walked away, trying hard to retain what was left of her dignity amidst the goading from some of those nearest to our table that had overheard the commotion. I sat down once more and looked across at Laurie. He was concentrating on buttering some slices of toast. I then looked at Christopher, he had resumed eating his breakfast. A minute or so later he put down his knife and fork and awkwardly picked up and drank his cup of tea. Then he quietly and unsteadily got to his feet and departed.

I gave him an encouraging smile, then shrugged my shoulders and carried on eating. A few seconds later came a call for attention from the House Captain.

"Good morning ladies and gentlemen. First of all, I would like to welcome the five newest arrivals to Manor House. They are..."

CHAPTER TEN

Royston's coffee table was really beginning to take shape from that morning onward. I managed to find and go with him to the woodworking department and it was there that we parted once more. Royston to the benches and me to Gordon's office and the continuing lessons in Rush seat making.

Gordon took me a bit by surprise when he produced a chair, a chair with no seat to it and invited me to get started.

"The Rush is suitably damp and I would like to see a good result, a really good result by coffee break time. I shall now leave you… Off you go."

Working with, or for, a Master Craftsman like Gordon, was nothing short of a genuine honour, for me that is. I had had a bit of a false start in his department in the early days but I was quick and keen to realise the potential of learning from Gordon and so, here I was, determined not to let him or myself down.

It was just before the bell rang that Gordon came back to see how far I had got with the task, but I still had at least five more minutes of work to do. Not only did I have to do the work quickly, I had to do it to the highest of standards as well. At least Gordon was astute enough to quietly turn away and leave me alone when he noticed how close I was to finishing.

He came back again a few minutes later, accompanied by someone else. I had almost finished. Just a few more strands... Then the bell rang out.

"Stop there please."

"But..."

"It's alright, I didn't really expect you to actually complete it. Now let me see... Hmm. Come here Royston."

Gordon indicated Royston to come forward and then there was a quiet minute or so while they studied the frame.

At this point it might be prudent to explain a little more about the ancient craft of Rush seating... and the way that I was taught.

English Rushes were mainly harvested from the Norfolk fens where they grow straight and tall. Traditionally they would have been cut close to the rootstock below water level and then they would be taken by Punt and by land, to a place where they could air dry in roof covered; open sided sheds. This process took several weeks during the late summer. A good indicator that the Rush was nearly ready would be when the long green shoots turned light brown in colour. A few more weeks of turning and drying and then they would be gathered, in, adolescent armfuls. (what a teenage boy could encompass in his arms) These tapering bundles would then be tied with two strands of Rush, one at the top; narrow end and one at the bottom, while the boy held them around the middle. The bundles of Rush would be stored for a while longer and then sold to the likes of Gordon White.

Properly, and traditionally air dried; bundles of Rush, will keep for years and it only needs to be wetted once more for it to last a great many years further. The wetting process would be to take sufficient Rush and roll it up in a wet blanket and then leave it in a cool place overnight. The Rush was ready to use when it could be bent and twisted without it breaking. Two pieces would then be taken and put 'top to tail' (thick end to thin end) and the remainder covered up with the wet blanket. At the start of making a chair seat, these two strands would be

94

tied with a single short piece of Rush to the side frame of the chair, then it would be taken from the base of the seat (untwisted) and the twisting together of the two strands would only begin when coming around and up and over to the top of the chair seat. In other words, the underside of the seat would be strands and the side and top would be twisted together. Down, up, around and over. Down on the opposite side, around, up and over, gradually working towards the centre of the chair seat. When two strands were about to be used up, two more damp strands would then have to be brought together, top to tail, and knotted together to continue the pattern, but they should always be knotted on the underside and woven in such a way that the knots were never to be seen in the finished seat. Shorter pieces (waste) would be used to pack out the interior spaces as work progresses and gradually the traditional pattern would appear. There are complications to consider if, as in most cases, the seat is wider at the front than the back. But I won't bore the reader with these.

Royston put down the chair and he and Gordon talked in the sign language for a few seconds. Royston then carefully looked around to find me. Having done so, he gave me a smile, and a thumbs up sign.

"It would seem that your work also merits the approval of Royston."

"You said, also, are you okay with it as well Gordon?"

"Yeeees" He replied cautiously. Now then! The others have gone across by now... Leave this, I shall tidy up... However, as for tomorrow... I will have to find something else to occupy you... because I will need this room for something else... have you any thoughts?"

"I wouldn't mind a bit of woodturning Gordon, if that's alright with you?"

"Have you ever done any?" Queried Gordon.

"Yes. I've even got me own lathe back home. I've had it for years, even before me accident."

"Right then..." Said Gordon in a surprised voice. "Right! Off you go."

There was an empty space at the dining table. There was Laurie, Christopher and myself, but no sign of the newcomer, Anita.

Out in the main hall again a short while later I was with Royston once more, but not for long. I encouraged him and watched as he went over towards the far end of the hall to join the small crowd gathering for mobility lessons. He wasn't very keen on the prospect of what was to follow, but it was for the best, so I hadn't made any attempt to dissuade him. Meanwhile, it was time for me to go and do something that I was not very keen on... Braille!

Wendy greeted us as we arrived in her department. Fag in mouth she asked for Jim and smiled as he acknowledged her. Just how he had become her star pupil I may never know, but he had. There was no doubt that Jim was keen to learn Braille. My natural inclination was towards the other extreme, but I had upset too many of the tutors so far during my stay at the Manor, so I was doing my best not to antagonise Wendy, and as such I was slowly learning the entire Braille system.

I got up to the end of book one that morning and began on the smaller, blue backed book which contained most of the, so called. 'Contractions.' I won't bore the reader with too much of the finer details of Braille Contractions, suffice to say that Contractions consist of series of collections of dots which have different meanings to the main context of the Braille language. I hope I have said that correctly. The truth is, I was feeling at something of a loss by this stage. I was working alongside Jim at the time, so it would have been difficult not to become involved with the system. I still left the Braille room at lunch time, feeling not all that much wiser than when I had gone in.

Jim came up behind me as a large group of us were approaching the outer doors of the Commerce building. He wanted to know what strategy I was going to adopt when we went into Pauline's domain after lunch. I hadn't got a strategic plan, or anything else. It had slipped my mind that at some time that day I was more than likely going to have to confront Pauline once more. I think I had behaved myself that day with Wendy. Could I now carry on and do the same in the typing department with Pauline? To find out, I was going to have to wait until after lunch. In the meantime, something else was about to happen.

There was no sign of Laurie, Christopher, or Anita when I arrived at the table in the dining room. I had been one of the last to enter the room and Laurie was usually one of the first. Feeling slightly puzzled I sat down and waited for my lunch and my companions to come. It did but they didn't.

A man on the next table turned around and asked me if I had B.O. I smiled and obligingly lifted up my arms to sniff and said. "No, I don't think so."

Apple pie and custard followed the salad. I was eating the last mouthful, when Beryl of the Care staff came across to me and asked me the same question that the man at the next table had. I went through the motions once more and smiled up at her and said. "I don't think so, I had a good wash this morning, I've got clean underwear and a clean shirt on. Where are they?"

"Shush... Come with me." Said Beryl mysteriously. I followed her out into the, as yet, empty main hall.

We stood near the bottom of the stairs while she asked me what had happened that morning on our table. I told her as best I could remember and then she asked me to elaborate more. I couldn't be sure what it was she wanted from me, so then she asked. Rather impatiently.

"Did Laurie use a four-letter word to the new girl. We have been told that he did and was very offensive to her. The woman, Anita, was most put out and she is insisting that we take action against Laurie, for his behaviour, but she is also insisting that we allow her to leave as well. This sort of thing could be bad for the image of Manor house in the hands of someone like Anita. It seems that her 'Father' is something with a newspaper."

I began working it out on my hand. Then I looked at Beryl and said.

"Yes. Laurie did use a four-letter word, but it wasn't the one you might be thinking of. It didn't begin with an F, it began with a P. That young woman, Anita, she was being abusive towards Christopher. Ask any of the others nearby... Laurie was only doing what he felt he had to do. He only said what I might have said if I had been quick thinking enough at the time. It's a bit of a shame but you might as well let her go home. She's not really Manor materi..."

The word remained incomplete and I immediately felt awkward. I could feel my face becoming hot. This feeling was doubled in intensity when Beryl looked at me in complete surprise and then started to walk away while at the same time she remarked sourly.

"Oh really! And who on earth, gave you the right to be judge and jury?"

The residents were leaving the dining room by this time and my apologetic words were lost on the back of Beryl in the ensuing noisy confusion.

I was dreading the thought of going to the typing department even more now. What the heck was likely to happen in there after what had happened so far?

I saw Beryl for a fleeting moment when I was about to leave the main hall. She was coming out of the Care staff office and completely ignored me as she made her way towards the lounge. I felt like going after her to apologise properly, but it was too late for that now. Besides, it might complicate matters further.

I was standing in more or less the same spot in the main hall that I had last seen Albert standing, just before he had departed on the Friday previous. Albert's sentiments began ringing in my ears.

"You should have been like me…You should have been like me Bob and kept a low profile."

Albert had gone home, and he had told me that he was going home to get his compensation claim sorted out. I was still here at the Manor. I hadn't kept a low profile, so where did that leave me? My compensation claim had already been dragging on for years, and I had no idea how much longer it was likely to drag on for. What could I do? I was only just beginning to come to terms with the dark and the thoughts of using a white cane in the dark. Could I dare to allow my troubled mind to venture further into the realms of obscurity and pluck out the next big problem for me to cope with? No! No... It was too much.

Still in a gloomy mood I sat down in the typing department and looked at the crude wooden box which was covering the keyboard. There had been no sign of Pauline or anyone else of authority when we had entered the room. I had vaguely reasoned to myself that as I had been moved from the cumbersome manual typewriters the last time I had been in this room, and been taken through into the other part where the electronic machines were. Then surely, I ought to be sitting in there awaiting my instructions for the day. Jim was sitting directly behind me and added weight to my convictions. He began insisting that I should go and join Josie and the others on the other side of the glass partition. I think I had decided in my own mind by this time that to go into that part of the Typing department without being invited to, would have been a bit impertinent of me. A bit of humble pie attitude won't go amiss here I decided... How wrong can a man be?

A few seconds later. The slim, dark haired, petite and middle-aged figure of Pauline, came and entered the room. I looked away from Christopher sitting beside me with his fingers on the hidden keyboard, and looked to the front instead "Good afternoon all." She said as she began making her way towards her desk. There was a mumbled reply and then, having put her papers down, Pauline began looking around the room... and noticed me... With eyes inextricably fixed on each other, she came towards me. Disarmingly; she arrived and faintly smiled down at me and said. "Whatever are you doing here Robert? Don't tell me that you prefer these machines after all? Somehow, I don't think you do. Would you mind? Oh! and please sit at the same desk as you did yesterday. There's another exercise on the tape recorder which is all ready for you."

What was I saying about humble pie? Pauline was coming behind me. Her manner was different to what it had been and what I had come to expect of her. Had I really underestimated her so badly? I was only just beginning to realise that, 'Yes' I had.

Pauline had told me the day previous that she was not the ogre that I and others believed her to be. Maybe, she and Beryl were right. Who am I to judge other people? when I couldn't even judge the ability to judge myself.

We entered the room in verbal silence. Which really, we should have both known better than to do, because there's not a lot that is more infuriating for a blind person, than to be deprived of the knowledge of what is going on around them. Except perhaps, too much of it. Anyway, for the time being, I sat down at the far superior machine than the one out there beyond the glass screen.

I could see a few of the others. They were out there, on the other side of the screen. I could just see Christopher's head and shoulders. Then there was a movement beside me. I looked up and watched Pauline as she silently turned away and closed the glazed door on her way out.

I was modestly, rather pleased with myself by the end of that session. But the real pride I was feeling was for the fantastic abilities of my wife. Who, in the first place and only a couple of weeks after the accident, when she alone had recognised a reason for my impatient frustration, had seen a need for me to learn a new skill whilst I had been blinded. It was Janet who had very wisely recognised the need for me to keep my hands and mind occupied. It had been Janet who had sown the seed of an idea even while I had been in Hospital. And that seed had germinated into the desire to learn how to type. And now, the fruits of her efforts, and mine I suppose, were now in front of me. I had a feeling that I had correctly written the long verse, as it had come to my ears over the tape recorder. It was Pauline's voice on that machine and she had dictated what I had to type, right down to when and where I ought to put the full stops and the commas and whatever else.

My work was finished and I was trying my best to read what I had written but with more than a bit of difficulty. Until, that is, a man across the other side of the aisle behind me got to his feet and offered me a magnifying glass, thanking him I then turned to look down at the page again and this is what I had written.

The Farmer's boy. Attributed to Charles Whitehead.

The sun went down behind the hill, across the dreary moor. Weary and lame, a boy there came up to the farmer's door.

"Can you tell me sir, if any there be, that will give to me employ,
for to plough and sow, for to reap and mow and to be a farmer's boy.
My father's dead and mother's left with her five children small,
and what is worst for mother still, I'm the eldest of them all.
Though little I am, I fear no work, if to me you'll give employ,
for to plough and sow, to reap and mow and to be a farmer's boy.
And if you won't employ me sir, one favour I've to ask.
Will you shelter me 'till the break of day from this cold winter's blast?
At the break of day, I'll trudge away, elsewhere to seek employ,
for to plough and sow, for to reap and mow and to be a farmer's boy."

The farmer said. "I'll try the lad, no further let him seek."

"Oh yes dear father." The daughter said, while tears ran down her cheek,
for them that will work it's hard to want, and wander for employ,
for to plough and sow and reap and mow and to be a farmer's boy"

At length the boy became a man and the great old farmer died.
He left the lad the farm he had, and his daughter to be his bride.
And now the lad a farmer is, and he smiles and thinks with joy.
Of the lucky day, when he came that way to be a farmer's boy.

I had somehow felt deeply touched by the sentiments within that verse. It seemed to be so appropriate to the way I was feeling at the time, that I couldn't help but wonder if there was deliberate intent? Or was it just by sheer chance, that Pauline had picked that particular verse, out of many, many thousands of verses; for me to type out that day... I could only wonder.

I dutifully escorted Josie out of the door at the end of the session and we handed in our typewritten work at Pauline's desk. Pauline, glanced at the page I offered her and then dismissed me with a half-smile and a casual wave of her hand.

I've said it before. Tuesday afternoons in the dining room are unofficially reserved for the new Intakes, and for those who haven't anything better to do. I hadn't anything better to do, which was why I was amongst the dozen or so residents in there that afternoon.

Gill Roberts had stopped me on my way across the main hall and reminded me that I hadn't got the rest of the afternoon off like everyone else had. In a short while I was going on a Mobility lesson instead. I could have gone to the Den I suppose, like Jim and Josie had. But I think I was more intrigued to find out if Anita was or was not still with us, and my way of reasoning was to go into the dining room to find out that way.

She wasn't there and when I asked one or two of her colleagues for her where-abouts, it turned out that they were no wiser either. A few minutes later I was heading out of the dining room, making my way to the prearranged meeting place by the railing overlooking the sunken lawn to wait for Gillian.

Coming out from the Porch entrance to the Manor, the wind was so strong that I was very nearly blown back inside. I was actually only a few yards from my destination and the expectant, black shrouded figure of Gill Roberts, when I suddenly realised that I hadn't brought the cane with me, so, with a quick turn so as to avoid what might have been a scathing look from her. I hastily made my way back inside. All the way to the lounge and then out again.

We spent less than a minute by the railings which overlooked the sunken lawn. It took less than that in fact for Gill to decide that it was much too windy to do anything useful. The high winds weren't really bothering me and I told her so, but my opinion didn't matter. "Steps today." She said. "I was going to take you up through the woods, but I'm not so sure if that would be a good idea. Come along, if we're quick we might catch Graham before he sets off."

One of her colleagues, Graham, was about to climb aboard the white mini-bus which was nearby. He was helping a young blind man inside. A few minutes later we were heading down the drive away from the Manor. And I found myself sitting beside Ian. I wanted to ask him where Jack Townley was, but I didn't get the opportunity. I noticed that Ian had a white cane in his hands and something akin to a sort of relaxed look on his face. He also wore dark glasses and was impeccably dressed in a dark blue suit with a matching tie and a white shirt. He looked as if he was going to a business meeting or something, rather than on a mobility lesson. I had mistakenly thought that he was going to have a mobility lesson but I was wrong. Ian was going into Torquay to buy something special for a rather special occasion. That was just about all that I could get out of him.

Gillian and Graham were in the front of the bus while I sat quietly in the back occasionally looking at Ian and to the front and out of the windows as we travelled to our destination. Wherever than might be, but I should have known.

We pulled to a stop in more or less the same place we had done the day before, outside the old junior school somewhere on the other side of Torquay. This time the children had all departed. I watched as Gillian climbed down from the passenger seat and came around to the back of the bus to let me out. The engine was still running which gave me a slightly odd feeling of relief that I wasn't about to have an audience. Even though one of the potential spectators couldn't see.

The rear door opened and in came a howling blast of cold air, bringing with it her floppy felt hat. I picked it up, bade farewell to Ian and climbed out into a gale force wind. I stood there for a minute watching the minibus pull away while Gillian composed herself. Then I followed her into the school yard and on into the warm confines of the school. Gillian chose a different route than the day previous. We eventually came to a spot at the base of some stairs. I was looking up and studying the layout of the twenty or more concrete steps before she could do her thing once more. She had just finished telling me that the corridor we had been in the day previous, was directly at the top of these stairs... I didn't like the thought of what she was about to do with me, but I was beginning to understand the wisdom of her ways. When it came into view, I thought. "Aha... Here's the blindfold coming out of her bag once more." I quickly looked back at the steps again, trying to build up a mental image before it was too late. The steps were about normal height and depth and about ten feet wide. There was a wooden handrail on either side and another one set on black iron rods coming down the middle. I quite naturally began to edge over towards the left-hand side at the base of the stairs, but she was much wiser.

"Stand still will you, and take your glasses off please... You know what I want from you... Or do you? Tell me? How would you tackle a flight of steps like these if you couldn't see them?"

"Carefully." I responded, with dubious enthusiasm. "Very carefully indeed."

"We shall see." She said, and proceeded to put the blindfold over my eyes.

"Right! Are we ready? cane ready? Good... Now then. Come over here. Ah! that's spoiled it for you hasn't it. You don't know where you are now. This is good as it happens, now don't worry... This, by the way is the same school where I had some of my training, blindfolded, just as you are... Now then... You didn't do so badly with the cane yesterday. You are, after all, getting the basic principles correct, but today is going to be ever so much different. Today we are going to ascend these steps, now obviously, you can't swing the cane from side to side going up, can you? No. So, here we have to adopt a different technique. First of all, if you are about to climb some stairs you have to find them. Go on, off you go, no, not that way, that is the way we came in. Over to your left... a bit more. That's better, there. You have found the bottom-step. Now what to do? Well, it wouldn't be a bad idea if you felt for and found the handrail. You'll need it at this stage. Good. That's it... Now, hold the cane vertically about a foot out and away from your chest, still keeping the cane in contact with the ground by your feet and in front of that bottom step. That's right... Having found the bottom step and the handrail, you might be aware that the cane is at an angle as you begin to move forward and starts to slope away from your chest towards your feet. Keep your right hand in the same position and take your first step up and you will notice the cane making you aware of the next step beyond that and so on... Keep going that's right... allow the cane to slip up and over the lip of each step. Carry on, I'm right behind you... All... the... way... to... the... top... There! Thin air. Nothing more for your cane to touch. No more steps. After you take the last step up shuffle forward a little so that you are out of danger and then you may carry on using the cane in the conventional manner. Now those steps are pretty well straightforward, but there are others that are more complicated. For instance, semi- ambulant steps, or steps with a wider step. Or even spiral steps... We have a flight of those in the Manor. Now then. You may not know that you have completed the ascent of a set of unfamiliar steps or stairs until you are certain that you have finally run out of them and there are no more in front of you. Your cane should give you all the information you need to make the correct judgement. It will all come with practice. Right. You can take your blindfold off now and we'll go back down and then come back up again with it on."

Twice more I blindly climbed those concrete steps inside that old school. I think she would have had me doing it a fourth time, if it hadn't been for the caretaker coming to let us know that our transport had arrived.

A bit less than half an hour later we were approaching the lights of the Manor up the long and dark drive. I was sitting beside Ian in much the same way as I had done on our way out. He didn't enlighten me on the contents of the carrier bag on his knee. In fact. He hardly said anything all the way back. I had had a feeling that something else had been bothering him, but I didn't yet know what that something was. This was going to come from Jack Townley later on. This, being the revelation, that this was to be Jack's last week at the Manor.

I was sitting on my own. beside the grand piano, in the lounge at the Manor. The evening meal had been a sombre occasion, with Laurie, Christopher and Anita, all three of them sitting and eating the anaemic looking cauliflower-cheese. It made me feel a bit depressed as well, to see their miserable faces and the food that evening, but these three weren't just depressed by the evening meal. Words had been said and feelings had been hurt. What did surprise me was that all three of them were still on the same table. In a way, I was glad to get away from them. So, here I was, in the Lounge, minding my own business and listening to the howling wind every time someone came in or went out through the French windows. A few minutes later, a short and fair-haired man came in and announced: -

"Good evening ladies and gentlemen. My it's quite a nasty night out there. Ah, hello. I do hope that I'm not disturbing any of you. I have only come to tune the piano and also to see if I can recruit any of you to my trade. Gather round please do."

I was already there, so I stayed where I was, watching and listening. The man carried on in his peaceful manner.

"Quite a remarkable occupation in actual fact. Although, a lot of people might contest otherwise. I've been doing this job for almost sixteen years now and I've also been teaching folks like yourselves for more than ten of those years. I've never been out of work yet. Touch wood, and there's plenty of it in this beauty. Harold Moss is my name, I come from Paignton. Now then, who wants to watch, or listen, to what I do and the way that I do it?"

I stayed and watched, and so did quite a few of the other residents. I saw him lift and prop up the lid and tweak at the mechanism inside and then go to the keyboard and tap at one or two keys. He did this a number of times for about five minutes or so until he came to a frowning stop and declared: -

"Oh dear...! Oh! dear me. What a mess, what a sticky situation. Chewing-gum, I think... It was the last time... No, something worse. Someone has spilt something down here and it's inside the works. Nothing like a challenge is there. I'm afraid it's too big a job for tonight though. I shall have to come back after lunch tomorrow and fix it. Now then... Who might I be able to sway to let me teach him or her my trade?"

I was interested, but not really interested enough to learn. My way of thinking at the time; was that you had to have a knowledge of music to be able to do that job. I could pick out a tune on a piano, but that was about all, and besides. I couldn't even read music. One or two of the others there proved his journey not to be a wasted one though. I left the scene at the cry from one or the residents that the cold sausages were now heading for the den.

The Den was where I met up with Jack Townley. The Den as usual at this time of the evening, was well and truly packed. I somehow managed to squeeze in and helped myself to some of the sausages from the tin tray before they were all gone, and then went and stood by the sinks to eat them, and watch the goings on. I could see Jack Townley and Ian nearby, but they were too busy talking for the moment to bother with me. I could see Jim and Peter and Josie. They must have been here for a while because they were in prime places seated at the tables. They were also too busy to notice me, but having said that, there was only one of them that might have noticed me there anyway.

I finished eating and turned around to rinse my hands under the tap, and turned back to face the room once more. It was just at the point when, having eaten their fill, the bulk of the residents were beginning to leave the den and go their various ways. It wasn't many seconds later, however, when there was a commotion in the corridor outside and a few seconds later, a group of seven people came in through the ever-open door. The first person I saw and recognised was Barry, he was followed by Samantha and Denise, and Shirley, and quite a few others that I knew to be the nucleus of the group of people who would be staging the music concert that coming weekend. There was a cry of dismay from nearly all of them when they discovered that they had missed the cold sausage supper that night. I then overheard Shirley speak and say.

"Never mind I'm sure it's for the best... Anyway... We just do not know what might be in those sausages do we? I mean, there could be anything in them and you wouldn't necessarily know it would you? I do not touch them myself; I just simply cannot abide them."

"What at gooin 'ave fer thee supper then Lass?" Queried Jack Townley over the general noise of the room. Shirley began moving towards the area where Jack was sitting alongside Ian, which was also fairly close to me as well.

Shirley seemed to be squinting through the glasses on her pretty face as she looked at Jack and said. "Oh, I shall make myself a sandwich. A jam sandwich perhaps, I don't know. First of all, I shall make a nice cup of tea for some of us. I do not mean you as well Mr Townley, I know how stubborn you can be. You can please yourself anyway, because I am not making you a drink. You nor Mr Weaver. Sorry! I did not mean it to sound that way, I do apologise."

"Apology accepted!" I said in mild surprise. Then came the crunch when I realised the reason for Ian's moodiness on our way back that afternoon in the minibus. Shirley stood at the side of Jack Townley and said.

"You're leaving us this weekend, aren't you?"

"Aye, I'm afraid so lass. Theyun finished with may an'it's back off wom come Fridee."

I watched Jack turn his head and look at the sad face of the young blind man at his side, then he shrugged his shoulders and gave a heavily suppressed sigh and continued.

"Theyat bay alrayt lad dunna worry thesen, ah've towd thee theyat bay alrayt. Thayse things'appen an'th's nowt much way c'n do abite it is the?"

I had been half watching the steady drain of residents as they left the room. I gave a hasty acknowledgement to the departure of Jim and Josie when they called out to me. I hadn't seen Peter go but I did notice then that there were only about a dozen people in the room by this stage and that was including myself. Shirley didn't seem to notice that most of her musical colleagues had already gone out as she busied herself at the worktop. I did notice, with some amusement, that Samantha and Denise had already taken the opportunity whilst Shirley had been talking, to have made themselves a hot drink, and they were now sitting in the corner nearest the high windows, each with a steaming mug in their hands. This was what I liked best of all, I thought to myself.

Watching what was going on, and hopefully, not being intrusive at the same time. I couldn't help becoming involved a few moments later however, when Ian started to get to his feet and said: -

"I don't know why you have to go. I need you to help me get better and better. There's nobody I respect more than you Jack… Now you're leaving and going home. I might never see you again..."

Those last few words carried a squealing hint of his former self, which gave some cause for concern from me and from Jack. I even noticed Shirley turn around to have a look as well. But it wasn't so much the way he had said what he said. It was what he said that hit the mark. At least with me it did. This poor lad never will see Jack Townley. If he stayed by Jack's side for the rest of his life Ian would never ever see him. How could he? This young man had been involved in a car chase which had caused him to run off the motorway, over an embankment and into a concrete rainwater run-off. The results of which had severed the optic nerve in both of his eyes. It may have been just a figure of speech from Ian but it had a hell of an impact on those who took the trouble to interpret it.

A few seconds later I was watching Ian and Jack as they got to their feet and Jack helped by escorting Ian towards the door. Other folk were still talking within the room, but I strained my ears and eyes, and managed to hear Jack say quietly. "Come on, dunna mak' a fool o'thesen lad, 'ere theyat, bloo thee nose on this."

With Ian and Jack now gone, I looked around the room once more. Most of those remaining were talking or doing their washing at the far end of the Den, so I quietly left them to it.

I phoned home earlier that night and then spent the next hour or so in the Lounge, playing cards with Royston. A few others joined in after a while and this took us up to bedtime, well, the Manor's bedtime.

I had just spent a pleasant and eventful evening amongst my Manor colleagues but, behind it all there had been something of an ulterior motive on my part. It wasn't raining out there but it was blowing a right old gale, and I had partly been hoping that I might have managed to get a lift down to the Lodge with someone; anyone. But no. Ten minutes later, there I was on my own under the stone arch of the Porch, with a squeaky dancing lantern above casting weird patterns of light, and with twigs and leaves swirling around my feet.

Tapping the sections of the cane together and uttering the words "Here we go!" I stepped out into the dark windy night. There was no one to accompany me and, to the best of my knowledge, no one to watch me either, but then? Who in their right mind would want to stand and watch me in the gale force wind blowing that night? What with all the debris blowing about as well.

CHAPTER ELEVEN

Early the following morning I was heading off down the drive from the Lodge once again. The wind had dropped, the day was calm but cold and the first hint of daylight was beginning to creep across the wide sky. I was on my own and heading for the Manor. I had been talking to Jim in the Den at the Lodge only a few minutes earlier. It was during our conversation that the subject of Braille was mentioned, this included Jim's likes and my dislikes. It was strange how we both seemed to have reached something of a conclusion, and for it to be disclosed, within the space of a few short minutes of talking, that for me to continue learning braille in Wendy's department was nothing short of a waste of time. Mine and Wendy's.

"She told you this did she?" I said in surprise. "She actually told you that it wouldn't bother her if I didn't continue learning braille... Why the hell didn't you say so sooner? Why didn't she? Why wasn't I told yesterday. I've been wasting my time all this while thinkin' the worst and that for some blasted reason those beggars back at th'Manor knew best when it came to me eyes. So, after all this time they decide as it's not all that important for me to learn braille. It's Ruddy marvellous that is. Just wait until I get back up there and have a word with her..."

Jim had interrupted me and said. "Perhaps it's just that you aren't showing enough enthusiasm."

"Well, whatever." I replied as I had got to my feet.

I wanted to catch Wendy and sort things out with her before the working day began. And so it was that I was out so early on that Wednesday morning.

I turned the corner by the gateway to the Lodge and began the journey up Middle Lincombe Road. The visual conditions were slowly getting better as I travelled. There was no-one else around and it seemed as if I had the whole of Torquay to myself, so quiet was it around about me. I hadn't gone many yards though when things began to get a bit more difficult. The footpath and parts of the road surface, for as far as I could see, were strewn with leaves, twigs and wind-blown branches from the nearby trees. I mumbled to myself. "It won't be all that long now until the others will be coming this way... A lot of them won't be able to see this... Where are the Torquay Council workmen? This's a job for them not me... Ah well!" Opting for a practical solution. I cleared as many as I could of the larger twigs and branches from the footpath and kicked them into the gutter as I went along.

l was in the Manor gardens waiting for Wendy to come down from her flat above the Commerce building and make her way over to the Manor for breakfast. I had already noticed the wind strewn mess within the Manor grounds and around the sunken lawn, which gave the impression that the area hadn't been tidied for some time and I felt sorry for the gardening crew who would be tackling that lot this day. I was reminiscing and re-living a few past events in my mind as well as observing as best I could of what was around me as I sat on the wall near the entrance to the Commerce building. At the far end and a few yards further on is the arbour where I had first met Cyril Thompson all those weeks since and after all that he had been through, he was now a married man, and happily married as well, judging by what I had seen of him since he and Ann had joined forces. With nowhere near as much pleasure, I was also remembering that first day after my glasses had been stolen down at the Lodge and I had ended up looking out onto the blurred shapeless world that was all too familiar to me. That had also been the day when Royston and myself had been given the task of clearing the entrance to the arbour of the thickly matted undergrowth of weeds and briars. It had mattered little to Len, the head gardener if you were blind or not. As long as you could do something like a reasonable day's work, that was all that mattered to him.

Gillian had asked. "What do you want to do. What career do you want? Typing, Woodworking... Crafts? Gardening or what?"

Or what...? I didn't know. How could I know where all of this would lead to? I was there in the gardens at the Manor and I had only a faint idea of what I wanted to do with my life beyond this place. I knew beyond doubt that I wanted to be able to work and support my wife and family just as I had always done, but how? I had lost my job on the Post through no fault of my own, and become lost and confused ever since. How could I begin to carve a new career for myself in that big bad world out there? A world where many a sighted, more able-bodied person had lost the battle. How could I cope? What could I do...? I got to my feet and went a little further to sit on a log at the base of the steps which marked the beginning of a path which wound its way up through the woodland. I could see the front of the Commerce building from here and even though I might not have been able to distinguish who it might have been from this distance. I could at least see well enough to notice if someone came out. I could also see the main building from my new vantage point. A car arrived and there was a fair bit of activity going on towards the other end of the Manor, but this was all too far away to serve as anything more useful than to tell me that the Manor was awakening and the Lodge residents must have begun arriving at the Manor. "Ah well..." I muttered to myself. "There's one thing for sure. Whatever I end up doing it won't be anything to do with Braille if I have my way."

Rather naively. I had genuinely convinced myself that if Wendy would go along with it, as I had understood from Jim that she might, then I could dispense with learning the Braille system completely and I would be a happier man for a chance to learn something new. Crafts perhaps?

Something was moving across the way. I saw the head and shoulders of the figure walking towards the steps. I waited for her at the top of the steps and it was here that I let her know who I was and what I wanted.

What I wanted; I didn't get. What I got was a pact. I still don't quite know how she managed to get me to agree to do it, but she did. Wendy got me to agree to at least, learn by heart if possible, the basic Braille system so that I wouldn't be entirely helpless if the worst came to the worst at some time in the future. I didn't want to think about the future and even told her so. Besides, I had, already learned the basic system. Wendy halted my mild protestations when she agreed that I had learned, but I hadn't stored it. Learning the basic Braille system properly was the only way she would let me have my way, so, by the time we had travelled the short distance to the Manor and stood outside the French windows for a couple of minutes more, I was beginning to see no other reasoning other than to begrudgingly agree to do as she had asked.

Wendy's parting words were. "I shall set you a test in your final week here, so don't you go letting me or yourself down. Do we have a deal?"

Wendy was a no-nonsense type of woman so when she offered her hand in my direction and I felt the soft smooth skin, I knew that I was now honour bound to comply with her decision. I watched as she opened the French window and entered the Lounge in an easy manner which belied the fact that she was blind. The glass door closed and I felt glad that I hadn't followed her inside. It was too noisy for my liking in there. I decided to wander around the gardens for a few minutes longer and see if I could find out what it was that I had seen a few minutes earlier. There was something mauve and purple and white which lay beneath the bushes that had caught my eye around about the same time that I had noticed a movement over by the Commerce building.

I knew from experience that the breakfast gong wouldn't be going to get a resounding hammering by an over enthusiastic resident just yet. I had got at least another ten minutes of quiet contemplation and discovery ahead of me before the day began again in earnest.

I headed back towards the arbour to where I had found peace and solitude on rare occasions in the past and soon found the clumps of Woodland Cyclamen beneath the trees and on further investigation I found even more of them. Very attractive they were and in the three colours I have mentioned plus differing shades in between as well. They were flowering in all their autumn splendour. There was an area just to the rear of the arbour where I had followed a trail of the naturalised plants and it was here that the largest clumps of Cyclamen were to be found. I carefully sat down on a fallen tree trunk and leaned forward to look more closely at what was at my feet and all around me, and I think I cursed my inability to be able to see those dainty flowers well enough, but then I reminded myself of how it could have been and then I looked up to the heavens and then back down again at the swathes of colour before me and I thought differently.

The area inside the arbour had been empty before, while I had been waiting for Wendy to put in in appearance. I had been feeling very confident that I would be able to have few precious minutes to myself, but I was wrong. I began to develop a feeling that someone else was nearby. Then I heard his voice. Soft and frustrated it was. He fell silent for a few seconds before crying out once more. "Who's there?"

"It's me... Bob! What are you doing Mike? And how did you get here?"

I went around to the arbour entrance to meet him. We weren't all that far apart and he carried on talking as I approached him. He was saying.

"...Jim told moe yow was wantin't'spoik to Wendy, towd me yown'n be waitin' near the engineering ploise for her. Thowt as I moyt foynd yow hereabouts."

He had. Once I had got over the initial surprise of meeting him like that and had commented on his unusual exuberance, we went back inside the arbour and sat down on the white painted seat. I had quickly developed a feeling that there was something Mike wanted to say to me so I waited for him to say it.

Long seconds passed and then he turned his near sightless eyes to me and said.

"Down't gow in fer breakfast yet Bob. In fact, down't gow in at all. Oye wants to ask yow a favour... Jim towd moy as yow moight be free from doing braille and oye wanted to ask if yow'd come and escort me loike, so's oye c'n dow some shopping. Mobility folk are tow busy and they won't let moy gow on moy own, but they moit if yoy gow with moy."

A few minutes later we were entering the main hall as our fellow residents were making their noisy way down the side of the wide staircase towards the dining room. I was feeling hungry but not unduly worried. Mike had promised me a cooked breakfast down at the Victoria Shopping Centre.

Breakfast was almost over by the time Mike and myself had sorted things out with the care staff. Some of the residents were coming out into the main hall just as we were about to leave. I had readily agreed to go with Mike that morning, so much so that it hadn't occurred for me to ask him just what sort of shopping it was he wanted to do. I decided to ask him as we walked down the drive away from the Manor. "None!" He replied. "Oye just wanted an excuse to get away for a whoile. This's moy free period. Oy wants a bit mowre than the Manor can give moy... Oye moight now a bit of shopping and I moight not."

I lightly kicked a small branch into the gutter as I wistfully smiled and thought of the lies Mike had just been telling the care staff concerning his urgent shopping requirements. Then I looked at him in his brand new looking light brown gaberdine trench coat and carrying a white cane. This attitude was a good thing to see in Mike and it pleased me. This was infinitely better. He was on something akin to a roller-coaster was Mike. His mood swings were up and down up and down. I suppose that this was all an inevitable part of coping with trying to come to terms with his problems. He knew it and so did I. He didn't need to tell me that it was the middle bits between the ups and the downs which seemed to be and were by far the hardest to cope with. I know. I've been there, done that and didn't like it, and to a large part. I was still doing it. Nevertheless! This outing was a welcome break from the usual routine of the Manor and we plodded on in good spirits.

We arrived at the Victoria Shopping Centre and there was an attractive, dark haired young woman there to greet us. She had on a short skirted black dress with a pure white apron and wore a white lace cap on her head. She beckoned us inside with a genuine smile on her face. Mike hadn't wanted to and hadn't needed to use his cane on our way here. Instead he had relied on me acting as his escort to get him to this place down by the harbour. Mike had only recently begun to have some proper mobility lessons and was still unsure with the cane he was carrying. We sat down at one of the clean white lace topped tables, while the pretty young woman looked on and waited to take our order.

After a good breakfast of bacon, sausage, egg and tomatoes. Which was all the more delicious because I didn't have to pay a penny for it, we got to our feet and headed off once more and spent a while just walking and talking around by the harbour. It was here that I discovered that Mike was something of a pianist. "You never told me!" I said.

"Yow never asked." Said Mike.

"How come you're not doing a bit for the concert then?"

"Oy'm not that good Bob but oye loikes playing when oye can… that one back at the Manor's more knackered than oye feels sometoimes."

I told Mike about the piano tuner and what he had said about the state of the grand piano, Mike asked when was he coming, and I replied.

"Before the weekend I hope, or else there's going to be a very frustrated pianist named Annette to deal with."

We gradually moved on to the gardens on the other side of the harbour where we walked and talked about families and so on, and then, quite naturally and, partly by design on my part, we went on down to the beach. A thought had just occurred to me, it was just a thought but I had a reasonable idea; that if it worked, it might do us both good.

The tide was out and it was here; by the water's edge, where the sand was the firmest that Mike realised that he didn't now need me to escort him, which was partly what I wanted him to realise. I casually mentioned about the time I had come here early one Sunday morning and how I had run to my heart's content along this same stretch of sand. I had no sooner said it when Mike stopped and declared that he wanted to do the same.

And so, gently at first, we began to jog along the beach side by side, and what was more, we enjoyed it. The sheer exhilaration of having the wide-open space around us, the sand beneath our feet and nothing to run into, except the sea; but I was on the seaward side. This was nothing short of a great and wonderful tonic for Mike, for both of us. And my earlier thoughts of concern if this all went wrong were quickly dispelled, for when we stopped for a breather after a steady jog of about two hundred yards or so, it turned out that Mike was so carried away by this new found freedom that he wanted to race me for another hundred yards or so, or until one of us collapsed, and that would have more than likely been me! I managed to convince Mike against having an all-out race, we settled for a short final burst to see who could out-pace the other. Mike won, but then. He was the younger man, and he needed a morale booster. He certainly got one, judging by the look on his face when we came to a breathless halt, which was more than halfway towards the Railway Station side of the Bay. We walked the rest of the way and eventually left the beach and went up onto the coast road and found a seat to sit on. It was here that we stayed awhile and just talked, but Mike's spirits began to sink again when I talked about my two girls. I managed to coax him out of it before he got too low and at the same time, he began to explain that, although he and his wife wanted children, they had decided not to have any because of the risk involved of passing on whatever it as that he was suffering from. A short time later and with Mike in fairly good spirits once more, we decided to go into town and find a place where we could have a bit of lunch before heading back to the Manor.

There would be plenty of opportunities in the years ahead, for Mike to do what we had just done, on this very beach and others nearby, but obviously, neither of us could have been aware of this at that moment in time. Or indeed where a casual conversation about the piano at the Manor might lead to.

Mike had got a session in the daily living skills bungalow for the first period of the afternoon and I had got a session in the typing department. I escorted him up to the bungalow. Not that he needed it, but I did it anyway.

On my way back along the front of the Manor I came across a group of people heading towards the Commerce building in the same direction as myself, and one of these people turned out to be Royston. He saw me coming and gave me one of his friendly pat-on-the-back greetings. I took this in the spirit in which it was intended and then I asked him where he was going.

"REMEDIALS" He replied, and then he followed this with… "WHERE ARE YOU GOING" I responded with "TYPING" Royston shrugged his shoulders and signed. "SEE YOU LATER" and off he went to re-join the group he had set out with.

I entered the typing room in the company of Josie. We both went straight through to the part of the room to the electronic typewriters. Much to the dismay of Jim and Peter who were still having to stay in the other part of the room where the manual typewriters were, but not for much longer, as we were shortly to find out.

This had been the first time that I had seen Jim since early that morning, but he didn't seem to want to ask how I had got on with Wendy. I could only guess that he had already got the information he might have wanted from Wendy herself while Mike and I were out that morning. There wasn't time for small talk just then anyway. Josie and myself had no sooner gone through the door into the other part of the room when Pauline came in behind us. I dutifully sat at the desk which I had occupied previously, and a few seconds later in walked Pauline and politely but poker faced gave me the sheet of paper that I had typed the previous day.

I decided to play safe and just took the paper from her with a mumbled "Thanks." Pauline then turned her attention to someone else in the room. I waited until she had gone before daring to look at what she had just given me. In big and bold red letters, at the foot of the page, she had written just one word 'Good.' Looking up through the glass of the dividing screen I couldn't be absolutely sure, but I did have a feeling than she had just been looking in my direction, but she was turning away from me now and approaching Peter. I watched for a few seconds longer and noticed Peter getting to his feet with Pauline assisting him. Then they came towards us. When they entered the room. I put my head down and got on with some work. Pauline sat Peter down at a vacant desk across the aisle from me and then she said.

"Robert and Walter? I wonder if you two wouldn't mind helping? You are the only two in here at present with anything like good vision. Peter has been having a little private tuition from me over the last day or so. I think he is now ready to come in here and join the rest of you. I would appreciate it if you would both give him any help if he needs it, which I am sure he will. Come down here a while will you Walter."

I was really taken aback by this sudden move on Pauline's part, and really pleased to see Peter in there with us. More so and especially in view of the fact that I knew just how badly he had wanted to be in here. The guy named Walter came forward and began earnestly helping Peter to set up his machinery and show him how to operate it. It seemed fairly obvious to me that he had done this sort of thing before. Pauline left us and I watched Peter and Walter for a minute or so more and decided that my services weren't required as yet, so I got on with what I was doing.

Having set Peter up, Walter turned to me and said. "Now it's your turn, just watch his paper, he should get through three sheets in this exercise. He'll more than likely have trouble feeding in from the back."

Peter was strangely silent throughout all of this and it puzzled me a little. If I had been him and knowing just how badly he wanted to get on these machines. I would have been more excited at the prospect of coming in here, but Peter wasn't. Or at least he didn't seem to be. An explanation soon became apparent.

Peter was so busy concentrating on what he had to do that he hadn't any time for getting excited or anything like that. I dutifully watched him and tried my best to get on with my own work at the same time. Thankfully, Peter wasn't constantly in need of my help. I only had to leave my seat twice during the rest of that session in order to help him and that was to put new paper into his typewriter. He was slow, but I put this down to him having to concentrate so hard. About ten minutes before the end of the session. I happened to glance up through the glass screen once more. I was just in time to notice that Pauline was standing over Jim and talking to him. Then I saw, and heard, Jim's delight as he got to his feet and hugged Pauline. Then the two of them went forward to the front of the class and came towards the door into this part.

"Looks as if Jim's coming in here to join us." I said to those around about me.

"Saints preserve us." Said Josie.

A few seconds later Jim came in and exuberantly announced his entry. Then he immediately headed for the one and only vacant desk directly behind Josie.

Peter was doing fine, and as Pauline was directly behind Jim, I thought it best to get on with my own work. I busied myself while Pauline showed an eager Jim what to do with his machines. Five minutes or so later Pauline left the room. Peter and the others were quietly concentrating on their work and it was all I could do to try and finish my own work and at the same time make sure that Peter was doing his typing properly and not typing on the platen. Add to this, the presence or Jim in one of his happy go lucky moods and it was no real surprise that I didn't quite finish the exercise set for me that day by Pauline.

116

The end of the session. Feeling a bit anxious I switched off and covered the machines and then followed my colleagues to placed my partly finished article on Pauline's desk, and just before I turned to depart and let Walter do the same. I forced myself to look at Pauline as I said. "Sorry... I er, I haven't quite finished it, what you gave me to do today that is..."

Outside in the corridor, I pulled Jim back and ticked him off, but it was like water off a duck's back. He couldn't care less now that he had managed to get on the electronic machines. "God help us tomorrow!" I muttered in Josie's ear as we left the Commerce building.

Just before we went in through the French window entrance, I thought to look around and also up to the sky in order to try and work out if the weather was likely to prevent Gill Roberts doing with me today whatever it was she had wanted to do the day before. The sky was a clear light blue but in another hour it would be dark blue if not black, still, at least it wasn't raining, or windy, and if I was going to have a mobility lesson here in the grounds of the Manor then it was pleasing to notice that from what I could see of it, the gardening crew had at least been working hard clearing the grounds of fallen leaves and twigs.

I was one of the last to step towards the French windows but a woman's voice from my right caused me to stop and look in that direction.

"Just hold that door for him Robert, and help him inside if you will?"

The woman was Sally and the man she was referring to was Gerry. These were the two in charge of the Crafts section which I was immediately adjacent to on this side of the Manor. Gerry was, as I have mentioned before, both blind and in a wheelchair. I never asked, and as a result, I never knew what had caused his blindness or what had caused him to be confined to a wheelchair, Jim, and casual talk seemed to suggest that it was Multiple Sclerosis, but despite his affliction nothing seemed to stop Gerry from being a very dedicated craftsman. What that man could do with a sheet of leather was incredible.

I waited a few seconds until Gerry came down the narrow path between the Manor and the green painted prefab that was the crafts building and then I helped him and his wheelchair over the threshold while Sally was securing the locks on the crafts building. Once we were inside, Gerry insisted that he would be alright and that I could go about my own business once more. I watched in silence while he wheeled himself away across the floor. As he went, over and above the general noise of gathered people talking to one another, I heard him cry out.

"Watch out! If you're total or not. One more total, coming through..."

I could only stand and marvel and speak my thoughts to no one in particular, while mumbling. "How the hell does he know where he's going?"

I think that was the moment I decided to replace the Braille sessions with Wendy and join Gerry and Sally in the crafts room. If the powers that be will allow me to that is.

I didn't bother going to the dining room for afternoon tea. Instead I resolved to go to the care staff office and discuss my alternatives with Sandra or someone else who might be in charge.

It was Sandra... and she agreed.

I was waiting in the main hall for Gillian to turn up. Royston had come and then gone with the ginger haired Mobility officer. Peter and Mike had already gone out with their own, respective instructors a few minutes earlier. Two women I knew, but not by name, went off with one more mobility officer and then I was left on my own.

It was a good ten minutes more before Gillian finally arrived on the scene, just as I was about to give up and find something else to do. She came up behind me and startled me somewhat by saying.

"I don't know! I really don't. There I was thinking that you were a man of initiative… and here you are just idly waiting for me when you ought to be out there trying out your new found skills."

I felt like saying something along the lines of… 'I can't win!' or something like that.

I didn't at that stage know very much about Gillian Roberts but I knew enough to realise that something had recently upset her.

"Oh, come on then!" She said. "I've had a sod of a day what with one thing or another, we shall stay within the grounds..."

"Suits me." I interrupted. "Let's go."

"You're too bloody smart and too keen for my liking." She said with a slightly sarcastic smile on her face.

"I can't win."

It was going proper dark outside by now, but along by the apparently deserted front of the Manor was okay for me. I had got the lights from the tall windows and the rooms within to light up parts of the tarmac where I was walking and using the cane. The trouble was. It was also confusingly easy as well. Gillian hadn't blindfolded me as she had done on our previous couple of outings and although I felt glad that she hadn't I also felt that things might have been better if she had. I know that may all sound daft and it is daft, but I knew this area well enough to have the courage to travel even in the dark and what I was doing here, with the cane... was easy. Almost too easy. New systems take a lot of getting used to. Surely, I hadn't got used using a cane this easily? I stopped for a moment and waited for the dark shrouded figure to catch up.

I couldn't see her face, but felt safe in knowing exactly where we were, but I also felt something of a fraud with the cane in my hand. This was all very confusing.

"You are, perhaps, wondering if it might be easier had I blindfolded you?" Said Gillian in a calm voice. "Perhaps it would be. Right now, what you are experiencing is no doubt confusing. I've said it many times... I would rather teach a dozen totals any day of the week than teach just one the likes of you... Your mind, your eyes and the place you are in are all confusing you. You can't see well enough and I dare bet you can hardly even see my face, but you know the area well enough, and the problem... If one can call it a problem. Is that you are seeing in your mind what you can't necessarily see with your eyes. You know this area. You have travelled this way often enough, but what you may not be aware of is that you are falling back on your previous experiences of this area and subconsciously using that knowledge to assist you in getting about. But don't worry. Where I am about to take you there won't be any lights or familiar surroundings to assist you. Have you yet been through the woods in the area behind the Pottery building?"

"Yes."

"Oh! I shall have to think of another area of the grounds to take you then, shan't I? An area you haven't been in before. But in retrospect. I rather think that it won't really matter where I take you. We might go anywhere in the woods but there is one element we will be leaving far behind us and that is, artificial lighting... Once we get up there it will be as if you have slipped on the blindfold once more because you won't be able to see a thing. The only snag is... I won't either, but rest assured I should still be able to see better than you... Come along. You are learning all the time and doing quite well if I may say; without fear of giving you too much confidence."

"Confidence is what I need." I muttered to the dark figure in front of me as she led the way towards the woods.

The dirt path was uneven and seemed to be cluttered with leaves, stones and twigs, some of them were quite large, or at least they seemed large when I encountered them. The path sloped upwards at too steep an angle, much more than I remembered it did. The only security was when we came to the steps. These had been constructed wholly and solely with the blind in mind. Each one of them was a set two man sized, and perhaps three female sized footsteps deep. On every path that I had trodden in these woods I had encountered the same pattern and I knew what to expect. It was pitch black dark and I didn't know where the steps began, or where they ended. This was something I had to rely on the cane to tell me, and when it did and I felt sure that it was indeed a step, in front of me. I would dangle the cane vertically and allow it to find the step and also tell me how high it was. An even bigger problem though was the way the cane and myself traversed this upwards sloping dirt path. On the level and on harder ground, the cane would tell me what was directly in front of me on my next step forward. Everything about this white cane technique was designed to tell the user if it was safe or not to put the next foot forward before the cane would swing across to find the place for the very next foot forward and so on. On an upward sloping dirt path like this it was all so very different. I just couldn't seem to get the balance right between my chest, my arm and the length of the cane and also the shortened distance, because of the upward sloping ground between me and the tip of the cane. The whole white cane thing was still new to me, but this was even more so. I just couldn't get into the routine, and I began to wonder if it had been a mistake in coming up here? Gillian was somewhere close behind me. I knew this much even though I had not seen anything of her since our entry into these woods. She wasn't speaking, she wasn't giving me encouraging words. She was just there close to and behind me. I wondered if she could see what I was doing and would she be able to help if I got into difficulties... What do I mean? If I got into difficulties; I was in difficulties! I was doing insane things. I was doing what I would never in my wildest dreams have thought of doing one week ago! Onward we slowly plodded. Onward and upward. How far before we turned back, I don't know, and I don't really care. She called a halt after about five hours but really after only about five or ten minutes.

"Right." She declared. "So far so good! We will go back down now. Turn around and I think we'll use the guide rails this time... If you care to reach out with your left hand, take one step to your left, a little more. There... you have it keep hold of the rail and give me your cane.

I breathed a great sigh of relief when we arrived at the base of the woodland path and we were in sight of the lights from the Manor once more. I reflected on and even said that the experience had been harder for me than either of the two visits to the school had been.

There was a pleasant surprise for me that evening. Laurie and Anita were sitting side by side on Laurie's side of the table and they were laughing. It appeared to me that they had somehow managed to resolve their earlier differences. Christopher came just as I was about to sit down. I was watching Anita for any signs of aggression, but there was none at all. She even smiled a squinting smile up at Christopher as he carefully reassessed the seating arrangements and then, regrettably clumsily sat down in what would have been Adrian's seat. So far Anita hadn't spoken to me. She was saving all of her words and looks for Laurie. All throughout the meal she avoided looking at me and even when the meal was over it surprised me quite a bit to hear her speak to Christopher just before she departed as she said.

"Are you alright Christopher? Ready when you are Laurie."

And off they both went. Laurie looked at me and said. "See you lads later."

I was running past events through my mind and kept coming up with the same conclusion. I slowly got to my feet and looked back down on Christopher and spoke my thoughts which left him with a puzzled expression on his face.

"Maybe she is Manor material after all. See you later Chris."

Down at the lodge around about eight o'clock that evening. I was doing my best to study and understand the braille transcripts which Wendy had insisted I learn. The early evenings were going to be the only time that I could spare in order to learn the braille system to the level that she wanted me to. I was also cheating a bit. I had noticed when I had been in Wendy's department, that if I leaned to one side at a particular angle to the daylight coming in through the window and held the braille book flat on the desk, then I could see the raised-up dots on the stiff brown paper. This meant that I was both seeing and feeling the dots at the same time and somehow this seemed to make it easier to understand the confusing arrangement of dots. I was now trying to do the same in my bedroom. I had just put the desk close to the foot of my bed and was sitting on the end of the bed making some fine adjustments. The single light bulb in the middle of the ceiling lit up the room and I shuffled things about a bit before I was satisfied that the light from the bulb was at the best angle to help me to read the braille language. But it didn't work very well. Not quite as well as it did in daylight, and then I remembered the rechargeable torch and set that up to cast a light across the page. The whole setup was a bit awkward and Heath Robinson 'ish' but it was passable, and I didn't feel guilty in doing this. Anything was worth a try if it would help me to understand the confusing language without having to waste too much time in doing so.

I had only been doing the project for about twenty minutes though when there came a knock on the door and Jim burst in. The back of the door collided with the desk and I had to hurriedly gather up the braille books and the torch before they fell onto the floor. Jim popped his head around the door and said.

"This is a bloody daft place to sit, right where folk might want to come in! What are you doing anyroad?"

"Learning Braille like the good bloody student that I am! What do you want Jim?"

"Nothing really. I'm just sodding well lonely, do you fancy going out for a drink?"

"No."

"Well, how about staying in for one then? I've a secret... there's some cans of beer in my room. I could bring them up here and we could have a chat and a cosy night in. How about that then?... I know it's not allowed and we shouldn't do it, but what the hell. Why should we care... We won't be doing any harm will we. Just two guys having a drink in instead of going out for one... We can't go down to my room. One of the men I share with might blab on us, besides I haven't enough cans to go around."

"Okay then. Thanks Jim go on. Hey! See if you can find Mike as well. If he's still here I bet he'd like a bit of company."

Jim came back sooner than I had anticipated, I was still stuffing my clothes in one of the drawers when the door opened once more. I couldn't help but say.

"We don't get far in life without a good woman to look after us, do we?"

"Isn't that true, so very true?" Said Jim soberly. "I found Mike, and he's coming in a few minutes. He's been here before hasn't he?"

"Nope." I said. "Not as I know of."

"Oh, sod it. I'll have to go and fetch him then?"

"No Jim. You stay here. I'll go."

I found Mike coming along the corridor. He was about halfway along and struggling to feel his way and hold on to the plastic carrier bag at the same time. "Jim's not the only one who can break the rules Bob." Said Mike with a rare and wry grin on his face as he purposefully rattled the bottles within the bag.

We arrived at my room and then the drinking began and it wasn't all that long before Jim became intoxicated and began to unwind and inevitably, there were the jokes which followed. The first one went something like this.

"There were these two guys, just two ordinary guys. They were both out one night taking their dogs for a walk and they came to a pub and one man said to the other man. How about going in and having a drink? The other man says. No. They don't allow dogs in there you know that. The other man says. Ah! but I have a cunning plan. Listen. So, anyroad. These two men. The first one goes up to the pub and goes on inside. Straight away the barman says. 'You can't bring that Labrador in here. There's no dogs allowed.' 'Ah, but I'm blind.' says the man. 'This is my guide dog.' Oh, alright then. Says the barman and he helps the man to a seat and gets him a drink. A minute or so later the other man comes into the pub and the barman sees him and he says... I'm sorry but you can't bring that dog in here. I'm blind. Says the second man, and this is my guide dog. But that's a Pekinese dog! Says the barman. Oh!... is that what they gave me at the guide dog centre? Says the second man as he bends down to feel the dog."

The evening wore on and it was good having Jim and Mike for company. In fact, it was very good company and exactly what we all needed.

Jim told us one or two more jokes but I hadn't got any jokes to tell them. I did have one thing to tell them about though and I was quite surprised when Jim fell about in fits of laughter. I had only begun to explain about the night that I had sat at the writing desk and about the rickety old chair which had given way beneath my weight. It was when I produced the bundle of sticks from the bottom of my wardrobe that Jim spluttered in his beer and fell on my bed in hysterics. Mike had become a bit inebriated by this stage as well, but I was quickly surprised by the way he seemed to sober up when the remains of the chair were offered to him and it also saddened, and sobered me somewhat, to witness the way his hands, instead of his eyes, wandered over the bundle of sticks that had once been a chair. I could see the funny side of the saga with the chair but I didn't really think it was all that funny. Anyway. Jim played it out for all that it was worth and then some.

It was rather sad that we should have to call it a day. Mike and I volunteered Jim to dispose of the empties in whatever was the best way that he could. And that, was the end of another day.

CHAPTER TWELVE

Thursday the 22nd of November.

I was one of the last to leave the Lodge and it was far too bright and sunny on my fuzzyheaded journey to the Manor. Jim had offered to wait but I told him to go on without me. I had no idea how Mike was, or where he was.

Joining the tail end of the residents at the Manor, I noticed Mike sitting in his usual place, soberly talking to a man on the next table.

The ongoing saga on my table came to some sort of conclusion that morning, which pleased me no end, Anita smiled at me as I went to sit down and it wasn't a false smile either, she then continued talking to Laurie. Meanwhile, Chris was carefully pouring some milk onto his cornflakes and didn't spill a drop. All in all, everyone on our table seemed content at last to let bygones be bygones and just carry on from here. Another pleasant thing that morning was when the retiring house Captain got to his feet and called for our attention in order to announce that we were to get a new house Captain from the following day and this was to be Ann. Big Ann. A chorus of cheers went up in the dining room at this news and the retiring Captain sat down with an exclamation.

"Well...! What it is to be popular."

I found Royston outside the Porch entrance. He was making no attempt to go over to the woodworking department, he was just sufficiently content to lean against the old stonework of the Porch. I waited until he had finished his cigarette and he shrewdly made me wait as well. I didn't mind. I was glad to be accepted in his company once more. When he had finished, he slowly pulled himself away from the wall and then gestured to me that he wanted to talk. I was aware that it was almost time to start work for the day, a lot of our fellow woodworkers were already making their way across the courtyard.

I was surprised to discover, by way of the sign language, that Royston had been made aware of the fact that I was going to join him that morning in the Crafts department. I think we were both glad. Woodwork and Crafts, together, in one morning. "GREAT" Was the word I spelled out on his hand.

The legs had been attached to the coffee table but the veneered top was still incomplete. Someone, it had to be Gordon, had gone to a lot of trouble to fix a dark brown veneer all around the outer edge of the table top. It was much too intricate a task for Royston to be able to accomplish. Or was it? I watched Gordon and Royston for a few minutes more and then, with the permission of Gordon I went through to the machine shop and waited for him to come and set me up on one of the two lathes in there as he had said he would. A good ten minutes later, in he came. I was keen to get started, but he wasn't. I had already explained to Gordon that I had got a lathe of my own back home and had been using it for quite a few years. I was trying my utmost that morning to be as diplomatic as I could and not to go and antagonise Gordon in a similar way that I had antagonised Pauline over in the typing department. These people knew their skills and I could, only now, begin to respect their feelings when it came to dealing with someone who threatened their way of doing things. Gordon had long since proved to me to be a respected taskmaster and I willingly submitted to his questioning before he could decide to allow me anywhere near a lathe. However, by the time the questioning was drawing to a conclusion, it was then getting towards the finish and coffee-break time. So! After all that, I didn't get a chance to have a go on one of those lathes after all.

I met up with Ann, and Cyril in the lounge, just after the coffee break. It was only for a brief half minute or so before they were whisked off by someone for matters more important, but it was sufficient for me to be able to congratulate Ann on her promotion. I was watching them leave when I noticed a man working away on the grand piano and one other, more smartly dressed man standing there with him. Looking closer, I noticed that the smartly dressed man was Mike. The Lounge was fairly crowded but I was intrigued sufficient to want to get closer. Something quite remarkable was developing here and if I couldn't be a part of it then I wanted to at least witness it. And Boy! Oh! Boy was this something fantastic to witness? For there was Mike, almost beside himself with excitement and bubbling over with a fast-growing enthusiasm; as he bombarded the piano tuner with question after question. Beryl; of the Care Staff was standing nearby. She noticed my approach and smiled a wonderful smile and then put her hands towards me in a calming gesture before looking delightedly back at Mike and the scene in front of us. Just then the piano tuner stopped what he was doing. He also had a broad smile on his face as he said: -

"Whoa, hold on a moment my friend. You asked my name… Harry Moss is my name and I can see I may have quite a remarkable student to take under my wing by the sound of your enthusiasm. Are you truly serious in what you are saying?"

"Too roight oye am." Said Mike with a wide grin and a keenness that I had never before seen in him.

Turning to Beryl, the piano tuner said, with deep appreciation: - "Thank you."

"That's quite alright." Responded Beryl with a smile, and then she looked at me with the same smile on her face and tapped the back of her wrist with her other hand. I looked behind me and the Lounge was deserted. Reluctantly, I left the scene, and the two men, and Beryl.

Looking back up the room as I stood poised on the threshold of the open French Window, I noticed the mismatched chairs and the high ornate ceiling and the dark green drapes hanging down in the bay window over on my left, and the same colour drapes near to, which I was holding to one side, and I was made aware of the almost indistinguishable shapes of the two men, together with the red dress of Beryl, all three of them standing by the dark shape of the grand piano in the far left hand corner of the room, almost out of seeing and hearing range of my senses now. Quietly, I let go of the curtain and closed the glass door.

I was kept far too busy for the rest of that morning to try and think about Mike and that truly momentous occasion. The Crafts room was busy and I was a go for... Go for this and go for that, for Gerry and Sally, just about the same situation as had been the last time I had been in here.

Towards the end of the period Sally promised me that she would start something with me on the following day and Gerry backed her up by asking me if I would like to learn something about leathercrafts.

Lunch was a sullen affair. Anita was miserable and this made Laurie, Chris and me, come to that, she made all three of us moody, and I felt glad to get out of the dining room and go and do something else.

Typing? I still hadn't realised that I had won. If, the descriptive word of 'won' is terminologically correct that is. And ludicrous as it may seem, I had been far too intent on studying the reasons as to why I had managed to upset so many people; to actually realise that Pauline no longer pressured me. This realisation only occurred to me later that afternoon, after Peter had asked me to check that his paper was correctly positioned, and then he asked me to see if the print was coming through onto the paper, and finally he asked me to check what he had written. I was glad to help him, There, but for the Grace of God go any of us and all of that, but all of this getting up and down was bound to attract attention and it occurred to me that Pauline might be thinking that I was just messing about. At the end of the session I stood behind Josie with others behind me and I sheepishly placed my nearly, but not quite finished article on Pauline's desk top and then reached for the doorknob to follow Josie when...

"Robert... Thank you for helping Peter."

I was already halfway out through the door and being forced further by the presence of my colleagues behind me.

"See! What did I tell you?" Said Jim as he caught up with me halfway along the corridor. "I said you could do it. You've beaten her. She's been as good a gold since the other day... I told you you could do it didn't I?"

"Shurrup Jim." Was all I could think of to say to him. He was embarrassing me in the presence of all these other people when all I wanted to do was to get away.

Mobility.
I was sitting beside the large desk in the tiny office and Gillian was standing by the tall and narrow window holding a cane and a needle and thread.

"We're not going out today." She said. "I am unwell and, I, am, pig, sick, of mending these things."

She was busy. My mind began to wander. I was beginning to realise by this stage in my stay at the Manor that these mobility lessons had begun to open up entirely new horizons for me. Just one week back I had hated the idea of the possibility of using a cane, I had not thought it was necessary, and I couldn't truly understand how they might have helped others, never mind me, but now, one week later, it was all so much different,

"Yoo hoo! I said, is there anybody there?"

I looked up at her and began to apologise. "Sorry I was miles away."

"I know you were. What were you thinking about? Or shouldn't I ask. Perhaps not. Well! I have one more, black elastic strap to do and then we shall see what we can do with you for the rest of the afternoon, if only to prevent your mind from wandering."

I only said a few words but these few words were sufficient to set the wheels in motion, for something that would soon be making a vast improvement in what this woman was doing to help the blind: - "You could do with some Velcro."

"Vel…" She gave a great sneeze and started again. "Velcro?"

"Yes. It's made at place called Selectus in Biddulph, near where I live… I know a man who works there, he's a good friend of mine, Reg Evans… short for Reginald but he's always been known as Reg… He's a nice guy. I used to work with his son Mark, on the Post, before all of this happened to me. If I tell Reg what we want it for I bet he'll send us some try out."

"Velcro? but how do we know it will work. I mean, will the totals be able to use it?"

"There's only one way to find out. I could phone my wife and ask her to get his works number for us."

A few minutes later I was standing in the alcove, having a premature telephone conversation with Janet. Ten minutes later I had phoned Selectus and was speaking to Reg Evans. I told him where I was and explained what it was that I wanted from him, and he being of a good and generous nature responded by saying.

"Hold on Bob… Sorry to cut you short but I think I've got the gist of what you say. If I get cracking right now, I might just about catch the last Post and you should get some by tomorrow morning FOC How will that do?"

"Great! Thanks Reg, Thank You."

And that, was the beginning of something really and truly worthwhile.

I was standing beside the oblong table in the hall at the Manor watching the backs of Royston and Sid as they made their way towards the large old oak doors. Royston had just been torn between going out with Sid and a few others or else stay in with me and a few others. The outing won. I couldn't really go though. My evening had already been booked earlier on, during the evening meal in fact. It was there that I had received a visit from Shirley and she had asked me to go with her that evening up to the bungalow where my help was to be required in preparing for the concert. As I hadn't anything in particular planned for that evening, apart from an ambitious idea to try out the cane once more. On my own! Apart from that, I had no other plans. Until Royston and Sid had come and found me at around half past six.

At a quarter to seven I was watching them go, and I had been and was still, genuinely torn between the pleasures of going out for a drink, or experiencing the joys of good live music once more.

The old oak door clanged on its great iron latch and then they were gone. I went back to the bench I had occupied for the most part of that early evening and looked up at the clock before sitting down beneath it. Shirley had said she would meet me here in the hall at seven o'clock.

Close to the designated time I eased my numb bum and wandered over towards the oblong table. A group of residents hadn't anywhere to sit as all the other benches in the hall were taken, so I let them take my seat. There did seem to be a few more people than usual hovering around the inside of the Manor that evening. I watched the scene for a short while and then a gasp went up from three women who were standing nearby. They could obviously see.

She came down the stairs wearing a long cream coloured sleeveless dress which looked more like a negligee than a dress Her natural blond hair was never straight but it seemed to be even more curly at that moment. The dress was perhaps just a little bit too ostentatious. Or over the top in plain English,

129

but she didn't seem to care. I was mesmerised by what I saw. She stopped for a moment about three or four steps from the bottom and looked down on me and smiled. Then she delicately lifted her skirts again with a dainty finger action and came down the remaining steps to meet us. She was obviously enjoying every single moment of attention.

"What's all this then?" I said incredulously when she was standing beside me. Stepping back a pace to try and take it all in I continued to look at her. I just couldn't help it, and a lot of others were doing the same as well. Glancing around me I noticed that even two women had come from the Care staff office to investigate the sudden commotion and they were doing the same, staring at Shirley. And of course, as I have already said. Shirley seemed to be enjoying every single moment. She smiled at everyone once more before casually throwing a wrap of the same cream coloured material as her dress up and over one shoulder, then she modestly declared that she had been chosen to do a solo performance on her flute at the forthcoming music concert and that she felt she ought to dress the part for this final rehearsal and, this was the result.

The words were on my lips and I almost said them out loud, but honestly, she really was an amazing woman.

There was a tightly packed dozen or so of us heading up the dark path towards the bungalow on the hillside overlooking the Manor. We had been delayed for a few minutes more when it was realised that it was raining. So, Shirley had to go back upstairs to her room to get a coat. Strange how having to wear a coat seemed to calm her exuberant spirits, albeit for a short while.

Shirley started to play the part she was so good at though once we were inside the bungalow. Most of the musicians as well as their instruments were there who would be there on the day of the concert, but even so, it took me some time to realise that one reason why there were not as many musicians, and especially violinists, was that some of them had already gone home. Shaun was one of those who had gone home, but he would be coming back for the concert. How many others might be coming back I had no idea. There were a lot of people at the Manor when I was there. Around a hundred at any given time. I am just trying to tell the tales of some of those I was closest to. Blind and partially sighted people were coming and going all the time and it was difficult to keep track of it all. However, back to this particular night which had been chosen for a final run down on the arrangements for the concert.

There were to be just a few programmes printed for on the day of the concert. Shirley had managed to grab a draft copy and Barry, our conductor, had one as well. Shirley began to introduce the various individuals and as much as I may have wanted to show how amused I was with Shirley's antics, the way she walked up and down the room and the way she kept on bending down to talk to and especially how she patronised the players. I couldn't let my amusement show through though and let my feelings spoil the event. I don't think that my mind was on anything else except watching Shirley as she blundered her way through that first twenty minutes or so in her attempts to organise everyone. Eventually, that last practice session did get properly under way.

One of the best parts of that rehearsal. And there were many, was when Denise got to her feet and faultlessly played the tune. 'Stranger on the shore' on her Clarinet. This had been about halfway through the rehearsal. We had already had a number of other excellent entertainers including Shirley and Rachel's combined rendition of a theme from Dvorak. Popularly known as the 'Hovis' advert. Rachael played the Violin while Shirley played the main part with her flute, and they really were brilliant. There was a violin solo that followed and then there was the Trumpet Voluntary from Laurie's friend.

It turned out that the show was to begin and end with tunes from Laurie and his bagpipes and as this last practice session drew to a close, I watched in a rather fascinated frame of mind as Laurie began to pump the bellows once more and I wondered what he would play for us next. I think we were all totally fascinated by the sounds which came from the assembled musicians and also from that weird looking green tartan bag. In actual fact, I rather suspect that there was no need for a programme of events. Most of the forthcoming large audience, wouldn't have been able to see to read a programme anyway.

Eventually that final practice session drew to a close and we all set about packing up for the night before heading our separate ways. The musicians began to depart. I helped Shirley into her coat and was even prepared to act as her escort on our way back to the main building if she wanted me to, even though it might have been a toss-up just who was the worst out there in the dark, me or her. And this was also in spite of the mild ribbing I got from the others who seemed to be implying that there was something going on between the two of us, but need I say that there wasn't? Shirley was much too much of a religious person to get involved with something the likes of which they were suggesting and I was much too much of a married man to do likewise. We two seemed to have some sort of a mutual understanding between us and I was both pleased and even proud of myself as I took her arm in mine and we stepped out into the darkness of night.

131

It had been a good practice session for the concert and I reflected on this on my slow and lonesome journey down to the lodge later on that night.

I had stayed in the Manor for my supper and to phone home as well. Shirley had changed out of her long cream dress and then joined us in the Den after a short while and she was a bit more soberly dressed by then in a dark skirt and jumper. I was still in the den when Royston and Sid and a lot of others came back 'home' for the night, but the two I mentioned had gone a bit overboard in their drinking and were fit for nothing more than a strong cup of coffee. I left them sipping the hot beverage that I had watched Shirley make for them and then she had begun to admonish them for their behaviour. I had also seen the crafty bemused look on Royston's face as Shirley took hold of his hand and signed as seriously as she could onto his hand and at the same time began ticking Sid off as well. I could tell that Royston hadn't bothered trying to translate for himself what Shirley had to say. He just couldn't be bothered and had switched off. It was good to see him laugh and then rub his hand on his trousers. A short while later I had left the scene and begun this journey to my 'home' at the Lodge.

CHAPTER THIRTEEN

Friday 23rd November. I had gone to bed late and got up early. My Granny Lil used to have a saying that she never went to bed the day she got up. I had gone to bed and got up on the same day and was now sitting by myself in the Den, with my mind intermittently on memories of my Gran and on what I had written in my room the night before. I had been writing an abbreviated account of what I had been doing in the early days of my stay at the Manor, but now, in the early hours of the morning after, I was rubbing my aching wrist in an attempt to shrug off the cramps that a short night's rest had not relieved. I tried to remember what significance there was in thinking about my Gran. My Gran had died six months before I had had the accident in 1981, I was thinking about my Gran, my writing, and this very crowded and yet so lonely place called America Lodge. At first, I couldn't pinpoint the cause of my train of thoughts and then it dawned on me at about the time of the real dawn outside. The only trouble was, this was also about the same time that the Lodge began to wake up, and the room I had had to myself for the previous hour and a quarter was gradually filling to capacity, as more and more residents came downstairs. A

132

few good-morning's and some pleasantries from people I knew and I decided that it was time to move on.

I had become intrigued by thoughts of my gran and I wanted more time to myself to think about her and the significance of thinking about her at such a time. It was only when I was standing outside the den in the dimly lit corridor that something stirred inside me and my stomach seemed do a backward flip.

Two blind women had just gone into the den. I was alone for a few moments, although there were voices inside the den and further up the corridor as well. I was standing near to the door of the typing room and something seemed to be compelling me to go in there. I quite naturally resisted, knowing what I knew about the place. And then it occurred to me just what the significance was between this room and my Gran. Or rather... The mysterious American and my Gran. Both of them were dead... That World War Two airman's spirit was supposed to occupy this room, and my Gran had been a Spiritualist in her lifetime. "Why am I doing this?" I found myself saying in a quiet voice. I had to find out if it was all true or just a figment of my imagination. But would I find out? and what would I find out if I go in there? Will that icy; mind numbing blast of cold air go right through me as it had done once before? There was only one way to find out and that was to turn the knob and open the door... And so, I did... and it happened, almost exactly the same as it had happened before. Only this time there was more than myself involved... I had unwittingly gone and chosen that particular moment to turn the brass knob when Mike and a few others had been approaching the den from my left. I hadn't noticed them coming. I had been far too engrossed in finding out what I was quickly regretting, and they all felt the unnatural icy blast as well.

I didn't turn around; I couldn't turn around; I was frozen to the spot once more the same as before and I'll swear that my hair was standing on end. I know the one's on the back of my neck were as the... The... Whatever it was went right through me.

Mike's voice seemed to come to me from a distance as I heard him say.

Boigh! Someone's just walked over moy groive and stamped hard on it loike."

"What the hell was that?" Came another man's hesitant voice. This man could obviously see as he touched me on my shoulder and said.

"What the hell are you standing there waiting for man? Get off in there and close that frigging window before we all freeze our bollocks off."

I had cringed when he had touched me on my shoulder, but other than that I didn't move at all, and I couldn't move. I had heard Mike's voice, I had heard this man's voice and I could now hear other voices coming from behind me and a bit further up the corridor from the direction of the Den, as other people in there joined in the protestations. The icy draught had ceased almost as quickly as it had started and then the warmer air from the corridor began to come past me in the opposite direction, and I was left wondering once more. I could move now. At last, and the man behind me was again prompting me to go into the typing room and close the window.

I did go in. I now knew that I could. The green, steel and glass French window on the opposite side of the room would not be open. There was no fireplace to have caused the phenomenon either. If there was one it had been bricked up long since. I stood for a few moments, listening to the sounds of normality returning. Then I walked past the desks with their heavy burden of cumbersome typewriters and made my way over to the French windows. I didn't look around me at the room, I knew there would be little to see and I didn't really want to see what the deepest most primitive part of my mind; might have wanted me to see. Instead, I went and stood beside the glass door on the far side of the room and looked out at the mutilated leafless trunk of a tree, which, in the recent past, I had helped to chop up, and I was wondering about light and life and the universe, and everything above and below. Heaven and Hell, and were there such things? And what is it that helps us to see. Our eyes, but it is more than that... It's millions of cones and rods and a blood filled pad called the retina and thousands upon thousands of intricate nerve endings all coming together at the back of that pad called the retina and they are connected to another part somewhere deep down in the back of our heads where the brain sees what we see with the delicate instruments we call eyes. The human body is a truly amazing intricacy of natural engineering and plumbing, but then so too is the same for any creature. But the most amazing of all and the one thing which separates us from all others is the one thing we cannot understand, and that is our brain, our mind. These weren't necessarily my words, or thoughts. I suppose I might have heard them from someone else somewhere and at sometime in the dark and distant past. Maybe I had heard it all here at the Lodge or else at the Manor I couldn't recollect where, or, who had said them, but it didn't matter. None of it mattered... I was in a unique place. It was a place crammed to the brim and full of a great many philosophical people. So many that I had never before encountered in one place, and it did frighten me. But then why should it frighten me? I was one of those very same people. But what was the reason for this feeling? It had taken me a while to find this out for myself, and now here it was staring me in the face. Only when we lose or are at risk of losing one of our most valuable senses... If not the most valuable, do we then begin to fall back on primitive feelings in an attempt to rationalise it all. But even then, we can't. We can only believe what we believe in. Nothing more, and it does help when we come across something that we cannot possibly rationalise. In a weird sort of way, it makes what we can't understand just that little bit more understandable. I can't explain the icy cold feeling which had just gone right through my body, again, but I had to believe, and it had to be something which was unexplainable, and it gave me a strange, comforting sort of reassurance, a feeling that there was something beyond all of this. My Granny Lil hadn't just ceased to exist when she had died. Janet's dad hadn't just ceased to exist when he had died, and there was something within this room which refused to not exist. I didn't know what it was, but it certainly wasn't a fault in the design of the building.

Nobody came into the typing room to disturb my thoughts while I struggled to pull myself together, sufficient for me to leave the room. I seemed to be in a strange sort of bubble, where all outward sounds were muffled. But, slowly, ever so slowly, some sort of normality began to settle inside me, and this building. Eventually, I forced myself to turn away from the scene beyond the French windows, to walk slowly across the room, and leaving the door open I quietly made my way along the corridor, past the noisy Den and then up the stairs to get my things together for another day at the Manor, and the last day of that week.

Ascending the empty stairs, I couldn't help muttering to myself. "That's a rum start to the day... I wonder what else is in store?"

I purposely involved myself with a group of residents as we made our way up Middle Lincombe Road that morning. I had had enough of being alone. Now I wanted company. Whether those around needed me, was a different matter and remained to be seen. I was mostly content to just be there and listen to people talking, blind people talking. They weren't talking about blindness, they were talking about normal things like, what they had done and where they had been the night before, and some talked about the weather. Half of them couldn't even see what the weather was like, but they had other means of knowing and they used these other means in a perfectly natural way. Some of them, particularly the four in front of our group were using their canes in a manner which seemed perfectly natural. They swung those symbolic white objects from side to side and made their way almost effortlessly towards their goal and the rest of us followed just as effortlessly in their wake. It looked like those in front were clearing the way for the rest of us. And that's partly what made the journey from the Lodge to the Manor seem so easy, so, normal.

When we arrived at the Manor I even went inside with that group of people and another group who had been congregating just outside the porch entrance. The main hall would be getting very crowded by now but I wasn't at all bothered. This was what I needed. I wanted to throw myself into the action. I wanted to involve myself with all of these wonderfully brave people. Having spent far too long on the fringes I suddenly wanted to involve myself with my fellow colleagues more than I had ever done or dared to do in the past and I wanted to learn more about them, and about myself as well, before it was too late. Up in my room back at the Lodge it had occurred to me that I only had twenty-one more days to go before this course would be over and I would be going home. I had missed out on so much. I was slowly but surely realising that now. Now that it was almost too late.

I seem to have set myself a tight and confusing regime during my stay so far. It had become a pattern that had caused me a lot of problems and a lot of misery. I still wasn't sure if it made any sense, but somehow knew that I had now reached a turning point. I didn't yet know it, but shortly, in a few days as it happened, I was going to be making some extremely hard and difficult decisions, decisions that up until then had meant more to me than common sense ought to have dictated. First of all, there were the people of the Manor and America Lodge. I don't think I made a fool of myself. I may have done to begin with, and I might have done if I had gone on any longer than I did, but that morning, I really threw myself into events concerning the place and the people around me. I did it all with a completely renewed vigour and with such a determined attitude that it came as little surprise that I managed to turn a few heads.

My new, involved mood was short lived however, and was to alter shortly after breakfast was finished. First of all, there was the breakfast itself and the incident on my table which had to be dealt with. The man with the camera, John, was retiring, and going home that day, whereas Ann. Big Ann, was our new House Captain and this was her inaugural speech, about halfway through breakfast. I could hear but couldn't see her from where I was sitting.

"Good morning lads and lasses. Thanks for making me your house captain until me and me husband leave at the end of next week... Never thought as I'd be saying this but, will all those of you terminating this week, please see Sandra as soon as possible to collect your train fare tickets home. Now, what's next? Oh yes! now then. Talent contest. Sorry, sorry! It's not a talent contest it's a music show... Concert! It says here that Shaun is coming back to give it a bit of a boost. You all remember Shaun. Anyway, that's it for now folks but if there's anything else. I'll tell you about it at lunch time. Now, all that remains is for you all to put your hands together for our retiring House Captain Thank you John and thanks to you all for listening."

Amid the noise and commotion following Big Anne's announcements, it was something Anita said which drowned out everything else and made me look directly at her stern features, as she said once more.

"I am leaving and she hasn't even bothered to mention it... And no-one cares either. "No-one?"

"Why Where're you going?" Was all I could manage to say in surprise. I could see that Laurie was looking rather surprised too, and just sat there gobsmacked and speechless. One thought quickly shot through my mind and was almost as quickly discounted. Maybe there had been something developing between these two over the past few days, but no. She wouldn't be leaving if there was. Or would she? Anita was slowly getting to her feet now. Her parting words echoed in my ears as she sullenly passed me by and started to walk away.

"Nobody likes me here and I don't think I could get to like this place anyway."

And then she was gone... and I never saw her again.

My new 'involved' mood had been dented, but not squashed by the sad looking departure of Anita. The real bashing to my new mood was to come in about ten, or fifteen minutes time. Meanwhile I carried on with breakfast and passed some of the toast to Christopher and the remainder of our time in the dining room went by in miserable silence, but only there on our table. The rest of the dining room was just as noisy as ever it was.

Out in the main hall a few minutes later I was 'involving' myself with other residents. I wanted to get to know more about more of the residents. It was totally going against the grain to attempt to do it this way but I felt that I really needed to get to know more about the people I was incarcerated in that centre for the blind with, and this seemed to be the only way that I could do it. I plonked myself down between two men of about my own age, both of them were blind and they were casually dressed, as was I. So, I naturally began thinking that we had a sort of kinship going for us already.

"Hello." I said. "So, what brings you two here?"

"Piss off." Said the man on my left with the dark glasses.

"Yes, Piss off." Responded the other man indignantly.

Neither of them had moved their heads to emphasise their words, there was no need to. They just carried on looking blindly ahead as they waited, impatiently, for me to, to not quite literally do as they had suggested. Getting to my feet, a little more dented but as yet; undaunted. I casually strolled across the crowded hall and as I went, I listened in to the various conversations that were going on.

"Braille. I love braille." Said one smartly dressed woman in a blue and white crisp looking dress. I think her name was Margaret, something or other. I had seen here in the Braille room. She was talking at that moment to Walter, my companion in the typing room. There seemed to be little or no chance of joining in with this conversation. Then I noticed Jim and Josie in with a group of five other residents. Jim had his back to me. I detected laughter and realised by the actions that Jim had just been telling them one of his jokes. I passed them by. I already knew a lot about Jim and Josie and I even knew some of his party as well. It was new blood that I was after. Stopping beside the huge grey stone fireplace I began to study the three people and was about to 'involve' myself, when the only woman there, looked between the shoulders of the two men and said. "Yes? what do you want?" I moved on. I moved towards the main entrance and the conspicuously spacious area immediately outside the care staff office. I always found it strange that this area was always left unoccupied by residents when the hall was as crowded as was. After all, how could the blind know how much room to leave in that area? One of Manor life's puzzles I suppose.

I came to a stop near to the door, the old oak door that had accommodated many a blind and partially sighted person, on the almost genuine pretext of studying the ancient grain and the heavy ironwork of the door. I was at the same time listening to the conversation between the group of five men, none of whom did I know by name. This'll do. I'll just listen and try and join in with their conversation when I see an opportunity. I'll soon get to know more about some of the residents this way… Fishing? They were talking about fishing. Two of them were as blind as they could be and they were the ones who were holding the other three spellbound with their tales of fishing. Now what did I know about fishing? Not a lot, except for the story about the time when I was about twelve years old and had been fishing with a friend on the canal and had caught a twelve-inch pike with a worm bait. Right! I readied myself for an introduction, but it never came. I was already too late to involve myself with this group because they broke up within the next few seconds and went their separate ways to ready themselves for another day of assessments.

I drifted around the hall and made one or two further, innocent, but fruitless attempts at trying to get to know some of the residents a little bit better, but they were all drifting away by now and it wasn't long before I was forced to decide that I ought to be trying to find Royston and we should be heading for woodwork. I was just about to temporarily give up on my quest for closer links with the other residents, when I noticed with a curious feeling, directed solely at myself, consisting of disgust, shame, and dismay... Shirley was near to the bottom of the wide staircase and she was doing exactly what I was trying to do, only better... much better. She was involving herself with the residents as only she knew how, and I had just been attempting to mimic what she was always doing and I hadn't even realised it. Until now... Turning away I went in search of my tall and deaf and nearly blind friend.

I ended up finding Royston over in Gordon's department. After searching the hall, the Den and even up the room we used to share, but he wasn't anywhere to be seen. By the time I was coming back down the stairs the hall below was conspicuously empty. Then I noticed the solitary figure of one man in a black suit sporting a white cane and an oriental kind of smile on his face. I stopped to pass a few pleasantries with Peter as he waited outside the closed door to the Mobility office. Just then, Beryl came out of the Care Staff office behind and to my left. Her clicking high heels echoed loudly on the wooden floor as she headed away from us towards the lounge at the far end of the hall. Peter said something and I had to ask him to repeat it. He began again.

"I said that's a nice sound, pity I can't see the body that goes with it."

The door behind him opened and out came Gill Roberts. She hesitated for a brief moment or two and I think she must have thought that I was there for the wrong reason. Then she looked directly at me and said.

"Half past three, not now, half past three. Oh' by the way... What you said the other day. Something about, Velcro? It's still on. I mean. It's not going to be too much trouble?"

"No." I responded eagerly. "No, it might be here this morning I'll let you know."

"Thank you." She then took hold of Peter's arm and escorted him towards the old oak doors. I followed at a discreet distance and once outside hurriedly crossed the yard.

"You're late!" Said Gordon as I tried to sneak in and hang my coat up. "Do you want to learn how to use a woodturning lathe, or not?"

"I already know." And immediately realised that I had said the wrong thing. Judging by the look on his face that is. My coat slipped off its peg and I bent down to pick it up and began again. "I mean. I've er, I've got my own lathe back home. It's not anywhere near as good as the one's you've got here, but I've had it for quite a few years now but I'd like to learn a bit more on how to use these bigger and better one's if I can."

'This is better' I thought. 'Butter them up, don't antagonise the tutors any-more.' But even this didn't seem to work.

"Don't patronise me young man."

Young man! Me, at thirty-six years of age! I nearly said something else but didn't. Sheepishly I followed Gordon as he led the way to the machine shop.

"Right." Said Gordon as we stood in front of the lathe. "As you profess to know how to operate one of these machines I might as well dispense with the usual routine of showing you how to use it. As you can see. I…" He carefully scrutinised my face and eyes, and then continued. "Hmmm. Well. As I was saying, there is a block of wood, Mahogany as it happens, already fixed to the faceplate. Faceplate, faceplate! This is the faceplate, beg your pardon. You already know that don't you."

"Yes." I said patiently. He's not going to antagonise me and I'm not going to antagonise him, but it was getting increasingly difficult. Gordon was very much the same as Pauline had been, the boss of her domain and here Gordon was acting in the same manner. He seemed to want me to learn right from the very beginning. I had fallen foul of Pauline. She and me were alright now but I couldn't do anything about what had already happened. I didn't really want to fall foul of Gordon and as his lathe was much larger than mine, I had to make a decision. I had used this type of machine in the past and I did know how to work it. Nevertheless, I decided there and then to let him show me how to use it and get this initiating ceremony over and done with.

"Go on… Show me, I admit, I don't know how to use this one."

I knew this would please him and I patiently listened as he began to go through the paces and principles of woodturning before he actually switched on the lathe. He also went through the motions of explaining what the various tools were for and how to hold them. I watched and I listened. I wasn't feeling frustrated, or smart. I was always ready to learn from a Master Craftsman.

It must have been about twenty minutes later that Gordon finally decided to start the lathe and the block of wood began to spin in a blur of motion on the faceplate. Gordon took the gouge and cradling the long handle beneath his right forearm he rested the curved edge of the gouge on the tool rest and gently eased the blade towards the whirring block of mahogany. Chips of wood immediately began to fly up and over the surrounding area and a few landed on me as well. This didn't bother me in the slightest and I edged in closer in order to see where he was going, and also to show him that I was still watching. He hadn't done all that much though when someone came in from the other room and demanded his attention. I watched him go and felt a bit disappointed that he had switched off the lathe which meant that I would have to wait for him to return. He came back and went away again and he did this a few more times before he finally allowed me to have a go myself. I stood there in front of the whirring, now rounded block of wood. It was about five minutes or so before the end of that session and I now had the gouge in my hands at long last. I offered the blade up to the spinning wood knowing full well that Gordon was watching me intensely and that the cutting angle of the gouge might not be exactly the same as my gouge back home was. If I didn't go in at the correct angle to the blade; I knew what the outcome would be. A lot of juddering, or even worse, a terrible snatching and tearing of wood on steel. Fortunately, I knew how to approach the potential problem and so I was just about able to avoid losing face with him. Was he playing with me though? Did he know that I would find it a lot more difficult to newly approach this block of wood when it was in the round rather than as it had started out; as an eight-sided block of wood? I did wonder, but I couldn't let this spoil my concentration. The blade edged in closer and closer to the spinning wood and then some fine dust like particles began to fly into the air. I considered myself lucky in that exercise. I had after all, very nearly got the cutting angle correct. I only had to come up with my arm a fraction and then I felt and saw the red shavings spiralling up and away from the mahogany and I knew that I was under way at last. The only trouble was. It was also very near to the end of that session. Just a couple of minutes of concentrated wood-turning and then Gordon was ordering me to stop what I was doing, then to switch off the lathe and follow him through into the other room. I had done it though. I had shown him that I could turn a bit of wood, maybe not as good as Gordon could, but as good as the next man could.

I was in the other shop, standing with Royston, studying his coffee table and had a deep admiration for the quality of craftsmanship that had so far gone into making it and getting it to this stage. I had played a part in the creation of this beautiful piece of furniture but it had only been a small part and I wanted to keep it that way. This was his project. I had had no part at all to play in the intricate decorative top that was now finished, and only lacked the time consuming task, of hand sanding the veneered pattern to a very fine finish and this would have to be done before the polishing could begin. Just for once in my troubled life during my stay it the Manor, I was fortunate, right there and then, to realise where this sign language and the studying of a fine piece of furniture might lead to. I had already done the lacquering of the coffee table legs for Royston. Gordon had helped him to make the top and I was lucky enough to realise that any moment now he might ask me to sandpaper the top for him. I would have done it if he had asked me to, but I knew that it really would be for the best if he did this part for himself, so I got in first and signed:-

"WELL DONE THIS IS GREAT GORDON IS SHOWING ME HOW TO USE A LATHE I AM DOING THE SAME TOMORROW COME ON TIME WE WERE OUT OF HERE"

CHAPTER FOURTEEN

I was standing inside the recess of the bay window in the lounge, this was adjacent to the rack where I had deposited the cane earlier that morning, so that I wouldn't have to carry it about with me all day long. The rest of the lounge was just as crowded as it always was at the time of the Postal round. I could hear Sandra but I couldn't quite see her, so I had to wait and listen, and then it came: - "Quite a large parcel for... for Mr R Weaver!"

"Over here." I cried out, and eagerly accepted the parcel from Sandra. I looked for the sender's name and saw the legend. 'Selectus' Biddulph. Staffordshire. Then I headed out into the main hall to do a Postal delivery of my own.

I knocked on the door of the Mobility officers' room and waited. Behind me, all the residents who had bothered to find out if there had been any Post for them, were now making their way towards the dining room for their morning coffee and biscuits. I waited a few seconds longer before deciding that there was no one at home. So, using a biro I crossing out my name and put Gillian's there instead, then I left the unopened packet by the base of the door and went for my break.

I had absolutely no idea how much Velcro Reg Evans had sent me in that parcel. It had to be a fair bit; I could at least tell that much. I also had no idea whatsoever where that simple act of obtaining a supply of Velcro would lead to. I had seen a problem with the black elastic on the canes and a thought had occurred and I had acted upon it, if only to help Gillian in a small way who was trying her best to help me in a big way.

I quickly forgot about the good Samaritan act by the time I was entering the Crafts department with my good friend Royston. There was to be very little time to think about anything else while I was in there that morning.

The first person to greet me was Sally, she seemed quite concerned that I hadn't started some project the day before. I wasn't about to get much done that day either, but we didn't yet know that. I told Sally I hadn't minded helping out the day before and would gladly do it again but that I was just as keen to get stuck into something, but I didn't know what!

Gerry came in in his wheelchair a short while later and with him came the remainder of the residents for that session. Amongst them were Jim and Josie and another 'J.' J for Janice Longford. A youngish woman that I was going to get to know a lot better by the end of the session. Janice was just about as blind as me without her glasses. In fact, she had a similar condition, but hers wasn't caused by a R.T.A (Road Traffic Accident) hers was caused by an operation which went tragically wrong. I'm still not entirely sure how the situation between me and Janice came about but within those first few minutes I seemed to have become attracted to her. I had seen her around about the Manor and more recently down at the Lodge as well, but this was the first time that fate had actually thrown us together, perhaps, so that I can now tell some of her story. Janice wasn't only near blind. She was also profoundly deaf, but this wasn't as it had always been. She had gone into hospital a few years previous in order for her to have what was supposed to be, a relatively simple operation; to clear blocked tear ducts. Sally carefully signed a message onto Janice's hand and Janice then looked at me and indicated for me to follow her. She was taller than me and I couldn't help noticing this as we walked over to a section of the long bench, she sat down and indicated for me to do the same. I glanced out of the window which looked out onto nothing more exciting than the drab grey exterior walls and the French window entrance of the Manor just across the way. I sat down to the pleasant but patronising voice of Sally as she quickly made use of this excuse for her and also an opening for me to get started somewhere. She began: -

"That's it, sit here with Janice and she will show you how we make our furry animals... You sign to Royston so you should be alright with Janice, she is also a very fine lip reader as well."

Sally left us to it and was off across to the other side of the prefabricated building to deal with a minor crisis. I didn't watch her leave, but I could hear her heels clicking on the vinyl floor and I immediately thought about what Peter had said that morning and I wondered if he was saying the same to Jim as he had said to me, when Beryl had crossed the main hall inside the Manor.
"Nice sound. Pity I can't see the body that goes with it!" Oh! the dilemma of it all. Still! No time for reflection. I could see that Royston was busy doing something quite large in cane; alongside Gerry. Then someone else demanded Sally's attention, and someone nearer was demanding mine. Janice was twenty-five, easy going, tall and slim. She had smooth dark brown hair which extended down her back just a bit lower than her shoulders, she had a nice neat fringe at the front and it soon became clear that she was a very meticulous and tidy person. Everything to do with the work she was doing had to be neatly laid out in front of her from the cardboard shoe box she had picked up from the large cluttered table in the centre of the room. Other residents had similar boxes. I watched Janice and a few others as they busied themselves. I noticed Josie as she came and sat down at the long wooden topped bench on the other side of Janice and started unpacking her cardboard box. I might have been wondering just how Josie had managed to find her own work amongst the clutter on the large table behind us, if it hadn't been for the oblong plastic label stuck to the lid which was dotted with Braille writing. Janice's box had the same sort of label. I was only being curious and picked up Janice's box lid to have a look, when she spoke her first words to me. Her voice came over in the sadly typical way of someone who cannot hear their own voice.

"What are you doing? put that down."

She looked at me then but to do so she had to do a quarter turn to her right and then she had to lean back in her chair in order to focus on me. Her glasses had quite thick lenses and were larger than mine, but obviously, more delicately framed, and they made her eyes seem quite large looking at them from this side. It was strange, but I couldn't help but wonder at that particular moment just how my damaged eyes must look to someone looking at me.

"You are a dreamer. I can see that." Came that voice once more. That same haunting, broken voice, with that ever so vital link, between mouth and ears undeniably lost.

"Sorry." I said, and then I remembered my association with Royston and indicated for her to give me her hand so that I could sign to her.

"Don't need to do that, I can read your lips." She said.

"Aye, but only if you're looking straight at me." I mumbled.

"Yes!" Said Janice, which startled me. I hadn't intended her to hear, to see me say that. She turned away from me just then and got on with her work. She was making a stuffed Penguin the same as Josie was. I must have sat there for at least a full minute watching the two of them. I didn't dare touch anything on the bench in case it spoiled her concentration. Besides, I didn't need to touch anything. This soft toy making didn't appeal to me. I wanted something more challenging to do, but I hadn't got a clue what that something was. It wasn't quiet in the room. There was a lot of talking going on and questions being asked and answered. There was also a relaxed easy-going merriment which was noticeably lacking in other departments. I had already had a few tentative looks around the room while I had been sitting beside Janice, this was in order to find out what was going on, but I had just been on the receiving end of a curious look from Sally; almost as if she was about to ask if I was feeling bored or something. So, now, I was bored. Having had nothing better to do than to look around and out of the window at the bland exterior walls of the Manor. There was no one sitting on my right-hand side and I was about five feet away from the entrance where we had all come in. This end of the long bench was empty, except for a wicker fruit basket which someone had made but not finished off. I reached out and picked it up more out of curiosity than anything else and before I knew it, I had Sally standing beside me asking me if I would like to finish it off for her. "Nah." I said. "I wouldn't know how to."

So, she showed me. I didn't learn much by it and it didn't take me all that long anyway. All I had to do was to take hold of a pair of pruners and trim the wicker strands back to the base of where they had been twisted to form the rim of the basket. Five minutes more and the job was done and I was looking for something else to do. I didn't have to wait very much longer. Janice had been putting the final touches to her work. With a flourish she declared. "Finished!"

While she waited for Sally to come, Janice reached for my hand and without bothering to turn to look at me she dragged my right hand across in front of

145

her, she then pushed it down, palm up, and began signing to me. The only trouble was, I found it to be very difficult to understand her. She was talking to me in two languages at the same time, and she was saying something different in each of them. with the sign language she was saying something like. "I HAVE SEEN YOU… YOU ARE T… MA… WHO LOS…… GLA… A FEW WEE… AGO" and with her voice she was saying. "Your skin is tough, you like working with your hands, don't you?"

Sally came and took the penguin away with her. Janice then turned to face me once more and we were then better able to hold something like an intelligent conversation. I managed to find out that she had had the operation which I mentioned earlier that had all gone tragically wrong and that they hadn't even managed to unblock the drainage tubes with the result that she still had a weeping left eye, and that she had gone into theatre with normal hearing and reasonable sight and come out with a loss of both, hearing and sight. That had been nearly three years since, and she, like myself was pursuing a claim for compensation, but unlike me, Janice was having to find an ongoing cost of a solicitor and pay him a fixed amount each month. I wasn't told and I didn't ask how much this sum was, but I got the distinct impression that she had already paid out a considerable sum of money and that she would have to pay out a lot more before she would reach anything like a conclusion. Then as now, I considered myself lucky that I had the Post Office Solicitors on my side. I explained this to Janice and she jocularly remarked that she wished she had been working for the Post Office. She was not bitter and I was quick to take a liking to her. And her voice, sadly afflicted though it was, had a faint and very pleasant Welsh accent to it.

I hadn't seen him coming up the room, the first I knew was when Gerry turned his wheelchair away and said: - "Would you like to come with me Bob?"

I think I mentioned earlier that it was amazing what Gerry could do with a piece of leather, Well, this was the day that I was going to begin to discover that fact. First of all, Gerry took me to one side and asked if I had ever done any leathercraft work. To which, I said; no. What followed was extremely good to witness and also to be a part of. Gerry was really in his element now and it showed. First of all, he opened a cupboard and pulled out a small sheet of stiff lightly tanned leather. It was smooth on one side and rough on the other, about A4 size and around 4mm thick. Gerry explained to me that this was tooling leather and he proceeded to show me some of the tools which he would be using in his demonstration. He got me to clear a section at the end of the long bench near to where Josie was busily working away stuffing another soft toy. When I had done what was asked of me, Gerry emptied a box of steel punches onto the wooden top and began to finger feel the working end and then put them to one side in an orderly regimental fashion. He then gave me a tin can with instructions to fill it with some water from the tap and bring it back, along with a cotton cloth from beneath the sink. By this time Gerry was almost ready to start and show me how to make an embossed pattern on new leather. First of all, he wet the cloth and wiped it over the smooth surface of the leather which made it go a darker colour. He then picked up a small hammer and the first one of the tools he would be using, then, his fingers wandered over the damp leather so as to find a suitable place to begin. The leather was laid flat on the bench top and before I could realise what was happening, it had happened and there was a pattern radiating out from the centre of the piece of leather. Gerry had placed the tool in the chosen spot and tapped it with the hammer and had then gone on to the next part of his pattern. When it came to a change of punch, he would put down the hammer and feel for the progress of the pattern in the leather while he reached for his next punch and then he would continue and the tools would leave a permanently deep mark in the leather. A few minutes later and his pattern was complete, while I just stood there genuinely mesmerised by this blind craftsman and the speed in which he had achieved such a uniform pattern. By this time, the leather had begun to dry out and the pattern was becoming more pronounced. It amazed me that Gerry had managed to make this in so short a space of time and to do it with such accuracy that a perfectly sighted person might find it difficult to match. Gerry turned his sightless eyes towards me and said.

"There, what do you think? Would you like to have a go now?"

I did, but my first attempts at leather tooling were nothing like as they should have been, and definitely not as good as Gerry's efforts.

One of the most important skills as well as one of the most difficult to achieve, was to hit the punch with the hammer at the correct angle and with a consistent pressure each time, this was so that the indented pattern in the leather was of a uniform and consistent depth. Gerry kept saying. "You only have one go, you can't keep hammering or going back, you will spoil the pattern if you do."

I had at least learned some of the importance of, if not some of the actual skills, of leather tooling before that session was over, and it was thoroughly enjoyable as well. I felt sorry when the session came to a close all too swiftly and without me having realised it. I told Gerry with unabashed enthusiasm that I would be looking forward to having another go as soon as I could. I even asked him if he could make sure that I could get into the Crafts department with him the following week.

I couldn't help but overhear Gerry's remarks to Sally as I, being one of the last to leave, went out of the door. He was saying. Yes! I think I've got him hooked!" Was he referring to me? He must have been, but I didn't mind, I didn't mind in the least. The long hard road was at last beginning to show some promise of better things to come.

CHAPTER FIFTEEN

I was one amongst many others who were taking advantage of the unusual mild spell during the brief interlude between lunch and resuming assessments once more. There were a lot of residents who were just walking singly or in groups around the sunken lawn and also there were quite a lot actually walking or else sitting down on the sunken lawn. I stood with my back to the Manor and was leaning on the railing looking on the scene below. Jim was down there, he was with Josie, but he didn't see me. I looked to my right and saw a group of women slowly coming this way, I knew all five of them. There was Denise and Samantha, and Shirley, and then there was Rachael and also the newly acquired knowledge and character in the shape of Janice. Janice and Samantha were both about the same near six foot tall. The other three were shorter. None of them spoke to me as they passed me by and I didn't expect them to for theirs was girl talk. I could tell by the way one or two of them went silent, which prompted the others to do the same, as they first came past two familiar looking men leaning on the railing a bit further along, and then the five came past me and did exactly the same. I turned my head to look to my left and watched them go by in their bright colourful clothes, and I couldn't help but notice with a slight tinge of sadness, at the way the empty sleeve of Samantha's blue cardigan fluttered behind her in the gentle breeze.

"Didna think as thee'ad it in thee mon, lookin' at a bit o'skirt. An' five on 'em at that."

I quickly turned my eyes away from the five women and feeling embarrassed and wanting to find an excuse, I looked to my right and watched Jack Townley approaching, and then there was Ian, tapping his cane from side to side bringing up the rear. I looked away and all around, except to my left again, while I waited the few seconds for them both to draw nearer. Then I looked at Jack and said.

148

"Does no 'arm t'look does it? Reckon I should thank God I can."

"Aye! maybe theyat rayte lad. Listen boooth on thee. Ah nades goo see Sandra. Look thee after Ian fer a bit wut Bob? Talk to'im, ay's bloody shadderln' may everywheere ah goos. Frittened stiff ah might layve'im. Here theyat, stay wi'Bob ah shonna be long."

A nod of the head from me and then from Jack and he turned about face and headed away for the Porch entrance and left me to guide Ian's furtive hand towards the railing.

With his back to the guide rail Ian relaxed a little and leaned back. I found myself looking upwards at what he would have been looking at if he could have seen it. The railings and the balcony above the windows of the lounge. There were a couple of people up there but were too indistinct for me to tell what sex they were never mind who they were, and besides, the sky was too bright for me to see in that direction for very long. Turning back to look at Ian I hesitated for a moment before daring to speak again. I had been given a hefty task here. One wrong word from me and Ian would be off and looking for his mentor, I could tell that Jack had been desperate for some time to himself and I wanted to give him that breather if I possibly could. "Have you got a girlfriend Ian?" I asked, as casually as I could.

"Nah!" Came the reply a few thoughtful seconds later. "But I'll tell you what... I don't half fancy Jack's youngest lass, Rita."

It was the way he had said it, and did I detect a twinkle behind those dark glasses? "You've been with Jack too long you 'ave." I said cheerfully. "Far too long. You'll 'ave me thinkin' you've spent half your life down th'pit the way you're acting."

"I anna acting. I'm bloody serious man. Ever since I first met her. She's just great. I like her and I want to get to know her a lot more, a lot, lot more... She hasn't got a boyfriend, I know, Jack told me..."

I was watching his dreamy face as thoughts drifted around inside his head, and I found myself trying to analyse this curious mixture of Northern and Southern dialects all mixed up amongst everything else inside this young man's head. I smiled then. Not at the woman going past us, but at the tremendous strides this young man had taken over the past weeks since his remarkable transformation and the eventual acceptance of his position, or, situation in the world of the blind. "Come on Ian." I said. "Show me how you use your cane. Let's see how good you are."

Jack was waiting for us by the time we had circumnavigated the tarmac path around the sunken lawn. As we approached him and his familiar outline started to become clearer, I noticed that there was something of a difference in his appearance and as we came to within a few feet of him, I couldn't help but wonder why, or how he had altered so much in so short a space of time. An explanation was quick to come from his smiling face. Although he kept his voice sternly regulated.

"The's good news an'the's bad news Ian... Good news is they'n kaypin may on fer another wick till theyst ready goo wom an'th' bad news is ah've got spend it wi'thee. Nah ah dost fayle abite that then eh?"

"Bloody marvellous Jack... bloody marvellous..."

There was about twelve inches separating the two men and in view of the circumstances, it was a touching scene, I watched quietly as Ian put an empty hand up to his face to wipe away a tear, and then there was the quiet way that Jack was tentatively reaching out to put a hand on Ian's shoulder as he started to lead him away... And then I was reminded by the scenes of gathering orderliness as groups of residents reformed and headed for the Commerce building and wherever else, that it was time for the afternoon shift, and for me, a spell in the typing section.

Pauline gave me a rather curious half smile as I entered her domain a few minutes later. I don't know why but I wasn't quite ready for her just yet, so I took the papers which she offered to me from her sitting position behind her desk and then headed for the sheltered part of the room where the electronic typewriters were. Peter and Josie and most of the others were already in there and about to start.

As I went to sit at my station, I noticed with some strange trepidation that Peter was already struggling with his machine. 'I won't be doing much today' I thought to myself.

With this thought in my mind I looked at the papers I had done the day before to see what Pauline's comments were. In red lettering near the bottom of the second sheet I saw the one word. 'Incomplete.' I was feeling a bit flustered and didn't quite know what to do. If I was going to win this woman's favour I should have to try and ignore Peter and get on with my own work. Or should

150

I? Surely, my helping Peter ought to account for something? I was torn between the two. I couldn't effectively do both. Peter was so determined to learn how to use an electronic typewriter that it was almost inevitable that he would make mistakes in his typing, and in his handling of the unseen machine in front of him. I did try to concentrate on my own work. I even gave Walter at the back of the room something of a mixture of a pleading look, as I put the paper in the back of Peter's machine for the second time, but either Walter couldn't see me or else he didn't want to, he had helped Peter before, but he wasn't offering any help now, and neither was Jim. I noticed Jim intently looking up at the wall on his right with his head on one side and his left eye close to the typewriter. He wasn't looking at the cream painted walls, or avoiding me, but concentrating hard on what little he could see. I sat down but not for long, a few seconds later I was back on my feet again. Peter had become frustrated and lost foot contact with the controls for the tape recorder. I patiently put him right once more and went back to sit at my own place again. Before sitting down however, I looked through the glass screen and searched out the features of Pauline. There she was, at the back of the room, bending down to look at something the large unmistakable bulk of Christopher had just done on his machine. Sitting down once more, I really began in earnest. But! Not for long.

"Bob! anybody! How do you spell 'Constancy?"

Needless to say, I was more than pleased to be able to help where I could, but I didn't get a great deal of my own work done during that session. I did get a bit more done than the day before though and that was a surprise in itself, because not only had I had Peter to see to, but I and the rest of the residents in that part of the room also had the exuberance and the eventually very frustrated person of Jim to contend with as well. The end of the session came around all too soon.

I joined the queue in readiness to hand in my papers. Josie was directly in front of me and I had Jim behind me. Peter and most of the remainder from both parts of the typing room had already gone out of the door. I wasn't feeling awkward when I gave Pauline my work, I had after all, done a bit more than the previous day, so what was there to worry about?

"Would you mind waiting for a minute or two Robert?"

Jim caught my eye and he just couldn't help himself when he pursed his lips and said: - "Ooh! Look who's got to stay behind after class then."

Pauline took Jim's paper from him and said: - "On your way James... Hmm... is this all that you have managed to do?"

Jim went out of the door while I anxiously watched the remainder of Pauline's pupils leave the room as well. I was thinking. 'Careful Bob, things have been alright over the past few days, don't go and spoil it now."

"Right! That's the last. This shouldn't take more than a minute. We don't want to keep you from your afternoon break, do we? now then. I shall come straight to the point... Do you mind having to help Peter? You seem to do. Or have I been misinterpreting your actions?"

"No, I don't mind, and yes you have." I responded with just as much forceful attitude as I dared bring myself to use under the circumstances, and bearing in mind that I didn't want to offend or upset her anymore. She smiled a faint smile just then which instantly dissolved all previous, present and any future antagonism between the two of us right there and then on the spot. I think I gave her a bigger smile back as I said: - "Just don't ask me to spell it."

"Spell what?" She laughed easily.

"That word... Misinterpreting."

"Go on... Get off with you... Oh! by the way... Thank you..."

"No, it should be t'other way around, me thanking you... Thank You."

She busied herself tidying the papers on her desk just then and dismissed me with a wave of her hand and her final words on the subject.

"I rather suspect we have both been wrong."

Jim was waiting for me out in the quiet corridor. We were the only ones there. Even the engineering shop at the far end was eerily quiet. Jim wanted an explanation. I didn't want to give him one in case Pauline should come out of her room, so I grabbed his arm and pulled him along and around the corner towards the exit. Once we were outside beyond those stupidly designed glass doors, I told him what he wanted to know and I also said how annoyed I was feeling with myself for the way I had judged Pauline. I finished with: -

"Anyway, I reckon she's alright."

"Huh' You weren't saying that sort of thing the other week. I suppose you're right; she hasn't been all that had to me come to think of it. Come on Bob."

CHAPTER SIXTEEN

The long hard road was at last beginning to show some promise of better things to come. I don't think I had quite realised it yet, but that conference with Pauline had done me a lot more good than I realised, and so it was that I headed towards the Mobility office after afternoon tea on that last day of the working week, in a far better frame of mind than I had been in for many a week. I was ready for anything... Well, almost anything. Cane in hand, I knocked on the door and waited. Gill came, beckoned me inside and I could tell that she was busy with something and it was only when I saw the two black rolls on the table top that I remembered the package that had come in the Post that morning, which I had left for her outside the door to the mobility office. My first surprised words were to ask what she thought of the Velcro and was it proving to be of any use to her. She thanked me and it turned out that she had been experimenting with the Velcro ever since midmorning and she was still finding new ways for its usefulness. I didn't expect or get a mobility lesson that afternoon. At least not with Gillian. The look on her face told me that I wouldn't be getting one.

"It is too cold out there this afternoon." She said; by way of an excuse. "Why don't we stay indoors? This really is remarkable material you've managed to get for me. I am really and truly convinced that it has monumentally great potential, especially for holding the canes together when they are folded up. One of my colleagues has even suggested another use for it but as you can see, I'm up to my ears in trying to find the best ways in which to use it for the canes. I don't need any more ideas just yet… Look. I know I am neglecting my duties here and I really should be giving you a mobility lesson right now, but I can feel this is such an important discovery that I want to exploit it to the fullest. You won't mind will you… I know! Tomorrow night I will take you and your friend Royston, both of you out for a drink down at the Hole in the wall and I'll give you both a mobility lesson on the way there. I think that you might find Royston in the den. He is, that is Royston, is with Andrew, we have excused him also. Andrew wants to get back here as quickly as he can so as to help me. So, the two of you can have the rest of this afternoon off now if you like. Go on, make the most of it."

I passed the other Mobility officer, Andrew, in the corridor leading to the Den and in confirming the whereabouts of Royston he hastened off back to Gillian.

Royston was sipping contentedly from a steaming mug when I attracted his attention and told him what Gillian had just said, and he seemed pleased with the idea. I wasn't feeling all that lucky, or pleased a minute or so later though. This was because of what Royston was about to suggest.

As we both now had the rest of the afternoon off, Royston suddenly decided that he would like to go down to the shops so as to get some cigarettes. Looking out of the tall window behind the sinks I decided that we would have, at the most, no more than three quarters of an hour before it went dark out there and, although I did feel more than a twinge of anxiety at the thoughts of the possibility of returning to the Manor in the dark, without the expert help of the likes of Gill Roberts. It was also true to say that I did feel a degree of confidence in the knowledge that I could do it now that I had had some mobility training, and also, that at least the outward journey, and probably most of the return journey as well would be undertaken during the latter part of natural daylight, but then, the nagging feelings began to return once more and I found myself wondering what would happen if my friend, or I, should run into difficulties out there? I looked away from the window, back towards Royston once more. He was standing beside the door now. Jacket on and ready to go. He even had his red and white stripped cane in his hands... How could I say no? I think it must have been my gestures as much as anything else as I spoke the words. "Come on then, we're burning daylight standing here like this... Let's see if we can get there and back before it goes too dark."

His face lit up and off we went, and despite the thoughts of what might happen if we ran into difficulties, I was feeling rather chuffed with myself as we made our way down that quiet and empty drive away from the Manor and I glanced at Royston and said to myself. "Is this number three, or is it four today as I've managed to please?"

We didn't rush. As we approached the entrance to America Lodge the daylight was already beginning to fade, but we knew about the perils involved in trying to rush, So, we didn't. We both kept to a sensible walking pace.

We were near to the Lodge gates when Royston stopped for a moment in order to light up and as he did so he showed me the now empty packet. I can remember saying something like.

"I don't know why I'm taking a risk like this, and encouraging you to kill yourself with fags into the bargain."

I don't know how much of that he understood, if any, but he seemed to know that I had said something as he stopped and gestured for me to sign on his hand, but I didn't. Instead, I just pointed to the sky and tugged on his sleeve at the same time to get him going.

We made it safely there and we made it safely back as well. We only had to use our canes on the last couple of hundred yards or so, and that was at the top end of Middle Lincombe Road.

We arrived back at the brightly lit Porch where we had departed from less than an hour since, jubilant and unscathed. I remember feeling especially pleased as I began to realise that this had been the first time that the two of us had ventured out under these strange and new circumstances. I indicated that I wanted to say something to Royston and this is what I signed.

"SO MUCH FOR MOBILITY PEOPLE"

He signed back. "WHO NEEDS THEM"

"We do!" I said out loud, and then I pulled his sleeve once more and signed: -

"COME ON LETS GET INSIDE"

Royston resisted me though and I quickly realised that all he wanted to do was to sit in the shelter of the porch and just idle away the time until five o'clock. I sat down resignedly on one of the cold stone slabs and watched Royston sit down and light up a cigarette. The place was quiet and we were alone. The tutors and the residents were all busy in the various departments. I looked up at the bright yellow light in the middle of the limewashed ceiling above, and then I looked out onto the darkness beyond the curved stone arch of the porch. There were no sounds out there either. It was as if we had the entire place to ourselves; which of course, we hadn't, this was just the lull before the storm. In a short while, we and all the other residents would be free for the weekend.

A few more minutes went by and then there was the sound of a vehicle. It drew up just a few yards away.

A few seconds later I heard the car door bang and then the sounds of footsteps coming this way. A middle-aged man carrying a large suitcase came into the Porch entrance. I seemed to know him and then I remembered who he was. This was Harold Moss, the piano tuner. He said hello but didn't stop as he turned to open the dark old oak door and then went inside, out of sight and was gone. A few minutes later Jean from the Care staff, came out and headed off into the darkness. She saw me and Royston but she didn't speak. I think she was in too much of a hurry. A few minutes later still and Mike was the first of the residents to come in through the porch entrance, with Jean escorting him, and once again Jean hadn't or didn't seem to have the time to stop and talk to us. I didn't say anything either, and Royston, wasn't inclined to. He was placidly sitting on the stone slab, enjoying his second or was it his third cigarette since we had both come back to the Manor. I spoke to Mike though, because he was the closest to me and I felt that I ought to. He instantly turned and just as the pair of them were about to disappear into the bowels of that ancient building, Mike picked out my location and said.

"Stick around Bob, this moight be the start of something big loike, what yow doin' anyroad? woy down't yow come with us, he can't he Jean?"

"If he likes." Said Jean. "I'm certainly not stopping him, but he does seem to have Royston to look after out here. Do you want him as well?"

"Woy not!... Come on Bob, bring Royston with yow."

I was intrigued enough to want to follow him by now, so I did. Dragging a reluctant Royston along with me, we went through to the inner doors and on across the brightly lit and as yet, empty main hall. Jean was heading for the lounge area to where the piano tuner was waiting.

He immediately put down his tools and greeted us all, but Mike more so. Jean guided Mike as he went to sit down on the piano-stool alongside the man. Jean then turned on her heels and went back out of the room and Mike quickly forgot about the presence of his fellow intake members, but I didn't mind and I don't think Royston did either. I was just glad to be there and have a chance to witness events and slowly realise just where all of this was going.

It seemed that Mike had found something, some new initiative of sorts that he could begin to get excited about. Although I didn't say anything to him for those first few minutes, it all fitted into place when Royston pulled on my arm and indicated that he wanted to tell me something. I looked away from the two men at the grand piano for a moment to look up at Royston and watch his

156

gestures. With quite a serious expression on his face he pointed across at Mike and then started to play an imaginary piano and then came the deep throated sounds of him trying to say something, and what he said I could understand. Mike would soon be leaving us and this was something that Royston already knew because he was now shrugging his shoulders in a matter of fact way and saying: - "Ome 'ome..."

And it was true. Although I didn't immediately get a chance to have my feelings confirmed, because less than a minute later the French doors at the far end of the lounge were flung open and in poured the noisy and jolly residents all ready for the start of the weekend.

It was strange how the noisy crowd didn't seem to spoil Mike's concentration as he listened to the man beside him, and not one of the residents interrupted Mike or his tutor in passing, or even as they congregated in readiness for their evening meal. I couldn't see any reason why I should disturb either Harold Moss, or Mike. I would get plenty of opportunities over the weekend to talk to Mike about the future. If he really was going, he wouldn't be leaving us that soon, things didn't work that way at the Manor... Or did they?

One of the many people who had come in through the French windows was Shirley. It came as something of a surprise to see that she was carrying a white cane. When she saw me looking at her, she came up to me and began to explain.

"Hello Bob. Just let me sign hello to Royston... There. Oh, he has such a lovely smile, hasn't he? Well! let me tell you something... I've just completed my very first mobility lesson outdoors, the one's that I have had so far have been indoors. Geoffrey, tells me that you've been to the school as well. Sorry, Geoffrey is my instructor. Isn't it exciting using a white cane? I mean... It gives you so much more confidence when you can actually feel something in front of you when you know you can't see it. Oh! it's going to be so wonderful... It's going to open up so many avenues don't you think so Bob? There's a snag though, there always has to be at least one doesn't there? You see, Geoffrey tells me that a woman like me, out on her own and using a white cane is seven or eight times more vulnerable to attack than a woman without a white cane. I told him that I would be more than ten times more vulnerable if I went out in the dark without a cane and not only just to marauding men either. It really is a sad, sad world, I mean when people with our sort of problems have not only to fear the problem but fear our own kind as well, by that I mean normal sighted people. Oh dear! I almost forgot. Do you know. I am getting so carried away that I nearly forgot to tell you something quite important. Oh, what is it that Michael is doing? Are you about to do a performance for us Michael? I wouldn't bother, it is very nearly time for the evening meal... Bob. Do you remember the Missionary healers that were in the area a few weeks ago? Well! Steven, you know Steven from the engineering section! Well... He is arranging an outing to Paington tonight... Is it too late for you to arrange to come with us? I would so like you to be there this time. Oh! I just can't begin to explain how wonderful it was the last time. If you only knew. Please say you'll come with us. It is short notice but it's probably the last opportunity you will likely get. Do say yes... you can bring Royston too if he wants to come."

I didn't fancy this idea of an outing, so I initially tried to sidestep the subject in order to try and distract her, but it didn't work. I started by saying. "You can't be too careful these days. A better idea for the likes of you would be to go out in a group. Didn't this mobility guy of yours tell you that?"

"Yes, of course he did. And a lot of other advice... But you are evading my question, here. Let me ask Royston for myself... Here goes... "DO YOU WANT TO COME TO A SPECIAL PLACE WITH ME AND BOB TONIGHT"

I could tell that Shirley was tickling Royston's hand but I didn't say anything. I just looked at her looking up at Royston through those glasses of hers as she waited for him to respond, and when he did a few seconds later, even I couldn't be sure if the smile on his face was really a smile of acceptance or else a smile caused by her hand tickling his.

Just then, the gong sounded off, out in the main hall and the crazy crowd I was a part of got even crazier as they headed as one towards the doorway leading out into the hall and the dining room beyond that. I held Royston back for a few seconds and advised Shirley to wait for those few seconds as well. I wanted to explain to her how Royton's smile could and most likely had in this case been interpreted in the wrong way. I did this, but Shirley remained unconvinced. I looked to the crowd and then back at Royston. He even smiled down on me when I had finished asking him if he really wanted to go to see the missionaries. That last word had been such a long one to have to spell out in the sign language that I couldn't be sure if he understood it or not. His smile gave him away however and this was sufficient for Shirley... I had lost.

On our way out at the tail end of the residents I noticed Mike still sitting beside the piano tuner. I somehow felt that Mike was getting his fill here instead of in the dining room.

Just before she left us to go to her own table, Shirley told me that Steven had arranged for all those going on this outing to gather in the main hall by six thirty. I didn't seem to be able to get out of this one, so I made a mental note to phone home earlier that evening.

I stopped beside my table and sent Royston on down to his with a friendly pat on his back. Then I sat down to a plate of cauliflower cheese followed by apple pie and custard, which wasn't too bad, but, cauliflower cheese! Twice, in one week! Ten minutes later I was on my way out and passing near to Mike's table. He was just finishing off his main meal and so too was the piano tuner sitting opposite him.

Later on. I was feeling a bit sad at only having about five minutes with Janet and my girls that night, I had caught them just about to start eating their tea. I was coming away from the phone in the alcove when Shirley came up from behind and grabbed me by the arm. How could I refuse that pleading look of hers? Oh' but I did try though, and rather shamefully too. I tried to tell her that I couldn't go out that night. No way! I tried to say that it would be totally foolish of me to go out in a strange and alien place after dark. Shirley was unconvinced and I found it to be very difficult to convince her or anyone else. All I seemed to be doing was to act cowardly. Steven looked at me rather sourly as we gathered in the hall awaiting our transport, I could tell that he didn't need this from me. I wondered though... Did he really know what he had allowed himself to get roped into? Indeed... Did I know what I was about to let myself get involved in? Yes, partly. I had been to these healing sessions before when I was back home. At our local church. The Guild of St. Raphael was nothing new to me. However, I had very little idea of how different this was doing to turn out to be at that moment though. Even so, before I could agree to the pressure from Shirley and from Steven and a few of the others, including Jim and Josie. I still felt that I needed an excuse not to have to go and I used the old complaint to what I thought to be good effect when I said that I felt that I needed some sort of reassurance from someone and that I would not, at any stage, have to venture out in the dark by myself. Steven was quick to try and assure me and even promised that he himself would make sure that I would get from door to door and safely. He finished by saying.

"Honestly Robert. Anyone would think that you're a total the way you go on... You're having mobility lessons, aren't you? Haven't you learned anything yet?"

I had lost the argument and in a way I saw no reason to doubt his previous words on my safety, but if the future could have been known, then I don't think that I would have gone that night, I suppose though that it has to be said that Steven's heart was in the right place throughout. After all, he was only trying to help me as well as others at the same time, and the inevitable as it happened was bound to happen. Steven managed somehow to convince me and it didn't take long to get myself sorted out in readiness to accept this unwanted night out.

A short while later we were climbing aboard one of the two mini-buses and then we set on our way, down the dark drive, out and away from the Manor. Destination? A Church or a Chapel? Purpose? Unsure, outcome? unknown.

I couldn't see who was driving, I only knew that it wasn't Steven up there at the front, because he was sitting opposite me on the other side of the dark interior of the minibus talking to the shadowy figure on his left.

Royston was sitting beside me against the window. Our surroundings were rather dimly lit and as such I could only faintly detect what I thought to be a smile on the face of my silent friend. He was happy, and I don't suppose it mattered all that much to him where he might be going that night. Just as long as he was going out, somewhere, anywhere.

We were on the road for about half an hour. It was much too dark beyond the glass to be able to see any familiar landmarks. Short of asking, I had no idea whereabouts we were heading, other than somewhere in or around Paington.

It was exceptionally dark and confusing when we disembarked from the rear of the minibus and this was where the troubles began. It had been raining, and the nearby puddles, reflected a curious and disturbing pattern to my eyes. The place that we were in seemed to be surrounded by some sort of a high wall.

The only lights around about in the immediate vicinity were the lights from other vehicles and the bright blue light which lit up the apex of a building over on my right-hand side. I could tell that there was more than myself who were going to have problems here. Once again, I was where I did not want to be.

"Where's Steven got to?" I asked the nearest dark shape. No one answered and my stomach flipped and churned as I stood there holding onto the rear door of the minibus. One or two of those coming down the steps seemed to think that I was doing them a favour by holding the door, but I wasn't. I knew the moment I let go of the door I was going to be in a rather serious predicament. If fact! The dreaded 'disorientation' had already begun to set my mind ablaze, as I feared it would the moment that we had left the security of the Manor behind.

160

There was hardly anything to see in the immediate locality, and worse, I had absolutely no idea what the surrounding landscape was like. Or where we were. I had a vague idea where we were going, but that was only apparent from the bright blue light some formidable distance away. Then something attracted my attention. The large and unmistakable figure of Royston came down out of the bus and stood beside me, and I could tell by his agitated movements that he too was frightened in some way. Probably more so than I was. If that was at all possible, and still there was no sign of Steven. I think I must have muttered something along the lines of. "I might have known this would happen."

We all seemed to be standing together in a rather tightly packed group. I felt the pressure of my cane on my back, I nearly got it out but I couldn't. After all, we weren't going anywhere just yet, and I hadn't even let go of the door. But then! The door was being prised from my hand by the soft fragrant hands of a dark and silent, unseen female. A moment or two later the minibus drove off and stopped a short distance away. I was still watching the red rear lights suspended in space when they flickered and went out. Royston's hand was on my shoulder now and I was near to badly letting him down. I could hear Steven's voice on my left-hand side, but couldn't see him. I wanted to ask him to come and help us but even as dark as it was, I could tell that Steven already had more on his hands than he would have liked, and if he tried to help us as well as the others then he wouldn't have been able to deal with any of us as well as I would have liked him to. He gave a feeble apology, but I'm not sure if it was addressed to me or someone else.

It was more by luck than by judgement that Royston and I, were, more or less, within the middle of our group and as we began to move, we seemed to be heading for the soft yellow lights, beneath the high up bright blue neon light ahead. Then there was the strangely comforting sound of the tap tapping of canes, this was coming from immediately in front of us. I couldn't use mine in this tightly knit group, even if I had wanted to, and yes, I did in a way, but that would have meant me and Royston breaking away from the group and going it on our own. Far better to go with the flow, I decided.

The journey was fraught with difficulties all the way but it wasn't long before we were climbing, with a bit more difficulty, some wide stone steps towards the yellow light and what seemed to be an awful lot of people as well. I can remember feeling a whole lot better once we were finally standing in the brightly lit entrance with the bright lights above bathing us in their warm yellow glow. Royston's grip on my upper arm was still quite firm. Steven may have unintentionally let us both down but we had got here, and the whole journey from dramatic dark to dramatic light had taken no more than a minute or so. There were a lot of people coming into the building and it wasn't long before we were being ushered inward and onward towards another set of doors and then through into a very large, oblong and brightly lit hall. My nerves were rapidly calming now that I could see where we were going. I noticed that the place we were in had quite a high ceiling with lots of complicated and ornate timberwork up there, and the walls were painted a pale blue. There was a half-moon shaped balcony stretching from one side wall to the other over near the back of the hall that we had just passed beneath, which was now above and behind us. I was looking directly ahead to where I had been expecting to see an Altar, but where an Altar should have been and more than likely once had been, now, there was a stage, and this stage seemed to fill the entire width of the far end of this room. There was a constant humming of voices all around us and the place was fast filling to its capacity. This was all just a bit too bewildering for my liking and I hadn't fully recovered from the shock of the great outdoors yet. There were some empty chairs nearby and no takers, as yet. It seemed as if most of the people were only too glad to stand where they were and talk to each other as they waited for, whatever it was that was going to happen, to happen that evening. I was still trying to take it all in when I felt a gentle push and at the same time a slightly familiar female voice rose above those around about me and urged me to move onwards over to my left.

"Go oh, the pair of you." Said Gillian. "Those chairs have been reserved for us, sit down before they are all taken." She gave me an exceptionally friendly smile and then urged me on once more. I wanted relief from all of this and one way out was to break away and ask Gillian about the Velcro, but the chance didn't come. A few moments later our group from the Manor were mostly sitting down waiting for the beginning.

I couldn't see the stage now. These seats were near the back of the hall and they had been reserved for the blind folk from the Manor. There didn't appear to be a central aisle, but there seemed to be a fairly wide aisle at least on the left-hand side of the hall and this was just a few feet from where we were.

Some music was being played just as I was beginning to look around at the faces of my colleagues from the Manor. I recognised the Manor staff, and Jim and Josie, then there was Samantha and Denise there as well. I also saw Peter... Malcolm Tipper was also there. I was on a nodding acquaintance with some of the others, those of them who could see that is, and there weren't all that many. The one person I was looking for wasn't there. I was of course looking for Shirley. I hadn't seen her since our departure from the Manor.

162

I had been surprised to see Gill Roberts there. She must have been our driver. I knew I had smelled that scent before and felt that soft hand on mine, so it must have been Gillian who had coaxed my hand away from the rear door of the minibus out there in the dark. I let my thoughts wander as the music began to get louder, and then the crowd seemed to be getting a little bit more excitable. The music didn't seem to have any meaning. I hadn't heard anything at all like this before, it seemed to consist of guitars and drums and a piano, and 'something else.' There was a steady background rhythm but that was about all I could make out of that 'something else.' A short while later, amidst screams of delight, came a man's voice, which was amplified in some way and reverberated all around the room in an eerie manner. Even this poor deaf guy sitting next to me seemed to sense that something weird was happening but, how could he? I studied his face for a few seconds. His head remained still but his dark eyes flickered about, left and right, up and down. It was almost as if he was looking for someone... Or something! And then I began to feel it too. The wooden floor beneath my feet was vibrating. At first, I thought that it must be all these people who were standing around us, but no. This wasn't the sound of a few; or even hundreds of feet tapping, this was a steady, constant vibration and it seemed to be slower and yet it was still in tune somehow with the music coming from the stage, somewhere up front, and every now and then came a man's haunting, strange and gravelly voice. "Do you Love God? I want to hear you, do you... Do you Love God?" He did this a few more times and all the while the music played on and the wooden floor kept on vibrating, but each time the voice sounded a little more demanding, and yet soft and almost hypnotically slow, which seemed to almost imperceptibly excite the crowd just a little more. None but the most sceptical would have noticed this. Everyone else. Including nearly all of my colleagues from the Manor were slowly being drawn towards a climax of some sort. It had to heading that way. I quickly looked around me. Even Steven was getting carried away with the euphoria. But Gillian wasn't, and I wasn't.

As the whole thing progressed towards the inevitable, I was concerned not only for myself. I was also concerned for Royston. He couldn't seem to understand what was going on and neither could I. I was further concerned when Royston picked his feet up off the floor and wrapped his arms around his knees and then he closed his eyes. He looked extremely vulnerable and I could tell that the poor man was obviously terrified. I didn't like to see this and yet, I just did not know what to do to help him. The mesmerising effect of the strange man's voice seemed to come from everywhere around us once more, but he was slowly changing his theme.

"If you love God and you want to be healed…Then you have to love him more... and more and more and more."

The captivating music continued and when the man next began to speak, I was very surprised to hear another voice there as well. This time it was a woman's voice. Soft and gentle and it was hauntingly penetrating to the mind. A few minutes more of this particular combination and I was very nearly won over myself. Royston obviously wasn't. I think that it may have been the concern I felt for my deaf colleague that I was able to avoid going the way of most of the others in that large hall. I had already given up attempting to sign some sort of message of reassurance when I had failed even to prise one of his hands from around his knees.

It wasn't very many minutes later when the standing crowd suddenly surged forwards and left a naked area directly in front of us. A few seconds later they came backwards and very nearly squashed all of us where we were sitting. I remarked soberly to Jim, who had just cried out to the crowd.

"Ruddy hell...!" I said. "We'll be needing a miracle if they do that on us again."

And all the time the music and the man, and the woman who were there, somewhere up ahead, just kept on doing their thing, and the musicians did their thing, and the floor beneath our feet did its thing, and it didn't take very much longer to reach the penultimate situation and the all-pervading voices began to invite us to: -

"Come forth and bring your afflictions. The lame shall walk away from here. The heavy of heart shall be lightened. The infirm shall be made well. The chronically sick shall be comforted. And the blind by the will of God shall see once again... In the name of God come forth."

There she was. I might have known it. Since we had left the Manor, I hadn't seen her up until that moment, but as soon as the commotion began in the aisle over on the left-hand side, I seemed to sense that Shirley would be involved somehow, and she was. There were three of our group already standing up and keen to go, and yet they were strangely holding back at the same time. Shirley was there, right behind them though, urging Denise and Samantha, as well as others to go forward, towards the stage. That was when I also noticed Mike as well. Now, what was he doing here? I looked around once more. I couldn't see Gill Roberts anywhere now. I remember thinking. 'Why doesn't she come and talk to me about the Velcro and bring some normality to all of this. I couldn't help but also think, and wonder, if she had gone and taken someone up to the stage to see the miracle workers. Meanwhile the music continued to be played, and the voices also continued, and donations were mentioned and I stayed glued to my seat as the tense atmosphere grew and grew all around me. Suddenly! There came a roar, and screams of delight from up ahead, and I knew in my slightly cynical heart, that someone else had been 'Cured' Barely half an hour had gone by since the music had begun and yet. Something was wrong. This wasn't the way it was supposed to be. I looked around me. I looked at the backs of those in front. I listened to the frantic cheers and the screams of adoration and muttered to myself. "This isn't how it's supposed to be, but, How is it supposed to be?"

A movement beside me brought my mind under control once more and it shocked me to realise that I was almost gone. Almost captivated by it all, but not quite. Royston was getting to his feet. He stood for a moment in an agitated fashion and I couldn't be all that sure if he wanted to leave, or else go down there to the front of the hall. I didn't know what to do about the situation either. If he understood any of this, and I doubted it. I doubted it very much. But if he did understand what was happening, had I really got any rights to try and prevent Royston from going to the healers and let them 'cure' him? Should I let him go and be dramatically cured? Or... dramatically; disappointed? I reached out and pulled on the sleeve of his jacket. He pulled away, but then; quickly realising who it was, he offered me his hand and then he suddenly changed his mind and reached out for my hand instead, and signed.

"DON'T LIKE THIS BOB CAN I GO PLEASE"

"Hey! Where do you think you two are going to?" Came Steven's voice which was drowned a second later by another loud cheer from the excited audience.

I called out. "Royston's frightened, doesn't like it... And neither do I." I added in a more subdued tone.

There was a man in a grey suit standing beside the main door. His stance was rather like that of a sentry on guard duty. I wondered if he was going to let us pass or not, but he didn't block our exit and a few seconds later the two of us, Royston and myself, were standing at the main entrance to this 'very' unusual building. I looked out into the forbidding blackness and the pouring rain. Then I looked back at Royston. The yellow light in the ceiling above lit up his face, then another, more unsteady light, lit up a quivering cigarette in his mouth.

No-one came in or went out through that door while Royston and I stood there, and we had to wait for at least a quarter of an hour before anyone did come. I could still hear the occasional loud cheering and the almost hysterical screams of delight, but I felt glad to be outside, away from all the confusing goings on inside that large hall.

The first to appear was not unexpected, at least; to me it wasn't. I was standing with my back to the door and just casually watching the rain falling on the stone steps outside, when the door behind me opened and out came a young man of about twenty pushing an empty, dark green wheelchair. Behind him, came the multitudes. They were noisy, excited and completely undeterred by the rain. In fact, they positively revelled in it and some of them even began to dance about on the steps and I could hear them out there in the darkness at the bottom of the steps as well. Very shortly we were joined by Steven and others of our group and not one of them had been cured of their blindness. I knew that none had, or would be. But I wished that they all could have been. Still! Never mind, at least they didn't all seem to be disappointed. Only a few of them... and Mike was one in particular, and I felt really sorry for Mike, but I didn't say anything. What was there to say after an experience the like of which he, and others, had just gone through?

On the journey back, the occupants of our bus were very subdued. Most of them had been expecting something to happen. Something really spectacular. Nothing had happened. I couldn't understand. What was it? What was it with those healing missionaries inside that old chapel that was so? so, unreal?

The bus pulled up outside the gates to America lodge and a few of us got out. I stood in the drizzling rain and watched the red tail lights of the minibus disappear, on its way up to the Manor. I was reflecting on the final words which Royston had just said to me.

"I DID NOT LIKE TONIGHT RATHER GO TO THE PUB"

I couldn't help but talk quietly to myself as I followed in the wake of Jim and a few unseen others. "Royston didn't like tonight and all I've got to say is, Amen to that."

Jim's voice called out from the open doorway, where the yellow glow cast a welcoming beam of light out into this darkness. "Bob! Are you coming inside or are you going to stand out there in the rain for the rest of the night? Come on in. Me and Josie are going to the lounge and she wants to know if you'll join us there."

I went inside, and then I went to carry out a belated telephone conversation with my wife, and afterwards. I made my way to the lounge. And what followed was about an hour or more, of painstaking dissection of the evening's outing, but over and above mine and Jim's, cautious, but rather sceptical comments. Came the almost overriding feeling from the half dozen or so others, including Josie, that the generous donations that they had all been encouraged to give had been money very well spent. Rather excitedly, they then went on to praise the wonderful healing missionary work that the people involved were doing. Surprisingly for me to say, and for a lot of others there to hear no doubt. I did try to assert my beliefs at one stage, by saying that I firmly believed that those who could genuinely heal and had got the gift of healing, should not, accept payment, for administering their God given skills. A few of them were still talking when I left them at just before midnight.

CHAPTER SIXTEEN

Up in my room I did not get much sleep that night. There was so much to write about which had happened that day, and I had completely lost track of where I was up to on my early day experiences at the Manor.

It must have been around three in the morning before I finally climbed into my bed, with just one thought on my mind. 'What was it that was so compelling for me to have to sit and write, night after night, in this lonely, lonely room?'

I was up bright and early the next morning, quietly enjoying the peaceful solitude of the Den. I had been in there for about half an hour or so when I heard someone coming along the corridor. I looked up at the clock behind the door and quietly moaned to myself. "Five past six and already the place is waking."

For obvious reasons, the blind will always walk with a lot more caution than sighted people, especially when rules ban them from using their cane inside buildings. Sadly, Mike was no exception. I waited for the slow intruder to appear in the doorway and then I dismissed my initial feelings and greeted him amiably when I saw who it was. I made him a drink and we sat there for the best part of the next hour and just talked about one thing after another. We discussed the events of the night before, and although he had been one of those of our group to have gone up to the front of the hall and been administered to by the healers. He was, nevertheless, unconvinced now, that the experience had done him any good. It's always remarkably surprising what sleep can do to the bubbling enthusiasm of the night before. But for all of that. Where did it leave Mike? And, where did it leave me and all the others as well? It took a fair while longer for the rest of the residents of the Lodge to wake up on that Saturday morning. After a while Mike got up to make us another drink of tea and I looked up at the clock and noticed the time of a quarter to seven. I was and had been settled in my own mind for a short time and as such I was rather unprepared for the surprise that Mike was shortly to give me. In a way, it wasn't really a surprise. I knew what was coming. I had been trying to find out ever since he had come in to join the solitary figure of me. Royston had been astute enough to have picked up on it the evening before. Watching Mike now and comparing him to how he had been when I had first met him, and knowing that this was nearing the end of our association, I couldn't help having had a feeling of high regard and a deep sympathy as well. He was only a few feet away, but it was much too risky to talk and spoil his concentration. The kettle was coming up to boiling point and the tea was already in the pot. I didn't say anything for fear of distracting him. It was good to see him display a degree of independence, but it was also rather sad to see the way he went about this task that was tricky at the best of times for anybody. He lifted the kettle and gently tipped the scalding hot water into the pot after having first located the opening and then he shifted his other hand out of the way. When he had listened to and worked out from the changing sounds that the pot was getting fuller, he stopped pouring and put the kettle down again. He then reached for the spot where he had placed the teapot lid and carefully placed it where it belonged. He then reached out his right hand for the two mugs, the sugar can and, gentler still, the bottle of milk that was at the back of the worktop, and he had done all of this whilst looking directly at (if that's the correct phrase) the green wall at the back of the worktop. He was still standing in exactly the same position, with his back to me while he waited for the tea to brew in the pot.

Then came the surprise.

"Bob… Oy moight be goin home tomorrow. For good oy moign… Oy've had to do some serious thinking during the noight and oy wants to be a piano tuner. Harry Moss wants to toike moy on as an apprentice, and oy wants to be one… What d'yow think, d'yow think oy'm daft?"

"No, No I don't... What about your mobility lessons though? And everything else?"

168

"Stuff everything else… Mobility, oye c'n get boye on what oy've done… Oy only let moyself be persuaded to come in the first ploice so that oy moight foind another career. Now, oy've found one. Oye should be able to manage with a small police pension and piano tuning... and me woife... Oye miss her Bob… oy miss her."

The room went quiet. What could I say, except: - "If that's what you really want to do Mike, then do it, we'll all be sorry to see you go, I can't help wondering if any of us will finish this course... of our intake I mean."

"Yes, yow will, an'Josie 'n' Jim. Moybe even Royston. Oy'm not sure about Peter... Peter's struggling a lot mowre'an he's letting on..."

Mike fell silent for a moment or two just then. I didn't say anything further. I could wait until he was ready to continue. The only trouble was. I'll never know if he was going to be ready, or not. I silently cursed as I heard the voices and the footsteps and the other noises too. Which heralded the Lodge residents awakening. I stayed a while longer and drank my drink and tried to talk some more to Mike but the noise of the other incoming residents made it difficult if not impossible and trying to get more information from him only seemed to unnerve him, so I excused myself and quietly left the Den, and left him talking to a coloured young man, Gerald who I remembered was Adrian's friend.

'Adrian' I found myself thinking, as I went out through the ever-open doorway of the Den and squeezed past a burly sixteen stone blind resident. 'I wonder how Adrian's getting on?'

"Well!" I said to myself once I was up in my room, standing there feeling perplexed and wondering why I had come all the way up here? I started to talk to myself again and said. "If previous weekends are anything to go by, I should be in for something weird and maybe... Just maybe, a little wonderful as well... Who knows? who knows? I wunna find out standing here though! Come on little white thing, let's go see what this day is going to throw at us."

I travelled alone on my way up to the Manor. I had tried to find Mike to see if he wanted my company, or my help, but I couldn't find him or even Jim or Josie. Perhaps it was all a bit too early for them to set off. Or maybe they just didn't want to partake of breakfast at the Manor.

As I walked, my thoughts were jumping from events to events past. One of the most recent being the most memorable. "Just what had it been with those healing missionary people, or missionary healers, or whatever it is they called

169

themselves?" I stopped and looked around me. There was a crowd of about half a dozen people a good distance behind me and a few others an equal distance ahead, but none that may have overheard me talking to myself. It could have been embarrassing to have been caught out, but talking seemed to put things into some sort of perspective. "Just dunna start answering yourself Bob! Now that would be summat to worry about...Yes, it would, wouldn't it."

I reached the Manor and went inside. Already the main hall was beginning to fill up with residents. Making my way to the far end beyond the oblong table I looked up to the clock on the wall and noticed that the time was just after twenty to eight. I just couldn't help it; the impulse was too great. I looked down at the two young women sitting there expectantly. Only one of them was looking up at me. I smiled as I spoke to Samantha and Denise and said: -

"Good morning! Just checking th'time... it's either twenty to eight or th'minute hand's fell off..."

Samantha turned her head to look at her friend and said. "There you are! what did I tell you? These men are so damned predictable."

I wasn't offended. I stood and talked to them for a few minutes while we waited for the breakfast gong, and all the while the hall was filling with more and more residents both from here and from the Lodge. Try as I might, and I didn't try very hard as it happened, but I couldn't get any response at all out of either of them concerning the events of the night before and my senses soon dictated that I shouldn't pursue that avenue after maybe less than a minute of trying. So, I turned he conversation to future events, the near future, and the Concert on the following day. "Are you both ready for the concert?" I asked.

Now that was a good move, and the next ten minutes or so went by rather quickly as they each eagerly delved into the programme of music that was to be performed the following day. It was only a call of nature on Denise's part which robbed me of their company up until breakfast time.

I watched them go. Neither of them were ever untidily dressed. Samantha had on a white fluffy jumper and a yellow skirt and Denise was wearing a dark blue dress with a black cardigan. It had come as something of a surprise when I noticed Samantha as well as Denise pick up a cane apiece from behind them on the bench seat and they then went off carrying their folded white canes.

This was all happening rather quickly and seemed to be all at once.

Suddenly and to my surprise, I realised that it wasn't just me who was getting mobility lessons. Almost everyone else I knew was getting them as well. I knew that Denise had had a cane for quite some time, maybe even before she had come here, but not Samantha. This wasn't the first time that I had seen her with a white cane, but it was perhaps, the first time that the real significance of it all actually began to dawn on me, and it was good, and yet, it was so terribly sad as well.

I stayed for a short while longer and then wandered around the main hall, but I did not try to do anything like I had attempted the previous morning. I wasn't going to poke my nose in where it wasn't wanted. No, way! but, I couldn't really help myself, curiosity seemed to have got the better of me.

I had wandered rather aimlessly around the hall, spoken to and said hello to people I knew and that was as far as I had gone, but when by chance, I found myself standing beside the wooden bench that was occupied and situated to the right of the grey-stone fireplace, nearest to the care staff office. I happened to be looking down at a dark haired and rather attractive looking woman, in an emerald green, short skirted suit. I had seen her before somewhere around the Manor. I couldn't be sure but I had a feeling that she was on the same intake as Big Ann. Not that this was of any significance, but what she was doing seemed to be significantly different; to what I would have expected her to be doing. I hadn't known her to be blind, to be one of the so called. 'Totals' So why was she just sitting there, staring ahead? Why was she doing it so intensely? Her eyes were open wide and seemed to be bulging with the effort of, of seeing? There was a white handkerchief and an open handbag on her knees and in one hand she was holding a pair of spectacles. I found myself being dragged along on a wave of curiosity. I didn't want to just stand there and stare at the poor woman. What would all these other, sighted people think, or say? I couldn't help it though; my feelings had got the better of me. I found myself thinking of Mike and the tragic way that his sight had deteriorated over the past couple of months and I found myself wondering if the same sort of thing had happened to this woman. It was all so sad, to witness one so young as Mike lose his sight, and now one so attractive as this woman losing her sight as well, and she was still so young. She could only have been thirty or thirty-five at the most. 'What use are those glasses for? I found myself thinking. 'Huh, they're about as much use by the looks of things as Ian's glasses are to him... Oh, oh! She's crying.' I looked away, and then glanced back at her. She was wiping her cheeks with the handkerchief now. I looked away again and then back. Should I offer to help her? Why isn't someone else going to help her? They're all too busy talking amongst themselves to bother. Them as can see that is, I thought scathingly. And them as can't, can't, or else don't want to help her. Could I console her sufficiently enough? Should I get involved with someone suffering such a tragic loss? Am I the right sort of person to try and help someone who looks so vulnerable?

"Stan? Are you there? Oh good! Can you spare a moment please?"

The man who had acknowledged the call, came forward and stood in front of her, partially blocking my view. This Stan person had noticed my nosiness. But he was polite enough not to use this knowledge to my embarrassment.

"You've got an audience." He said to the lady. "Suppose I tell him eh? what you've just been doing?"

"Yes... If you must, I don't want people thinking I've gone all doolally."

The man, Stan, turned to face me and disarmingly introduced himself. He knew me as well, but I couldn't place him, I had seen him around but not really to talk to. He said. "Right... mister Bob. You seem as if you've been wondering what Carol's been doing for the past few minutes. I would have thought it was obvious, you having been a contact lens wearer yourself. Still not got it eh? Oh well! Thick as a plank and thick as they come... Sorry! No offence. I'd better tell you before the gong goes off. Carol was doing what she was just doing so that she could force her eyes to make some tears, and now she's putting in her contact lenses. Look, see! She does it every morning, has to in fact. Here we go... Time for breakfast everyone. Come on people."

I watched the crowd moving almost as one towards the opposite side of the hall as they headed for the dining room. The man, Stan, obviously knew the woman named Carol would be able to cope with the necessaries which followed her concentrated efforts. I only looked back at the woman one more time before I too headed for the dining room. She had already got one contact lens in place and was now doing the other one. Just as I was turning to go, she looked up to me with what I knew would be watery eyes and gave me a feeble, unsure of what she could yet see sort of a smile. I went on my way feeling puzzled. I had been wearing a contact lens on my good eye for almost a year by then. (Before losing it, here at the Manor, or more accurately, the Lodge.)
It was a hard contact lens and often troublesome, and in all that time, no one had ever told me about this neat little trick. It had never occurred to me to even think about the benefits of having a wet eye to begin with before putting a piece of plastic against it, but then... Given the short time that it took to realise it, I began to realise that I didn't as yet have to go through the same eye

straining procedure. Usually, I only had to think about the hard contact lens as it would be approaching my eye, to make it water.

Entering the narrow corridor leading directly onto the dining room I couldn't help but express my thoughts. "Hmm, might be useful to remember that little trick."

I sat down to an empty table. There was no sign of Laurie or Christopher. The dining room lady placed my breakfast in front of me and smiled as she said.

"Frightened them all away have you dearie? None to worry mind… I hears that nice young lad is a coming back on Monday... ooh yes! yes he is, and we're to be having a lot more intake that day as well... My we're going t'be busy. Bye bye love."

Well, what a morning that turned out to be. I had thought that something was bound to happen. I was still thinking along those same lines when ten o'clock came... and went. Most of the people I knew had either not bothered to come up here to the Manor, or else they had gone out on the town of Torquay, before I could even think about the possibility of going with them. Meanwhile, I had come out here to the main hall once more and found a quiet place to sit and... observe... and... to talk. But there was hardly anyone to talk to never mind see. I sat for perhaps a further twenty minutes, just basically twiddling my thumbs. There was a group of about four or five down at the far end of the room and a blind woman in a red dress was just coming to the bottom of the stairs. There was a tall man standing by the huge fireplace. "Studying the stone carvings" I mumbled to myself. And then I got to my feet in order to look for something a little more exciting than this.

I finished up in the lounge, and this was only slightly more occupied than the main hall or even the Den was. The Den had been occupied by a group of about half a dozen women, most of them blind, but they were managing well enough to do their washing between them. Not a place for the likes of me though, so I only stayed long enough to get myself a cold drink and then I left them to it. And now I was about to sit down in the lounge at the grand piano.

Someone had left the lid up and the sight of those ivory keys were tempting. I looked around the room. Hardly anyone in sight. Flexing my arms and my fingers, I then threw back my shoulders and then hunched them up again and started to pick out the only tune I knew how to play on a piano. Beethoven's 'Ode to Joy.' In E flat major, or minor, plus a C or D or two, and with just one finger.

173

I was very soon getting a bit carried away. I think it was having to concentrate, together with the fact that I was humming the tune. "Oh, oh... sing a song of love... so early... in the mor...ning... Oh, sing a song of love so... so early in the morning." All of which prevented me from noticing that I had acquired an audience. One man, his voice was familiar, cried out.

"Can't play, can't sing... trying to play and sing solo, but not so low that we can't hear you."

"Ah very funny Jim." I said, feeling more embarrassed than anything else as I looked up and saw the group of residents nearby. Barry was there, and so was Shirley and a lot more that I knew. Mike was also there, but he was to the rear of the group and he kept trying to raise his head above the others, I don't know why. I kept my eye on Mike and realised that he wasn't trying to see anything, he was trying to get through, to the front, and when he did and he was standing on my left beside the raised lid of the grand piano, he was now gently fingering the prop as he looked towards me and said.

"Oy hope yow've not buggered it up... Here mowve over Bob... Better still, shift your ruddy arse."

I quickly did his bidding and all I wanted to do then was to beat a hasty retreat out of the room and away from them all, but Barry checked my exit, saying.

"Don't take it to heart Bob. The tuner's spent a lot of time on that bloody thing. We thought we wouldn't have it going in time at one point. What's it like Mike? alright?"

Mike had begun playing the tune I was playing, only better, a lot better. And he was playing with both hands as well. I looked back in astonishment. I hadn't realised that he could play so well. Mike was beginning to show up to be a bit of a dark horse by my reckoning.

"Sounds alright." Said Barry.

Barry was joined in his verdict by some of the others within the group. As a way of defending my actions I felt like saying something along the lines of... 'If it can't take a bit of use from the likes of me, it isn't going to be much use tomorrow.' I didn't though. I didn't say anything. I just stood and looked at Mike as he got to his feet to make way for the voice of a dark-haired woman to sit at the piano. This was Annette, the lady who had been embarrassed so much by some of the residents here in the lounge. She didn't seem to be

174

embarrassed now though, quite the opposite in fact, and it was good to see her displaying such confidence.

Annette was sitting at the piano now and began playing a soft familiar melody, whilst I was unobtrusively leaving the room, still wondering how and from where all of these people had come from. I was also trying to remember the tune that Annette was playing. It didn't come to me. Something else did though. A few minutes later, no more than five, and the big gong sounded off as I stood beside the oblong table, feeling surprised and wondering where the morning had gone to.

Lunch comprised of, ham sandwiches, an apple, or an orange, take your pick, and a cup of tea if I you wanted one. I didn't. I didn't like the empty table either, so I took my sandwiches and apple and headed off in the direction of the Den. 'There's bound to be more folk in there I thought.' Wrong! The place was almost empty, there was just one man, a man I knew, a blind man and he was feeling about in the drum of one of the washing machines. He stopped what he was doing when he sensed me standing there and called out.

"Who's there? It's not you Ann. Who is it?"

"Hello Cyril, it's me, Bob... Don't tell me your wife has got you doing the weekly washing."

"I like that bit, 'Wife'... The washing! Oh, well. I had to do it before I met Ann. I don't mind. Besides! she wouldn't have it any other way."

Cyril had got to his feet by now and he had carefully felt his way along the worktops with his left hand as he made his way towards the part of the room I was in, then he said: -

"Do me a favour Bob. I've counted four pairs of socks and one odd one, there's still one missing, see if you can find it."

I went and picked up the dark coloured sock from where it had lain on the floor near the front of the machine and folded it in with its partner and placed them on the top to the contents of the wicker washing basket. I began to feel that he could sense me looking at him and I was, I was looking at the terrible scarring on his face and around his eyes, or rather, where his eyes used to be. This poor man must have gone through sheer hell to get this far. He was better now though than when I had first met him all those weeks ago.

I broke the momentary silence by offering to make us both a hot drink and then I told him what had happened in the lounge just before lunch.

"I once fancied being a piano player." Said Cyril, in a matter of fact tone of voice, then he went on to say. "When I was a youngster my parents wanted me to learn. I had an uncle who could play, he was good enough to play the piano at concerts and such like. I never seemed to have the inclination somehow. I did learn, but only the basics and I only did that to please my Father and Uncle Ned. Now, I wish I had learned. You hear of blind pianists, don't you? That young man on your intake, I hear he's a bit of a pianist and he's going to learn how to become a piano tuner isn't he. Who'd have me as a piano tuner eh? Never mind a piano player. Frighten the ruddy life out of most anyone, me looking like this. Does it bother you?"

"No. If you aren't bothered by my scars why should I be bothered by yours? Don't forget Cyril, we've both been through a similar thing."

"Yes, but you can see me and you can see yourself..."

"Huh." I interrupted him. "What makes you think as I go looking at meself, I dunna go looking in mirrors at all if I can help it... Someone's coming, d'you think it Might be Ann?"

"No," Said Cyril. "that isn't her."

And it wasn't, a few seconds later two women entered the den and neither of them saw us. They knew that we were there but they couldn't see us. They both had coats on and they were each carrying their white canes. We let them know who we were and where we were, then we let them get on with making themselves a hot drink which was what they had come in here to do. A few seconds later one of the women commented on the emptiness of the Manor and asked us if we knew where all the people had gone to. I had no idea except to say that I thought that the one's involved with the concert might just be over in the bungalow having a last practice run. This was quickly confirmed by the arrival on the scene of Cyril's wife.

"Aye, there were about a dozen or more of 'em all heading for the bungalow about ten minutes ago. Got their instruments and the lot. Right then me love, have you done that drying for us? Oh good, this is it is it? Hiya Bob, hello Maggie, bad timing again, no, don't bother, I can make meself a brew it's alright. Listen luvvy... Not you Bob, I mean Cyril... Listen, you know you said you'd rather stay in this afternoon, are you sure you don't mind me going out to do a bit of shopping. Ah, bless you, I'll bring you something back, what do you want?"

"Just you." Said Cyril meaningfully.

Ann bent down to lift up the loaded wicker basket and as she tucked it easily under one arm I watched as she adjusted her eyepatch with her other hand and then she grabbed hold of Cyril and gave him a rough and ready kiss on his forehead before saying."

"Bless you. See you all later then, toodle-oo."

And then she was gone, out of sight out into the corridor. A minute or so later and after one of the two women had quietly and valiantly struggled to find the sink, and the necessary, in order to wash their cups, they too left the den. This meant that Cyril and myself were on our own once more. It didn't take him long to pick up on the threads of our earlier discussion, but then he began to open up. I felt a bit uneasy at first as he probed deeper and deeper into his own past. I could tell that he wanted to talk. I also realised that this was akin to the situation I had been in in this very same room many weeks earlier when Elizabeth Dakin had opened up to me and told me what she had told me about her life and the loss of her sight. I sat; listening to Cyril as he talked and I just hoped that he would not go too deep, but he did.

"...have you been as close to death as I have Bob? I mean really, really close?"

"Yes..."

"Horrible it was Bob, the day the rear of that car transporter loomed up towards the windscreen of my bus. Pushed into it I was, by some bastard behind me, but that wasn't all. The worst part was when I started to come round after the accident and then after the operation's they had done on me. That's when you start to begin to realise your weaknesses, how vulnerable you are. We all think we are immortal in a way don't we, I know I did. Don't no more though. I can still remember that day but it was more than just one day, it was a period of time. I found out more than once that there was not much hope, they thought I might die. Once, I remember them standing over me. It was on the day, the day it happened. They were talking about me; they must have thought that I was unconscious. Too badly injured to hear, or understand what they were saying. One of them said to another one. 'I wonder what his insides are like with facial injuries this bad? It's a wonder he's still alive.'

177

Another, Bob, another was saying. 'Where do we start?' They shouldn't have said that. They should have known better, but I couldn't say anything... I couldn't even move could I... I couldn't talk either. It was months before I could do that. They had to wire up my jaw, it was broken in a couple of places. They had to scoop out what was left of my eyes. It's a good job I was under the anaesthetic, I would not have liked to have heard what they had to say about that. It was bad enough when it happened and the days, and weeks, and the months that followed. I went to deaths door a lot of times in those days Bob. When you're lying there or you're trying to find your way about and you start thinking, this is it. This is how it's going to be for the rest of your life. No sky. No faces No open road in front of you. Nothing... And then you get that feeling in the pit of your stomach. That horrible feeling when you think again just how vulnerable you are. And you think. How long before I die... How long have I got? Do I want to live like this? Will anybody want me looking like I do. I don't know what I look like Bob, but I've a pretty good idea. Still, none of it seems to have bothered Ann... She's a good woman Bob... I'm glad I met her. Oh! What now! There's never a lot of peace to be had in this place is there?"

What Cyril had just been referring to was a noisy gathering of residents out in the corridor, coming this way. A few seconds later and in they came, five of them, three blind men and two more, not so blind. They had just come back from a trip into Torquay and it was obvious from their actions that the two sighted men were in charge. One of the three others seemed to want to break away from their group and when he realised that we two were there he started edging over towards us, but the tables were in his way. I wouldn't have minded just sitting there and take this opportunity of getting to know another, if not a few more of the residents, but Cyril had other thoughts on his mind. He wasn't aware of the approaching blind man, until he heard him colliding with the tables, and that was when one of the two guardians stepped in. He came around the tables and caught hold of the man's arm and said.

"Come on Derek, I've cleared a space over here, now don't you go bothering these two, I'm sure they've better things to do than get involved with us."

 Cyril was sitting beside me, I leaned over to whisper in his ear and said. "Shades of Shirley here Cyril. Shirley in the shape of a feller."

"Good God," Whispered Cyril. He didn't say any more for fear of being over-heard. Instead, he got to his feet and started to walk towards the door. I followed in his wake and nodded to the men as I passed them on the way out.

178

Cyril was out in the corridor by now and it did occur to me that he might need some help, but then I quickly realised that he seemed to be doing just fine, and he was, and also, sort of, honouring the code of the Manor by not using his cane indoors, at least, not extended. I was walking close to and behind him, we had taken a right turn out from the Den, and were now heading towards the door leading through into the main hall.

I had seen the short sections of scratch marks on both sides of the corridor before, but only now did the significance of them begin to have any meaning. There weren't a lot of them, a few were clearly etched fairly deep into the plaster beyond the green paint and they were more pronounced on the right-hand side of the corridor than they were on the left. They were of a height of just below waist level to most people, and Cyril and his kind were the cause of it all. Cyril's cane was in his right hand, three times I saw him put out his arm and tap the wall with one end of his folded-up cane. I could just see his left hand extended slightly in front of him, and he was using these methods to get him to where he was going, wherever that might be. It was all so intriguing, to follow behind Cyril and patiently watch as he pulled the door at the end of the corridor towards him, and a few seconds later we were out in the main hall.

Apart from a couple of staff members, there was no one else around, it was very quiet and peaceful and it wouldn't have been a bad place for us to continue talking, but Cyril had other ideas.

"Why don't we go outside Bob, I know just the place where we can talk in peace."

And he was right... Well, almost. The place he wanted to go to was the very place where we had first met, and this was the arbour over at the far end of the Commerce building. We came out from beneath the Porch entrance to the Manor and Cyril immediately unfolded his cane and compressed the sections together with a sharp tap on the hard ground, I walked beside him as we went along by the front of the Manor. I didn't say much, mainly because I didn't want to spoil his concentration, and I also wanted to watch and see if he knew where he was going.

The afternoon was bright and cool and there was no one else around, except the two of us. I found it to be rather uncanny, the way that Cyril stopped when he neared the top of the concrete step leading down to the Commerce building and there he smiled and said.

179

"The steps are just about here on my right aren't they Bob. Good eh? I've been pacing it out ever since we left the porch. I've done this journey enough times now to know that much at least. This next bit's going to be harder though. I haven't been this way, at least not as far as the arbour for a few weeks now. I think I can still find it. Don't help me just yet. I want to see if I can get there under my own steam."

Cyril didn't quite make it on his own. I ended up helping him soon after the Tarmac ran out and the thick and crunchy gravel took precedence, which naturally made things rather difficult for this blind man and more particularly, his cane. Still, I only ended up having to escort him for the last forty yards or so of our journey. We entered the arbour to the gentle swish of the wind in the nearby trees and surrounding bushes. There were no other sounds except for those of the woodland bird songs. As I slowly escorted Cyril over towards the white bench; a blackbird took offence to our being there and darted off into the undergrowth uttering that familiar high-pitched cry of alarm. There were no other sounds or intrusions. Well, not for a while... We sat and talked and I attempted to divert him away from going back to the topic we were talking about whilst we had been in the den, but the strategy didn't work. It wasn't long before he was describing the gruesome aftermath of his accident once more. It was almost as if he wanted to get it off his chest, so to speak, and so it was that I had to listen to, all over again, most of what I have already mentioned and a fair bit more besides. Cyril then went on to explain about a follow up operation where the specialists had considered fitting him with artificial eyes but had then discovered, on the operating table, that he was unsuitable. He had awoken from the anaesthetic to be told by his neighbour who was visiting him that he had collected a bit more scarring and nothing more, and it was all to no avail. It was around about this time that the topic was brought to a sudden halt as I hushed him and said: -

"Listen! Did you hear that? There it is again. Music. It seems to be coming from over near the boundary wall."

I think we both heard the beautiful melody at the same time. It was the sound of a wind instrument and I strongly suspected that it was a Clarinet.

"The crystal sweet clarity of a clarinet." I mused, as much to myself as to Cyril. "I wonder if that's where it got its name from? What a beautifully haunting melody."

"Yes." Whispered Cyril. "I wonder who it can be."

"Who cares." I replied quietly. "It seems a shame to disturb him, or her, whoever it may be... Let's just stay here and listen for a while. If this's a taste of what we'll be getting tomorrow, roll on tomorrow."

We sat and we listened, and it was good to be there. The repertoire was varied and interesting but it came to an abrupt halt after about ten minutes. We waited in silent anticipation for whoever it was to continue, but no more haunting melodies came our way, and that was when the desire to find out who it was, began to take hold of me. I already had a good idea of who it might be, but I wanted to check it out. I couldn't just get up and go looking and leave Cyril there on his own though. I had taken on the responsibility of looking after Cyril the moment we had set foot outside the Manor, and so it was that I didn't get to confirm my feelings for the identity of the mysterious player. Not until the following day, the day of the concert, for this was to be when she valiantly played the piece she had been out here practising, and in front of a lot of people, but most importantly, she did it in front of the person she liked the most... But more of that later, at the appropriate time. Eventually, other sounds returned to our ears, these were the ever-present woodland sounds of the wind rustling in the trees, together with the cries of the resident bird population, and just to remind us that we were close to the sea, there was also the booming sound of a ships horn somewhere out there beyond the trees and the boundary wall.

A while later. Twenty minutes, half an hour... Who knows! After resuming the story of the gruesome details of his accident once more, and of his life since the accident, I started to try and think of a way of calling it a day without offending Cyril. In the end I had to resort to a tactic I felt reluctant to try out. I said. "What does Ann think of all this then?"

"Oh. I haven't told her all this, I've tried, but I don't think she wants to listen."

"Probably happy to just have you the way you are." I replied, and then. "It's getting a bit chilly now, should we go back t'th'Manor."

We must have been in the arbour for about an hour, I hadn't noticed the time on our way out but I did now that we had got back inside. The hall was just as devoid of life as it had been on our departure and now, we had both just walked the length of it and we were standing beneath the clock on the wall. I looked back at Cyril and said. "Twenty-five past two... What do we do now Cyril?"

His hand was already caressing the clock face as he responded by saying. "So it is, I don't know. Haven't you got anything more important to do? I don't mind if you have. I wouldn't want to keep you."

I misunderstood him, his mood and what he had just said. I only meant my reaction to be a friendly one. I even laughed a little as I said. "Oh, you've had enough, want to get rid of me now do you?"

"Suit yourself." Said Cyril moodiy.

I was looking at his badly disfigured face just then and I think it was something to do with the way his face seemed to be more contorted than usual that made me realise what might be going on inside his head. I lowered my voice and said. "Sorry Cyril... had enough eh?"

"I could do with a lie down that's all."

A bit less than five minutes later I was coming out of the care staff office from where I had handed over the care of Cyril to a more competent person. I was just about to go through the door, outside once more, when I noticed Sandra and another lady coming out of the care staff office with Cyril between them, heading for the stairs... Cyril's head was hanging down, almost touching his chest. I was automatically pulling on the old oak door at the same time as saying to myself while still watching the threesome slowly climbing the wide staircase.

"Poor sod. I've gone and really knackered him."

A hand dropped on my arm through the open space and then a figure in a long dark blue open fronted coat went and thrust a white cane into the gap, then she stepped forward and demanded.

"Knackered who? Who are you and who are you talking to? May I come in please, or are you all; both, or whatever... are you going to stand there and block this entrance all day?"

She had dark glasses on her smooth oval face and her blond hair was cut short and curly. There were so many faces and so many people, and changing all the time. I knew this woman, but I couldn't remember her name. Her bright red lips moved once more. "Well?" She demanded irritably.

"Sorry... Only me, just the one, only me." I said at the same time as pulling the door wider in order for us both to go our separate ways.

I was sitting in the Porch a short time later; feeling a bit guilty with myself. I should have been able to pick up on Cyril's condition, but I hadn't... I began wondering, about this man in his late thirties with the stamina of more like a man in his sixties, and I also wondered what Ann might say when she returns from her shopping expedition.

I must have been in the Porch for about ten minutes when the residents began returning to the Manor. They came mostly in small groups and odd ones at first, and then they began to come in their droves. The blue minibus came and pulled up outside, packed with first, and second week residents. Terry was the driver; he drove away as I watched the last of the residents from the bus go indoors. The place fell silent again for at least the next few minutes and then there came the sound of many people heading towards the main entrance. As soon as the first ones came into view, I realised who they were. I tried to say hello to Shirley and managed to say hello to Barry and most of all the other musicians that I had come to know over me past few weeks. At the tail end of the large group there was Samantha. It seemed strange for her to be without her best friend and constant companion. Samantha didn't see me as she went inside, she was too busy talking to Ken, the drummer. This musical association made me begin to wonder where Mike was and this worried me, it worried me a fair bit. Had he already gone home? How would I know, how could I find out? Not from these people, they were far too keen to get indoors to stop and talk. When they had all gone inside and left me on my own once more, I just shrugged my shoulders and waited for the next thing to happen.

By this stage of the day's events it must have been turned three o'clock. You could still get an afternoon cup of tea and some biscuits in the dining room but mostly, anyone, apart from the newest Intake, who wanted refreshments at this time of day would normally go to the Den. Should I go to the Den, or should I stay where I was? This was the dilemma facing me. Or should I just go down to the Lodge and stay there, and maybe do something useful up in my room. Like... and then I remembered what Gill Roberts had told me the day before, that she would take Royston and myself on a mobility lesson of sorts down to the Pub called the, 'Hole in the Wall.' "Come on Bob..." I muttered as I forced myself to get to my feet and do something other than to just sit there being miserable, and on my own. "Let's see what the Den's got to offer... then I'd better see if I can find Royston... and Mike."

Finding Mike was going to prove to be a rather difficult task. Finding Royston however, was going to be a lot easier than I imagined, he was sitting beneath one of the tall windows in the Den having a game of cards with his and my friend, Sid. As soon as he saw me, Royston did his classic act and immediately gathered up the cards from the table, much to Sid's annoyance, mainly because he seemed to be winning. Anyway, having gathered the cards up in his large hands he then put them down again and signalled for me to make my way around the tables towards them both. We were only a few feet away from each other and I was on the side of the room where the brewing facilities were situated, Kettle, teapot and so on... There was a lull in the usage of this area, so I indicated that I wanted a drink. Royston had been watching me very keenly with his limited vision. I was just as keenly watching him at that moment so that I could be sure that he could understand me. One moment there had been a rather bland expression on his face and then the next, there was a careful shift of his head and then a cup from the table was offered in my direction. I got the message... I also took hold of Sid's offered cup and began to make all three of us a hot drink.

I stayed with Royston and Sid for the rest of the afternoon after that, and we played cards and talked, and then played more games. People were coming and going for the rest of the afternoon and into the early evening as well. We three were the constants of the room, until the gong sounded. When Sid told Royston that it was time for tea, he gathered up the cards once more and made me feel like he must have made Sid feel when I had entered the Den an hour or so earlier. I was winning that hand of pontoon.

We had all three, along with a few others, just come along by the side of the wide stairs and I was both pleased and surprised to notice that the hall was more like its usual crowded normal self once more. We were about to pass through the gap from the base of the stairs and the oblong table in order to go down the other side of the stairs to get to the dining room, when a voice called out. It was a woman's voice and I turned to look at Gill Roberts. She then said.

"So, this is where you are. I'm glad I've caught the pair of you together. I hope you haven't forgotten about our arrangements for tonight. I was wondering just now if I might be wasting my time hanging on after five."

"When do you want us to be ready?" I asked
.
"Six o'clock do? Here at six o'clock? Okay, see you both here at six o'clock, bye for now."

184

With a swish of her long black coat and with a steadying hand to place her black felt hat on her dark short hair, I watched her leave via the large old oak doors. Royston had held back when I had stopped, Sid, had gone on with the others and the main hall was almost deserted once more. I stayed just long enough to explain to Royston what had just been going on and then I indicated for us to get a move on.

It was a nice evening meal, consisting of a salmon salad with all the trimmings, there was plenty of bread and butter as well, and to follow, there was ice cream and a good cup of tea, laced no doubt with bromide, but what did I care. Just as long as it wore off before I went back home to my wife.

I looked for Mike while I was in the dining room but there was no sign of him on the table he had occupied ever since coming to the Manor. That table was made up with knives and forks and spoons and so on, in just the same manner as it always had been, except that Mike was not there.

I was on my way out after enjoying that meal, which had been spoiled by the absence of Ann and Cyril at their table and Mike at his table, and those on mine. I wondered if there might be enough time to at least go and look for Mike before the six o'clock date with Gill Roberts.

I mentioned the missing ex-policeman to one or two other residents and to the dining room staff as well, but none of them were able to offer any insight on the subject, and in a curious way this seemed to make things better than I was imagining, because if the dining room staff weren't aware that Mike had gone, then maybe he was still here. I really did want to get a chance to speak to him at least one more time before he went and left the Manor.

"As I went down to strawberry fair, singing, singing buttercups and daisies... I met a girl with bright red hair, fol-deree..."

"Someone's in a good mood." I said as I went to go past the blind young man of about eighteen or nineteen years old. We were in the corridor leading from the dining room towards the main hall.

"Well... why shouldn't I be?" Came the cheerful voice once more. "I've only been here a week and I've just met the most gorgeous girl ever..."

The meal was over and it was perfectly natural that a lot of people should be leaving the dining room at that moment. One of these turned out to be Jack

Townley, he had heard the lad singing as well. He gave a nod and a wink in my direction and said.

"At they gooin tell the lad or shall I? Aye alrayte... ah'll tell'im... Another wick or two on bromide lad an'theyst wonder what they't singin' abite... Oh, bloody gormless... Theyst best spell it ite fer 'im Bob... goo-on."

"What a weird way of talking! What did that man just say?"

Encouraging the young man to go with me so that we wouldn't block the corridor, I then stood him beside the oblong table in the main hall, and after discovering that his name was Nigel, I explained what it was that Jack had been referring to. The look of incredulity on this young man's face was a sight worth getting a photograph of, more's the pity I hadn't got a camera with me.

This young man, Nigel, ended up taking it all in good heart though and after pretending to poke his fingers down his throat he then exclaimed to one and all. "That's the last time I touch a cup of tea in this place." He then asked me whereabouts the stairs were so that he could get himself a bearing. I showed him and he then felt his way around to the other side of the table before heading off in the direction of the lounge and singing his song a bit louder. Soon, he was gone, out of sight and I was left with the task of finding Royston and then stick with him until six o'clock.

CHAPTER SEVENTEEN

We were sitting on a wooden bench nearest the door of the mobility office, we had been here for more than a quarter of an hour, a lot of people had come and gone but we stayed where we were. We were playing a game of cards in the empty space on the seat when Gill came on the scene. She didn't come out from the mobility office as I had expected her to do, she came down the wide stairs instead; and she still wore the same long black coat and carried the same floppy felt hat in her hands that had become a trademark of hers.

"Are you two ready?" She asked, as she put on her hat. "Right... Well tell him Then, tell him we're ready and to put those cards away... come on, get a move on."

A few minutes later we were standing under the curved arch of the Porch entrance. I was looking out onto the dark of night and feeling just a bit more fearful than I would have liked to have admitted to. Looking behind me to where Gill stood with Royston beside her, I thought to myself. "How am I going to see or know where she is when she's dressed as dark as the night?"

Shrugging my shoulder's, I unfolded the cane, tapped the section together on the stone slab beneath my feet and then said out loud. "Ah well! I'm ready when you two are... I think?"

Just before we stepped out into inky blackness, Royston nudged me to indicate that he waited to say something, and this is what he said: -

"NOTHING TO IT BOB JUST CLOSE YOUR EYES AND THINK OF ENGLAND THAT IS WHAT SHE JUST SAID TO ME"

And then we were off. Two blind guys, at least, now we were, as good as, and I didn't get a chance to respond to that last statement, as much as I would have liked to have done because this slightly mysterious woman who was there, behind us, somewhere... but where? and I had already lost sight of her and that was the way it was going to stay.

Little did I know it at the time but I had last seen Gillian in the Porch and I wouldn't see her again until I arrived at the Hole in Wall Pub.

Meanwhile, Royston was keen... by heck he was keen. I could hear his long cane tap tapping on the hard ground ahead of me. Stopping for a moment I looked around but couldn't see anything except the yellow light of the Porch entrance and a few other lights to the left of that one. But where was Gill Roberts in all of this? I should be able to hear her even if I couldn't see her. Where the devil was she?

Her voice came to me from in front and a little over on my left. "Come on you..." She said. "Royston will have started on his second pint before you've even left the grounds of the Manor at this rate."

I was still only a few yards away from me Porch entrance, still within reach of sanctuary, but just then there came the sounds of what tuned out to be quite a sizeable group of residents, who were about to leave the Manor for a night on the town. I remember feeling a bit uneasy, and vulnerable, standing there in the dark. I can even remember feeling rather awkward as well, mainly because of the white cane in my hands. I was alright with Gillian, she expected me to use this cane, and Royston did too, but what about these other people coming towards me, what would they make of all of this? Would they make fun of me and the cane? This whole cane thing was still in its infancy with me and I didn't entirely know what to think, or do...

Gillian's voice came to my ears from a dark distance ahead. "Will someone give that man a nudge, tell him to get a move on."

The group who had just left the Manor seemed to be all around me now, there was at least one female amongst them but the half dozen or so others were all men, and by the sounds of things there was only a few of them who could see.

One man, in the background, somewhere, was getting verbally agitated as he began frantically tapping his cane at the loss of his escort and he seemed to be wandering further and further away. If I could have seen well enough, I might have gone to help him, but I couldn't help him now, or even a short while later. In fact, I could barely help myself...

"I'm alright." I said to the faceless man who was trying to escort me down the drive in the direction Gill and Royston had gone. "It sounds as if you'd best go and help whoever it is over there, sounds like he needs more help than I... this is daft this is."

Gillian's voice no longer penetrated the darkness and I had a feeling that she had deserted me. I began to see this as a golden opportunity for me to turn around and go back the short distance to the safety of the Manor and leave her and Royston, and anyone else fool enough to want to venture out here in the dark to just go ahead and get on with it.

The agitated man had been between me and the Manor entrance, but now he was going the other way with the man who had offered to help me, and they were so close that I felt I could touch them.

"Sure you don't want to come with us Bob?" Said the man. And then, I recognised his voice. This was Malcolm, Malcolm Tipper.

"I'd get back indoors if I were you, and right smartish, before that mobility woman comes back..."

I interrupted him and said. "That won't do any good, she'll only find me again, and give me a good old bollocking for wasting her time, besides, she was supposed to be doing me a favour, she was taking me on a sort of mobility lesson, we were supposed to be going down to the Hole in the Wall pub. I bet her and Royston are half way there by now."

"Aye, and the group I was with as well." Said Malcolm "That's where we were all heading for. You don't know Arthur here do you Bob? Blind as a bat he is and twice as daft. At least a bat can find its own way in the dark. Not like him, or you, apparently?"

Malcolm's companion interrupted him by saying. "I'm not daft. I can manage well enough thanks, once I know which direction, I'm supposed to be going in... Come on Mal, what're we waiting for? Just point me in the right direction and let's get to the pub."

Gillian could have been standing a few feet away, silent; and waiting, just waiting for me to turn back, to see what I would do. My silent friend Royston could be waiting beside her as well, what would he be thinking? His problems were worse than mine, so... "Come on Malcolm, come on Arthur... Come on Gillian and Royston... if the pair of you are there that is... let's go."

Well. What a character that man Arthur turned out to be. Off we went, down the drive away from the Manor, just the three of us. Malcom, Arthur and myself, there was no sight nor sound of Gillian and Royston. Arthur had a cane but didn't use it properly. I had a cane and I wasn't using it properly, but this was mainly because I couldn't yet concentrate on what I was doing. I began to think that I could have done a lot better on my own out there in the dark, but then? If I was on my own, would I be daft enough to venture out at this time on a Saturday night on a journey to a pub? Malcom didn't have a cane. I almost wished he had, at least then he would be on more or less equal terms with me and Arthur. I knew Malcolm was watching me and he proved this by constantly trying to help me, which was very much to the annoyance of me and my independent streak, and also the frustrated needs of Arthur as well.

I somehow knew that we had now lost the company of Gillian and Royston. I commented on this to Malcom and Arthur and I went on to say that it was probably just as well that Royston was now able to have a one to one with his tutor. Malcolm reminded me that he and Arthur had also lost contact with their group and with this statement he began to hurry us along a bit faster than safety dictated we should. I managed to slow him down but then he speeded up again in order to try and catch up with the others, of both parties. I still don't know if Arthur was having us on, or not, but he didn't half cause a lot of confusion on that journey. At one point, I was the one in the lead, this was just after I had somehow managed to convince Malcolm, that I could manage this thing with the cane a bit better on my own and without someone walking directly in front of me, and I did, until Arthur caught me on the ankle with his cane, this was when I dropped to the rear once more, and then I found that I was doing the same thing to Arthur. Was he genuinely struggling? or was he deliberately slowing down and then speeding up, just to confuse me? It didn't take me all that long to realise that this really was the way of things and he wasn't trying to confuse me, or Malcolm. I soon decided to relax my attitude over the white cane in my hand, especially in the way that Malcom and even Arthur, had not really poked fun at me, but had both encouraged me to use the cane, and Malcolm in particular, had, after a while, jokingly pleaded with me not to put too great a reliance on him. By the time we had got to the bottom end of Middle Lincombe Road, I realised that I was beginning to develop a liking for these two. Arthur really was as blind as blind can be, but this fact didn't prevent him from enjoying himself, on the contrary, he rather put me, and Malcom to shame over our respective eye complaints, because we weren't the one's hopping up and down off the kerb as he was doing shortly after we had gone past America Lodge and were on Higher Woodfield Road heading down towards the harbour. It soon became clear to me that Arthur was on familiar ground now, but I wasn't, and this part of Torquay was much better lit up than the part we had just left behind us. The scene before my eyes was frighteningly incomplete, fragmented and confusing. I began to see Arthur's antics reasonably clearly as we approached a street lamp and cringed at the thought of an impending collision, but none came, Arthur's swinging cane sounded against the base of the lamppost and he immediately stopped to assess the situation. I watched as best I could as he negotiated around the street lamp and then carried on in much the same manner as before. Malcom hadn't warned him and I began to realise that there was no need to warn him. Arthur was right in what he had said just before we had embarked on this journey, when he had more or less said.

"Point me in the right direction and let's get on."

We were getting near to a busier and more brightly lit part of Torquay and Malcolm had by now, almost disinherited Arthur because of his antics. The two of us, Malcolm and myself, were walking side by side and although I held the cane out in front, I was no longer swinging it from side to side. There was no need to. I instinctively knew that Malcolm would make me aware of any serious obstacle that I might miss, and if he couldn't see well enough, there was always the tip of my cane that I could still rely on, and it was working. We had been walking side by side now for at least the last eighth of a mile or so, and in the brighter spots where I had been able to see things a little bit more clearly than at other times, there would be Arthur, messing about. Just as Jim was the resident comedian in our Intake, just so was Arthur of some other Intake. I remember a curious feeling as I walked down towards the harbour with these two men. There was Arthur with not an apparent care in the world, he seemed to be taking everything in his stride, this excursion in particular. I continued looking directly ahead into the gloomy darkness as I commented to Malcolm on the audible, but momentarily unseen person ahead of us.

"Hardly a care in the world has that man, and here I am frightened stiff as I might bump into something. How does he and others like him, do it?"

"Ah! That's the big difference isn't it?" Replied Malcolm as we trudged along. "From what little I've seen and been told about you I would say that you can only see well enough in good daylight. It makes no difference to Arthur and others like him, whether it's light or dark, day or night, it's all the same to them. I would have thought that you were intelligent enough to have realised all of that by now... How long have you been at the Manor?"

"I sometimes think I've been here too long, but it isn't that... I've seen people like Arthur. I've watched them, worked with them and helped them as well. And I've even been there myself... I've been blind and I suppose it has to be said that I'm damned near as good as blind out here in the dark as well. But folk like Arthur. I find them really fascinating... I mean, they're what the staff back at the Manor call totals aren't they? I don't like that word myself but I suppose that's the way it is, but it doesn't bother them, being out here like this I mean. It only bothers us, folk like me and you, the one's as the title givers refer to as RVs or the one's with residual vision. I mean, can you see Arthur, can you see him right now?"

"No... But I can still hear him, I can still hear you Arthur, you still alright?"

"Fine, are we nearly there yet?"

"There!" I exclaimed. "That's what I mean... He can't see where he's going but he's getting there all the same... and he's cheerful about it as well... How many times has he travelled this route? How he does it beats me."

A few cars had already come up the hill and past us on our downward journey, another was just coming towards us with its dazzling headlights blazing, and every time one had, and now this one too. I had become aware of the manner in which Malcolm had stopped talking and had tensed up in an anxious fashion, and more than a few times he had even stopped walking as well. Only when the vehicle had safely passed us did he calm down once more. I knew a reason for most of this. It was simply that he was concerned for the safety of Arthur... A man who had apparently got himself lost right outside the Porch entrance to the Manor and yet here he was humming to himself and still occasionally stepping up and down onto and off the pavement. Now though, there seemed to be more vehicles than previous and I realised that we were near to the main road, there were more people in this area as well, and as I have already said, the street lighting was much better and brighter. So much so that I soon began to see more and more of Arthur as his outline was lasting much longer in my field of vision.

"There's a method to his madness you know Bob." Remarked Malcolm. "Have you any idea why he walks so close to the road... Plain foolishness if you ask me but he does it so that he can follow the edge of the footpath. It's the best way he's found I suppose but it doesn't half scare the likes of me, he's done it all along though, and he's survived. Come on, not much further. Once we get past the Victoria centre it's just a short distance and around a corner and then we'll be there, I could murder for a pint of best. Figuratively speaking I mean."

Well, we got there, and as we went in through the ancient and low doorway, other members of the Manor were there to greet us... I quickly took in as much as I could of my immediate surroundings and just managed to catch a glimpse of Gill Roberts before the fog closed in and misted up my glasses. It was warm here and cold outside, I knew this would happen. While Malcolm and Arthur edged forwards into the crowded bar I stood and wiped my glasses before venturing any further. I was putting them back on again when a group of three young women and an equal amount of young men came towards me and the way out. I squeezed into a small recess beside the outer door to let them pass and felt rather conspicuous, standing there with the extended cane still in my hands, I couldn't fold it up either, not until they had gone that is. Then, a delicate, but firm hand touched the back of my hand and I looked up to see Gillian standing in front of me.

"Where have you been?" She said. "We've been here ages; Royston was beginning to get worried. Come over here by the fire and join the others."

The Hole in the Wall public house was every bit as one could expect an old sea port public house to look like. Warm, smoke filled, low beamed ceilings, bare stone flagged flooring, copper topped tables and an ancient looking Bar, making the whole place look no different than it had done for probably a hundred years or more. The only significance being the dim electric wall lighting and the modern telephone which was over in the recess by the entrance. There was quite a sizeable gathering of Manor residents in the corner

192

of the room beside the roaring log fire. Royston beckoned and pushed Jim out of the way to make room for me, but Jim didn't seem to mind, he went over to sit beside Josie. Gillian came back from talking to Malcolm over by the Bar and complained that Jim had pinched her place, she then went and sat beside Peter and I could hear her advising him on the amount he ought to regulate himself to drinking that night. I squeezed in to sit beside Royston and took hold of the glass that he had clearly been saving for me. I gave him the thumbs up sign by way of thanks and brought the tempting brown liquid up to my lips.

Then I felt something move behind me and instinctively just about managed to put my glass down in time, before Royston's hand came down between my shoulder blades.

"I think he's pleased to see you." Laughed Jim. "Gill's right though, you certainly did take your time getting here. What took you so long?"

I looked at the faces around me. Gillian was still talking to Peter. Jim seemed torn between pressing me for an answer or else carry on where he had left of with talking to Josie. He soon chose the latter when he realised that I hadn't got an immediate answer for him. If the truth be known, I was still in something of a state of surprised relief, that I had actually got here, in the dark and, mostly under my own steam, so to speak. I was also just about realising the fact that if it hadn't been for the distracting antics of Arthur, I might well have been more anxious about the journey than I had been. I wasn't feeling much like talking to anybody at that precise moment, far better to just to sit and reflect on this stupendous recent achievement, drink my well-earned drink and watch those around me.

There were five more Manor residents who were part of the group I had just joined but their choice of topic separated them from us, they were headed by Barry and I noticed that Ken, the drummer; was there as well, then I was momentarily distracted by two people coming towards us from the bar area. I had managed on our journey down here to get an occasional glimpse of Malcolm's features. He wasn't tall, only about five foot four, slim built and he had very dark short hair and his eyes seemed somehow mysterious. He was looking in my direction but he didn't say anything as he came to a stop a short distance away with the man called Arthur, who was looking in my general direction, but not at me, or anyone else for that matter. Arthur was bigger and thicker set than Malcolm. He was a man in his early fifties, wearing a brown tweed jacket and dark trousers, and he sported a bright and almost luminescent green and yellow tie. I felt like commenting on that tie and say something like. "Wow! With a tie like that, who needs electric lighting? I wasn't quick

193

enough. One comedian recognised another and then, Jim uttered, more or less, the same words that I might have said, given the opportunity. I still didn't say anything. I just continued to watch the two men and thought to myself. So, this is the man whose back I had seen a fair bit of on our journey here, and now I could actually see the man himself as he waited patiently beside Malcolm and sipped at his beer while we shuffled around in order to make a space for them to join us. I soon found that I was casting my mind back a bit further to when we had left the Manor earlier on. This had been when Malcolm had taken charge of Arthur and they had both come past me within touching distance. "Why hadn't I noticed that brightly coloured tie then, I wondered. Surely my eyes aren't that bad that I couldn't pick up on something so vividly coloured as that while we were still within the Manor grounds? He must have had it covered, maybe he was wearing a scarf. Oh well, I drank some more of the beer and then I managed to find my tongue and said, just as Malcolm and Arthur were sitting down almost opposite me.

"Gillian… How did you know I would come?"

"I have my ways; I have my ways. One doesn't do this job without developing an astute sense of what one's students are capable of. Even if they don't. Besides, you might like to ask your friend that question, he seemed to know that you would, right down to getting you a beer ready."

I looked then at Royston and gave him the thumbs up sign once more and he acknowledged this with a shrewd smile and then downed the contents of his glass and wiped his mouth with the back of his hand before offering me his empty glass.

Fortunately for me, and my financial resources, I only had to buy drinks for myself and for Royston throughout the remainder of the time we were there at the Hole in the Wall. Most of the others seemed to have adopted a similar solution to what could have been an expensive evening.

A bit later I became aware that Gillian, it seemed, had a suitor by the name of Peter. Or maybe that should be the other way around. I know Gillian was dedicated to her duties when it came to her role as a Mobility officer, but I don't think she was quite this dedicated. It was almost a shame, the way she seemed to be allowing the situation between her and Peter drift towards, but then, perhaps it was just my imagination. Maybe she was just being thoughtful and kind. I didn't know, and it was really none of my business.

Little did I know it but it 'was' very soon, going to be something to do with me... Meanwhile, I looked across the tables at Jim and Josie and reflected. If we really did get a regular dose of Bromide, or whatever, back at the Manor, and the women got it too, then Josie's dose was working perfectly, but then, I knew it was nothing like that in reality. Josie was the way she was, with, or without, intervention. Was it working on Jim...? No. Mind you. If Josie, or any other woman dared to bare all. Then I think Jim would have run a mile. He was harmless enough. Just then the musicians amongst us got to their feet, on instructions from Barry that they should be getting back to the Manor on account of their busy schedule of the morrow. It was damned good timing as it happened, because just then, a man came inside, took the cap off his head and said out loud.

"Taxi to the Manor."

Until they were about to go out through the door, there was a bit of confusion amongst those who couldn't see, but it didn't last long, within a minute or so Barry and his team were gone and this left the rest of us with a bit more space between us. Gill helped Peter to his feet and they came from what had been the fringes of our group to a spot nearer the fire. Which was all a bit of a waste of time because Peter then decided that he wanted another drink and would I go with him to the bar in order to get one.

The two of us were standing against the crowded bar waiting our turn when I casually asked. "Who fancies who Pete, between you and Gillian?"

"Mind your own bloody business." Hissed Peter angrily. "You're not getting her."

"I don't want her!" I said in desperate surprise at the tone of his voice. Some of the locals around the bar area turned their heads to look at us and this made me look back in the direction we had just come from. I was fearful that those from the Manor might have heard the commotion. From what I could see though, through the dim lighting and the smoky atmosphere, all seemed to be normal back there. I was torn between going back to my seat and leave Peter to fend for himself, or stay and help him to do what he wanted to do, and as there was no softening of his attitude, I felt like doing the former, and hastily too. But then. A bit of wounded pride shouldn't get in the way of helping someone less fortunate, should it?

We both ordered our drinks separately and we paid separately, then I carefully carried Peter's and Gillian's and mine and Royston's back to our tables on a tray kindly loaned by the pleasant barmaid, then I went back for Peter.

I was still feeling surprised and taken aback somewhat; by Peter's reaction to my seemingly harmless observations. To say anything more might have set him off again, but to say nothing at all, might be construed as a sign of feeble and sulky weakness on my part. In the end, I took hold of his upper arm instead of letting him catch hold of mine and I led him back as quickly as I safely dared to and then left Gillian to finish off the finer part of helping him to sit down.

That incident tended to spoil the evening coming to the pub as far as I was concerned. I sat down for a while and occasionally looked across at Peter, he was sitting beside Gillian on the right-hand side of the roaring log fire, while Josie and Jim were sitting on the other side. I had no other room in my mind for Malcom, Arthur or Royston, or any of the other three from the Manor. Strange thoughts were in my mind and almost on my lips. After all that I had done to help Peter, in the typing room and other places, and for him to be like this with me now? I could tell that he was still annoyed with me by the way he had pulled away when we arrived back with the others.

It's weird how those you help the most, apart from those nearest to you, seem quick to reject you and become abusive. I had noticed this strange phenomenon of human nature many times in my life and I still could not understand it. One such incident was a childhood incident with another Peter. Peter Harding.

I come from a poor background. One of six children. Poorly shod, none of us more so than Mum. I saw her many a time shoving cardboard in her shoes. A lot of second-hand clothing used to come into our house, mainly from the W.R.V.S. (Women's Royal Voluntary Service) Any other all used to get washed, or boiled, and then washed some more. We never really went hungry in our house. There was always bread in the cupboard. Twenty-six loaves a week we used to have, and more sometimes. Bread and beef dripping with a dash of salt, always tasted better scooped out of the chip pan. Co-op Red Seal margarine and watery Raspberry jam with loads of woody seeds which lodged in-between your teeth. And there was always the squabbling over who should clean the jam jar out. We had a cold house in winter where we would go to bed with more clothes on than we had worn all day, and wake up shivering to thick ice on the window panes. We had a good mum and a sometimes good and hardworking dad, Step-dad in my case. Others on our Council Estate weren't so lucky. The Harding family was one of them. Peter Harding was the same age as me, he was one of more children than I can remember. There always seemed to be a filthy, snotty nosed child crawling around in their littered front garden and it must have taken me many of my younger years before I realised that it was a different child every summer. The Harding's front garden was a weed infested battleground of old pram parts and other things and a haven of play opportunity for us local lads. Their back garden was even better, or worse, depending on whichever way you want to look at it. The old wooden shed with no roof and only three sides was a good place to play, but most of us would not go anywhere near the far end of the garden where the old mattress's lay in a musty smelly heap. Not many would venture that far, not even Peter or his many brothers and sisters. We would all steer well clear, because the yellow and brown stains told us to. I never saw Peter's dad. I used to imagine him to be a huge burly man. A boxer perhaps... I befriended Peter at around the early age of eight or nine. We went to the same junior school together and went on to the Secondary School together as well. It was there that I began to share my food with him and help him with lessons. I even stole some cigarettes from my step-father one day for him, but only the once. The consequences of being found out gave me nightmares for weeks. It was at around the age of thirteen that it all changed, and alarmingly sudden at that. I may have said something, or nothing. I just don't know. It was all so long ago. I was on my way home from school and taking the usual short cut through the Vale where the Howty Brook waterfall disappears into a hole in the ground. There's a high old stone wall nearby and sometimes the bigger, and braver lads would climb up there and spit on us as we went by. This day it was Peter up there, and he, what we call, gobbed on me. I looked up expecting to see Ian Wainwright, or Eric Shaw. Or even Michael Gorman. Or even all three, but not Peter Harding, on his own. It didn't end there either. In the weeks that followed, there happened to be a very curious relationship between Peter Harding and me, which was strange, and strained, sometimes friendly and sometimes downright terrifying. Our friendship finally ended one day in a fight, at the top end of the Vale, right outside the Chip shop where Valerie lived. A lot of us boys fancied Valerie. Her dad, Mr Price, had lived at the Chip shop for many years, I often thought that maybe he chose to call his daughter after the nearby shortcut of the Vale. I can still remember that hot summer Saturday afternoon when my brother and me and two of our sisters went to the nearby sand quarry with Valerie and took it in turns to toboggan down the bare yellow scars on a tin tray and see who was the quickest to get to their feet at the bottom before the cascade of loose sand hit them. The danger of being engulfed was real enough, but no problem to us sure footed youngsters. We could never understand why the grown-ups shouted at us so much. But, to get back to Peter Harding... I never did understand or find out what I had done to offend him. Maybe he liked Valerie, and in some juvenile screwed up mentality, took offence at me and my association, mainly through my sisters, with Valerie. I had helped Peter Harding with his lessons. I shared my lunch with him many a time because he was, like his many siblings, always hungry. I had been a friend and he mine for years. And then the fight happened…

"He's bloody miles away... Hello, I said hello, is there anybody home?"

I looked up; Jim was standing over me with his head on one side in that peculiar manner of his. "Sorry... er, sorry Jim... what?"

"Do... you... want... some... crisps? I was just going to get some from the bar. Yes or no? Come on then, give me your money, I'm not buying... Buy for one of you and I'll end up buying for all… Plain crisps?"

After delving deep into my pockets, I began to look round about me once more. I felt a bit uneasy, almost as if I had been caught out doing something I shouldn't be doing.

When Jim came back, I tried to involve myself with these people, my colleagues from the Manor, but it wasn't much of an effort. I didn't really want to be here, in this pub with all these people. I wanted to be at home with my wife and my family. Even Gillian started to be concerned. She leaned forward and said.

"You're not fretting about the journey back, are you? You shouldn't be, there's no need, I told you, we shall be having a lift, so come on Robert, snap out of it."

"Hey!" Said Jim. "I've got a good joke, who wants to hear it?"

We all looked at him... Those that could. Half said. "No." while the other half and some of the locals nearby said. "Yes." Josie muttered something under her breath but Jim ignored this and said.

"Right, by popular consent, here goes... There were these three blokes, all friends. There was an Irishman a Welshman and an Englishman. They all three go for a job interview for a new building site. Foreman's a bit keen though... doesn't want just any old Tom, Dick or Harry on his team, so he thinks up a test, a sort of intelligence test if you like... Only trouble is, Good for the three guys as it happens, Foreman's too busy, so he sends in his secretary. She's the original dumb blond, she doesn't think on as she ought to interview the men separately. She asks the first one, the Englishman... What do the letters T.U.C. mean? The Irishman whispers to him. Trade Union Congress." Then the Englishman says it out loud. "TUC stands for Trade Union Congress. Good, says the dumb blond... And now for number two, Mr Jones? What do the letters R.U.F.C. mean? That's easy says Taffy... Rugby Union Football Club... Good. says the dumb blond again. You've got a job as well... And now for number three. What do the letters D.I.Y. stand for? The Irishman's struggling a bit at this stage... Sorry Josie... I..."

"You always say you're sorry but I don't think you mean it, indeed I don't. You might as well carry on I suppose. Go on make fun of the Irish... See if I care... Gillian? Wherever you are... would youse be kind enough right niow to be arranging a taxi back to the Lodge please... I'll be giving you some money for the phone of course."

"I was just about to go and do exactly that." Said Gillian. "I'd like to hear the end of Jim's latest wit, but I don't think I will. Come along Josie, to the loo for the two of us and then I shall phone when we get back... Who knows? by then they might have all stopped laughing."

It took a lot of coaxing to get Jim back in the mood to tell us the finish of his latest joke... Gillian and Josie had been to the toilets and come back and were now heading towards the entrance and the phone. Jim had his back to them. I don't think he had seen them. If he had then we would have had to start at the beginning again... In the end. Malcolm promised to lubricate Jim's tonsils, if he in turn promised to finish telling the joke. Jim smiled at this and his smile encouraged a couple of the locals who seemed to know Jim to offer him a drink as well. By my judgment, the two women were in danger of returning before Malcolm and the others came back with the drinks. And they did. They nearly all came back together.

"Oh, I see." Said Gillian. "Got to whet his whistle; have you? He is not really sulking you know, are you James? This is just a ploy to get folk to buy him drinks... These aren't all for him, are they? It must be going to be a good joke."

In the end, the two stayed to hear the end of Jim's joke and it was Josie who actually and finally managed to get Jim to finish it off. We had to wait a few minutes more, while he downed two of the pint pots in front of him. Nicely inebriated, he began a bit previous to where he had left off.

199

"Well, alright then, here goes... Where was I? Oh yes... This interview .... this er, 'other' man. He's sitting there and the dumb blond has asked him what the letters D.I.Y mean and the other guy, the one that he helped earlier... the Englishman... He whispers to the Irishman and says. 'Do it yourself.' 'Sure.' Sorry! Sorry! I won't do me Irish accent."

"Thank the Lord for that." Interrupted Josie, and then she continued. "Go on will youse, the taxi will be here soon so it will."

"Right." Said Jim, firmly and a little drunkenly. "The other guy has already whispered the answer to the initials D.I.Y Do it yourself, by a way of helping him, but the other guy the Irishman, he turns on him and says... Do it yourself indeed! Sure, but didn't I help you with the TUC question?... Good eh? Now wasn't that worth a few drinks and a bit of waiting?"

Somewhere around about half an hour later, I was making my way upstairs to my lonely bed at the Lodge once more.

CHAPTER EIGHTEEN

Sunday.

This was to be the day of the music concert. As I lay in my bed for those first few minutes, my mind wandered over the rehearsals leading up to this event. Then I remembered Mike... Where was he now... Was he already preparing to leave? Would he go without saying goodbye? Will he be one more resident I had befriended only to lose contact with, simply because of the fairly common understanding that...

"There will always be more important things to do than to keep in touch with one's fellow Manor residents."

How many times had I heard that phrase since coming here, and how many opportunities had been lost to me, and to many others?

Twenty minutes later, I was washed and dressed and on my way downstairs.

The Den was eerily empty, looking at the clock on the wall I couldn't help expressing an opinion to the desolate place. "Flipping heck... ten past five. No wonder the place's empty." Then there were footsteps out in the corridor. Seconds later she came and stood in the entrance, filling it with her large body. She looked at me in dismay and said.

"You again... I might have known... What are you doing up at this time on a Sunday morning? Going to get an early confessional, are you?"

I was a bit slow in taking in what she said, and when I did, I smiled and replied. "Good-morning to you as well Ruth... No... I'm Church of England."

She didn't make any further comments on that subject, instead, she mentioned something a great deal more interesting.

"Well, you're not the first. That blond-haired young man is already up and about. I think you know him, don't you? wasn't he on the same intake as you?"

"Mike!" I said in surprise. "Where is he? He's supposed to be going home today from what I've been told..."

"Oh, don't panic..." Said Ruth. "His train won't be going until half seven at the earliest, so there'll be plenty of time to see him off, you get something to eat while I go and see if I can find him, he can't be all that far away... You might pop him a round or two of bread in the toaster, he hasn't had anything to eat yet. You just carry on while I go and search for him. I shan't be long."

It was just as well that I didn't follow Ruth's advice with regard to the toaster, because it must have been at least a good few minutes before she finally turned up with Mike in tow. She sat him down at the table and left us to it, saying as she departed out of the ever-open doorway: - "There you both are... I'll leave you to yourselves for now... I have to see to a few other matters before the place gets wild once more... Bye for now."

Well. One look at Mike and I began wondering if this had been a good idea after all. The slumped shoulders, and the sheer and utterly miserable look on his face made me unsure of what to do next. I gave Mike a few seconds to settle down and then said: - "I'm doing a bacon butty here Mike, do you want one?"

"No... No thanks. Oye just wants to go... Oye didn't think anyone would be awoike yet... Taxis coming six... catching seven o'clock train North. Look Bob... Oy don't like goodboise. It's bad enough as oy've promised to say goodboie to Josie without yow as well..."

Mike fell silent, I switched the grill off and then turned around to look at the smartly dressed, but utterly miserable man on the other side of the tables, and waited... An eternity of silence passed by and then he took out a pen and a small black notebook from inside his jacket.

"Listen Bob... just put your noime and address in here and, and, oy'll troy'n get in touch..."

Mike's chair grated on the hard floor as he pushed it back and got to his feet, and with a hard to control trembling to his voice he continued.

"Oye, oye should be glad... chance of a new career loike... but... here... just dow it."

Silently, I scribbled down my name and address and gave the pad and pen back to him. For one brief moment I thought he was going to shake my hand, but no, he carefully turned towards the way out and disappeared into the gloom of the corridor and I remember feeling just about as miserable as he must be feeling... I turned back to the cooker in silence, and then decided that I couldn't allow him the privilege of leaving without at least a respectable farewell gesture. So, making the area safe in case someone less fortunate than myself should come in I then went out into the corridor to catch up with Mike, stopping, momentarily by the old brown clock, I looked at the time and murmured. "Twenty to six. Where have you gone Mike?"

Josie's name had been mentioned, her room was here on the ground floor. It was to the far right of the large assembly room next to the lounge, it was only a small room, just big enough for one. I had seen it just the once, shortly after Josie had been moved down here. I made my way along the corridor beside the stairs on my left and then the corridor opens out onto a large square area with a glass chandelier hanging down from the middle of the ceiling. The chandelier wasn't lit at that time of the morning but a couple of lights on the cream walls above the dark wood panelling were lit up and they gave an amber glow to the surroundings. I couldn't help noticing the rather large pile of suitcases against the far wall. These could only belong to one person, they were well out of the way of causing a hazard to the not so good at seeing, but they were also close enough to the main entrance so as to afford a quick and efficient getaway for

Mike. There was no sign of Mike though. In fact, there was no sign of anybody. The place was just as silent as it had been when I had come down here near enough an hour earlier... I hesitated by the door which would lead to the other door and Josie's room beyond. With my hand on the brass knob, I was trying to convince myself that it was fated that I had woken up at the time I had done, and thereby been given this unique opportunity of saying goodbye to Mike. He had to at least allow me to say goodbye for myself and on behalf of Royston and the others.

I had developed a really healthy respect for Mike, despite our occasional differences. To be afflicted with blindness in the manner in which he had been, and to cope with it the way he had done throughout our time together, was nothing short of truly and amazingly brave. I couldn't just let him go...

Quietly, I opened the door and stepped into the large, well-lit room. Ruth was there, standing beside the other door which was open and led through into Josie's room. Ruth watched my cautious approach in complete silence and then she came towards me, touched me on my shoulder and then made her way out of the room. Watching the door that I had just come through silently close, I then quietly edged towards the other door and the faint voices beyond.

Perhaps I ought to have announced my presence. I don't know. In a way, I am glad that I didn't. I just stood there half in and half out of Josie's bedroom and watched the scene unfolding. Josie was dressed respectably enough in a long dark red dressing gown. I looked up at her face and for the first time since I had got to know her, I was seeing her now without the dark glasses on her face, her dark eyes perfectly matched her short dark hair. Both she and Mike were within touching distance but neither of them seemed to realise that I was there. Mike was saying goodbye and it was hard on him, Josie too, and me... but I couldn't say anything, to do so would have destroyed the moment. Josie wasn't trying to hide the tears like Mike was. I watched as she turned around to try and locate her dressing table and the box of tissues lying there, blindly she reached out to where she thought the dressing table should be but she was just a bit short of the front when her hand came down. Instantly disorientated she floundered like a fish out of water for a few seconds while she tried again. I should have stepped in at this point, even though it would have spoiled things for the two of them, but thankfully, Josie found the edge of the dressing table and in so doing she also found her location, and the tissue box, and pulled a handful out. Wiping away the tears, she softly called Mike towards her and they hugged each other. When Mike finally pulled away, I could see the beads of moisture trickling down his cheeks and could hear his gentle sobs. He couldn't see her and she couldn't see him, but they looked at each other all the same. An arm's length apart they held on to each other and then Josie drew him towards her once more before finally saying.

"Nigh, Michael you'se promised to write and I'll be holding you to your word... Be off with you... I'll tell the others... go on nigh... go."

Mike turned quickly, and surprisingly efficiently; on his heels. A remnant of his Police Force days no doubt. I quickly pressed myself up against the wall outside the doorway. Unsure of his reaction if he realised that I was standing there, I held my breath while he came out of the room and past me. Cautiously looking back at Josie I could see her sitting on her bed wiping her eyes. I turned my head and silently watched Mike as he walked carefully over towards the other door leading out onto the entrance hall, and before he could open it, he reached into his pocket and drew out a hanky to wipe his face. I continued to watch, and wait, while he composed himself, then he reached for and found the door knob.

The sound of the knob turning brought a cry from the other room.

"Michael... Michael... God bless you and keep you safe... and, and thank you for the dressing gown... Mi... Michael... What colour did you say it was?"

I was still looking at Mike... His whole body had frozen to the spot. I was the same, I didn't dare move a muscle. Mike didn't turn around. His voice was trembling.

"Dark red Josie, dark red with gold braiding."

"Thank you, dear Michael."

A few seconds later, he was gone. A few more tortuous seconds later, Josie came and pushed the bedroom door to. I waited about half a minute or so and then I edged carefully and quietly towards the other door.

I was now in the entrance hall. The inside door was propped open, and at the other end of the short, well-lit corridor, the outer door was also open. There was a cold breeze which brought in with it a few brown leaves from outside, but there was no sign of anyone. I was surprised to notice how quickly the pile of suitcases had disappeared from the spot they had been occupying, and then I heard the voices just as I had decided that it was now or never if I was going to get a chance to say goodbye to Mike.

It was Ruth's voice carried in on the cold early morning wind. "You take care now young Michael and good luck for the future. Yes, yes, I'm sure he will understand, they will all understand, I will explain everything, goodbye now. Make sure he gets on that train won't you Lesley? Goodbye now Michael, and take good care of yourself."

By the time she had finished, I was almost standing beside her but already too late... All I could see were the twin red lights at the rear end of the dark coloured taxi as they slowly moved away and on into the inky blackness of this hour before dawn. I stood, half in and half out of the front door, half of me bathed in a yellow light from above and behind and the front half of me looking out into the darkness. I didn't say anything. What was there to say? Ruth didn't say much either... except, as she turned to go back inside, she said.

"Oh! I do hope he manages to make a career for himself out there?"

"So do I." I responded quietly. "So do I... Goodbye, and good luck, Mike."

Mike did write to me. Three times over the following three years he wrote to me. The first was sent to me in the late spring of the following year, and in the letter, Mike explained that his wife was being transferred to the Devon police force, and that they were going to set up a new home in a cottage in Paington, so that he could be nearer to his piano tuner tutor Harry Moss.

The second letter came in nineteen-eighty-six, to let me know that he had nearly finished his training and Harry was so impressed with him, that he had made Mike a partner in his piano tuning business.

The third, and final letter as it happened, came late in nineteen-eighty-seven.

Mike was so much in demand as a professional piano tuner, that his wife had given up her career so as to drive him all over the Country to tune Concert Hall and many other types of piano. Leaving his business partner Harry, to deal with the Manor Grand piano, and the many others on the south coast.

CHAPTER NINETEEN

There was nothing more that I could do now. Mike had gone and that's the way it was and had to be. I thought just then of the way that Mavis had departed, and then began thinking about the others, like Daniel, he had gone home to his wife and young family within the first couple of weeks. Then there had been Brenda. She hadn't been able to cope with the regime, and more importantly, the residents, particularly those residents of the room she had to share with. Then there had been the departure of Albert just over a week previous… "And now Mike's gone as well." I sighed once more, then I took a deep breath, turned around and went back inside.

I had almost forgotten about my breakfast, until that is, I smelled the bacon just as I was about to go upstairs. I let go of the ornate newel post and made my way along the side of the stairs.

Approaching the Den, I began to hear voices, male voices. One of them I recognised to be that of Barry, the man who was to be the Concert Conductor. I turned the corner and entered the Den just as the three men in there were about to sit down to the tantalising smell of bacon and eggs. Barry looked at me and then at the other two and said. "Don't tell me... That first batch under the grill was yours, right? Oh dear, Ken's just about eaten it... You could try and make him cook you some more... but..."

"Nah, it's alright, I'll cook some meself."

"Ah, well now, you see..." Said Barry. He was half smiling as he adjusted his glasses and then continued. "Erm... It's all gone, the bacon I mean, there's plenty of eggs left, but for some inexplicable reason, there doesn't seem to be enough bacon... Just too bad isn't it, Sunday morning and no more bacon."

Barry and the others knew that Mike had gone, but they hadn't tried to do what I had done. They had respected his wishes and said their goodbyes sometime the night before. Barry did offer to give me some of his breakfast but I declined and settled instead for a few rounds of toast and jam.

Within the next quarter of an hour, Barry and his two colleagues, and myself, were on our way out of the Den, these three to head off up to the Manor while I was going to go up to my room to sort things out for the day ahead. It had been quite cosy in the Den, until Ken, (the drummer, from Kingkerswell) suggested we should perhaps vacate the room before others came downstairs and discovered who had eaten the last of the bacon.

We parted company beneath the Chandelier, where I promised Barry that I would be there to help him with whatever he wanted me to do at around nine o'clock up at the Manor. I was part way up the stairs when the front door closed on the sounds of their voices and the place fell silent.

There were a few people queuing outside the bathroom in the long corridor at the top of the stairs. I said hello to those I knew and then Jim came out of the bathroom just as I was going past.

A few minutes later I was about to lie down on my bed for a short nap. The day had already proved to be a long one, and what lay ahead I had very little idea, but I instinctively knew that forty winks now would help keep me in good-stead, for whatever else this day had to throw at me.

At about half past eight I met up with Josie and Jim and we spent the next half hour or so reminiscing about Mike and the others. We parted at the Lodge gates, them to Church and me to the Manor.

I was approaching the main gates when I became aware of the group coming towards me. As they came closer, I recognised Samantha and Denise, and the one in front was clearly the unmistakeable figure of Shirley.

I asked Shirley where she was going. "Why to Church of course." She said seriously.

"What about the concert?" I asked.

"What about it? The concert doesn't start until three o'clock this afternoon. We shall pray that there is a good attendance and that all goes well, so you don't have to worry... Why don't you come to church with us?"

"One man, with three attractive women. What would me wife say. No, you're alright, besides, I've promised to help Barry."

"Oh, that is a pity. Never mind then... Come along girls, or we'll be late."

Shirley went striding off and just before Denise and Samantha set off to catch up with her; I couldn't help but notice the look on Samantha's face. Then she linked arms with Denise and said. "Don't ask Bob, just don't, ask."

207

I watched them go and a few seconds later they had merged with a rather large group of residents coming the other way, and there seemed to be an even larger group behind that one. I turned and continued on my way.

I couldn't have timed it better, or could I?

I was just in time to see Peter coming down the wide stairs in the main hall. I mumbled to myself. "Should I? shouldn't I?" There were a lot of other residents milling around near to the oblong table. I must have been just one more vague shadow as far as Peter was concerned. I had already reasoned to myself that I had overreacted the night before and was ready to make amends. So, throwing caution to the winds I said. "Good morning Peter, did you sleep well?"

Instantly, his head swung in my direction and he replied. "Bob, Bob... About last night."

"Oh, that's alright, forget it." I said easily.

"Forget what, why should I? You're a first-class prat do you know that? God you're sensitive. I suppose I've gone and hurt your feelings again now?"

"Nah... Sorry, can't stop Peter... I've got to see a man about a dog."

A bit of a lame excuse I know. But there's one thing about dealing with blind people. If you don't let them know which way you're going, they can't come after you. His voice rose above the general noise of the hall as I heard him say.

"Going to see a man about a dog?"

Sandra was just coming out of the Care staff office, in a bit of a hurry. She caught sight of me as I hesitated, trying to decide whether to go to the Den or go outside for a walk in the gardens.

"Now this is what I like to see, someone who doesn't know which way to go, it shows he's not going anywhere important and he can come and help me, come Robert, with me please."

A few minutes later, after she had rounded up a good half dozen of us, we were going out through the main doors when the breakfast gong sounded.

208

Neither I nor any of the other men were asked if we had had our breakfast or not. I know, I asked them, quietly, as we came back with our first load. Sandra had more important issues on her mind, like getting us to carry dozens of chairs in from another building around the back of the Manor and carrying them on through into the Lounge, where a few other 'volunteers' were gathered to space them out in orderly rows, I spent the best part of the next hour doing that job and getting a bit knackered by the end of it. Sandra and one other care staff lady had their work cut out as well. They had to deal with the blind Sunday morning drifters within the main hall, and keep them out of our way.

There were ten of us and we were having a well-earned rest for a few minutes sitting on the fruits of our labours, when Barry came into the Lounge, followed by a handful of his musicians. He was alright at first and was pleased to see our efforts and commented on this to us, but other than that he didn't bother us. Then, as the minutes ticked by, he began to seem a bit agitated. Finally, he called out. "Where is she... Do any of you know where Shirley is? she was supposed to be here a good ten minutes ago."

 I volunteered the information he required but nevertheless didn't want to hear. Then he exclaimed: -"Good God! Why has she gone to Church this morning of all mornings for heaven's sake?" He stopped himself and laughed uneasily. "Now, that is a contradiction of terms, if ever there was one."

The ten of us and some of the musicians as well, went for a cup of coffee at around half past ten and still there was no sign of Shirley, or Denise or Samantha. There was no sign of Laurie either. Barry was in a state fit to pull his hair out, but there was very little, if anything we could do to help him, we would just have to wait until these important people turned up themselves.

I tried to coax Barry to come with us but he wouldn't hear of it, so I left him and headed for the dining room in the wake of the others. I didn't get there though. I had only gone halfway across from one side of the main hall to the other when I heard the unmistakable sounds of an accordion, and when I looked around the crowded hall for who I hoped was playing it, there he was... Shaun. The little Irishman had come back. He was standing in very nearly the exact same place I had last seen him before his departure nine days previous. There was a large crowd gathering around him and I was soon one of that same crowd. Josie was there and then I saw Terry, we acknowledged each other and then he said.

"No bowling and no outing to the pub today Bob, it would have been nice for Grace and her husband to take time out to come here, but alas, they cannot."

Terry and I, and others, all turned our attention back to Shaun. I was very intrigued by the appearance of Shaun. He was different, he was certainly more amiable and he seemed to have more confidence than I had known him to have had. He was smiling now at the many words of encouragement offered by those in the crowd, and then he began playing again. It was good to know that Shaun had returned and it was also good to hear that unique sound once more. Someone else had heard it too.

Barry came up from behind me and pushed his way into the centre of the crowd. He was impatient but at least he had the decency to let Shaun finish playing his piece before he interrupted and broke up the crowd, by gently taking hold of a bewildered looking Shaun by the arm to lead him away in the direction of the lounge. The group broke up, Terry went to the care staff office and I went up to Josie and said. "It's good to see Shaun's come back, I was just going to go and get a cup of coffee... coming with me Josie?" But; I didn't get there, and Josie declined my offer anyway. I had barely got to the other side of the oblong table when I heard the large oak doors open and then close with a rattle of ironwork and who should be there looking all wet and bedraggled? Shirley, Samantha and Denise. Some bright spark cried out...

"Is it raining?"

"No Jim... We've all just got out of a bath. What do you think?" Retorted Samantha, impatiently, this was not like her. I was a bit taken aback, but then, she had had the company of Shirley for the past hour or more to contend with, and by way of a demonstration of what she must have had to put up with, I noticed how she first took off her own coat and shook it in order to get rid of some of the excess rainwater, and then she brushed away Shirley's offered hand and helped Denise off with her coat and all of this, with just the one good arm. I didn't hear what she said to Shirley just then, all I heard Shirley say, were the words.

"Well really, I never did..." And then Shirley came as if directly towards me and then turned sharply to her left and began climbing the wide stairs. Her blond curly hair was curly no more and her short coat and her dress were wet. I suspect she hadn't seen me, or anybody else for that matter, because her glasses must have been wet as well. Soon, Shirley was soon out of sight on the balcony above and my attention was drawn once more towards the entrance, where a much larger group of residents had just come inside. I gave up then on the idea of getting a cup of coffee, because someone was going to have to go and tell Barry that Shirley had returned, but first, I stepped forward and spoke to Samantha and Denise and said.

"The rain came on sudden did it? There wasn't any sign half an hour ago when we fetched a load of chairs in. You two had better go and change, it isn't going to spoil things is it, the rain?"

Denise had been quieter than her usual self. She turned her blind eyes towards me and softly spoke the words. "No... don't be silly... We can't let a bit of rain spoil things."

"Or even Shirley." Chipped in Samantha with a half-smile. With that, the pair of them seemed to merge with others in a similar wet state as they began to climb the stairs. When I looked around, there was no sign of Jim. 'Has he gone to tell Barry.' I thought. No such luck.

Barry's reaction to the news was not good. "Go away Bob, that's twice this morning you've brought me bad news."

Even Sandra thought it best to keep out of his way. Sandra was standing near the Bay window and I was in the corner nearest the door. There were others as well, all of us like statues wondering what might happen next. I was leaning on the panelled wall and watching Barry from a reasonable distance while he paced up and down. And then he stopped his pacing and looked around the room before clapping his hands together and declaring.

"Right! Let's get going, 'Again!' shall we? Come on Sandra, I'll be damned if I'm going to stop now."

I had always thought of that wall which I was leaning on to have been a rather solid wooden panelled wall, but I was wrong. I was looking at Sandra now as she came toward me, faced the wall and got busy, and the next moment the entire wall began to move. It was all in sections and it was beginning to fold concertina fashion, to expose another room behind. This other room was beginning to appear to be just as wide as the Lounge and about half its size in length. I began to realise just then that it hadn't been a mistake, as I had thought, in putting the first row of chairs so close to the front. It had occurred to me that there might not be enough room for the entertainers to do their thing, and one or two others had even mentioned this, but no one else had seemed to take much notice. Now though, all was being revealed. I stepped forward, out of the way. Those large, floor to ceiling ornate panels were being almost effortlessly folded one into another until the two halves were against opposing walls, and one woman had done it all, in the space of a couple of minutes. I was standing now, looking at the nearest panels, at the secret hinges and the really amazing carpentry, but there was no more time. My assistance to help move the grand piano was now required. This took the efforts of all the half dozen or so men in the room while Sandra directed the operation.

Now moved to its new location, I took a breather and looked up at Barry over the black shiny top. It seemed as if the extension to the room, together with the effort of moving the piano had given him renewed vigour. He was more confident now and it didn't seem to matter that Shirley still hadn't put in an appearance. All that mattered was getting on, and it was contagious. Five minutes previous we had all been quietly standing around, full of apprehension and now we were as busy as bees. Some five minutes or so later, in came Shirley, dressed in the same long cream dress I had seen her wearing a few days previous. She seemed subdued at first, but the mood of all of us soon rubbed off on her and she too was soon involved with the process of preparing the room for the concert. The high-backed easy chairs which were normally scattered about the room all had to be neatly arranged in rows at the back of the room nearest to the French windows. I couldn't help but smile at the un-lady like way that Shirley was taking on this task, the dress seemed to be hindering her as she pulled another chair towards herself and began dragging it along. Then a familiar Scottish voice interrupted my observations by saying.

"Don't just stand therre mon, give the poor wee lass a hand."

Many others came into the room soon after that, and we seemed to be busier than ever while everyone sorted themselves out in what they were supposed to be doing. A few minutes later and the sounds of musicians tuning up, or else practising their pieces was coming from all corners and parts of the Lounge.

Barry, Shirley and a few of the staff, began having an intense conversation while we others carried on working. Time flew by and suddenly it was time for lunch. The lunch gong rang out, Sandra and her team left us, and then the others went and there was just Barry and myself about to leave the room. As I looked back, I said to Barry. "This's going to be good, I can feel it."

"It better had be," Said Barry. "I want something good to remember this place by when I leave next Friday."

"And you need this concert to do that?" I said in mild surprise.

"Well, no... What I mean is, I want something good to be remembered by when I leave next Friday. Come on Bob, I bet you're hungry since we scoffed your bacon. Let's go and get stoked up ready for a busy afternoon. It's still raining out there by the looks of it... I hope it doesn't put people off coming."

Sandra, Terry, Ken, Barry, Shirley, myself, and quite a few others were back in the Lounge with hardly any time to let our lunch go down, and I could now see why Barry had been so concerned over the absence of Shirley at such a crucial moment earlier on. He really needed her to be there. To many people; there at the time, Shirley appeared to be an interfering busybody and I suppose she was, up to a point, but in reality, one of her finer points was that she really was a good organiser. We had no sooner entered the Lounge when she was gracefully given free range by a melodramatic bow and a wave of the hand from Barry.

"Off you go Shirley... Do your stuff and do it good."

"Why thank you." Said Shirley demurely.

And then she was off. She began by organising the incoming musicians and directing them where to go for the time being. I caught a worried glance and raised eyebrows from Ken, the drummer, as much as to say. "Hey-up, here we go..." And then he got busy himself as he started to set up his drums in the new addition to the lounge and in the opposite corner to the grand piano. Ken may have been thinking that he could do his own thing and thereby avoid Shirley, but he was wrong. He had only been working on his setup for a minute or so when Shirley went over from the middle of the room and began insisting that he should move to a more central spot. Ken's mild protestations about getting too close to the piano were near enough ignored.

"That may be so." I heard Shirley say. "but have you considered the acoustics? no, this is where you ought to be, here in the middle... Now come along, would you like me to help you'?"

"No... no, it's alright, you just tell me exactly where you want me and I'll do the rest by myself."

A few seconds later, Shirley was heading in a new direction. My gaze went back to Ken as I watched him push his spectacles back onto the bridge of his nose and then he went to lift one of his drums with a visible, if not audible sigh.

213

"Robert?" She clapped her hands to catch my attention as she leaned forward in front of me, I looked down and then slowly upward, from the hem of the long cream dress, up to the nice face, the glasses and the blond hair. Her cleavage was, thankfully hidden by the long wrap of the same colour material draped over one shoulder, otherwise I might have been unavoidably looking down the inside of her dress at that precise moment. I followed her as she straightened up and said. "I do hope you're not planning to sit here all day and just watch. There are things to do you know."

"Just keeping out of the way until you're ready."

"Well, I am ready. Now then, as you profess to know very little about music, I have the very job for you where you can be most useful. Sandra and others of the care staff will be administering the monetary side of the concert. So, I would like you to help the audience to their seats as they come in. Oh, along with a few others of course. We wouldn't expect you to do this entirely on your own. Could you manage this for me... Would you be an usher for the day? the residents should start arriving soon, definitely within the next half an hour, I hope, because that way we can get most of the blind seated before the guests from the locality begin arriving."

I was curious to ask at least one question, maybe I shouldn't have, but it didn't really matter. After all, it was for a good cause. I got to my feet and said.

"What's the admission fee?"

"Oh, it's only a pound. Look, there's Sandra, over by the door, you can go and pay her now if you like."

I left Shirley talking to Denise and one or two others and I was wondering if everyone would have to pay for the privilege, even the musicians. I gave a bewildered looking Head of Care Staff my one pound, and informed her of my new found duties. This, and the first part insistently done, I stepped back and waited by the door for the first batch of the audience to arrive.

Annette. Our pianist for the day arrived a few minutes later. She wore a long black dress with no sleeves and her dark shoulder length hair was done up with a white head band and a small red rose to one side. It pleased me no end to see that Annette had her sister Rebecca as her escort. I went over to them and said:

"Wow! It's good to see the two of you, so you were able to come after all then Rebecca?"

214

"Only with thanks to whoever changed the day. I can't say how thrilled I am to be here. Everyone is so amazing. And doesn't my big sister look lovely Bob?"

"Yes, you look fantastic Annette, I hope everything goes alright for you…"

"Oh! It will now Bob." Said Rebecca; with a huge smile, and a slight quiver to her voice. "It's the red rose you see. I always used to present Annette with a red rose for her hair before she gave a performance.

The two sisters went over towards the Grand piano, and then I saw that Denise was already in the room, she was wearing a short red dress and was now seated just in front of where Ken was softly practising his drums.

CHAPTER TWENTY

People were coming and going but I couldn't see Sandra taking any money yet, so I didn't bother with my duties either. Just then I saw Samantha heading my way across the busy main hall. She had the same long blue coat on that she had been wearing when she had come in from the rain earlier. She came directly up to me and softly asked if I could help her. Being careful not to mess her long fair hair I removed her coat and held onto it for a moment while she stood there all beautiful, in a short sleeved, knee length yellow dress which had pleats in it. And I couldn't help but watch, and wonder, why I had never seen her do this before, as she self-consciously adjusted her limp right arm within a white sling which went over her left shoulder, then she adjusted the pink eyepatch over her eye and asked for the whereabouts of Denise. I pointed her in the right direction and even offered to take her there, she refused, naturally, so I watched as she made her way towards her friend.

I had just helped Christopher Hills to a seat when we were blessed, or cursed, as one resident nearby declared, by the arrival of Laurie. I stepped out into the main hall and both heard and saw Laurie, in full Highland dress, making his solemn way up the length of the hall playing the bagpipes, and just like the pied piper there was a remarkably large crowd of people following him. I had heard the sound, albeit faintly, a few minutes previous and then it occurred to me that Laurie had been outside the Manor and giving an impromptu solo performance. Well? maybe not outside, outside, because his green tartan nor his white hair; seemed to be wet, whereas some of the others clothes did. But whatever! Here was Laurie, and this was where we were going to start getting busy as the mix of residents and local people began lining up to pay their entrance fee. I nudged the blind man beside me, the one who had been doing the moaning, and encouraged him to clap Laurie into the Lounge cum-Concert hall.

There were eight of us to help people to their seats. Only two of them I knew by name and those were Jim and Malcolm, we were soon far too busy to bother with such niceties. All seemed to go fairly well for the next quarter hour or so. Not quite the way that Shirley had envisioned it in getting the residents to their seats before the bulk of the locals arrived, but it didn't seem to matter. In fact, it was probably just as well that we filled the seats regardless and in a methodical fashion from the front to the back and mixing everyone together, the blind and not so blind, and the rest, at least this way; there was no unfair segregation. A while later I chanced to pop my head outside to see if the queue was diminishing any, and no, it wasn't. By this time, we had more than half filled the room. I went out into the hall again and stood by the oblong table to get a better look, the queue stretched the length of the hall and out through the propped open old oak doors and, how far beyond that, I had no idea. I was then surprised to see an officious looking group and a man with a pointed hat and a large chain around his neck. A fuss was being made by Beryl from the care staff, but I could hear the Mayor saying. "No, no special treatment please...We shall queue and pay just the same as everyone else...I insist."

Just then I was called back inside and a couple of minutes later it was Jim who snatched the privilege of escorting the Mayor and his consort to their seats. Special treatment or no, they got the best seats in the house anyway, right down near the front. I had wondered who the 'Reserved' half dozen seats were for. We helped other people to their seats and then I noticed a man taking photographs and encouraging the audience to "Look this way" One or two visitors actually had the audacity to physically try and move their blind companion's heads in that direction. I had just escorted Malcolm's colleague, Arthur to his seat, and was coming back with two more people when I noticed the visitor next to Arthur advising him of where the photographer was standing and then she mistakenly went to move his head. He caught hold of her hand and licked it and panted like a dog at the same time. I thought that she might be offended but the lady seemed to take the reaction of Arthur in a friendly enough manner and even laughed as she tried to pull her hand away.

Someone, somewhere had seriously underestimated the turnout. The queue in the hall was very much smaller by now and there was a trail of wet footprints all the way back to the main door, but there was only seating room for about another dozen people right at the back of the room and there were at least another twenty or thirty or so out here where I was standing wondering what to do... Just then, Barry came out to have a look for himself and I couldn't help but express my opinion to him.

"What were you saying earlier on Barry, something about hoping that the rain doesn't put them off? Where are we going to put them all?"

"Quiet...Not so loud Bob...This's better than I had hoped for... come on back inside, we'll find the space don't you worry."

And we did. It meant that the likes of me had to stand for the duration of the concert... But that didn't matter, even though I had paid for a seat. There was one last extra seat that had to be found though, and that was to be one for my forgotten friend, Royston.

I was out in the main hall about five minutes later. Everyone had been accommodated, almost everyone. I had just witnessed a very pleased head of care staff walking towards her office carrying a heavy looking box in her arms, and I had just noticed some members of the dining room staff enter the large room near the entrance to the Lounge, where Ann and Cyril's wedding buffet and reception had taken place. My enquiring look brought this response from one of the ladies.

"Refreshments love, for the interval. You look as if you could do with some now. Been busy have you getting them all seated. You just stay there, I'll get you something to keep you going, won't be a tick."

I welcomed this opportunity and whilst waiting for her to return and the noise in the Lounge, sorry; Concert Hall, to diminish, I was looking around the almost empty hall and at the wet trail on the pine floor, and then I looked up at the solitary figure who was standing on the landing at the top of the stairs.

The figure on the landing didn't move. Just then the lady came back with a glass of lemonade and a couple of sandwiches, saying. "Here you are love, my what a turnout, who'd believe it? I was just saying that I hope we have enough refreshments to go round. Oh, who's that up there? isn't that your friend? you know, the deaf man? What's his name?"

"Royston...Royston, ruddy hell, I forgot all about him!"

I quickly downed the fizzy drink and gave her the glass and the small plate back, before heading towards the stairs.

Seeing me, Royston reached out eagerly and took one of sandwiches out of my hand and ate it. Then he reached out again and gestured that he wanted to sign something to me. What he said was: - "RAINING NOTHING TO DO"

There was still a lot of noise coming from downstairs, but it was more music than voices now as the musicians finished their warming up. Then Barry began his introductions. But Royston couldn't hear any of this. He didn't seem to be aware of what was going on. I coaxed him down and we were standing on the opposite side of the oblong table when he noticed the trail of wet footprints coming at a slight angle from one end of the hall towards the other and his curiosity got the better of him. He then followed the trail towards the lounge and stopped in his tracks at the sight just beyond the doorway.

I gently pulled him back and signed to tell him what was going on and then he went back again and on inside to see for himself. By this time the concert had just begun with a tuneful rendition of a Scottish anthem from Laurie and his bagpipes. Not many took notice of me and Royston entering the room but Royston stopped momentarily and pointed at the green tartan clad figure and then he put his hands up to his ears, looking carefully at me he then pointed down to his feet. I realised then that he might not be able to hear the music, but he probably could feel it, and what bit he could see of it, he would.

I knew by now that there was not going to be a seat left for me. In fact, I wasn't alone, Jim was standing nearby and he was looking across the room, only he wasn't. He saw us and with a bit of an embarrassing shuffling, he managed to persuade some of the people near the front row to make room for just one more. We left Royston sitting beside a puzzled looking man who was staring at the floor as Royston was, but obviously wondering what Royston might have lost.

"He'll be okay there Jim." I murmured. "He'll most likely feel what music he wants to hear through the floorboards.

I stood with Jim near to the entrance as we watched and listened to the concert. There was no stage, as such. All the performers would be playing on a level with the audience but this didn't seem to bother anyone.

After Laurie had finished the opening piece, I could see Shirley make her way to the front and face the audience.

"Thank you, ladies and gentlemen. And a special thank you to Laurie... For our next performance, Annette... Who is one of our residents, will play a wonderful piece on the piano, accompanied by, her Sister, Rebecca, now, although Rebecca will be standing close by, it will not be necessary, for fairly obvious reasons, for her to be a page turner, Rebecca's role on this occasion will be purely for moral support. Annette will be playing this piece purely from memory... This item in the programme is by Franz Shubert and is called Ave Maria. I present to you; Annette ladies and gentlemen."

I watched as the two sisters held each other's hands and then Rebecca helped Annette to sit at the piano and then stepped back a pace to proudly watch her sister's performance. I leaned closer to Jim and said quietly: - "Rebecca's the woman I met on the train. I'm really pleased she's been able to get here."

Annette began playing and a few moments later Jim turned to me and said: -

"By heck the guy did a marvellous job tuning that thing. Hey I hope Mike manages…"

 "Shush!" came the voices from the audience nearby.

It was almost comical the way that Jim tried to glare back at his chastisers, I didn't want to let my knowledge of his affliction show too much but I couldn't help but smile as Jim looked in the only way that he could at the couple concerned and yet glared at the backs of the people two or three rows in front.

That piano solo by Annette was played brilliantly and brought a long applause from the audience. Annette gave a bow and then we were assured, by both sisters that there would be another performance later, if the audience so wishes. Which brought another round of rapturous applause.

Next, it was Barry's turn to come to the front; to the sounds of violinists tuning their instruments in the background. He began with. "Thank you, Annette. Well done, well done indeed, and now for something rather innovative... I say... Innovative. Mainly because of the fact that if we had held this concert just a couple of weeks earlier, you would have then had a rather remarkable resident violin quartet to entertain you this afternoon. However, be that as it may have been, we wouldn't then have discovered this rather remarkable local duo, would we? So, it is now my pleasure and I am very proud to present, a quartet, consisting of two very talented 'local' violinists... Jane and, and Jane! Same names, but entirely unrelated, and yet they both originate from nearby Kingkerswell. There must be a lot of musical talent in Kingkerswell by all accounts... Here too, amongst the residents of the Manor I hastily assure you... Now then, the two Jane's will be performing with our own equally talented resident violinists Rachel and Gary. They will... Yes, I know I am waffling a little, but I think they are nicely tuned up and ready... Yes, yes, I think they are, so, now we shall have a piece by Amadeus Mozart. I've been wanting to say this to you, and I have been practising. Here goes... This piece is called, Eine Kleine Nachmusik... The first part... Thank you Jane, Jane, Gary and Rachel."

False start, unfortunately, but no one seemed too concerned, especially not the four violinists, and thankfully, they resumed without too much delay. What those four could not do with the violin was not worth bothering about. They stood at the front of the audience. They were casually dressed, all four of them, but that didn't matter. What did was the quality of the music that they played and it was fantastic.

We were still clapping enthusiastically when Samantha escorted Denise to face the audience, and the violinists stepped back a little, then Shirley came on from the side to stand beside Samantha and Denise, and said.

"Thank you... Now wasn't that splendid ladies and gentlemen? Now then, Oh! This makes me feel so proud, to present to you today, one of the finest Clarinet players it has ever been my privilege to meet. May I present Denise, Denise is completely blind, one of those commonly referred to in this establishment as a total... She suffered a terrible accident a number of years ago now, along with her best friend Samantha, but tragic though it was, that accident has not prevented Denise from continuing with her love of music, or her friend Samantha, as we shall see shortly. Well, ladies and gentlemen, it now gives me great pleasure to present Denise, Denise will be playing a Clarinet Concerto in A major, second movement by Wolfgang Amadeus Mozart with violin accompaniment... Denise, ladies and gentlemen."

Samantha stayed close by Denise and was talking to her. And then the Clarinet went up to her lips and Denise began to play, along with the four violinists. The piece started very soft, and stayed soft throughout. About a minute into the performance I noticed Samantha surreptitiously creeping off to one side but she was back there beside her friend just as soon as Denise had finished a few minutes later.

The hall fell into complete silence for at least five seconds before the rapturous applause began. I think. 'Stunning' is the operative word to use here.

Next came a bit of accordion music from our Irish friend, Shaun, with the local lad, Ken Hutchins, on the drums. Barry gave the introductions this time and he began by relating to the audience how Shaun had left and then come back.

"Shaun, ladies and gentlemen was a former resident, who has kindly returned to help us with this concert, assisted by a colleague of his from a splendid organisation called The Diamond Accordion Band... The, diamond accordion band are an excellent band of Irish musicians, and one of their group, Eric, will be performing pieces made famous by the popular group called the 'Shadows' in our second half of the programme today. Meanwhile Shaun will now play a few medleys of popular songs for you on his accordion, together with Ken on drum accompaniment. Thank you."

Shaun started with... Tie a yellow ribbon round the old oak tree, and then went on to play... Send me the pillow that you dream on and... Take these chains from my heart and set me free. He played others of a more obscure nature but they sounded good all the same and he and Ken finished off after about ten to fifteen minutes with a very appropriate piece of music called 'Nobody's child.' And I found it to be very touching when almost the entire audience joined in with the words to the music as Shaun reached the part of the song where the words go; "And I'll walk the streets of heaven where all the blind can see, and just like all the other kids, there'll be a home for me."

Once again, there was a rapturous applause.

Just then I saw Jack Townley and his family, with Ian as well and that was a sight worth seeing. Everyone seemed to be thoroughly enjoying themselves... Barry was standing close to me and I almost had to shout in order for him to hear me:- "Is this good enough for you Barry? Can it get any better than this?"

The clapping was fading when Barry started towards the front again, but just before he did, he turned to me, adjusted his glasses, and with a wide smile on his face, he uttered a classic... "Stick around kid. You ain't seen nothing yet."

Rachel and Shirley stood side by side whilst Barry introduced them, and the tunes they would be playing on their flutes over the next five minutes or so.

"Ladies and gentlemen, we now have a piece called dance of the blessed spirits. Originally scripted by one Christoph Gluck to be played for you by Shirley and Rachel, thank you."

They were good, particularly the very versatile Rachel, who I felt was one of the unsung heroines of the entire show, but she didn't seem to have a care and was just glad to be a part of the whole. There seemed to be two different flutes that they were playing but the sounds produced had a unique and beautiful harmony which is hard to describe.

When their repertoire had come to an end, they too received a heartfelt applause from the audience.

Next came Laurie's friend with his Trumpet, and yes, he played the 'Trumpet Voluntary.' He was good, very good. So far, this concert was going way beyond my own expectations, and a lot of others too, judging by the many happy faces.

What happened next, came as a complete surprise. I knew that Samantha used to play the piano prior to her accident, I think it was she herself who had told me. Something unusual and rather special was about to happen. I wasn't quite sure what it was, but began wondering as soon as Samantha and Annette got to their feet at the same time.

I watched very keenly as Rebecca escorted Annette over towards the piano, while Samantha followed behind on the arm of Barry. I couldn't help but wonder what was going to happen. Was Samantha going to be the page turner? No, not much point there. I was becoming more and more intrigued as Samantha sat down on Annette's right-hand side. There was a concerned look on the face of this young woman. A look of anxiety, which was quickly replaced by a timid smile, as the lady dressed in black spoke quietly to her companion in the yellow dress. Just then, with a little prompting from our compere, the two women began to, 'tickle the ivories to warm up,' meanwhile, Barry turned to the audience and announced the next item. A piano duet.

The two women were going to play a piano duet... Now I realised the reason for the sling which Samantha was wearing. Somehow, she had to keep her right arm out of the way while she bravely played the piano alongside Annette.

I was so full of admiration. One blind woman and the other, half blind and half paralysed... I did wonder why Denise wasn't beside her friend giving her a bit of moral support, but then, Samantha was okay. She looked my way. There

222

was a soft twinkle in her good eye. They had both warmed up sufficiently now and were about to start playing.

"Right, ladies, gentlemen, and our distinguished guests, we shall now have Annette, accompanied by Samantha and they will be playing for you a special 'duo' version of Arabesque, by Claude Debussy. I have to say people, that I have seen these two playing and I feel that I have had the highest honour to have helped them in their practice sessions. I just have to say... that I am truly... truly, proud of them both, with no more ado, Annette and Samantha... Thank you."

A few seconds into the performance I was aware that there were at least three of the dining room staff ladies jostling for a look from the doorway, one of them said. "Well I never... Who would have thought she could play that well? God bless her."

Just how the woman could determine who was playing what, I don't know.

The recital that Annette and Samantha were giving us was very bravely and very brilliantly played. This was a piece completely unknown to me, I hadn't heard anything like it before, but that's not to say that I didn't enjoy it, I did, and so did many others as well. What do they call it? What do we give when musicians play really well? A standing ovation? That's what these two women got. A standing ovation and deservedly so.

We were about a quarter, maybe a third of the way through the concert by now and it had already turned out to be far better than I had imagined it might be. Could it really get any better than this? Yes, it could, and it did. Barry came to the front and waved his hands in a calming manner. It took a while but eventually, he managed to say what he wanted to say.

"Very good. Thank you, thank you. Now! What... what we have next was thought to be much too ambitious, but some of us thought differently. You all heard how good Samantha and Annette were just now... Were they not brilliant ladies and gentlemen? Yes, you may give them another round of applause if you like. Annette and Samantha..."

"...Now... Where was I? Oh yes. Ambitious. This next item may just turn out to be something to regret. No, seriously. What you are about to hear will be conducted by myself and played by the two Janes, together with Garry on violin, Denise on Clarinet, and with Rachel and Shirley on flute. What we are

223

about to present for you is, to quote the details on my piece of paper. Dvorak's symphony number nine in E minor, opus ninety-five… From the new world. Now I am not altogether sure if that is the correct title in this instance but I would like to add, before we begin. We are not, obviously, anywhere near the size of even a small orchestra, so please bear this in mind. There is just one further, tiny detail that I would like to point out. This is mainly for the music critics amongst you. Denise and others have all assured me that it is acceptable to play the relevant parts on the instruments that they have. All I know is… I have heard them, I believe them, and, I know that it sounds good. So! Without further ado… Oh! it's the Hovis theme… You've all heard it, thank you, ladies and gentlemen."

How can I best describe those following minutes of pure musical nostalgia? Magic? Fantastic? Incredible? How about all three and more. Even Jim was finding it hard to restrain himself. Mind you, this wasn't hard in his case. They were about a quarter of the way through the piece, when Jim started, but at least he didn't draw too much attention to himself as he said the words.

"Eee… brread just like me mother used to make."

About twenty minutes later, after Shaun had given us another medley of tunes on his accordion. Barry went to the front and announced: -

"Right. Following on from the next item on the agenda ladies and rabble will be a twenty-minute interlude… Now, it is with great pride that I present our next item before the interval… and this is our resident whistler, No, not Rex Whistler, the artist… the painter artist, that is, no, this is our very own mouth and hand whistler from Liverpool. May I now present to you Roy, ladies and gentlemen. Roy! Oh, please don't panic at the interval, there will be plenty of refreshments for everyone… Roy! Ladies and Gentlemen, Roy."

Barry mentioning that there would be plenty of refreshments for everyone, was an opinion not shared by others nearby, because there was a sudden movement behind me, I turned just in time to see the dining room ladies scurrying off, and one of them to say.

"I wish he hadn't said that, I do wish he hadn't said that."

Roy was fantastic, far better than I had ever heard him before that day. His was a completely solo performance, there were no drums or anything else of that nature, and to my knowledge he didn't have any reeds to hold between his fingers or any other type of equipment. All he had were his hands and his mouth, and a fine set of lungs as well. He began with a selection of bird sounds; mainly native ones and I could have sworn at one point, that there were two blackbirds calling to each other from different parts of the room. How he projected those birds sounds I have no idea, but they were so realistic that it wasn't just me turning my head to look for the real thing. Completely captivated I also watched and listened, to the, "oooh's" and the, "ahhh's" from the audience between each of the fantastically realistic bird sounds. The look of absolute delight on the face of Terry and Sandra and others nearby, was also an incredible thing for me to witness. Roy was blind, a 'total.' Barry was ready to assist from a point a few feet away and when Roy finished his performance with the soft twittering call of a Robin. Barry stepped forward to take hold of Roy's arm and stood with him in anticipation of what he seemed to know was about to happen... Once again, a momentary and complete silence descended on the room, and then there was the applause. And the ecstatic applause; came not just from the audience, but also from the other musicians behind Roy, and now Barry also, and then more of the staff began to line up behind them, and then everyone in the audience stood up and clapped and clapped...

CHAPTER TWENTY ONE

What followed next was to quickly force me out into the main hall as the audience began to surge towards me and the way out.

I went and stood near to the oblong table out of the way and watched as the talkative and excited audience came out into the hall and then began turning to their right and on through another door into the room where the refreshments were being served, and thankfully, the hall floor was now dry. A minute or so later and they started coming out of another door further along to the left, laden with paper plates of food, and drinks in paper cups. Then I realised I was in the wrong place for the refreshments queue, the tail end of that was inside the Lounge, but I was here on the outside, in the main hall. There was no likelihood of me jumping the queue. Not unless? Yes, why not. There was Peter, and he seemed to be having a bit of difficulty with the stranger. Well he was... I didn't hesitate a moment longer. I went forward, excused myself in order to get past Beryl who was guiding people into the other room and then I caught hold of Peter's arm and explained. "It's alright. I'll help him."

Peter seemed to be a bit bewildered at first and then he tried to resist me. It was too late by then of course, because we were in front of the food now. I did try helping Peter to make his selection from the tables but it didn't get me anywhere. Or him come to that. I very nearly left him to his stubborn self but fortunately, one of the ladies filling our plates seemed to recognise that Peter was a special ease. Diabetic and all that, and so it was that she filled his plate for him. He still needed someone to help him out into the main hall though and it was either me or the stranger over on his right. My remarks of. "It's alright. He's just a bit confused by it all." Didn't help one little bit. We left the room with Peter holding on to my upper arm, and we only got as far as the oblong table when he decided he had had enough of my assistance. He pulled away from me with such force that he nearly spilled his and my food and someone else's. This made me feel embarrassed, so I left him to it and went to sit on the stairs like a lot of others were doing. Royston was already there, sitting and eating, alongside Jim.

A short while later we were joined on the stairs by Josie and a few others that I knew. The hall below was noisy and people seemed to be packed together like sardines in a can. Jim mentioned that it was still raining outside and he thought a lot of these people would rather be outside than inside. There was nothing we could do though. Soon it would be time to go back for the second half.

There was a narrow passageway up the right-hand side of the stairs which had sensibly been kept clear of obstructions. It was towards this gap that Sandra, Head of care staff, was now approaching. As she was just about to go past me, I looked up at her and mentioned a problem that had been bothering me for the previous few minutes. "Sandra?" I said. "How are we going to get them all back inside in the right places?"

She looked down at me and then looked back to where she had just come from and then back at me and Jim and said. "Oh dear. I hadn't thought of that, I wonder. Will it? Oh, I don't know. Problems, problems." With that, Sandra turned away from us and went back down the stairs, still muttering to herself as she forced a passageway through the crowd.

Jim nudged me on my arm and said. "I'd leave them to it if it were left to me... Let them find their own way back to their seats. It'd save us a heck of a job if they did. I know that much."

I don't know why Jim said that, because he didn't mean it, as events were shortly to prove. I glanced idly over the handrail to my left. No one else was coming out of the other door so I presumed that the refreshments were probably finished. I saw one lady in a white overall going around the main hall carrying a large plastic bag which was gradually being filled with the rubbish. I particularly noticed, as she came near to the oblong table, just how she coaxed and guided the hands of the blind amongst us to deposit their paper plates and cups in the bag. Another of the dining room ladies in a white coat was heading towards the Care staff office carrying a heavy looking glass jar which seemed to be full to the brim with coins. Just then my attention was diverted by a happening even closer... The Gong, on the other side of the stairs from where I was sitting, reverberated loudly as someone struck it a number of times...

Jim and I both stood up and looked as one over the handrail. Sure enough, there was Shirley. I thought I had seen that unmistakable figure in the long cream dress; making her way through the crowds, but then she had been lost to me, only to turn up here... She looked up at me and Jim and one or two others and said sheepishly.

"Oh dear, I seem to have got rather carried away there didn't I? Sorry er, it's time for the second half... the only way I could, sorry."

Barry's voice reached us over above the dying sounds of the noisy gong, and the crowd. "The second half will begin shortly ladies and gentlemen. If you would all just stay where you are. We seem to have developed a slight problem. If you would just bear with us for a moment... Could I just ask for those who were helping with the seating arrangements earlier, to come to the lounge please? Now!"

"That's us Bob he means us, come on! Right folks, Peter, excuse us... Excuse us, let us through please, that's it... Yes, let us through. Come on... we're the ones who're going to get your bums on the seats, so come on let us through., Sorry Vicar... Oh! you're not... never mind, coming through folks..."

The look that the Mayor gave us when he turned around as Jim tugged the back of his Regalia chain, made me wish I wasn't bringing up the rear... The Mayor smiled at our passing though, so I didn't feel too bad, just as long as he didn't think it was me who did it. We eventually reached the Lounge entrance and this was where Jim showed his unique ability at organisation, which was something I had seen very little of from him over the past few weeks. Jim stood at the entrance to the concert hall and announced.

"Right Ladies and Gentlemen... Qui... Quiet please, that's it, yes quiet please if you will. Now then... Listen folks... This is important. Those of you who can see, I want you to please come this way, but before you do, will you please look around and see if you can recognise a resident who was sitting near to you in the first half... If you can, would you please bring them over here with you and help them to their seats as well... Not too much to ask... That's it. Good, this way folks."

Well... it worked, surprisingly effective as well, and this was another valuable exercise in public relations... For a task that I had seen as a rather large one which might very easily have taken the best part of the next ten minutes or more, had taken around five minutes to do and no more. Some of our team of ushers were in the room assisting where necessary. I should have been there with them but I was too fascinated by the orderly fashion in which people were coming past me for me to be needed, or want to help. I saw and acknowledged, amongst a great many others, people like Ann and Cyril. Ann had two more people holding on to her other arm. Then there was Jack Townley and Ian, and Jack's youngest daughter Rita. She must have come down especially for the concert. Or was it for some other reason? Then I saw Royston and his barrel shaped friend Sid and Sid was doing more or less the same as Ann and had brought a couple of residents in with him as well. It was around about the time that the Mayor and his lady consort came in to the room, each of them with a blind person holding onto their respective arms, that Jim said that the worst was over and all we would have to do now was to go out there and help the care staff bring in the remaining stragglers. I still had nowhere to sit and neither did Jim so, having made sure that everyone else was seated, Jim and me and the rest of us helpers began to relax and look forward to the second half of the concert where others would be doing all the hard work by way of entertaining us.

Shaun and Ken were the first up. Ken played the drums while Shaun played some well-known tunes on the accordion. Then Barry helped Shaun to one side while Ken limbered up and then did a drum solo for the next few minutes. After this it was Shirley's turn for a solo performance on the flute. She played really well and what sounded like Irish folk music... I looked around to where I had last seen Josie and there she was, about twenty feet away, I didn't have any difficulty in being able to see that she was delighted with it all, just as everyone else seemed to be as well.

After Shirley had left the stage area, to an almost deafening applause, I continued to watch as Barry came up to face the audience and announce the next item.

"Ladies and Gentlemen. Thank you... And now for something rather special. You all heard this young lady playing earlier on, when she played the er, the Hovis theme. What you are about to hear is rather special and I do not wish to embarrass Denise by saying any more. This sweet young lady and her Clarinet will say it all for me... and you...Denise Lockhart ladies and gentlemen."

Nobody knew yet that it was going to take a little longer than anticipated, but, something special was indeed about to happen. Sandra and Beryl of the care staff knew. The dining room ladies knew... and Terry knew as well... Even Jim seemed to know something more than I did... It was written on all their faces.

I looked back to where Barry was positioning Denise in front of the audience. First of all, there was a welcoming hand clap. Then, Barry, having done his bit, started to back off, and this young woman in her early twenties, stood there in a red dress as she held onto her clarinet with one hand and self-consciously tried to pull the hem of her dress down a little further with her other hand, she then put the instrument up to her lips and quickly pulled it away, and embarrassed now, she tried to retreat, but she had no idea of which way to safely go... The silence in the room was deafening. I felt deeply for her but could do very little to help. Whatever it was she wanted to play she wanted to do it so badly that she just could not do it. Barry went back up to her and so did Shirley... there was a soft moan from behind me, I didn't look round, there was no need. All eyes that could see were on the young woman in the red dress standing in front of the audience and desperately trying to get away. I looked for Samantha. Where was she? Where was Denise's constant companion, the two of them were inseparable. Where was Samantha? I moved forward to get a better view and then I noticed the yellow dress and the arm in the white sling. Samantha was sitting in the third row from the front, blocked in from all sides and then I saw Beryl go and squeeze in beside her and the puzzled expression on Samantha's face told the tale that she knew little of what had been previously planned. However! The best made plans of mice and men and all of that. There were a few mutterings from the audience and then Barry's voice drew my attention away from Samantha for a moment.

"Sorry about this. I think it's best if... Oh, just a moment..."

Laurie, seemingly recognising the dilemma, was coming forward with his bagpipes. He went and stood beside Denise while Barry remained on the other side of her with his arm around her shoulder and then Laurie put a hand through his pure white hair and looked at the audience through anaemic eyes and said in his broadest Scots accent.

"Och, will ye noo look at the lass's legs and look at ma'own if a raise ma kilt fer ye... That's betterrr... Noo let the lass abee and play her piece fer ye... It's that, or ma kilt gooes higherr!"

That broke the ice. Somewhere in between cries of "Go on then." and loud clapping and other cries of. "Let's see what he's got under his kilt." From somewhere, I don't quite know from where, but there came a very calming situation for all of us and for the shy woman who was still standing facing the entire audience but unable to see any of them. Then, a smile broke out on the face of Denise as Laurie gently took hold of one of her hands and lifted his knee up towards it. She didn't try to back away, which was a bit surprising. I heard cries nearby. "What's going on now?" Looking to where the dignitaries were sitting, I couldn't stop myself from smiling just as they were doing, and then I said. "You don't want to know."

Laurie stayed beside Denise; Samantha stayed in her seat. Barry moved out of the way and everyone else stayed where they were and just as I was beginning to think that the dreaded silence would descend once more, there came a gentle clapping from the audience which seemed to set a firmer footing and to bring the required response from Denise.

Those of us who could see, watched in admiration as well as in anticipation, as Denise brought the Clarinet up to her lips and began playing her solo version of the tune... 'Stranger on the Shore.' She faltered a bit during those first few moments but valiantly carried on and even though Denise was obviously not used to playing in front of an audience, it soon became clear that both she and the Clarinet were as one. She was a natural when it came to playing this instrument and when she had got over her initial embarrassment and maybe, maybe it might have been because she couldn't see. She knew we were there, but that didn't matter now, not any more...

After Denise had finished playing and being reminded once more of the audience in front of her, by way of the cries of delight and the ecstatic hand clapping, she began to take it all in her stride now and I noticed how her hand drifted to one side and Laurie took hold of it and seemed to squeeze it. Then I noticed a huge difference in her face as she smiled, straightened up, and quietly, but a little falteringly, she said the following.

"Thank you... I would like to dedicate this next piece to my friend Samantha. I, I wouldn't be here without her... I mean. She is a lifelong friend and I love her more dearly than I could love a sister. I know you are here Sam... Thank you, this, this is for you."

An anxious silence descended on the room once more but this time no one was bothered, least of all Denise... Laurie was surreptitiously stepping one pace backwards. I continued watching and even found that I was holding my breath as Denise brought the Clarinet up to her lips and began to play...

'Bridge Over Troubled Water.'

I listened, we all listened, I wanted to know what the others were doing, all of those around about me... but I didn't and I couldn't bring myself to look at anyone... I just stood there looking, watching; while I could, at the beautiful, brave, Clarinet player in the red dress and then, after about half a minute I noticed Annette as she began softly playing an accompaniment on the grand piano, and then, from behind Denise, the four violinists slowly got to their feet, came forward and formed a half circle behind Denise and began to play their violins, very softly, so as not to overpower the beautiful, beautiful sounds of the Clarinet... I could feel the warm wetness running unrestricted down my cheeks and then my vision began to go blurred. Denise carried on, oblivious to the effect she was having on me, and, although I couldn't yet know it for sure, a lot of others in that room as well. Jim was standing immediately behind me. I knew this even though I didn't turn around. I began to feel a bit awkward just then in case anyone was watching me and I quietly cursed myself for being such a sentimental softy. I looked towards Denise once more and was filled to the brim with admiration for her, for her and for the tremendous example she was setting herself and for others like her... I could hardly take any more. I wanted to let go and unleash my pent-up emotions, but grown men aren't supposed to do that sort of thing, are they? I looked away from Denise and the truly wonderful sound of her Clarinet. And there was Annette, wonderful blind Annette in her long black dress, her white headband and the Red Rose that was so synonymous to her rise from the ashes of despair caused by blindness. Encouraged by her sister Rebecca... and, the Magic of the Manor... I thought I could avoid the aching confusion and the other feelings brought on by looking at Annette, Denise and the violinists, but I knew I couldn't and didn't want to avoid listening to that all-pervading beautiful sound. I looked beyond Denise, and only then did I become aware that Ken was gently playing a skiffle on his drums in the background. The dining room ladies were back. I could hear one of them behind me... It wasn't so much what she was saying as what she was doing. Only she and one other person in front were close enough to make a difference. Looking at that other person now I felt reassured... Barry had an eyesight problem just like the rest of us. Barry's was with his left eye. He wore dark framed glasses and the left lens was blanked out and painted white... I didn't know, I had never asked what his eyesight problem was. He was standing at right angles to me and looking straight ahead, as best he could.

231

He was looking at the side view of Denise and Annette and the others... and there was a hand and then a handkerchief moving slowly towards Barry's good eye. I was strangely comforted by this sight and that of the dining room lady behind me as she blew into her handkerchief. I kept telling myself that, 'Grown men don't cry,' and, we shouldn't let our emotions show, at least not in public. I stole a sideways glance to my left, at the audience. The tune 'Bridge Over Troubled Water' was winding down now towards the end of a truly magnificent performance, and the audience? The audience were absolutely and completely captivated. There was a soft wheeze from the Clarinet and then there was silence, and more silence. Then there was a sigh that seemed to come, not just from the people but from the walls and the ornate ceiling of the room, there were a few murmurs and some noses were blown and then one man cried out.

"Bravo!"

Then more and more voices cried out. "Bravo, Well done." And then they got to their feet and the handclapping began... and it went on... and on... until finally, Barry's voice called for some order... He was ignored of course. It was only when Sandra went up to the front and began escorting Denise away from the centre of attention that things began to quieten down... Denise, Samantha and Sandra came towards me. I wanted to add my feelings to those around me. I wanted to make a personal comment. I wanted to... but I couldn't. All I did was to return the smile from Samantha as she was the first to come past me, clearing the way for the heroine in the red dress. I turned with their passing and watched them go out through the doorway, I could see Jim now beside me, and his eyes were unashamedly wet. Jim's sentiments would have been my own if I could only have dislodged the lump in my throat. We both stood there with our backs to the audience as Jim said.

"There goes one heck of an amazing woman... Nothing... Nothing at all... Bloody nowt will touch that... everything else from here on will be like an anti-climax, compared to what that girl's just done... Bloody mar... bloody marvellous."

We stood there, me and Jim, and we let the silent tears flow, as freely as they should do, even though it was only for a few more seconds while the hand-clapping faded and the room came to some sort of order once more.

When things finally settled down it was Shirley who now occupied the compere's position facing the audience.

"Well... well, ladies and gentlemen. I am all choked up... I don't mind telling you... I do believe most of you are too... Never in my entire life have I experienced the like of what has just happened here, this day. I am not really sure if we can go on after such a response from such a wonderful and truly appreciative audience, I... Oh! I haven't my list... I have no idea who is to play for us next. Tell me... What would you like? Who would you like for your further entertainment this afternoon? I shall leave the choice to you... but please, please, for what should be obvious reasons, please do not ask for Denise to return. She really did do so well just now and I do not think that she could go through all of that again, indeed I do not think we ought to ask or expect her to... Now then."

Shirley clapped her hands and leaned forward and then straightened up and threw the cream coloured wrap further up and over her shoulder and waited expectantly. It began quietly from somewhere nearby... Just the one word to begin with. "Shaun." Then that name spread and was echoed throughout the room and grew in its intensity until Shirley raised her arms high and declared.

"Alright. That would have been my choice too, but is he willing? and what would you have him play for you?"

"Nobody's Child" Came the chorus of voices from somewhere in the middle of the room.

"Again? Fine, excellent. Can someone find him though? He doesn't seem to be here, is he willing may I ask?"

It started quietly and was caused mainly, and kept going by the residents. A chant began and quickly grew in volume... "Shaun, Shaun, we want Shaun. Shaun, Shaun, we want Shaun."

They didn't get Shaun. Not just then anyway. Sandra came back into the room and made her way towards the front, facing the audience, she said.

"Could I have your attention? Please could I have your attention? Thank you. It would appear that Shaun is unavailable for the moment and I do honestly think it would be rather wise, if some of you calmed down a little, you really are not setting a good example to our guests and..."

"Nonsense my dear lady." Interrupted the Mayor's voice from over near the piano. "Nonsense, this is by far the finest concert I have attended in this year of my office and I would like you all to know that. Never have I experienced

233

such talented musical entertainment. I for one will second the motion to command that fine accordionist to entertain us once more. Now, where is he?"

Fortunately for Sandra, and one or two others, who were all concerned for order, but unfortunate for the Mayor and most of the audience, Shaun remained unavailable. No one seemed to know where he was. We didn't realise. How could we... that, although blind like Denise and a lot of others, Shaun had just witnessed the effect that Denise had had on the audience and decided that there was no way that he could match, or better it. Ken came past and went back to his drums without saying a word. Jim leaned forward and whispered in my ear. "I think I know where Shaun is, don't say anything, just come with me when someone else gets up and does something."

It didn't take long for Shirley to show her unique organisational abilities once more and before we knew it; she had Annette playing another piano recital for us instead of the intended and much demanded performance from Shaun and his accordion. Annette was safely into the first couple of minutes and the audience had settled down to listen when Jim nudged me in my back and reluctantly, very reluctantly, I followed him.

We went diagonally across the deserted main hall, skirted around the oblong table and down the left-hand side of the wide staircase. Jim opened the door to the green corridor beyond and indicated that I should proceed the same as he was doing. We almost tiptoed along that corridor and turned in to the left to enter the Den. There was no one to be seen. Jim looked surprised. Then he went and put his head around the partition wall further up the room on our left-hand side, the one that separates the washing machines and ironing boards from the dining part of the Den. Sure enough, there was Shaun sitting on an upturned wicker washing basket.

"Hello Shaun, don't worry." Said Jim soothingly, he then turned to me and said. "I saw Ken take him out of the other door of the extension to the lounge, I watched them cross the hall and somehow knew he'd be in here."

Shaun was confused and even seemed to be frightened. He explained to us how he felt and that he didn't want to play any more music. He told us how he too had been affected by the way that Denise had played the Clarinet and that. Although he did not want to be the star of the show, he felt that anything that he might play for the audience might not be appreciated in the same manner that the audience had previously appreciated him."

"There, I told you he was confused Bob."

And so were me and Jim after another minute or so of listening to Shaun.

There seemed to be no way to persuade Shaun to go back to the Lounge and play for us once more, so Jim and I had a quiet discussion of our own in the other part of the Den while we put the kettle on to make us all a drink. Jim decided we should stay with Shaun for the next few minutes, but I desperately wanted to get back to more entertainment. We wouldn't be needed back in the concert hall for quite a while yet, but to miss more of what I had seen and heard so far was painful to have to endure, to say the least.

We managed to somehow persuade Shaun to come and sit on a more comfortable form of seating. I poured the tea while Jim got to work on convincing Shaun of his worthiness. The clock on the wall above the ever-open door to the Den had moved a painfully slow ten minutes, from ten past five to twenty past and still we were no further forward in our attempts to get Shaun to voluntarily go back with us to the concert. At around twenty-five past five there came a noise from the corridor. A few seconds later we were all three aroused by the sounds of familiar female voices coming this way. A few seconds later with barely enough time for us to compose ourselves, in came Samantha and Denise.

"Oh!" Exclaimed Samantha when she saw the three of us. "What are you doing here?"

"Who is it Sam?" Said Denise timidly. Samantha explained and then asked us again, what were we doing there in the Den, so I told them, despite Shaun's embarrassed objections. This was for the best in the end, because it was the only thing which seemed to stir Shaun into accepting some sort of reasoning for his somewhat jealous behaviour. I knew Denise well enough to know that this was the last thing she needed, to be made to feel guilty over Shaun after all that she had been through that day. She began to show her discomfort as well. She even said. "Let's go Sam."

Neither Jim nor myself wanted them to go. We wanted them to stay and help us to encourage Shaun to go back with us and play some more music and forget about this problem of his, and the quicker the better as far as I was concerned. Samantha had somehow seen the difficulty and managed to sit Denise and herself at the table.

Denise was the first to speak. "I wasn't really that good Shaun, not as good as you think... I was scared stiff out there without Sam beside me... Why did you do it Sam? Why did you leave me there on my own?"

"It wasn't my idea, I told you... it was Shirley who wanted me to sit in the audience. I knew how you would feel but you know how she can be, you all know that don't you?"

There was a nodding of heads. Even Shaun was pensively nodding his head as much as to say. 'Yes, I know how Shirley can be.' Jim placed a cup of tea in front of Denise on the table and we watched as Samantha automatically guided it into her companion's hands and then took the other offered cup of tea from Jim.

Jim was in a thoughtful mood, he sat down and said. "I think we all know how she can be... but for all her faults. If it wasn't for the likes of Shirley and Barry, we wouldn't be sitting here now mulling over who was the best musician and who wasn't and in my humble opinion there was no wasn't at all... Everything about that concert, that concert out there that's still going on in our absence. Everything about it was and is bloody great. No one person is any better than another... That's what you want to hear me say isn't it, Denise? And it's true... By 'eck you stirred my emotions out there, Bob's too... when you did your solo performance for Samantha here... but you were all good. When Shaun played, it plucked at my heartstrings a heck of a lot. Can't say as I was all that impressed with the wailing bagpipes, but even so, you've got to hand it to Laurie for doing his bit. Still... I will say this much against Shirley... She shouldn't have separated the two of you. No, that she shouldn't... Look, I could go on all afternoon and it may not get us anywhere. What we have to decide here and now is this... By the way? Are you staying over tonight Shaun? I take it that nod is a yes. Well there we have it... you don't want that long journey all the way from Ireland to be a complete waste, do you? No... of course you don't and it hasn't been. If you don't go back in there you've done your bit but don't you think you owe it to yourself and to us and those back there to at least be there for the finale... Come on... let's all of us go back in there and show them what we're made of... By God! Just think what could be done if someone out there took you and Denise and Samantha and what's her name? piano player? Annette, Annette and all the others... if someone took you all under their wing? Well, just think what an impact you could all have on the world out there. 'The Blind Orchestra.' or, or something better than that... You've all got what it takes, dedication to your music... Oh, I've said enough."

Jim sat down and then got to his feet again and began gathering the empty cups off the table. None of us had spoken or made a sound since he had stopped talking and then Shaun gave a cough to clear his throat and murmured.

"I've a job... I start after Christmas. Diamond accordion band, in Ireland... they want me to play with them... offered me a job they have, and they sponsored me to come here, one of them is in the audience, he was the man who brought me here last night. They might have a recording contract soon."

Denise cried out and her eyes lit up... as best they could for eyes that couldn't see, and then she said. "But that is marvellous, really, really marvellous Shaun. I am really truly happy for you."

"Yes, so am I." Smiled Samantha.

"Bloody hell, that's fantastic." Chipped in Jim from near the sinks. "Just look at Bob he looks proper gobsmacked."

"He is." I said. "Well done Shaun."

"I am sorry if I've caused any bother." Said Shaun. "Jim is right. I'll go back to the concert. It's silly I've been and silly I am... would youse be coming back with me Denise, and all of youse?"

At just before twenty-five minutes to six, four of the five of us were in good spirits and walking out of the Den, heading back for the remainder of the concert. The fifth one, was feeling a bit miserable just thinking about what I might have missed out on whilst we had been gone.

"Going back to face the music." Was what I heard Jim saying as we crossed the main hall. I had to smile at that statement because it had suddenly taken on a whole new meaning. Back up North from where I come from, we were more used to the phrase 'Going back to face the music' to mean going back to face a problem of one's own making. Not literally 'To face the music.' Ah well! Now I was getting confused.

The four violinists were playing a soothing melody as we approached the Lounge. Two people were standing by the door. Shirley and Barry. They both came towards us and Shirley cried out. "Oh! you've found him. Well done Robert. Well done."

I don't think Shirley heard me when I said that I hadn't done anything. The next moment she was brushing past me, arms outstretched towards Shaun and she was saying. "Shaun, Shaun, what can I say?" I turned to look back at those who had been my companions for the best part of the last half an hour and it was the way that Shirley had just said what she had and the way she was gesturing with her arms, that made Jim say what he did and very casually he did too. "Shirley? have you got Jewish ancestry in you?"

"I'm sure I just don't know what you mean James. I am extremely glad to see you all... especially Shaun... Now then, you do remember don't you Shaun what you promised. The finale. Yes? You, just you and Laurie. Amazing Grace? Ah! the signs of recognition, look, all of you. I am on next, this is my last piece, we were getting worried in case you didn't show up Shaun... I am so glad you are here... I am on next and after that it will be the finale... Denise… Samantha. You both were fantastic! Look, I have no more time. I am sorry but I shall have to go... Barry? Barry can you take over from here and, and let's have them all back inside please... I don't want to worry unduly, I shan't... Oh, I must dash,"

And with that she turned, went back inside and disappeared around the door to her right. The rest of us dutifully followed Barry as we entered the room to the dying sounds of hand clapping. Barry turned to me and said.

"I don't know what she's in such a hurry for, I'm the one who's got to introduce her. You lot stay here. Bob, Jim. Just make sure you look after these precious girls. Shaun, come with me,"

I watched Barry and Shaun go and then I looked to make sure Samantha and Denise were alright. It was no use even considering trying to find these two a seat at this late stage and I think they both knew this anyway. They seemed alright now and just like me and Jim they contented themselves to enjoy the rest of the concert from a standing position.

"Ladies and Gentlemen! Thank you... We have two last pieces scheduled for your entertainment this afternoon, but first of all I would like to say that Shaun has returned and he will be playing in the finale alongside Laurie and Ken, but before that, it is with great pleasure that I introduce Shirley, who will now sing a song for us, a song which is called. 'At the end of the day' I now hand you over to, Shirley."

A few minutes earlier when we were in the main hall, I had noticed the way that Shirley's nerves were beginning to get a little frayed, and it was small wonder really, but now, now she was standing in front of the audience exuding her usual confidence once more. I particularly noticed the way she raised her hands, palms outwards close to her body and at shoulder height and then did a sweeping outward curve as if to encompass the entire audience within her arms, and then, with a verbal signal to Annette on the piano, and following the first few bars and then a resumption to the beginning again, the song began...

Shirley's arms and body became and were an extension to the gestures in her fine voice as she sang, softly and in low key.

"At the end of the day... just kneel and say,
 thank you Lord for my work and play.
I've tried to be good, for I know that I should,
that's my prayer for the end of the day.

So, when the new dawn; begins to break,
just lift up your eyes... let your heart awake,
be ready to meet what the day may send,
and be ready to greet every man as a friend.

Nobody knows, what a power you have found,
So, do what you can for the others around.
Carry them high... when they seem to be low,
as on, your way, you go.

At the end of the day, just kneel and say...
Thank you Lord for my work and play,
I've tried to be good, for I know that I should,
that's my prayer, for the end, of, the, day."

Stunned silence seemed to have been the norm throughout this entire concert, and when Annette had finished on the piano and Shirley followed with her finish a few seconds later, there was a pause and then Shirley straightened up and went on to say.

"May God bless you all... Bless you… and, thank you."

The silence crept over the room like a veil, and this time the silence lasted for what seemed like an eternity. Then the applause began and if ever there was a moment of public appreciative glory in Shirley's life, other than that day there at the Manor, then that moment must indeed have been a truly special one... I have never seen such admiration shown for such a woman as this, a woman who was so dedicated to her fellow man and woman, and such a diligently hard worker, and who was such a good musician, and an excellent organiser. Aye, and sometimes a pain, as Shirley.

I clapped my hands, we all clapped our hands, I clapped may hands hard and loud, until they hurt, and then some, because she deserved it.

I think that Shirley was supposed to introduce the finale but she didn't in the end... She stood there for a moment, at first just basking in the gratitude that through all of her hard work she was justly receiving applause for, and she seemed to be enjoying it, but then it all seemed to be getting too much for her and I noticed with some alarm that she seemed as if she was about to faint.

Sandra was the closest to her, but she didn't go to her aid... I later discovered that she couldn't, because she, being head of Care Staff meant that Sandra was supposed to constantly watch over the audience in case of a mass emergency whereby, she and other strategically placed staff members would have to execute an orderly evacuation. Sandra had already broken the rule once that day, and so it was that instead of Sandra dashing over to help Shirley, it was me who quickly stepped forward and helped her to one side where she could be taken care of. Barry came up to me and asked if Shirley would be alright, but before I could say anything he quickly turned around and took Shirley's place and then he began reassuring everyone as he tried to calm things down.

Someone came up behind me and gave me his chair. I got Shirley to sit down in a corner while I tried a bit of reassuring of my own.

"I don't know Shirley. You're as bad as me missus. She never knows when enough's, enough, but I suppose we're all a bit like that. Come on... cool down and calm down, it's nearly over now and you've done more than your share... Would you like me to fetch you a drink?"

Jim came up from behind me and said. "I'll do it. What does she want? a stiff whisky?"

Shirley didn't say anything and I was getting more and more worried by the second... She was breathing normally. As I was kneeling down in front of her now, I noticed her eyes behind the spectacles seemed a bit vague, almost lost. She hadn't fainted I knew that much. I looked up at Jim and said. "I don't know what it is. Just sheer exhaustion I suppose, but she won't say anything?"

"Now that is something to worry about. Shirley not having anything to say." said Jim still trying to keep things light-hearted, but I could tell that he was just as concerned as I was. Jim then suggested that we take Shirley outside into the main hall, he said, at least out there we wouldn't attract the attention we were attracting here in the Lounge, which all made sense, and he went on to further suggest, that if we did take her out then Barry and the rest could get on with the final event of the day.

There were a few expressions of concern as Jim and I helped and half carried Shirley out of the other door at the side of the extension to the Lounge, but once we had her sitting on a bench in the main hall we were joined by others of the care staff and also Terry, the Intake tutor, and then Shirley began to recover some of her lost composure.

"Listen." She said weakly. "listen, Laurie's about to start. Oh, let's go back inside, please."

"No." Said Terry. "We can hear it all from out here. You just stay where you are... What is it? What's wrong?"

Shirley looked at Terry, then at Jim and finally at me. Then she closed her eyes, took a deep breath and said. "No breakfast, no lunch and no refreshments this afternoon. I'm afraid I just got too worked up that's all... I am sorry, really I am, for causing so much concern... Oh please! can we talk about this later? I do so want to listen to Laurie and, and Shaun..."

One of the dining room ladies came with a glass of milk and some cake, and stood over her while she ate and drank. Then Shirley closed her eyes again.

The gentle wail of the bagpipes had begun a spine-chilling rendition of 'Amazing Grace' Barry came and quietly sat down beside Shirley while Jim did the same on the other side of her. There was no space for me so I leaned on a part of the old stone fireplace, Terry and the others went back and jostled for a place at the Lounge entrance a short distance away...

There was no one else about, the rest of the main hall was empty. We were still and silent, and then the lesser but still audible sound of Shaun's accordion joined in with the sounds of the bagpipes and what came to our ears from the other room was slightly muted but it was glorious and fantastic and great and... I closed my eyes...

Amazing Grace was drawing to a close when Shirley and the rest of us stirred once more. I watched as Barry helped a more composed Shirley to her feet, and then Jim and I followed them back inside. Shirley had only had about five or six minutes rest but this, and the refreshments, must have been sufficient for her to recover enough to see her through to the finish.

We re-joined Samantha and Denise who were where we had left them, standing near to the entrance. Then we watched as Shirley and Barry made their way to the front to face the audience, there they waited and just as the applause was beginning to die down, I noticed Shirley and Barry rounding up the musicians. Barry indicated for me to bring Samantha and Denise to the front and this I was glad to do... I had a good idea what might be coming next even if these two and Jim didn't.

It didn't take all that long to organise. Within a few minutes those of us who could see were looking at a long line of musicians all standing smiling facing the audience. All of them, that is, with the exception of Annette who was still sitting at the piano, and Ken who was sitting at his drums. I felt more positive when Ken did a familiar drum roll, and when Sandra asked everyone to stand, I knew for certain just what was coming. 'The National Anthem.'

Me and Jim were already standing, as we had been all along. I turned to Jim and said. "This is a good ending to a good day."

"Only good! Only good! Bloody fantastic I'd say..." Said Jim, as Annette on the piano and Ken on the drums led us all in good voice right through to the end of a really good concert.

CHAPTER TWENTY TWO

Five minutes later I was sitting at one of the recently vacated seats near to where I had been standing and I was feeling a bit sad. The concert was over, finished. I had missed a lot of it and yet, I had been involved with a lot of it... but now, as I watched the backs of the excited and talkative audience filing out into the main hall, I couldn't help but feel a twinge of sadness that it was all over. Jim was sitting beside me... he was feeling the same... Sandra had gone to supervise an orderly exit from the Manor for everyone else.

Just before she went Sandra had told us that we could, "Relax, for now." and we were relaxing, but that emphasise of hers on the words 'for now' gave me reason for a little concern. Shirley and Barry were still shaking hands with and seeing off the visitors. We stayed in the Lounge and when the crowds had thinned out sufficiently, we made our way to the far end to where the French windows are and opened them and stepped outside for a bit of fresh air... We got that and we also got the rain. It was the sound from inside, which only came to our ears because the Lounge was nearly empty, which had brought us out here. Neither of us could believe that it could have rained for so long. We didn't venture far, the rain seemed to be coming at an angle and we could feel the wind whipping around the corner of the building tugging at our clothes... Thin clothes in my case, which had been perfectly adequate for what I had been doing indoors... but not for out here.

"Excuse me." Came a familiar female voice from behind us. This was Wendy, blind Wendy, the Braille teacher. We both turned around to see and let her know that it was us two. She was standing silhouetted in the light from the Lounge and came towards us.

"Going back to your flat now?" Asked Jim, raising his voice to be heard. Then he went on to say. "You'll end up like a drowned rat if you try in this lot, even for that short distance."

Wendy ignored him by saying. "I'm not waiting for this to go off, excuse me, if you're in my way get out of it." With that she came towards us, pulled a hood over her head and holding it there, she set off into the rain and the darkness. She was lost to sight within a couple of seconds and we couldn't even hear her footsteps because of the rain. I knew how difficult that short journey was to undertake, in the dark, and this woman had come and gone past us, out there, in the rain and the dark, blind, and without any qualms about it at all.

Jim quickly realised this as well, because he turned to me and voiced his opinion on it. "This place, and the folks in it, never ceases to amaze me Bob, and she hasn't even got a cane with her."

"Years of practice, must be." I muttered. I then turned to look back through the open door. The room inside was a lot quieter now. A few of our colleagues not too far away were doing what we should also be doing, and just to emphasise it, Sandra was coming this way. She came and stood where Wendy had stood only a few seconds earlier. I looked up. Sandra's face was lost to me now, darkened by the lights from behind her. Her voice reached us clearly enough though.

"This is where the two of you are. Now, I know you have both had a busy day, haven't we all? but listen, I would appreciate your help in tidying the Lounge if you will, and I've a special surprise in store for you when you have finished, so, are you coming?"

I for one, felt extremely relieved when Sandra asked us to stack all the spare chairs in the extension to the Lounge. I didn't fancy lugging them outside to where we had brought them from earlier that day, in the dark and the pouring rain as well. The job, stacking the chairs, must have taken the original eight of us, and a few other volunteers, around about ten minutes or so to do. Then we moved the grand piano back to its original position within the Lounge and when we had finished, we stood and watched as Sandra and Terry unfolded the ornate wood panels and closed that section off from the rest of the Lounge. All that remained now, was to rearrange the high-backed chairs in their usual placcs around the room.

Ten or fifteen minutes later we all stood around the piano, some of us leaning on it for support, and I think we were all thoroughly exhausted. Even Sandra and Terry. Sandra went off. Jim chose that moment to tiredly crack one of his jokes. He lifted his head out of his arms spread across the shiny black top and said.

"Hey... what's the difference between a fish and a piano...? You can't tune a fish... Tuna fish Tu... Oh, forget it." His head slumped back down again.

Sandra came back a minute or so later, she smiled on all of us and said.

"Right... Everything has worked out just fine. The hour is late... the rest of the residents have had their evening meal while you have all been of such tremendous help in here... I mentioned a surprise earlier... So! my boys... Come with me."

We followed her out into the main hall where everything seemed to be normal, for a Sunday evening. There were residents scattered around the room, either sitting on the wooden benches or else standing in small groups. It was perhaps, noisier than usual but, judging by what had gone on that afternoon it was of little surprise, for that and the main topic being discussed. Sandra asked us to stay beside the oblong table while she went around the room talking to some of those there. She came back towards us followed by a sizeable gathering. Then she mysteriously led us all down the right-hand side of the staircase in the direction of the dining room.

When wc cntered, all the musicians, including Shirley, were already there, and we were warmly greeted by John, the head Chef, and the rest of the dining room staff who had prepared a delicious meal for us. I looked around for and then, at Jim. Even he was dumbfounded by this pleasant surprise. We joined our friends and colleagues and sat down to the finest Cod fillets, delicious chips, corn on the cob, and home-made apple pie and cream, washed down with plenty of tea. The Manor's way of thanking us, for helping them.

About an hour later I was sitting on my own near to the alcove in the main hall tired but content. Annette and her sister Rebecca had just a few minutes since departed to a nearby hotel. Annette would be coming back to the Manor but Rebecca was going home the following day and it was a bit sad to see her going but at least I now had an address that I could write to. Jim and some of the others had left about fifteen minutes earlier to go for a drink. Royston and his friend Sid had come and then gone out for a drink as well, the only difference with these two was that Sid had arranged for a taxi to take them out. I was almost tempted to go with them, but had decided to stay where I was so as to phone home at nine o'clock. There was no one using the phone but there were a lot of people about, they were mostly in small groups and a few like myself sitting on our own. I got to my feet shortly after Royston and Sid had gone out through the old oak doors, and went across the room to check the time, to come back with the decision in mind that ringing home ten minutes earlier wouldn't do any harm... no, too late. Ah well, I would just have to wait a bit longer while Josie used the phone. A minute later I was sitting near the alcove and the phone once more. I wasn't deliberately eaves-dropping, besides, the folk in the hall were rather noisy anyway. I couldn't help feeling a tingle of pleasure though to hear the way Josie explained to her family all about the concert.

I must have still been smiling to myself when the young couple came and stood in front of me. I looked slowly up from the immaculate black shoes, the pristine grey suit of the man and the dark blue dress of the woman and then I was looking up at the faces. Both of them were smiling benignly down at me and I began to wonder what it was they wanted. They didn't waste any time, the man spoke first.

"Mr Weaver? forgive us, we don't wish to interfere, were you about to go somewhere? Jenny, er, of the care staff, she's just pointed you out to us... I hear you were part of the organising team for the wonderful concert we all enjoyed so much... I am sorry... allow me to introduce. This is my wife Anthea and my name's Brian, Brian and Anthea Palmer. We represent the Torch Trust for the blind, the local officials you might say... erm... would you mind if we sit?"

"Here we go, I thought as I indicated for them to do as this Brian guy had requested, and then I said. "Sorry. I've never heard of it... but I'm not blind."

"Oh yes, we know that." Said the sweet voiced, petite, and dark-haired woman. "You don't have to be blind to be a part of the trust. Although I suppose the majority of our members are blind. We have been told that you are learning Braille... It's people like you who we would like to help the most. Oh hello."

Josie had just come away from using the phone in the alcove. I was quick to notice that someone else had promptly jumped in there ahead of me. Anthea stood up and talked to Josie for a minute or so and then she helped Josie to the stairs and watched her going up before coming back to sit down beside me once more. She carried on where she had left off, with: -

"Sorry about that. That was one of the ladies I was telling you about Brian. Now then, Mr Weaver. Where was I? oh, yes... What we produce is a Braille magazine which covers aspects of life in general but more specifically, articles on the teachings of the Bible. You are Church of England yes? Not that it matters, you see, what Brian and I expressly concern ourselves in is the drawing together of different religions. We are small cogs in a much larger mechanism, an engine if you like... our task is to reach out to people like yourself and offer you a chance for you to become involved with the Torch Trust, and to take advantage of the publications, all free of course…"

"Why don't you come to one of our little get togethers." Interrupted her husband. "Gillian Roberts. I saw you outside the school with her a week or so ago... Gillian will be bringing some people to our house tomorrow night, why don't you come with them. There is no obligation of course and I... We, we can promise that we are not out to convert you. Eight o'clock? will that do... I think Shirley will be coming along as well... you do know Shirley? of course you do you helped her this afternoon didn't you... Sorry..."

He looked to his partner for help. She said. "Doesn't everyone know Shirley? I saw how poorly she was this afternoon, what a shame, but what a spirited person she is, don't you agree? she seems to have become almost one of the family after all of these weeks... Oh, his friends, yes... I do believe that lady just now is one of your friends, of your intake? yes? Josie? Two others are Jim Grice and Peter Pugh. Please say that you will come along Mr Weaver. We would like you to be there."

I was surprised to hear Peter's name being mentioned and it must have shown. I only said the one word, but it clinched the arrangements as far as these two were concerned, when I said. "Bob." Brian said, good, and then they were off in search of someone else.

Watching them go I muttered to myself. "Hooked once more. Oh' well."

I quickly got to my feet just then. There was a man coming towards me, hands out in front of him, feeling for any obstacles that might be in his way. I could tell that he was heading for the alcove and the phone, so I beat him to it.

Twenty minutes or so later, I was sitting in the Den having a nice cup of hot drinking chocolate. There were about a dozen or so residents there and it was no surprise to me that the main topic of conversation was that of the concert. I joined in and before I knew it the time was fast approaching ten thirty and bed time for the Manor residents.

It was just before Jenny from the care staff came that Sid and Royston dropped in for a night cap. The barrel shape that was Sidney, took off his flat cap, and shook it in an exaggerated manner, then declared.

"And it's still raining... that storm we had this afternoon, are you listening people? has apparently done a full circle out in the Atlantic, over Ireland and come back to us, it's a wicked night and I don't envy anyone going out there, and that includes you Bob."

"Thanks."

His coat wasn't all that wet, and neither was Royston's, so I assumed that they must both have come back in a taxi. I was beginning to get a little bothered by then though.

I had purposely stayed on at the Manor that night in the hope that it might have stopped raining before venturing down to the Lodge. I had no cause to doubt Sid's remarks, especially when two more residents came in, followed almost immediately by Jenny, to say it was bed time. Those other two residents, both men, were carrying a white cane and a dripping umbrella apiece. I wondered for a moment just how they might have managed out there in the dark with a cane in one hand and a brolly in the other. I tried to picture the scene, and then heard Jenny saying.

"Be quick then... You know the rules and we have all had a rather busy day, haven't we?"

With that, Jenny turned and left the room. Royston made his extra careful way around the tables and came to sit down beside me. I could tell that he had had quite a few drinks that night but he still wanted a nightcap to finish off the evening. He signed a request on my hand and I in return directed his gaze across to the grey jacketed bulk of Sid's back, as he stood in front of the worktop, preparing what I assumed was a good hot drink for both of them.

"You'd better make it good and strong and black Sid." I said. "He'll snore the place down tonight if I know him at all."

"Yes, I know." Responded Sid without turning away from what he was doing. "I'm just glad I'm sleeping on the other side of the Manor. Do you know! He's cost me a small fortune tonight has Royston?"

Sid turned just then and quickly put the two steaming mugs back down while most of the remaining residents said their goodnights and left us. Then Sid picked up the mugs again and came around the tables to join us. There was just one other person in the room besides us three and she was doing some ironing out of sight for the moment on the other side of the partition wall. That person was Denise. She had been at that end of the room, minding her own business whilst quietly and methodically doing hers and probably Samantha's washing, I had thought it best not to disturb her. The Den was much quieter now and I could hear the steady rhythmic thud of the iron and thought of this blind young woman who had played the Clarinet so beautifully that day and the remarkable way that she coped with her life after the tragic death of her boyfriend. And then, there was the unique bond between her and Samantha, who had also lost her boyfriend at the same time, and I thought for a moment longer about how fate had dealt them both a double tragedy in their own personal injuries... and then there was a nudge in my ribs and a packet of playing cards was thrust in front of my face... I had to sign to a very disappointed friend of mine and tell him that it was too late to have a game of cards that night. Sid reached out and signed something on Royston's hand. I don't know what was said but it seemed to cheer Royston up a bit. A few minutes later the pair of them left me to wash their cups and mine and off they went to their beds. This left just me and Denise in the Den.

In the almost deathly silence that followed Sid and Royston's departure I heard a click of a switch from the other end of the room, which was followed by a scraping sound on the floor and then an audible sigh and a grunt and then Denise came into sight carrying a wicker washing basket-full of clothes. Her voice was soft and gentle. "Are you still here Bob?"

"That looks heavy." I said by way of a response.

"Oh, I can manage thanks... I think Sam's gone to bed and forgotten about me, she was very tired and so am I, especially after doing this lot."

"Here, let me help you. Come on, lead the way I'll carry this upstairs for you."

She let me help her and I was glad.

We were soon on the balcony at the top of the stairs and then the lights below us went out. Denise didn't stop or hesitate. I know she didn't or else I would have bumped into her. I stopped though, I came to an abrupt stop and hesitated before moving on once more. I thought of calling over the railings to whoever it was below to switch on the lights for a moment or two longer, but then the much dimmer night lights came on and these gave me sufficient light to get to the fire door and the exit from the balcony.

The lights in the corridor beyond the fire door weren't all that much brighter while I continued to follow this quiet girl in front of me, the one who was carefully minding where she was going, blind, and unaided by a white cane or any other means of knowing where she was going, except for the occasional outstretched hand where she would stop and touch the wall and then carry on her way towards her destination.

We presently came to a stop outside a dark wooden door set in a deep recess which told a tale of the solid construction of this fine old building. Denise knocked gently on the door and then turned to hold out her hands. It seemed as if she was beckoning me towards her. Her facial features were a bit hard to distinguish and her arms were still outstretched and waiting when the door opened behind her. I gave her the basket and turning on my heels started to walk away.

"Bob." Came her quiet and ever so soft voice. "Bob." She said once more. "Thank you... goodnight?

I reached the fire door at the same time that I heard the click of the door latch in the empty corridor, which was now some twenty feet or more behind me. I stepped out on to the balcony and stood in the dim yellow light, and found myself trying to find a reason for the long pause which allowed me to get to the fire door before Denise went into her bedroom. No reasoning came to mind so, gingerly making my way around the balcony in the eerie darkness I made my way as quietly as I could down the wide stairs and across the hall towards the Lounge.

The lights from the Care staff office cast an elongated creamy yellow shaft of light across the dark floor. There were voices coming from that direction as well, both male and female. Some of them I seemed to recognise. Suddenly, an irrational thought flashed through my head as I was reaching for the Lounge door-knob and I said to myself.

"Why bother going all the way down to the Lodge? I could get me head down for the night in one of the chairs in the lounge. Yes, No... Shurup Bob, just get your stuff and get out of here... storm or no storm."

The Lounge was in pitch black darkness, but not for long. Looking around me everything seemed to be back to normal. The high-backed chairs, the piano, the wooden panelled wall on my right, the smoky atmosphere. It was as if the concert had not happened, but it had happened and I had been a part of it. I moved forward at last, now that I could see where I was going and went across to the bay window area where the wooden rack is. And once again I was talking to myself. "If that cane isn't where I left it this morning, if it isn't, there's no way I'm going out there tonight."

It was. There were three canes, I couldn't decide at first which one was mine, but then I noticed with a tingle of satisfaction that one of them had a strip of Velcro around the four sections. There was also a piece of paper with a message: -

> *Just thought you would like to be*
> *one of the first to try a Velcro strap.*
> *Kind regards,*
> *Gillian.*

I smiled and looked around the room once more. "Yep, I'll try it out alright. I'll probably end up like a drowned rat before I'm finished by the sound of the rain out there, but, what the heck!" Then I looked at the cane in my hand once more and murmured. "I must be bloody mad."

I was just about to open the big old oak door at the other end of the main hall when the shaft of light from the Care staff office grew wider and longer as the door opened, and the voices and the people from within came out. There was Jean, and Shaun, and another man; a man who looked just like Hank Marvin

250

from the 60s Pop group called 'The Shadows.' He even had the same type of hairstyle and black framed glasses, and just to make me wonder more; he was carrying a guitar case, Oh, and Shaun was carrying his precious accordion. Jean was speaking: -

"It should be here any minute now, oh! hello Robert, what are you doing here at this time of the night? Robert is one of our residents. A willing helper, but a bit of an insomniac. I wonder Shaun, Eric? Would it be possible to drop Robert off at the lodge on the way to your hotel? It is a filthy night as you know."

"No problem Jean… is it Robert or Bob? Said the man named Eric.

"Bob, Thanks, I'd be very grateful if I could cadge a lift…"

"Cadge, I haven't heard that expression in a very long while. Are you a musician Bob?"

"No, I can just about play Beethoven's Ode to Joy on a piano, but that's about all."

"Yes, I've heard him." Said Shaun.

"Was he any good?" Said Eric.

"No, not all that good at ten pin bowling either, but like Jean says, he's a good helper and now we can help him. Thank you, Jean, for all that you and every-one has done to help me."

"Bob! I don't know it you know; but this small in stature, but huge in abilities man here; is about to become a star attraction in our Diamond accordion band of entertainers. What a truly marvellous concert that was today. It was a great pleasure to have done my bit as well… What did you think of my performance Bob?"

"Sorry, I must have been somewhere else, helping out."

Jean was smiling benignly at Eric as she said. "That was the finest rendition of apache I have ever heard since Hank Marvin played it in the sixties, and like I said earlier, you even look like him."

"One of my all-time heroes is Hank… thank you for the compliment Jean… I have to say, this place… What a rare gem of a place it is. How you work together and in complete harmony is, is nothing short of unique. You must be proud to be able to work here Jean."

"Oh, I am, believe me, I am."

Just then the big door opened and none other than Les Freeman of Freeman's Taxi service looked in, and then we were off.

There wasn't much time on that short taxi journey, other than to ask Shaun if it would be alright to keep in touch, to which he readily agreed and told me to tell Jean that it would be alright for her to give me his address.

A few minutes later, I was standing outside the gateway to America Lodge and watching the red tail lights receding on into the rainswept dark of night, having just shaken hands and wished Shaun and his friend and companion Eric, all the best for the future.

Shaun and I kept in touch, for a year or so and then we lost contact. I understood and was glad to know that he was busy, touring and playing concerts and the like with the Band.

CHAPTER TWENTY THREE

"Ladies and Gentlemen. On behalf of my Husband and I… On be… Yes, yes… alright…"

The dining room was full and noisy. Ann was having difficulty in getting the messages across, so she tried once more.

"On behalf of me and my old man, is that better Stan? Quiet please, the rest of you. Now I would just like to make my final speech if you don't mind. Thank you… Yesss, yes, we are leaving today. It is sad to be leaving the place where I met my husband and the people who have been so good to us over the past couple of months, but it's time we moved on. Them as want it have got our address, or will have soon. Now then… I'm sure you'll all agree with me that yesterday's concert was an astonishing success. Our thanks to the organisers and the musicians and all those who helped out, but most of all. I think our thanks must go to the local community who bravely turned out to support us on such a cra... I mean horrible day. You'll be pleased to know that the show raised so much money that they are still counting it and all that money, however much it is, will go to being used for facilities here. Yes... Go ahead, give yourselves and those who did it a good clap. Clap I said, C.L.A.P! Honestly! Now... back to business. It has been a great privilege and an honour to have been your house captain, even though it has been for a short period of time... Now then! 'Apparently' now nobody told me this until this morning, but when there are special occasions the likes of what happened yesterday, the current reining house captain is supposed to be involved, make some sort of a speech, or maybe I should have given a bunch of flowers to the Mayor, or something like that, but nobody said anything to me, and in a way, I'm glad they didn't. Now, while we are talking about the concert of yesterday, I would just like to say, on a personal note, that it was the best bloody concert... Yes, go on... I was about to say it! A round of applause for all those who did so well yesterday... Yesss... Yes... Yes... Wow! Thank you. Your new house Captain is Graham Sutton. You picked him! Anyway, he's alright! What are you on about, yes, he's a total, what's it matter? He can feel the shape of your money and he's got a good memory, so don't any of you go trying to fiddle him when you give him your den money. Where is he? Come on Graham stand up. There you go. Now then, I'm not one for soppy things, soppy people, or soppy farewell's, as most of you know, but I would just like to say that before I came to the Manor, I used to think my problem with me wandering eye was the biggest problem in the world. Now, I know different. And. I've got meself a good man into the bargain. We won't be leaving until later on today and we will be coming round to see most of you before we go. That's it, folks, Thanks for having me as your house captain?"

Christopher attempted to say something legible about the final part of Ann's speech and the left side of my face and glasses were spattered with toast crumbs. "Sorreee, Bobbb." Came his deep sounding voice full of apology. Laurie, meanwhile, was quietly trying his best to suppress a smile.

It appeared that we would have to wait until another occasion for Mr Graham Sutton's inaugural speech. The dining room had by now returned to the normal buzz of many voices. Breakfast over with, Chris and I got to our feet and followed the many others all heading for the way out. We hadn't gone far before there was a thud in the middle of my back. This was Royston. He pulled me to one side so that the other residents could go past us, and then he gave me a piece of paper. Christopher carried on, slowing some of the residents down but in a curious sort of way being supported by them as well.

I looked back at Royston and then unfolded the piece of paper.

1/ Morning			3/ Afternoon		
Royston	woodwork		Royston	Gardening	
Bob	same		Jim	same	
Sid	same				
Jim	same				

Lunch

2/ Morning			4/ Afternoon		
Royston			Royston		Mobility
Bob			Jim	Braille	same
Sid	all got crafts		Bob	same	same
Josie			Josie	same	same
Jim			Peter	same	

Royston barely gave me enough time to read it before he slapped me on my back once more and indicated the importance of the first session for the day and that I could keep this piece of paper containing the timetable for that week.

On our way out into the main hall he stopped me again and signed and told me that it was Sid who had taken the initiative to find out what the schedule was for that week. At least it saved me a job. "Right." I said as I looked around the crowded hall and then at the piece of paper in my hand again. "Right. Let's go then." With that statement I moved and indicated to Royston to go with me towards the old oak doors, but Royston was suddenly anxious and pulled me back. This surprised me a little because I knew how keen he usually was to get over to the woodworking department. He took hold of my hand just then and I realised what was the matter with him when he signed the single word of

"SID"

It took Sid about five minutes to get to us and in that time, I watched the other residents and the gradual emptying of the hall. We were standing just outside the Mobility office door when I couldn't help but take notice of the chubby young man sitting on the bench nearby, he had mousy coloured hair and jet-black glasses, together with a pale grey suit, black shoes, white shirt and a tie. He also had bright, blood-red ears. I could tell straight away that he was a newcomer. Another resident was talking to him. This was a man who had been there for a few weeks, his name was Gary I had seen him around, and down at the Lodge but not really to talk to. Gary had never struck me as a talkative man but here he was quietly and casually talking to this young new arrival. Gary said something else and the young man responded indignantly and loud enough to turn many heads, mine included.

"Twenty years ago, I was nothing, I did not exist. Then my Mother had me and I exist. When I die, I will not exist, nothing before life and nothing after life, and nothing in between for me, so just go away will you."

Beryl came out of the Care Staff office to investigate the commotion. I caught the look on her face as much as to say. 'Oh dear... Another problem child.' Then she came past me and Royston to stand in front of the young man and said.

"Now, now, young man, there's no need to talk like that. Why don't you come upstairs? I can show you to your room now if you like..."

"Well I don't like, and who the hell are you?" The young man's chubby cheeks and forehead went red to match the colour of his ears, as his rage grew inside him. Beryl just sighed and turned her attention to Gary.

"Stay with him will you. I'll be back in a few minutes."

"No way!" Said Gary. "I'm due in the pottery building right now, so I'm off, you'll have to deal with him yourself."

Beryl then turned to me and gave me a pleading look. I, in turn looked up at Royston, he seemed to know a little of what was going on because he pointed at the young man and said, "Pah pah pah." and then dismissed him with a wave of his hand. Gary walked away and then I looked back at Beryl and said.

"Don't be long then. When his friend Sid comes, we'll all have to go over to Gordon's place."

Beryl headed hurriedly for the main door at the same time as she was saying.

"Oh yes! the coffee table, I haven't seen it yet... I must have a look. When? I do not know."

I didn't say much to the young man, except to let him know that I was there and to ask his name. "Piss off and mind your own business?" Remarked the young man vehemently. Then he started pulling vigorously at his ear lobes. This habit was to later earn him the nickname of 'Jumbo.'

Sid came down the wide stairs at exactly the same time as Beryl came in through the old oak doors. With her she had a man and a woman, both in their early forties, both of them were smartly dressed. The woman, obviously his mother, came up to the wooden bench while I got out of the way so that she could sit down beside the young man and say: -

"Simon! Now what is all of this? I thought you promised us you would behave. Why, we hadn't even gone back to the car when this nice lady came after us..."

The man impatiently interrupted the woman and stood over the young man saying. "You know it's for the best son, I thought we had an agreement."

"Your agreement, my sentence." mumbled the young man. Sid pulled on my arm just then, commanding me to go with him and Royston, and so ended this brief first encounter with this blind young man called Simon Braithwaite.

I got into a bit of a bother that morning in Gordon's woodworking department. It was my own fault though, for being too clever. It all started about twenty minutes or so after we had arrived and after we had all had a good look at the progress of the coffee table. Gordon's main task was to make sure we all had something to do, which was no mean feat for one man to take care of twelve. I was quite prepared to wait until Gordon had settled everyone else, but was pleasantly surprised to be one of the first when he singled me out for a stint on a lathe. I eagerly followed him through into the machinery department and there we began. He couldn't spend a lot of time with me and I didn't want him to. All I wanted was to get cracking on turning a bowl or something.

There were two lathes in that shop as I think I've mentioned before, the one I was to work on was the bigger of the two... I had already assured Gordon on the previous Friday of my ability to work the lathe, which I had done, albeit for a short while. There was just one slight problem to begin with and this was that someone else had been working on the lathe previously, and Gordon was now struggling to get the faceplate off the lathe spindle. There were others to see to besides me, so I offered to try by myself and told him that once I had got the faceplate removed from the driveshaft spindle, then I would come and let him know before doing anything else. His face said one thing. 'If I can't do this, what makes you think you can?' His mind must have been telling him another though. He should be elsewhere. Both he and I knew that he would have to be present at the start-up of the lathe for safety reasons. He reminded me of this important requirement, and anyway, he was probably thinking that I would still be struggling to remove the faceplate when he came back. So, he reluctantly left me on my own to get on with the task.

It didn't take me all that long to confirm what the problem was. The faceplate and the threaded drive shaft spindle were made of steel, the same as mine. What had happened here was exactly the same problem that I had had to solve many years since on my lathe back home. With both the faceplate and the threaded spindle being made of steel, they needed something in between them, a washer, something of a different metal, or material, so that when the faceplate was threaded onto the spindle, the two steels would not friction bond to each other and cause the tightness that I was now having difficulty with. I knew what I was doing. This machine was bigger and a whole lot sturdier than mine, so it could take a bit more than the hammering I had had to give mine to solve the same problem. Gordon wouldn't like what I was about to do, but if I was quick about it, he might never know. I stopped for a moment, feeling very puzzled. Now that I knew what the problem was, I couldn't help expressing myself and put my thoughts into the spoken word.

"He doesn't know what's causing the problem. He just doesn't know. This is incredible... For a man of his skills, it's really, incredible... Ruddy hell!"

I looked at the lathe again and then towards the closed door at the other end of the room. Then I went and found a large spanner and began to tap the steel collar immediately behind the faceplate and pull on the outer rim of the faceplate at the same time. The idea was to send small shock waves along the steel in order to jar the threaded sections apart, just sufficient to allow the two to unscrew.

Half a dozen strategically placed clouts around and behind the faceplate and I knew I was getting somewhere. Then I gave the faceplate one good pull from the top; towards me, and away it came, spinning on the thread until it came away from the spindle and into my hands. Great! I was feeling really pleased with myself. Next came a search around the workshop for something to use as a spacer.

Gordon came back while I was rummaging through a steel tool box, and still feeling rather pleased with myself but, unfortunately, the subtle art of diplomacy had flown out of the window as far as my ego was concerned.

Gordon came up the length of the room and asked me what I was smiling at and also what was I doing, so, I explained, leaving out the bit about the spanner, but when I told him about the need for a different metal to act as a spacer. "A brass washer, or a fibre one perhaps?" He scoffed at this suggestion, which, sadly, only added fuel to my earlier convictions, and then Gordon went on to tell me to stop wasting time. I was speechless, which was probably just as well under the circumstances. More's the pity I didn't stay that way...

I continued to watch as Gordon picked up the block of wood he had already prepared and began to attach it to another faceplate with some screws. I found my tongue and persisted. I knew the same thing would happen all over again if he put this onto the spindle and I didn't want the same problem when and after I had turned that lump of mahogany into a bowl. I knew the solution, but did Gordon? And, would he listen? I was questioning his judgement, his skills, and his knowledge. I was so damned sure of myself that I unfortunately abandoned any sense of tactful diplomacy, and he did not like it. We didn't argue, there were no raised voices, but the atmosphere and the disagreements were heavy. In the end, I foolishly, but as it happened, successfully suggested, that Gordon should phone the Engineering department and ask Steven or Brian's opinion.

"Alright. Maybe I ought to pack you off over there out of my way as well... You are nothing but a shit stirrer but I shall do it, I will have a word with Steven and then perhaps you might stop wasting time my man. Brass washer on the back of the faceplate indeed... between it and the threaded drive shaft... is that it? the way that you, you, would describe the solution to the problem? Right then! We shall see."
Off he went, leaving me in a very reproachful mood with myself. My self-confidence was failing fast, and he had left me with stern instructions not to touch anything in the room until he came back.

Gordon was gone a long while. He went out through the door we had come in by, which meant that he was going to have to go all the way through into the main workshop and come out on the opposite side of the small yard, unless he came back and went out this way. I went and stood by the glass and steel doors to look out onto the cobbled courtyard and at the building with the door opposite. Gordon was a long while coming out of that door and I could only guess that he was having difficulties with one if not more than one of his other wards for the day. Looking to my right; at the other building, and then over to my left at the high brick wall and the curved arch in the centre, I remembered that these buildings had once been the stables to the big house, the Manor, which I could just see the front wing of. Those glass and steel doors, gave the machine room a bright airy appearance and seemed to have been the only part of the external structure of the original stables that had been altered. Where I was standing must have once been stable doors. Wood, instead of this glass and steel. Across the way, on the other side of the yard must have been more stables, or a Coach house, or even a Tack room. The other building, on my right, was, more likely where the hay and food stuffs were stored. The three, adjoining buildings surrounding that small courtyard were all single storey but with high tiled roofs.

There had been a damp autumnal coolness to the air when I had come with Royston from the Manor to this place, half an hour of more since. I looked out and upwards again as a cloud masked the sun, it must have been a small cloud because the sun came out again and the brightness hurt my eyes and prevented me from seeing the roof of Gordon's workshop opposite. I almost missed Gordon himself just then as he came out of the other door. There was a brief glimpse of a white coat in the sunshine, and then he was gone, out of sight, through the archway. How long he would be gone, I had no way of knowing... I reasoned that he wouldn't be able to stay away for more than a few minutes because any one of the other men and women across the way may need him at any moment. As for me. I had had my instructions. "Don't touch anything until I get back."

I turned and looked around the room, searching for a distraction and tried to think what this place must have looked like when there had been horses in here instead of woodworking machinery. It was difficult to imagine, but when I looked upwards to the space above the cream painted brick walls, I realised that one part of this building hadn't altered, when I noticed the beautiful old beamed roof trusses above my head. After a few minutes more; boredom, and frustration began to settle in. I hadn't achieved very much in the time spent so far in Gordon's domain, and now I had questioned his integrity, his know-ledge, and, his skills...

"This is Pauline's all over again?" Shrugging my shoulders, I continued mumbling to myself. "It's all academic now, damage done, or is it? Whatever! This is mainly all my own fault though, just when I find something that I can really get my teeth into. Given half a chance that is."

An opportunity to work this lathe had given me renewed enthusiasm, but an enthusiasm that was fast waning now as the long seconds ticked by while I waited for the Master to return. And what would he be like when he does return?

The glass and steel door behind me opened with a resounding clatter as it swung back on itself. Spinning around in alarm, I expected a shower of broken glass, but it didn't happen. Gordon sternly stepped inside, immediately followed by Steven from the Engineering department. They didn't speak and neither of them looked at me, they went directly to the lathe and Steven began examining the headstock. I stayed out of the way and even moved a little further up the room. Gordon had his back to me which left me wishing I was somewhere else. They began a discussion. I tried not to listen. Then I caught the words Steven was quietly saying. "What harm can it do?" and. "I know that… Yes… look, why don't I go and get some brass shim and we'll see."

One man in a white coat, Steven, turned without looking at me and disappeared out into the courtyard. The other man in a white coat. Gordon White. Came up the room towards me. He didn't look at me either. He spoke though.

"Don't you dare touch anything until I get back."

He had said it with such venom that all I could do after he had gone out of the door was to lean back, and then quickly pull away from the smaller lathe and say.

"Oh dear, what have I done."

Jim came in, and a few seconds later, a few more faces showed themselves. All of them were asking the same question. "What the hell have you done to upset Gordon?" Jim stayed with me until Gordon came back.

One sour look from our Tutor and Jim went out faster than he had come in. A few seconds later and in came Steven, via the same door he had exited a few minutes earlier. He carried a small box in his hands. Between them, Gordon and Steven worked on the lathe and then Gordon started the machine up and did some turning and then he stopped the lathe and did something else and then resumed turning again. Steven had stepped back out of the way of flying wood chips, and as for me... I was closer to the door now and within an arm's length of getting out of the room. Just then, Gordon stopped the machine and I stopped in my tracks. Steven edged forward while Gordon did something to the headstock area of the lathe.

"Well I'm blowed!" Came the exclamation.

It was a sound which seemed to reverberate all the way down the room, off the walls and the roof and from everywhere, straight towards my ears. They both looked down the room at me, and then they turned as one back to the lathe once more. Their faces were too far away for me to have had a clearer way of knowing, but Gordon's outcry, and now his distinct aggressiveness at the lathe seemed to tell the tale that he was trying to disprove what he now knew was right. The whining sounds of the electric motor ceased once more and this time Steven was the one who stepped forward, while Gordon stepped back. Then Gordon quickly stepped forward again and the two men put their heads together. Some very long moments of inaudible mutterings followed and then they examined the lathe once more and then, eventually, they both came up the room towards the spot I was glued to. I was cringing, I didn't want to be right and I didn't want to be wrong.

Steven was the first to speak. "You can have a job with me anytime." He smiled, turned on his heels and walked back down the room, the tails of his white coat wafted out behind him in the breeze which was coming in through the open glass and steel door, Steven turned to his right and disappeared out of that same door while I slowly became acutely self-conscious of the other man in a white coat standing beside me.

I was thinking of a time when other men in white coats had stood in front of me. But that had been at a time when I was blind and couldn't have seen those other men in white coats. Those men were Surgeons and one of them had leaned over me and told me that because of the injuries to my right eye they may have to operate and remove it. They had explained the gruesome details. They had to... But then they had gone on to say that they would have to wait until Mr Gupta came back on the Thursday. That day had been a Monday... When they had told me. When Mr Gupta came back on that Thursday, he had me down in his darkroom, and announced to the other, astonished specialists, that the patient's right eye was a hundred percent better than it had been the week before. Those men in the white coats had frightened me... Gordon was standing beside me, in his white coat, and he was giving me cause for concern... Granted, I wasn't feeling as frightened or as intimidated as I had been with the Surgeons, but I still wanted to get out of there. He was smiling and saying something.

"Well done... That's a problem that has now been solved. Well done, but I'm afraid that it's too late now for you to do any woodturning. I am sorry about that. Maybe tomorrow."

'Maybe tomorrow? Those words hung in the air as I watched Gordon leave the room. And why was he smiling? Why had he spoken to me like that? Was he patronising me? I didn't want to be patronised.

Gordon's voice beckoned me, I took one last look down the length of the machine room and closing the door on my way out we went through to the main shop to where the others would be waiting.

"Another session wasted." I mumbled to myself.

Royston's coffee table was looking good at this stage. The veneer work on the top had now been completed. All that remained to be done prior to the hard work of putting on layer upon layer of polish, was the even harder task of sanding the whole table top to a fine finish. I was admiring Royston's endeavours for the few minutes leading up to our departure over to the Manor for our coffee break. Just then, Gordon came out of his office, stood in front of me and asked.

"Are you thirsty?"

"Pardon?"

"I said... Are you thirsty? It is a simple enough question, are you thirsty? Are you ready to go over to the main building for coffee? Or would you rather stay here and help me to find out something about you?"

"What?" I asked quizzically.

"Never you mind about that. Are you willing to stay behind for a few minutes after these others have gone?"

"I suppose so."

"Good..." Then he raised his voice and said. "Alright; people, you can start tidying up now?" He turned back to me and said. "Go ahead Robert, I shall let you tell Royston to get ready?"

I helped to carefully wrap the coffee table up in hessian sacks and watched as Royston gently tucked it up beneath the workbench, as if it was a sleepy child. He then straightened up and waited, seemingly for me to go with him in the wake of the others, including Sid and Jim. I signed once more to tell him that I was staying and he should go. He could find his own way over to the Manor, so it wasn't that which was preventing him from leaving. Maybe he didn't trust me within the vicinity of his prize workmanship. No! it wasn't that either, or he wouldn't have let me touch it the way he had. The answer was quite simple... it was just sheer and simple nosiness which had compelled Royston to want to stay behind with me, with me and Gordon.

While all of this was going on, Gordon had left the two of us and had now come back after escorting a particularly ambitious blind man over to the Manor. Ambitious in the project he was working on that is, which was another coffee table. There was no doubt that Royston was proving to be an inspiration to the rest of us. Anyway. Gordon came back to find the two of us waiting for him. I explained and mentioned that I would look after Royston if he would allow him to stay.

"Oh, I'll allow it alright..." Said Gordon sardonically, and then continued in the same tone of voice. "I don't quite know what it is that makes you think Royston can't look after himself, but it might just help to serve the purpose I have in mind. Come along, come along, this way."

We followed Gordon, and he led us through to the machinery shop. Then he stood by the door and beckoned us to go on inside, ahead of him.

"Go down the room to the lathe if you will. Then I shall explain..."

"I wish you would." I said; without thinking.

"Oh, I will... All in good time."

I stood in front of the machine over which I had caused so much bother and waited for the repercussions. Royston was also curious. Probably more so than me, at least now I had a reasonably good idea what it was that Gordon would be wanting me to do. I began to wonder if Royston had ever operated a lathe. So, I decided to ask him. Gordon had left us for a few seconds to go and rummage in a wall cupboard nearby. Royston reached out for the tailstock handle at the other end of the lathe. I reached out and indicated that I wanted to sign to him... He offered me his vacant left hand while he continued to study the tailstock with his other hand and what was left of his vision. It was very awkward signing to him this way round and ask him if he had ever operated a lathe before, but I think he got the message. His hand came away from that area of the lathe and he stepped back a couple of paces, I supposed, in order to try and take in the overall image within his restricted field of vision. He stood in a thoughtful manner for the few seconds after Gordon came into his and my field of vision. Having noticed our Tutor and then looking at me once more, he shrugged his shoulders in a perplexed manner and then vigorously shook his head.

"I take it that's a no." I said solemnly.

"Right." Said Gordon firmly. "When you two have finished gossiping, here you are… These tools should suffice… When you are ready, start her up and let me see what you can do."

I was right. This was Pauline's place all over again and I was just beginning to realise. They must have seen me as a threat to their skills, talents, abilities. Call them what you may. I didn't see it that way… Janet had taught me how to type when I had been blind and on the long road to recovery… Others had helped too…

Albert and Shirley Williams. They had helped me to learn how to type, in their own way. How could I refuse, how could back down, even if I had wanted to? And I didn't, especially when, that day a couple of weeks after the accident, when Albert and Shirley had come to visit me in Hospital. They had heard that I wanted to learn how to type and that night a rather large and heavy parcel was plonked on my legs while I lay in a Hospital bed. "There you are." Albert had said. "There's a thousand pages of A4 paper to be going on with."

I had eventually learned how to touch type, and a couple of years later when I had come to this place I had fallen foul of Pauline. One of the many tutors, simply because I had learned and could type, properly. Now, the big question was… Could I do some woodturning, properly?

Gordon was looking at me expectantly. I picked up the gouge and reached for the on switch only to be suddenly stopped by the reprimanding sounds of.

"Ah ah ah… What should you be doing first? Oh! Clear the area man, clear the area, make sure you aren't going to cause injury to those around you. Come on you ought to know that much at least. How long have you been working in my department? but then you haven't, have you? Come on man, shape up."

In my own defence, I honestly thought that Royston would be alright standing where he was. He wasn't within reach. At least, not me to him… His arms were longer though. When I looked around and surveyed the situation, I didn't think that flying woodturnings might pose a hazard to him. Royston was curious but he wasn't daft. So, what was it that Gordon wanted from me? Gordon wanted me to check and make sure that he, and Royston, both knew what I was about to do. So, I signed to Royston and told him that I was going to do some woodturning. Of course, he already knew this. The puzzled look he gave me told me so... That and the signed message. "GO ON THEN"

"You have not told me." Admonished Gordon, as I turned back to the lathe once more. "You haven't told me and I am just simply about to walk past you and your lathe, you know I am here and you have not told me what you are about to do. I could be a Total for all you know. Come on... tell me... This is something I have to do and instil in my workforce all of the time. Tell me what it is you are going to do."

I was feeling chastised and also feeling rather silly. This was a bit like play-acting, but I told him, I told Gordon that I was going to do some woodturning. His response was typical.

"And if either of us should come anywhere near you during your wood-turning? What should you do then?"

"Stop the machine and warn you, or watch you... Or tell you to bugger off and keep clear."

"Come now... This is serious."
"I am serious." I said defensively. "I have worked with machinery before now you know... and I've got my own lathe back home."

"Alright." Said Gordon. "But just you bear in mind that there are others to consider, all of the time."

Gordon was right of course and he had every right to be cautious. The rebel in me recognised that fact and it made me respect Gordon even more than I thought I could. His teachings then, and also in the few, all too short weeks ahead, were to come in useful on many occasions in the future. For the present, I still had to prove that I could indeed begin to turn an almost shapeless piece of mahogany into something more attractive and useful.

Royston knew what to do, and so did Gordon. Keep out of my way, but I made sure they did anyway... Then I started the lathe up and at long, long last I was actually doing something that I really wanted to do and could do.

I had barely got beyond the 'chipping stage' which was to remove the outer roughness of the bowl and get it to a point where the eventual outside shape could be determined, when Gordon interrupted my concentration and said.

"That will do Robert. There will be another class coming in just about now, so you two had better be making yourselves scarce. I shall reserve judgement on your efforts for now. Off you go... I will tidy up."

Oh, me and my cynical mind. The first thought that came into my head immediately after Gordon had finished saying what he said, was. 'Is this another one of his tests? Should I leave him to tidy up after me?

No, I didn't. Ignoring his suggestions, I picked up the woodturning tools and went to put them back in the cupboard where they had come from, and surprisingly as I turned to go back to the lathe I couldn't help but smile as I saw Royston pick up a broom which had been leaning against the wall and he began brushing the shavings into a neat pile. This made me feel proud that he was a friend, that he had taken the initiative without even being asked to help.

Job done and the area made safe for whoever was to come in next, and all within no more than a couple of minutes. I continued not to look at Gordon, but looked at the lathe and decided that this was my bowl that I was going to make and no one else, so, I should be justified, and satisfied over the earlier issue, if I could only bring myself to step forward and remove the bowl and the faceplate, in order to put them to one side for the next time.

"Don't." Said Gordon when he realised, too late to stop me.

"Sorry." I responded, as I gave the outer rim of the faceplate a pull towards me and prayed at the same time that it would actually come free... and it did.

I didn't know what to do now and this made me feel awkward. It was the seemingly long silence that made me turn away from the lathe to notice that Gordon was signing something to Royston, then he looked at me and I asked the question that I had wanted to ask.

"How have you been getting the faceplate off the spindle?"

"Always with some difficulty, but a few well-placed blows from a hammer usually did the trick... but ... it is not the sort of thing that I let my people see me do. So just you keep that bit of knowledge to yourself my man... Off you go then!"

CHAPTER TWENTY FOUR

There were a lot of people coming out of the Manor by the time we got as far as the Porch. I knew it would serve little purpose to go inside, so we took the right-hand route around the front of the Manor towards our next rendezvous,

Sid had done me a big favour that morning in getting a listed timetable together, but we still had to find where we were to be for the first part of the afternoon, which was something Sid had strangely omitted. A lot of those around me were completely blind and some of these had no idea where to go next, I had seen this on many occasions... It happened most Monday mornings until they all had a chance to learn the timetable for that week...

A rather large crowd had just come out of the French window entrance to the Lounge of the Manor and it was this group that was preventing us going any further. Our destination was the dark green door at the other end of the narrow path between the Manor on the left and the prefabricated Crafts building. We waited patiently while the other residents filed out of the Lounge and either came towards us or went where we were supposed to be going.

There were two people I had no difficulty recognising, they were heading where we were going, or we would be soon. Going on what I knew of the Manor and its people, I had already assumed at breakfast time, that Ann and Cyril might be gone before I could have a chance of saying goodbye, but now it looked as if I was going to get that chance after all. The prospects though had suddenly made me impatient. I was looking for a break, or a chance where I might create one when a familiar voice came from behind. It was Jim.

"Where the hell have you been? Why did you stay behind? Here, there's a letter for you... Well? Why did you stay behind?"

We weren't going anywhere for the moment so I told Jim while we stood there, and immediately I had done so he turned to me in a rather alarming manner and said.

"You cleaned up as well? And all that with the lathes... I thought you had a compensation claim coming up... What's up with you?"

I looked at the letter in my hand, Janet's handwriting, I had been feeling elated in what I had achieved in Gordon's shop up until the moment Jim had come on the scene. Even a letter from Janet couldn't raise my spirits now, and I didn't even know what was in it yet. I put the letter in my pocket and looking directly at Jim, which was more than he could do at me, as I said.

"I didn't think on... I never think, do I?"

"Come on you daft bugger, come on, bring Royston and let's get inside. Just do me and yourself a favour when we get in here Bob. Take it easy... And don't keep on making out you're better than you really are. Come on... idiot."

Little did I know it, but that little incident was to be another small piece of the jigsaw. Things would get better... I would have a clearer idea of where I was going, it was going to take a little longer, but I was getting there. The mood of the moment was well and truly shattered for now though.

I entered Sally and Gerry's department a hell of a lot differently than I had left Gordon's department a few minutes earlier... and all because of me and Jim and…

"What the bloody hell's the matter with you. You look as if you've lost a pound and found a penny... Hey Cyril... Come over here and give Bob one of us cards. That's it... yeh those... the one's with our name and address... Smart eh? What do you think of these then? Which one do you want? There's Braille one's and there's good old fashioned bold black print one's... Wendy made those folks, the Braille one's that is... Cyril wanted to make 'em but I told him not to...if he did, chances are we'd end up getting no Christmas cards this year or next or ever from our blind chums would we..."

Ann moved her large bulk closer to me and quietly said.

"Cyril can't do Braille... thinks he can but he can't. Anyroad... I'm rabbiting on... You haven't answered my question yet... I heard you did alright over in Gordon's place this morning. Stirred him up a bit, pompous ass... So, why the miseries?"

I think she must have seen the question on my face, because she instantly said.

"Sid. Royston's friend Sid. He's told me just... over in the Lounge. Hey don't let's forget anyone Cyril me love, should I take some of those and give 'em out? yeh that's right come here love let me help?"

Absentmindedly, Ann began to move away from me, so I reached out and took one of the cards out of her hand and shoved it in my pocket alongside the letter from home. Then I watched events for a short while. I saw Royston doing just about the same as he had been doing on the Friday before. He was going around the room in his usual helpful manner before settling down to work on his own project, a wicker washing basket that he was making. I noticed Gerry in his wheelchair going about the business of teaching his skills to those who would learn. Sally was doing much the same, only she was more of a, 'Spread it around person' whereas Gerry was a one-to-one person. Neither of them had noticed me yet, so I knew I could dither a bit longer, if I wanted to.

"So long everyone! Me and Cyril are going over to the commerce building now, maybe we'll bump into some of you a bit more before we go, bye for now. Come on love, this way."

Heads looked up. Unfortunately, that was when Sally noticed me standing there with nothing to do.

I rather enjoyed helping Jim to help Janice Longford stuff a fluffy rabbit for the remainder of that troublesome morning.

Lunch consisted of some sort of corned beef and mashed potato, together with carrots and sweetcorn. Apple pie and custard was what followed. I looked at the carrots and looked around the room. I was looking for someone who had shared those moments with me way back in September when I had helped pick some of the Manor's own carrots out of the red earth up on the hillside behind the Manor. Were these some of those same carrots? If they were, then there can't be many of them left by now, just as there aren't many remaining of the folk who picked them.

When the apple pie came, my head was already hurting. I remember thinking, is this some of the same apple pie we had last night, in payment for helping with the musical concert. I looked up. I wanted to see where Shirley and some of the others were, but that hurt my head as well. So, I didn't look up any more... I just wanted it to go away before it got too bad. This one wasn't going to go away though. What the hell's triggered this? I'm going to need some of the special tablets, but they are down at the Lodge. I hadn't had any for just over a week, I was doing rather well... Until now...

The table moved, a voice, Laurie was saying. "Come on Chris, he's lost in a worrld of his own... Noo good asking. I'll take ye over to the commerrce building maself."

I felt glad that it was neither sunny nor raining as I made my groggy way down Middle Lincombe Road. I still had to shade my eyes though and try to control the painful and colourful flashes of light. These always gave me cause for concern because of the damage they might do to my vision.

Within minutes of arriving at the Lodge and somehow managing to reach my room and collapse on the bed, a couple of tablets were fizzing away in the cup nearby and the sounds of popping bubbles seemed unreal.

The yellow lights always seemed to be the worst, these were a forerunner and a climax, and for most of the time in between. They started somewhere in the vicinity of my nose, and even with my eyes shut, I could still see them. They started near my nose. On my right they went in a clockwise direction, while those on my left went in an anticlockwise direction. The hardest part was always in trying to get the tablets inside me, even though they were dissolved in water, it was mainly the effort of having to lift my head up from the pillow, or wherever I might have laid my head at the time. 'These tablets must not be taken on an empty stomach.' That was what my Doctor had told me. I had always considered myself to have been one of the lucky ones. At least I had never been sick during one of these attacks. "Just lie here Bob." I moaned. "You've had your lunch so just stay here until the tablets get working."

It hadn't been my intention to actually go to sleep. I awoke suddenly and for the first few seconds had difficulty in remembering where I was... Reaching automatically for my glasses I swung my feet off the bed. "I should be up at the Manor, but where at the Manor?" I had no idea. I didn't know what the time was either. The tablets were working but the bad headache hadn't quite gone away, so I knew not to let myself become anxious in case it returned with a vengeance. This didn't stop my momentary outburst though and for my exclamations to come bouncing back at me from the four walls of the room.

"Come on Bob, get up and get going."

A car passed me, going in the other direction while I continued my slow, unhurried way up Middle Lincombe Road... I was late, to rush would cause more problems with my head... Wherever I was supposed to be they would just have to wait a bit longer... A vehicle was coming along the road from behind, but I didn't take much notice of it, until it pulled to a crawl beside me. The driver said. "Come on, get in." I did as I was told, I didn't want an argument with Tim Dunce, the Occupational Psychologist.

Where have you been? Torquay... Some shopping? No? Are you alright? You don't look all that well. Come along, lost your tongue have you?"

As we drove in past the gates of the Manor I said. "No, just a bad headache."

He parked his car and then he asked me to follow him. "The sun is bright, you are obviously having some difficulty, would you like me to escort you?"

"No thanks, go wherever you're going, I'll be okay."

"But you are coming with me Robert, this is why I came looking for you, come along, this way. Call me Tim, may I call you Bob? Thank you."

He took me to a small room at the back of the Manor and to get there we had to go under the archway to the left of the Den windows. I had a thought in my mind that we were heading towards the yard where the dustbins were at the rear of the kitchens, but no we weren't. A short distance further, we came to where there was a flight of black painted steel steps on our left, and on the wall nearby, was a sign saying. Keep Clear Fire Exit. We climbed those steps with Tim still leading the way. At the top was a narrow path on our right, sloping up through a gap in the trees and low shrubs to where I suspected it would connect with the path leading towards the Pottery section. On our left, was a narrow steel bridge, this was about ten foot above the ground and eighteen foot or so long and connected to a dark doorway at the other end. By way of an explanation Tim told me: -

"This is the quickest and shortest way to get to where my office is Bob, it may look rickety but this bridge is quite strong so you don't have to worry. This way."

He opened the door at the other end of the bridge and we went down a short corridor to where there were two more doors, one went off into the bowels of the Manor and the other; on our right was his office, there was a nameplate on the dark brown door, with nothing in it.

The inner room was square in shape, it had cream walls and ceiling, a dark wood stained door and doorframe, skirting board, floor and window. There was also a matching dark wood desk in one corner, opposite the door, and there was a small window in the right-hand wall which didn't let much light in. There was a green vinyl upholstered chair in front of the desk and another one behind it, and other than an indistinct picture hanging on one wall, there was nothing else within the room, apart from the shaded light bulb hanging from the ceiling that is... There were no rugs or carpets on the floor and the whole place seemed to say... And not just say, but it seemed to shout. 'Interrogation room' Of course, this was mainly my imagination once more, and a still fuzzy head. I was here, with a clever man, an Occupational Psychologist no less. What did he want with me? Well, not a great deal as it happened. That's how it seemed anyway, because I wasn't in there for very long, a bit less than half an hour by my reckoning. Tim began by asking me a few questions about my life and the accident I had had in eighty-one. I didn't feel any need to hold anything back, in fact I was actually feeling rather relieved that I hadn't upset him or, seemingly anyone else in my late return to the Manor, and that I didn't have to do anything more strenuous than answer his questions. I can't remember everything that I told him. I may have told him a lot or a little about myself. I just don't know... He very cleverly brought me forward in time a short while later and stunned me somewhat by asking me what I wanted to do with my life from that point in time... After some thought I leaned back in the chair, looked straight at him and said truthfully. "I don't know." He seemed to know. Though I still don't know how he or any of them knew, considering that at that time I had only the vaguest idea myself. Tim fingered his beard as he studied me and then said.

"I think you're best suited to craftwork, Woodturning perhaps? Or, Rush seatwork? Now there's a skill if you like... Oh, oh Yes... I have had a word with Gordon as it happens... and he tells me that you did alright working with Rush, but he also got the impression that it was perhaps; insufficiently challenging for you… However, there does seem to be something else here to do with you… Something even I cannot put my finger on... What do you suppose that something is?"

He was asking questions I didn't have answers for. I just shrugged my shoulders and sat there. What else could I do? Tim got to his feet just then and came around the desk. He stood over me, calmly and matter of fact, he said.

"You may go now if you like... it's quite close to the mid-afternoon break... would you like me to show you the way back?"

I declined his offer and as I left his little office I couldn't help wondering, who had the most confused look on his face... me, or him.

The headache and flashing lights were gone, which left me with a fuzzy; dazed sort of feeling, but not sufficiently dazed to prevent curiosity from taking me along the path at the other side of the bridge, which was after I had left Tim

Dunce's place, and yes I was right in my Manor grounds geography guess-work.

I had gone down the steep tarmac path to come out onto the yard in front of the Porch when I came across Royston and Jim and a few others. Jim was speaking "I'll say she was... Acker Bilk, eat your heart out. Hiya Bob."

Jim wanted to know where I had been. When I had finished, he said.

"I've been asked to take Royston to see that same guy after tea break... How does a guy like that get a name like that? I ask you... Tim Dunce! Weird or what? You don't fancy doing me a favour here do you Bob? You see, I'm at a good stage in learning braille and I'd rather be there than do this with Royston... Can you take him for me? I'll tell Wendy what you're doing, besides, you don't like her place, so come on Bob, before we go inside, say you'll take him for me... Please."

We were in amongst a lot of other residents as we were about to enter the main hall, and someone up ahead was holding the old oak doors open for us. I was momentarily distracted by something, someone, but couldn't be sure. Whatever it was, was lost now in the thick of the crowd. Absentmindedly I responded to Jim's continued prompting and said. "Yes, alright... but will you do me a favour as well?"

"Yeh... name it, if I can I will."

"Something's bothering me and something else is now... What's that up front? is it a dog? Oh, we'll see in a second or two... Anyway Jim. I had been thinking that I would have typing this afternoon but apparently, not now. Can you find out why, without making a fuss I mean."

"No sooner said than done... I'll call in at Pauline's before I go in Wendy's place, I want to know why I'm not down to be with her this week as well, leave it to me Bob... Mind! ruddy hell Royston, don't do that... Did you see that? he bloody near walked into the table... This way... Come on. Hey! It is a dog. There, going in through the door to the dining room, thought they weren't allowed inside. New intake Bob, must be... probably doesn't know."

The crowd got thinner inside the dining room. Seats scraped noisily on the wooden floor as folk went and sat down... I left Jim and Royston to go over to the far side of the room to where me, Laurie and Christopher... and! I stopped in my tracks. Denise collided with me. Samantha gave me a puzzled look for stopping the way I had. I apologised and moved on out of the way...

Yes! It was him. I wasn't mistaken. This was Adrian. Adrian had come back. And he had a dog with him, a guide dog. A black one. There was a lot of commotion going on around our table, people were wanting to stroke the dog. I saw Sandra coming up the aisle. She looked at me and I at her and then she said, rather sheepishly, as if I deserved, or warranted a reason or an excuse, for what was going on. Which I didn't consider I did, but I got it all anyway, and more, when she said.

"Dogs shouldn't really be inside, especially in the dining room... but you only have to see him... Adrian is such a changed young man... Now, Robert, I would like you to do me a favour if you will… Christopher here; has an appointment with Tim Dunce, that is where you have just come from I believe, so would you be kind enough to take Christopher to Tim's room after the tea break… "

"But…"

"Allow me to finish if you don't mind Robert… As I was saying. If you would just take him, and afterwards, bring him back to my office if you will. You may then have the remainder of what would have been your session in the Braille room all to yourself. Do this for me Robert and I will be grateful. Is that alright with you Christopher? Robert will take you just as soon as you have both finished here. Ah, just look at Adrian."

I had to squeeze past the small crowd who were making a fuss over the animal, so as to sit at the table in my usual place, while the young man that I could hardly recognise stood proudly with his dog in the aisle... Not for long though. Laurie distracted my attention by reaching across the table and got me to move from my usual place and over towards the wall, then he told me to help Adrian to sit down beside me.

Well! What a change in this young man. What a transformation. Could this really be just because he had got himself a guide dog? He had only been gone for a couple of weeks... This was amazing. Really and truly amazing... More's the pity that the break wasn't longer and I could spend more time with Adrian. There was so much I wanted to say, to ask, but, although Adrian was brighter and of a much-changed personality. He did seem confused by all the attention he and the dog were getting, so I thought it better not to intervene, it might only add to the confusion. The poor lad was still completely blind and nothing was going to change that side of his being.

I had no sooner drank my cup of tea when I noticed Royston coming up the aisle towards my table and me, followed closely by Jim, presumably; to make sure I kept to my word... I could tell that Royston was full of anxiety and this was what made me have to get to my feet... the action of which caused Chris to hastily, and clumsily get to his feet as well, which brought a yelp from Dollar, a cry of anguish from Adrian, and a cursing from Laurie.

"What the! will ye noo be moorre careful Bob."

Just to compound the situation further, Ann and Cyril were also heading up the aisle. I dearly wanted to stay but I couldn't because Christopher was getting anxious as well, and all of this would take too long to explain to Royston. I wanted to have a better opportunity of saying hello to Adrian and goodbye to Ann and Cyril than this.

Squeezing past Adrian, I bent down to stroke his dog and straightened up just in time to receive a whacking great blow in the middle of my back. Ann was laughing at this as I turned to see a nervous smile on the face of my friend.

Someone nearby on one of the other tables asked Ann what time would they be leaving. Ann told him that a taxi was coming at five o'clock. "Good." I managed to get a word in. "I'll try and catch you before you go. See you in a bit Ann... Cyril. Looks as if Royston's getting a bit anxious as well as Chris, I'd better be off. Jim can bring Royston, while I help Chris, please Jim."

Royston ignored the dog which was now seeking a quiet place beneath the table. A few others were beginning to leave the dining room so, off we went.

We were just going out into the corridor from the dining room when I heard, over and above all the other sounds, a high-pitched male voice which had a hint of its Jamaican origins and a curious American slant to it. "Adri! Adri my man."

I didn't want to hang around the main hall too long. Christopher was getting more and more anxious. We stood by the oblong table as I tried to tell him there was nothing to worry about. I couldn't be sure if he was happy enough with this explanation, but what else could I do? And one look at Royston and then a quick glance at the receding figure of Jim, left me wondering what sort of nonsense Jim might have been filling his head with. Royston was certainly frightened over something. I tried telling him about Tim Dunce and his job. and was halfway through spelling the title of. "PSYCHOL... ogist." When Royston quickly withdrew his hand and threw up his arms in despair.

By this time a lot of the residents were coming out into the hall to congregate for a few minutes before setting off for me next round of assessments. Chris was shuffling about nearby. A smart looking young woman with dark glasses, dark hair and wearing a blue trouser suit, came forward out of the crowd and reached for the oblong table. Having found it, on her own. I watched as she fingered her way to a point at the far end and stood there as if she was waiting for someone.

Jack Townley and Ian were there as well. I noticed Jack say something to Ian and then he went to the blind woman in me blue suit and offered to find her a seat. In the general noise, I heard her say.

"Oh no... Thank you all me same, but if I sit down someone is sure to come and make a fuss. It happens all the time. All I have to do is to sit down, anywhere, and someone always comes up to me, so I would rather stand if you don't mind... I think a man called Terry? He's supposed to be meeting me here... I only started today you see."

Jack turned away, noticed me and then he gave me a wink with his good eye.

I was just about to indicate to Royston that it was time to go, but then I became aware that Christopher had moved closer, and he was now speaking to me in that slow deliberate way of his

"Do, d,d, do I have to go with you, Bobbb?"

"Yes, Chris, it seems that you do. A bit of help from Jim would've been good but."

"Sorree." Said Christopher apologetically. I looked up at him. He was nearly as tall as Royston, but broader across the shoulders. I was sandwiched between the two of them while the hall was fast emptying around us.

"Come on Chris, you don't have to apologise."

It wasn't an easy task, getting a deaf and half blind man. As well as a crippled, half blind man, out from the Porch, across the yard and up the steep slope around to the back of the Manor. There were plenty of others who might have helped me but didn't. They were all going to the daily living skills bungalow, or gardening, or towards the Pottery. Thankfully, Christopher was pulling himself along by using the silver guide rail but his progress was painfully slow. Royston was managing by himself, but he was impatient, and I still couldn't tell if he just wanted to go and get it over with, or not go at all... In the end, as easy going as Royston was, even he couldn't force himself to hang about any longer... He came back down the path to me and indicated that he wanted to say something. I held out my hand.

"GOING FOR A SMOKE TAKE HIM FIRST"

I indicated an area of the gardens for Royston to stay within. The last thing I needed was to go searching for him when Tim Dunce had finished with Christopher. It wasn't a deliberately planned outburst, I was only speaking my mind, when I said.

"And what do I do when the psychologist has finished with Chris?"

Oops! Christopher wasn't deaf, he wasn't daft either. A little out of breath, Christopher came to a stop behind me and looked back down the path, then he turned his attention to me and said.

"I th, erm think I... Sorree, I think I c,c,can get baaack on on my own."

I felt guilty now.

"No way Chris, forget I said that, I didn't mean it to sound like that. Come on my friend we're nearly there. Mustn't keep the 'Occupational Psychologist' waiting, must we?"

A bit further on and we were on the path in front of the bridge. Christopher took one look at the narrow, steel footbridge with its handrails either side and backed off in trepidation. I went forward and like a fool bounced up and down in the middle of the bridge to show him how study a construction it was... I even muttered to myself. "I hope I'm not going to have to do the same as this for Royston." Then I managed to coax Christopher onto the bridge, and said.

"That's it, come on, we're only about ten feet up from the ground, look, well, maybe not... Sorry Chris... sorry, I'm not sure how much you can see."

"Eeenough." Came his cautious and concentrating response as he stepped forward on to the bridge.

Tim Dunce greeted us at the inner door, the door to his office. He seemed surprised that I should be there and he asked me in as well. I declined, so Tim took hold of Christopher's hand and helped him inside. The door closed and I went out and across the bridge to stand in the shade of the Manor and the surrounding trees. There was a tantalisingly cool, late autumn breeze in the air. There were multi-coloured leaves on the ground, in shades of gold, green, brown and red. I looked up at the bare branches of some of the trees and at the green of the evergreen trees nearby and then at those higher up the hill and then I looked at the slowly darkening sky high above. It was so peaceful and serene and the cool tranquillity of my surroundings were helping enormously to calm my fevered head. I began to think of home... They had already experienced the first snows of winter back home. Indeed, I had too, when I had gone home for Janet's dad's funeral. Here though, two hundred miles or so south, there was still the climate altering effect of the Gulf stream to keep the worst of the winter weather at bay. I correctly anticipated that Christopher might be in there for a while longer than I had been earlier on, so I went to check that Royston was alright and then came back.

I hadn't anticipated the possibility of having some help, never mind the task being done for me, in getting Christopher back to the Manor, and I was quite surprised, not to mention taken aback, when Tim Dunce and Christopher came and crossed the bridge and then set off on the way back. This left me feeling a little flummoxed, to say the least. So, I called out.
"There's none so blind as them as can see."

They both stopped and Tim turned around and said. "Ah that is where you are, I rather thought that you had gone and left us... Would you mind repeating what you just said?"

"What? There's none so blind as them as can see?"

"Quaint, I must try to remember that one. Here you are then, I am handing you over to Robert now Christopher. There you go, and now I need to find Royston Hickman. Christopher tells me you three came up here together, do you happen to know whereabouts he is."

"Over there on the other side of the bungalow, there's a white bench, he's there, just follow the smell of tobacco. Will you bring Royston down or shall I come back for him?"

"Last one of the day, I shall bring him back, you don't have to worry, now where did you say?"

Christopher and I waited by the guide rail just long enough to make sure Tim found Royston and then off we went.

No one else was about, except for a group of three men who were doing a spot of gardening, they were too far away and indistinct to make out just who they were. This was the last assessment lesson of the day. All of them were assessment lessons, where the powers that be, were constantly assessing each of us for our abilities, talents, skills or whatever. But they were also assessing each and every one of us for the way we coped with our own, particular, and unique eyesight problems. Everyone was different. There seemed to be more cases of blindness through Diabetes, than any other cause, but even here, there were differing degrees. I was the only (RTA) Road traffic accident, in the whole of our Intake. I was waiting for an outcome to my claim for compensation. The accident had happened at the end of June 1981, now it was the end of November 1984... Near enough three and a half years since it all began.

CHAPTER TWENTY FIVE

The main building was silhouetted against a darkening blue sky. We entered via the Porch and I left Christopher with Sandra. Job done, the finale for me that day, was to be Mobility, so it seemed perfectly logical to stay in the main hall and wait. Surprisingly, there were quite a few other residents dotted around the hall as well. Nearby, just outside the Care Staff office, stood a neat pile consisting of six large suitcases. I nudged Malcolm Tipper and said.

"Those cases. I suppose they must belong to Ann and Cyril... It'll be a shame to see them go."

"Can't say as I'll miss them Bob, they're just ordinary looking cases, as far as I can see... Only joking. Salt of the earth is Ann, and Cyril isn't too bad himself... They'll both be missed... Won't be long now Bob before it's your turn. Got any ideas on what you want to do when you leave... Buggered if I know what I'm going do. Oh aye! almost forgot. Wendy's... Braille! Come in, come in Bob. She gave me a message to pass on to you... wants to see you after school, you've to go over to her place when you get back from mobility. Da, da dada da dada dada dada...funeral march...Hey up, here they come. Grab your canes, grab your hats and grab a bum folks, here we go. Sorry

Helen. Message from Jim as well, Bob. Typing tomorrow, first half of the last half. No, no, I'm wrong, Tuesday tomorrow. Pauline's on Wednesday though, you caaan't get away."

Gillian Roberts and her associates came on the scene. There were four of them, and six of us. It didn't take all that long to sort us out, and the only female Mobility officer amongst the group, was the one who got the lions share to deal with.

We were standing just outside the Porch entrance; it was going proper dark now and we were beneath the pool of yellow light which shone down from above the archway. The woman named Helen went off, away and down the drive with the bearded man; Andrew, the quiet studious man. The sound of a cane, tap tapping on the hard ground gradually faded away into the distance, the same as it did with the next one to go. The tall, bespectacled figure of Janice Longford went off around the front of the Manor with another man. Then a man whose name I couldn't remember, went off with another mobility officer, whose name I also could not remember. This left Royston, Jim and myself... and Gill Roberts. Jim was in a bubbly mood and he was prancing around in front of us... Royston didn't seem to have any idea what to do, he looked even more confused than he did before going to see Tim Dunce, so he just stood there with one hand on my left shoulder and then I heard Gillian saying to herself... "What have I done to deserve this?" By this time, it must have been around half past four, or maybe just a little after. Half an hour, or less. Not much time left in which to say goodbye to Ann and Cyril. Or even get in a mobility lesson. As for the mobility lesson? what a lesson that nearly turned out to be.

"Come on you three, line up... stop that James."

"Oooh, James is it now?"

"Oh, please, will one of you tell Royston to line up?"

"I'll do it, I'll do it." Chirped Jim.

Gillian, in her long black coat swished around us within the pool of light, and when she seemed satisfied, she came and stood in front of us and I could now see her face, which was lit up by the light from above. The evening darkness wasn't the pitch-black sort of darkness that we had to contend with. That was perhaps another half an hour away yet. This was the something past four; onset to winter darkness, where there was also a cold chill and the smell of autumn in the sea air. I was feeling alright now, the headache had gone and it had left me with a weird light headed and slightly euphoric feeling. There wasn't much to see beyond that pool of light, but I didn't feel afraid of what lay out there anymore... What with the confidence that was slowly being instilled in me, and the use of a cane, and in the grounds of the Manor, then I knew I could face this old terror of mine, or did I? Another test was about to come.

Before Gillian said, what she was about to say, there came voices and the clicking of a cane to my ears, then the voices became clearer and I recognised them to be those of Jack Townley and Ian. They came around the corner from the front of the Manor and as Jack saw the four of us, he came towards us.

"Way wunna disturb thee, lads and lass just want t'get past and inside. Wayve just bin up in t'th'woods may an'th'youth'ere, an'aye's doin'alreet atna lad? At they alreet Gill? Cost manage theyse thray by theesen?"

Jim chipped in with a pronounced translation. "Are you alright Gill. Can you manage these three gentlemen on your own?"

"Not bad Jim." I found myself saying. "Not bad at all for a Manchester man."

"Aye not bad." Said Jack as his voice and a faint hint of movement and the sound of a cane on tapping the tarmac went off ahead of us. "Tell thee what 'ay conna spayk it rayte I'll bet, not like way con Bob."

"And may too" Exclaimed a younger male voice. "Come on Jack."

And with that they were gone, inside the Porch and out of sight. Next came a complete surprise from Gill Roberts as she got my attention and said.

"I've thought of something... I was going to tell you to go and see Wendy at five o'clock but you can go now I think, yes, and it might prove useful training for you if I let you go there on your own..."

I interrupted her. "Easy, I can get from here to her place with no trouble." Just for once, I was devious and quick enough to realise an opportunity for a venue of a more important nature.

"Not, the way I am sending you, you won't, I want you to get to Wendy's by going around the sunken lawn. I don't know if you have noticed on your travels around the gardens, but there is a small path which leads off to the right on the far side from here, do you know it?"

"No."

"Well I want you to find that path and when you do you will come across the commerce building, turn to you left... Are you listening? turn to your left as if you're coming towards the main buildings, go along the path and turn to the right at the corner and the rest of the way to the entrance should be familiar enough... have you got all of that? Off you go then, I shall explain to Royston, either I or James will before the three of us make our way down to the lodge, and use your cane, go on… Shoo."

The silver guide rail was found soon enough. On my way I had been making a token gesture, I did tap the cane on the ground in front of me a few times, just to let her know I was using it, but once I had my hand on the guide rail, I began thinking there was less of a need. Gillian wouldn't be able to hear me now anyway, so I moved on and followed the curve of the path and rail as I made my way to the far side. I knew that Gill had hastily devised a test for me and the cane, but this was almost too easy...

I should have done it first as last. It would have been far easier if I had stood there long enough for Gill, Royston and Jim to go their way and then backtracked on myself and gone and done what I really wanted to do before it was too late. But, daft as I am, I went the way she had wanted me to go and when I arrived at the far side of the sunken lawn and could see the windows of the typing room set low down against the dark outline of the commerce building, with a sea of shrubs and small trees between me and what should have been my goal. I stopped then and began to take stock and looked up, straight ahead to where the disembodied lights from the windows and the dark shadowy bulk of the Manor towered high up above the embankment. I could only see the lights of the Manor now, the building itself was lost in the background of darkness. No one else was around. I had come this far easily enough and without having to use the cane... apart from that token gesture a few minutes earlier. I had been feeling pleased with myself, but it was darker now. Much darker, and where was that path? Ever gullible I had allowed this to happen, to be stuck here, in the dark looking for a path I wasn't particularly interested in finding and hadn't even known to exist. Gill had told me there was a path which would take me through the dense shrubbery between the sunken lawn and the commerce building, but where was it? "Sod this, I'm going back before it's too late.

Mission unaccomplished. After leaving the rail and the darkness behind me, I was now standing beneath the curved stonework of the Porch entrance once more and made my way inside.

I heard them talking as I went to open the inner door. Ann and Cyril and quite a few others were standing in a group. As soon as she saw me, she came and threw her arms around me.

This was an emotional moment for them both; but, unlike most of the other residents I had seen depart in the past, it seemed as if Ann, if not Cyril, wanted to make the most of the occasion. Ann was pulling me into her ample bosom and almost smothered me with affection. There was a small group of residents nearby who they had clearly just been saying goodbye to, and then, just as if to emphasise the sadness of this parting of the ways, a man came and opened the door, saying. "Taxi for two, Newton Abbot station."

Ann stopped abruptly, straightened up and let go of me. The whole place fell silent for a few moments. I looked at Cyril and then at Ann. Was there a tear in Ann's good eye? It was hard to tell. Her voice, when it came, was controlled but it was also high and excited as she became instantly busy. She no longer looked directly at any of us as she moved towards the suitcases, but the taxi driver and Sandra were ahead of her. She stopped with her back to us, she fell silent again and so did everyone else. Then I saw her adjust the eye patch, and did she surreptitiously run her sleeve against her face? I doubt if Cyril could have looked any more miserable than he had done since the moment the Taxi driver had arrived on the scene. I had only ever seen Cyril one stage worse than this and that was when I had first met him in the gardens all that long while ago... Ann was the first to speak, she turned and said.

"Well folks, time to go. Bye Sandra, wish the rest of the care staff all the best from both of us. See you Frank, Bert, Alan, bye Jessica... So long the rest of you."

I wanted to be there. And yet, I didn't. This was such a sad occasion. I had been trying to prepare for this event all day long... I might never see these two again and I wanted this parting memory to be a good one, I think we all wanted that to happen, but how can sad farewells ever be good, or even memorable?

The task of carrying the suitcases having been done for her. The only thing Ann needed to concentrate on now, was to stay in control, at least for these last few minutes and help her husband towards the way out. The final leg of the journey through life at the Manor was almost over for these two. It was always going to be hard for all but the most cynical. Those large old oak doors were being held open, a new life out there was beckoning two more people. It was time to go, to leave the Manor behind and begin that long journey home and throughout the rest of their lives together. But before they could begin to do all of this, there was something that Cyril wanted to say. There he stood, in his grey suit. Small in stature, but tall and proud in his achievements, and I could tell that he was trying to visualise his surroundings and all of us standing there as he slowly moved his head, and said.

"There is a God... he's inside us... he's what we are... he's in this place... he'll be in our home as well... That lad just now... he was wrong... I know he was wrong..."

Ann took hold of his arm and they moved silently towards the door. They didn't turn, or look back, and we didn't follow. Some wanted to and moved forward, but Sandra stopped them.

"It's best this way." She said softly. "We don't want to see a big tough lady like Ann break down, do we?"

We all stood in silence for wants of something better to do as much as anything else... Ann and Cyril had gone. They would be getting into the taxi, the engine would be running and, in a minute or two, they would be moving off, down the long drive, away from the Manor and away from those of us who were left behind.

The silence didn't last long, thirty seconds or so at the most... Then, just as we were about to break up and go our separate ways, there came a cry of dismay from the balcony above. I instantly recognised the voice to be that of Laurie. He hastily made his way around the balcony and came down the wide staircase carrying his bagpipes. Without any further delay he came past me and out through the main doors. I looked at Sandra and all she did was to shrug her shoulders before going back in her office. As she was about to go out of sight, I heard her mention something about 'an old Scottish tradition' to one of the other ladies in there.

A tall, well-dressed figure I knew only by the name of Alan, was standing closest to me. He turned to me and said. "I'll miss those two... I suppose a lot of us will... Never mind, at least I've got their address."

"Aye, so have I." I responded eagerly, reaching into my inside jacket pocket and pulling the card out. With the card came the letter, the letter from home that Jim had given me that morning, I hadn't had an opportunity to read it. I excused myself and headed for the Lounge to read my letter.

Behind me came the sounds of many voices as the residents came into the hall in readiness for their evening meal. Ahead, from the open doorway to the Lounge there came even more of a noise as the crowds came in by way of the French window entrance and were quickly filling the room. I did think about going somewhere else but where else could I go? Anyway, I might just be lucky enough to find a quiet corner in the Lounge.

I had no sooner gone inside when I had to quickly step to one side out of the way of Shirley. The look of anger and disgust on her face, and her eyes bulging behind her glasses, made me look and wonder just what had happened. She looked at me in passing and said.

"Really, I have 'Never' heard anything so disgusting in all my life."

I watched her go and then my attention was captured by a thin looking man in his late thirties. The crowds coming in to the Lounge from the far end were noisy, but this man and the group with him were even noisier. The man had thinning black hair and dark glasses and I knew him to be one of the so-called Totals, he was within a group of about four or five other men and women and most of them were laughing, but this man was laughing the loudest as I heard him say.

"I only said I'd farted in the bath last night and I thought I'd done something else, but it was only the bar of soap. What's Miss prim and proper getting all worked up about something like that for?"

I didn't say anything. I just made my way to a spare chair near the bay window and sat down to read the letter from home. It read...

Dear Bob   *23ʳᵈ November*

Frank Pepper came today with some papers from the Post Office Union Solicitors. They want to know when you will be coming home and if they can contact the people down there for a progress report on your rehabilitation. I didn't know what to say to them, can they write, and if they do who do they write to, I don't know. Ian Allwood's been here as well. He sends his regards and he said that he will call to see you in the new year to sort out how he can help you when you come home. The girls are fine but they miss their dad and I miss you too. It won't be long now before you come home.

I'd rather have you than this money they keep sending me. I miss you Bob and I Love you. Can you ask someone there who the Solicitors can write to please because I don't know what to say to them.

I Love You.
Janet, Carol and Paula.

P.S. Your Mum phoned a few days ago, she wants you to phone her and she said you can reverse the charges, you know your Mum.

"Yes. I know my mum..." I muttered to myself... And then, a shiver ran down my spine and I looked up... A lot of others looked towards the windows as well... None of us could see out, it was too dark now, out there. The gong reverberated loudly out in the main hall behind me, the familiar sound came in through the open doorway, calling us to our evening meal, but the sounds of the gong were an intrusion to that other sound coming to our ears. The entire room had fallen into suspended silence... All ears were listening to that other sound, that mournful wail out there in the darkness. Someone quietly opened the French windows at the other end of the Lounge and a cool but gentle breeze filled the room, bringing with it the heightened sounds of Laurie and his pipes.

There was a fellow Countryman of Laurie's there with us in the Lounge. It was he who was the first to speak. He spoke softly.

"Ah, the Piperrr's lament, a lament for the loss of his Princess... He walks the heath beneath the dark cloud invading his lands, the brraken strrewn hills beckon and hold his soul, and noo man has a way t'goo fer fear of walking in his footsteps the while he plays."

286

Trust someone to break the spell. Jean came to the open door of the Lounge and called out. "Come on you lot."

I stayed long enough for the room to empty except for me and two others. One of whom was Jim. The other person was sitting patiently in one of the easy chairs nearby. Jim had edged over towards me as the others were filing out into the main hall. We were both in the bay window recess, looking at the jet-black shiny glass. Jim had his head on one side in that all too familiar way of his, I looked back at the window and out into the impenetrable darkness and said. "I thought you didn't like the pipes?"

"I don't." Was his simple response. There was silence... I looked back at the man in the chair. Then Jim spoke again. "I don't, but by God he can stir your emotions. He's finished now... Come on let's go and get some snapping before it's too late... Are you going to bring Royston, or shall I?"

"I'll do it. You go on ahead Jim."

Just as he was on his way out of the Lounge doorway, Jim turned and said.

"Hey... Laurie was playing that for Ann and Cyril I'll bet."

It was my turn for a short and simple response. "Yes."

"Hey, how did you go on with Wendy, Bob?"

"Oh damn, I forgot."

There we were just the four of us. Adrian, Christopher, Royston and myself. There were others of course, but we were mostly left on our own. The four of us were sitting in the Lounge where we had been for the previous half an hour or more.

Adrian had been extraordinarily lucid in his descriptions of the guide dog training centre where he had spent the last two weeks learning how to handle the dog that was now his prized possession, but it was more than this dog, which, incidentally, Adrian and I had brought in from the dog kennels behind the Porch entrance, almost immediately after the evening meal was finished. This dog, named Dollar, was Adrian's lifeblood, they were bonded and it was easy to tell that it was by more than just Dollar's training. Dollar was what Adrian had always wanted, ever since the operation to remove a tumour had robbed him of his sight. It was what he had set his heart on and what had kept him going, and now, now that he had finally achieved his ambition, all he could do was to talk about her and the places they had been. He had told us of an open space, where there were buildings which echoed and sounded empty, and lots of dogs barking, and men and women handlers, and of going along the streets in a small town, which was not really a town but a mock-up of one where there were loads of obstacles, like cars parked on pavements and lampposts on the edge of the kerb, and other lampposts which were set back on the inside of the footpath, and Pelican crossings. And people who pretended to be aggressive people who hadn't any time for guide dogs or blind people and didn't want them blocking the footpath. Then Adrian had trouble describing a new and intriguing invention for us visually handicapped people, especially when it came to him pronouncing the texture of some areas of footpaths when he tried to get his frustrated tongue around the word 'tactile' Once he had started to talk, it was as if he had to try and get it all out and tell us what it was like before he forgot it all, and the poor lad had already forgotten my name on two occasions since we had come out of the dining room. On more than one occasion, but at one point in particular, he began to seriously wander in his narrations. With a bit of difficulty, I managed to get him to calm down for a few minutes to give him a rest, and then I looked at Royston, sitting in an easy chair nearby. He hadn't heard a single word of what Adrian had been saying and he was at the wrong angle to have been able to lip read. I continued to watch as Royston idly allowed his limited vision to wander. He hadn't seen me looking at him. I looked across to Christopher. He hadn't said much either, he had seemed happy enough to just sit there and listen, to be allowed to be a part of this small group. I had seen a lot of people shun Chris in the time he had so far spent at the Manor, and it had been good to notice a sort of kinship developing between him and Royston. When we had all come into the Lounge and Christopher had managed, with difficulty, to formulate the words he had wanted to say and ask if he could join us. Even though Royston had not heard his request he welcomed Christopher's presence with the ever-friendly pat on the back routine.

Having rested for all of one minute and I doubt if it was a second longer. Adrian suddenly started to speak again... This was at around about the same time that Jim and Josie came into the Lounge. Jim noticed us and came over towards us. Behind Jim, I noticed another man entering the room, this man was more smartly dressed than Jim and he also walked a lot slower and he had lost his oriental smile. This was Peter. I hadn't seen him all day long. I gave up my seat to Josie, partly chivalrous I suppose, but more to do with going to have a word with Peter, but I had got to my feet and moved away without remembering to explain to Adrian that I was no longer there, and the poor unfortunate just carried on addressing a bewildered looking Josie. Until Jim started to put him right that is. I went over to Peter and managed to persuade him to come and join our little group but thought it best not to press him for a reason for his misery. Looking around me at the familiar faces I was reminded of a simple fact that there was not a decent pair of eyes between the seven of us. There was silence within our group. Adrian had stopped speaking again, but not for long. It didn't take Jim many seconds to get Adrian and most of the rest of us talking again. After a while, even Peter seemed to abandon his crestfallen look and he actually joined in with part of a conversation. And there we might have quite happily spent the rest of the evening, or until supper time at the very least, if it hadn't been for the intervention of Shirley and a vaguely familiar couple in their early twenties when they came in and headed towards us.

CHAPTER TWENTY SIX

They were dressed for going out, and I for one had forgotten about the promise made the previous evening, to go to a meeting concerning an organisation which the young couple represented, called. The Torch Trust for the Blind.

Of course, Jim knew all about it. His attitude was a lot keener than mine was. All I wanted to do was to stay there and glean a bit more information from Adrian about the guide dog training centre, but before I knew it. Shirley had stepped over to Royston and signed to him, something which obviously excited him. Then she rounded on the rest of us, and as there was no escape route, Shirley managed to somehow get all of us, Adrian, Christopher and Peter included, to go with her and the young couple to where a mini bus was waiting near to the main entrance.

On the way to get our coats I managed to sign to Royston and ask him for a reason for his willingness to go out. The beaming smile and the reply I got, was.

"GOING FOR A DRINK"

I turned to Shirley. "You crafty beggar... going out for a drink indeed."

We went out, from the corridor leading to the dining room where we had just retrieved our coats and joined another group standing beside the oblong table.

There were five people in this group. Our seven, and the three organisers, made a total of fifteen. Six women and nine men... While Shirley ran around us like a sheepdog herding sheep, I looked at each of those around me and was trying to decide just who and by how much I could depend on my fellow residents as well as the organisers for a bit of help out there, in what I intuitively knew would be strange territory. And then I began to look on the problem in a different way. 'How many of these-folk might want me to help them? I had been in this situation before, and I had a pretty good idea that I was going to need some help. How many were going to need some help that night I wondered... Royston? Maybe. Christopher? Certainly, someone was going to have to help him. And then there was Peter, and yes, Adrian? Adrian has got his beautiful black dog. Any opportunity to go out with his dog seemed a golden opportunity for Adrian, and it might be interesting to watch what happened, if I could. At any rate, Dollar shouldn't let her master down, even out there in the dark. Yes, Adrian would be alright... Three of the five others were completely blind and these were all women. I only knew one of the other two men by name and that was Frank, one of those earlier on who had seen Ann and Cyril off. One of their many friends, and any friend of Ann and Cyril was a friend of mine... but Frank didn't quite see it this way. Frank appeared to be able to see about as well as I could, which doesn't say a lot but at least I thought he may be able to help with some of those who couldn't see. Frank had other ideas though. As soon as I approached him as a possible ally, it was as if I had suddenly developed a bad case of body odour. He moved away from me, and indeed, he even moved away from the entire group, and this was despite, or maybe because of the herding techniques of Shirley. I watched him walk quickly away and climb the wide stairs to disappear behind the balcony rail. Shirley called after him but then she had to double her efforts to keep the rest of us together while the two organisers of this evenings outing, just stood looking rather perplexed at the antics of Shirley. I wanted to go too. I wanted to stay within the safe and solid confines of that ancient building, but one more glance around the people standing there made me realise that there were friends of mine within this group who were about to go out there, to goodness knows where, for an evening out. I couldn't desert my friends. Or, could I? I would have to, but just for as long as it would take to go over to the Lounge and get the white cane... I had a pretty shrewd idea that I was going to need that cane a fair bit earlier than I had originally thought I would that night.

"Robert, where are you going?" Cried Shirley.

"Back in a minute."

I had come out from the Lounge and was making my way diagonally across the floor of the main hall when I noticed something amiss, something was wrong, and as usual, Shirley seemed to be at the centre of it all, but I was wrong. Shirley was trying to help someone who was at the centre of it all.

This was a man of about average build, aged around forty and he was sitting on one of the benches surrounded by Shirley and a few others who were tending to his bleeding nose. Sandra came from the direction of the Den, she was carrying a wet tea towel and asked me to move out of her way. This I did and then looked around me for an explanation. Then I noticed the strangers in our midst. They were standing near the main doors. Three of them. Three men in their late teens, all dressed in blue track suits and white trainers on their feet. Sandra, having placed a cold compress on the poor unfortunate's face, then stood up and looked at the three men and asked.

"How did you say this happened? You were out jogging, the three of you, and you ran into him? Couldn't you see he's partially sighted? Or are the three of you blind?"

"Sorry," Said one of the men. "But we did bring him back here..."

"I should think so too... What else might you have done? Left him lying out there?"

Another of the men turned defensive and said. "Where's his thingy? I didn't see one. If he'd had one of those white things we would have known. He should've been using one if he couldn't see us coming."

"That is no excuse as far as you are concerned young man." Reprimanded Sandra. "This isn't the first time this has happened, the night before last? I can't understand, of all the places in the whole of Torquay, your Coach sends you along Higher Woodfield Road... Why?"

"It's one of the hilly parts." Said the first man sheepishly.

"Go on... Get off with you. I shan't be asking your names, but I shall be questioning your Coach's so-called training methods when I catch up with him... Go on boys, before I change my mind."

The old oak doors opened, they closed, and the three men were gone. Sandra then turned to our group and singled out Shirley and asked her to leave the man alone and go and do whatever she was supposed to be doing before all of this had happened. I was close enough to see that Shirley had got some blood on her hands, which meant that she had to go off and wash her hands before we could finally leave for the destination that I was so unsure of.

While Shirley was gone for the two or three minutes it took to wash her hands, three women and one man broke away from our group and scurried off as fast as their respective limited vision would allow each of them to go. That one man, was Royston. In the general confusion, Jim had told Royston that we were not going to a pub after all.

Jim and I stood watching the back of Royston hurrying towards the Lounge, as he was telling me what he had done. I would sooner have joined Royston if it hadn't been for the curious advances which were now being displayed by Peter. He was asking for me by name, and Christopher was pushing him in my direction. Peter stood by my side and gave one of his best oriental type smiles and said.

"Sorry about the other day Bob... Having a bit of personal trouble that's all... I'd appreciate a bit of help tonight."

"So would I."

"Oh, does that mean you can't help me, I wanted to go to this group Bob, I'm beginning to come over all religious."

"Come on... Shirley's here again, there's no escaping now... let's get going."

Adrian was in the lead. Jim suggested that this was the best thing to do, so as not to confuse the dog. Our two hosts were next, followed by Jim escorting Josie, and then there was myself with the dubious honour of escorting both Peter and Christopher. The one remaining person who had been a part of the fivesome standing by the oblong table a few minutes earlier, was now attempting to do as his colleagues had done and slip away. Shirley was bringing up the rear though and she wasn't going to let this one get away. He did though, but his escape opportunity would not happen for a few more minutes yet. I took one last look back at the scene we were leaving behind and felt saddened by what the scene reminded me of when I thought for a moment about Ann and Cyril, but then I looked at the lonely man holding a cloth against his face, and Sandra's attentive attitude towards him. Then there was Shirley coercing the man behind me to go along with the rest of us.

We stood for a few moments beneath the arch of the Porch entrance. The yellow lantern from above threw a pool of light out in front of us, beyond that there was nothing but the black of a moonless night, and there was a cold wind blowing. Brian and Anthea Palmer had just introduced themselves to us and tried their best to put us at ease. Then Brian had gone out into the darkness to bring their minibus a little closer to where we were waiting.

I unfolded the cane and tapped the sections together. "Better to be ready." I whispered to Jim. I then watched as he and Josie did the same with their canes. Then, Peter pulled a cane out from beneath his jacket and did the same as we had done. I looked quizzically at Christopher, and then there was Shirley. Where was her cane? Shirley was standing behind us, no doubt blocking any chance of retreat for those of us who might have a change of heart, and a lot had, so far... I could hear the engine revving now as the transport moved nearer. I looked behind me once more and dared to ask the question which turned a few heads including those who couldn't see. "Where's your cane Shirley?"

A reply was quite remarkably slow in coming, and as it did, the rear doors of the minibus were already opening to welcome us aboard. Shirley moved forward and quietly admitted that she had stubbornly declined offers of mobility. Jim scoffed at this and suggested a different theory as he stopped his and Josie's forward momentum and said.

"None of them will teach her Bob, because she's the one who tries to do all the teaching."

Of course, truth or not. Shirley had to defend herself and as she was doing so, I couldn't help but notice the stealthy method the unknown man adopted as he quickly and quietly slipped away down one side of the mini-bus, out of sight, preferring an excursion into the black of night to a trip out with the likes of us. I didn't say anything, I stepped into the spot he had just vacated and climbed aboard, pulling Christopher in behind me.

Shirley never even missed the man, until we were more than halfway along Middle Lincombe Road.

Shirley and the woman named Anthea, talked incessantly all the way to our destination, which was in a village of sorts somewhere around five miles from the Manor. They both tried their best to involve the rest of us in with the various, mainly religious topics that they covered and the now famous concert. Shirley seemed to have forgotten about the mobility incident, but I hadn't and neither had Jim... It was at a particular uphill climb when the old engine up front screamed and complained when Jim leaned towards me and said.

"What say we have a word with Gill Roberts or someone and get Shirley sorted out, she needs help with mobility and she should get it."

Talk of teaching mobility, I was glad to have been taught more than just a little about white canes by the end of that evening.

The first thing we had to do upon disembarking from the rear of the minibus was to sort ourselves out and then walk about fifteen yards to the front door of the white house across the narrow street. The ground beneath our feet was covered in thick gravel. There was the gable end of another brightly lit white house situated on our left, but this was at an acute angle to the one opposite and so too was the pub over on our right. No building seemed to be in conventionally straight lines. I knew there was a pub on our right by the amount of people nearby, but more so because of the coloured lights and the smell of beer drifting downwind. There was a tall tree close to and the wind was rustling in amongst the branches and more than likely tugging at the few remaining leaves. There was good street lighting and plenty of welcoming light coming from the place we were heading for.

Adrian and one or two others began to move off across the narrow street. I remarked that we could have brought Royston after all, but Shirley chipped in with a reminder that we were not here for the beer, we were here for matters of a much higher plane. I tried to take in as much as I could manage to see of our surroundings before deciding to follow in the wake of the others. I looked upwards to where the apex of the cottage on my left stood out stark and white against the night sky. Cars were strangely absent from the scene. Apart from the vehicle we had arrived in there were no more that I could distinguish in the area around us. Christopher had just gone with someone else, and I began to feel concerned about our immediate surroundings and having to get Peter safely across the road between that gravel strewn patch and our destination. As I have already mentioned, the street lighting was good, but the scene at ground level, for my eyes at least, was anything but good. It was too patchy. Still, I only had a short distance to go to where the others were already waiting and encouraging us to join them.

From what little I could make out of our shadowy surroundings I had already developed an image in my mind of a village street like a scene out of a Miss Marple film. Jim called out once more. I stepped forward, and took Peter with me. I may have managed to be foolish enough to think that, on my own; I might have been able to cross that narrow street without using the cane, but not with Peter in tow... In the back of the minibus on our way here we had both managed to resolve our differences and to agree how daft we both had been towards each other. I couldn't let an error of judgement spoil all of that now, so, with Peter holding on to my left arm I began swinging my cane in the conventional manner as we stepped forward. The only trouble was, we had no sooner gone from the gravel, plus a few paces across the hard surface of the road, when Peter started swinging his cane from side to side as well. This was alright, at first, at least we seemed to have some sort of synchronisation going between us, but that didn't last for more than about five or six paces, then we began to have a clash of canes. We battled, good humouredly, he still continued to hold onto my arm, and we made it, all the way to the front of the well-lit cottage, where the others were waiting for us. We then started to follow them down two steps to the wide open, well lit, low front door.

I was the last to step down and inside, and just before I did I looked at the cane in my hand and I think it was at about this particular moment in time that I began to really accept that white cane, not just for what it stood for, but for what it could do to help me.

The interior of Mr and Mrs Palmer's cottage was warm, inviting and very cosy. They had the sort of seating which seemed to wrap itself around you, floral and thickly upholstered. It was obvious that they did a lot of entertaining of one sort or another, because there were two three-seater settees and four armchairs in their surprisingly spacious lounge. The floor was covered in a plain beige carpet which was thick and new looking. The low heavily timbered ceiling made for the general atmosphere of cosiness, the walls were white with just three pictures, one on each wall, and with a rather large ornate mirror over the fireplace, but there was no roaring fire in the grate, instead, there was the bright red glow of a gas fire. In the corner to the left of the fireplace stood a dark wood and glass display cabinet. This was directly opposite the door that we had come in through. There was a pair of dark red curtains hiding the window which was to the left of the front door. To the right of the fireplace was an opening to the dining room and then the kitchen beyond that. Anthea and Shirley had just disappeared into the kitchen and I could hear the tinkle of china coming from somewhere around the back of the chimney breast. Brian stayed and expertly got us all seated, he was so good at this that he even took each of our canes and casually talked to us as he folded the sections together, before putting them to one side. Something about one cane in particular caught his attention though and stopped him in his tracks.

"Oh." He said out loud. "This is something new, is this what they call Velcro? whose cane is this then?"

Well, that broke the thinnest of thin ice as far as I was concerned. I had already been made more than welcome. We all had, right from the start. They were a really nice couple. They were both young. In their late twenties I would have guessed, and yet the furniture of that cottage seemed to be more in keeping with a couple in their mid-forties or fifties, but what did that matter. It all suited their personality anyway. Given his opening opportunity to explain about the Velcro, I modestly... Yes modestly, told them about the project that Gill Roberts and I had begun. Even Josie seemed intrigued by it all and she wanted to feel the Velcro for herself. I was watching as the cane got passed around and gave an explanation to the effect that I had only been the go-for and that it was Gillian who was developing the idea. "Talking of which." I said. "Where is Gillian? I thought she was supposed to be coming here with us."

"Oh, she was otherwise detained." Explained Anthea, as she walked in carrying a tray of crockery. I watched as she bent to put the tray down on a low table and then she straightened up, and smoothing her dark green dress she looked at me again and continued. "...but never mind that. What has a gopher got to do with helping Gill Roberts. A gopher is an underground animal isn't it?"

Jim was quicker than me, but that was no surprise. He laughed easily and explained. "What Bob means is that he was a 'go for' not a 'gopher' You know... go for this, go for that, go for the other... He got the necessary and Gill's doing the rest... Anyroad... Let's have a proper look at this stuff then... No not you, me first Shirley... Aye, it's alright is this... When can I have some on my cane? It's better than black elastic... I'm going ask Gill for some of this. It's alright for Adrian, look, he doesn't need a cane now."

Dollar was sitting by his feet and Adrian was sitting low down in an easy chair and had one hand on his dog all the time. He didn't say anything, he quietly accepted the refreshments when they were offered to him and on the whole, I think he was just simply enjoying the pleasures that his new eyes brought to his life.

Adrian and Peter were the only ones who didn't handle the cane. By the time that cane of mine had been handed around and the rest of the occupants of that quaint cottage had each had hold of it and tugged and pulled at it and done up and undone it, the inevitable went and happened. Shortly after Christopher had managed, with quite some difficulty to handle the cane, look at it, and then hand it over to Josie, and considering that this was only one of the very first prototypes, it was little wonder that it came apart after being handled such a lot, and it was a shame it did just that; just as Josie was trying to feel what it was like. The Velcro and cane became separated. Josie was quick to show concern for what had happened. Jim immediately changed his opinion of it. And when I looked across at Peter to see what he might have to say, I was genuinely surprised to notice that he had gone to sleep. Brian handed the two components back to me with a sheepish grin on his face and then we tried to console Josie as well as Christopher, because they both thought they had damaged the cane in some way. Suddenly. Everyone's attention was drawn to the corner of the room to where the slumbering figure lay, feet stretched out in front of the fire and with his upper body half buried in thick floral upholstery, Peter gave out another deep grunt, buried his head further into the cushions, and began snoring. One person spoke. "Really, I don't know." Said Shirley in a soft, slightly embarrassed voice.

Well... With the obvious exception of Peter, who readily agreed anyway, when he eventually woke up later on and had had his tonsils lubricated. We all ended signing up for the Torch Trust for the Blind. If signing is the operative word. Which it isn't because we didn't sign anything, we just agreed that Brian and Anthea could put us on their mailing list, so that we could each get a Braille magazine three or four times a year. Free of charge, courtesy of our new found friends, and the free postage for the blind service, run by the Post Office.

Tea and biscuits, good and intelligent conversation. And, much to the dismay of his wife, together with a welcoming nod and then a cry of "Sacrilege!" from Jim, when Brian stepped forward and poured a drop of the hard stuff into his second cup of tea. Avoiding the reproachful looks he was getting from his wife, as well as from Shirley. Brian continued by saying. "It will help to keep out the cold... Sorry Jim, I didn't realise you may prefer your brandy neat... It won't do any harm Anthea... At least none of them are driving tonight."

The look of dismay on Shirley's face, and the polite refusal, was a picture in itself. Josie and Adrian declined as well, but I didn't and neither did Chris or Peter. At least this was something that could and did wake Peter up.

About an hour later we were in the mini bus on our way back to the Manor, and I had a warm comfortable feeling in the pit of my stomach. Two tots of brandy, pleasant company and I was content, and just about in control. Adrian sat by the rear door with one arm around the neck of Dollar. She was a good dog and had remained in control all evening.

I'm not sure how we managed to get from that cosy cottage to the Palmer's mini bus, but we somehow did, and I vaguely remember trying to help Peter again, and then, Jim, Peter and myself seemed to lose all decorum, by having a sword fight on the gravel near the back of the mini bus. It didn't last long.

Soon we were being helped into the back of the bus, and apologising to Anthea and Brian, and Shirley, and Josie, for our behaviour. I tried to help Chris, I shouldn't have, but I did anyway, tried I mean... He was wobbling all over the place. Jim suggested something about Chris not being able to hold his liquor and I think he was right. Chris had enough trouble keeping his balance in normal circumstances, without this as well. Fortunately, Brian and Anthea were able to see an amusing side to all of this, and I think we would have had a bit of fun anyway, even without the drink. Theirs was such a welcoming place, a warm and inviting place, a place where you could unwind, go to sleep even, but generally, anyone and everyone could relax in their company and in their home. Brian and Anthea were proud of their cottage and its contents, but were not possessively proud. The soft furnishings and that deep beige carpet were there for the purpose of being used, not just for looking at, but then... How many Manor residents who had been there to the Palmer's home, could indeed look?

They stopped outside the gates to America Lodge to let us out, and the Palmer's carried on up to the Manor with Christopher, Peter, Shirley, and the two inseparable's, Adrian and Dollar. I stood and watched the red tail lights receding into the distance and then I unfolded the cane and followed Jim and Josie up the drive.

CHAPTER TWENTY SEVEN

I was about half an hour late in phoning home that night and quick to settle that little problem, then I looked in at the Den and decided that it was already crowded enough without adding my presence, so I went upstairs to do an hour or so revising and learning a bit more of that damned Braille system.

The Manor's rules were such that it was a case of lights out and in bed by half past ten. At the Lodge there were no such rules, you went to bed when you were ready, but another five minutes of running my fingers over a multitude of

298

dots and I would have been ready for the mad-house. I had to get out and the only place I could think of to go was downstairs.

The long corridor had seemed busy enough with residents coming and going along its length, but the scene was very different when I arrived downstairs standing in the dimly lit corridor near the Den. Hardly anyone was about. I could hear the steady rhythmic sound of someone typing in the room ahead and to my left. I looked up at the large face of the old brown clock and noticed the time was twenty-five past eleven. I glanced through the partly open door of the typing room but couldn't see who was in there. The Den was a lot quieter than it had been earlier and a lot less people in there too. There was Barry, our music conductor of the day before and Jim and Josie. Josie was pulling some clothes out of a dryer at the far end of the room. Jim had already been reprimanded for attempting to help Josie with her 'smalls.' He told me so, and advised me not to offer my assistance. Barry was sitting on the other side of the table, near the cooker. His slumped posture and his quiet manner told me that he must have been out for a drink, and maybe more than one drink at that. This was Barry's last week at the Manor. He had something to celebrate in the success of the concert, but he also seemed to have something to be sad about at the same time, and it showed, he just didn't seem to know what to do with himself, and strangely enough, he didn't want to talk to us either. A few more minutes of self-imposed misery he got to his feet, mumbled something of a "goodnight." and off he went to leave the three of us mulling over his departure and his moodiness, the concert, and to also discuss the events of the evening and our visit to the Palmer's home.

At somewhere just after twelve o'clock, Jim and Josie decided to call it a day. I still wasn't ready for bed so I stayed. It wasn't long after they had gone when I became acutely aware of that old slumbering building and nearly all of its people safely tucked up in bed, but in the knowledge of what I knew of America Lodge, the sounds of silence were a little unnerving to say the least.

I made my way to the sink and began to wash my cup, but didn't relish the thoughts of having my back to the ever-open entrance to the Den in case someone, or something, should come in behind me.

Someone did… So quietly did he approach that I just did not hear him. I instantly jumped and the cup fell to the floor when Jack Townley's voice penetrated the silence.

"What's they doin'ere? Ah thowt as owe on yer'ud bay in bed be nah. Theyat rayte jumpy atna? Thowt ah were bad enough. Anyroad, dunna mind may Bob Ah've only come dine'ere from th'manor, ite o'th'road."

For the benefit of those who need it, here is a translation of what Jack said.
"What are you doing here? I thought as all of you would be in bed by now. You're right jumpy, aren't you? Thought I were bad enough. Anyroad, don't mind me Bob. I've only come down here from the Manor out of the road."

I bent down to pick up the broken pieces of the cup as Jack came into the room to pull out a chair and sit down with a heavy sigh. He waited a few moments before continuing. He didn't want the drink I offered to make, he said he just wanted to sit and think. I got ready to leave him to his thoughts, but rather suddenly, he changed his mind and asked me to stay.

"I'm bloody mithered dust see Bob. It's yon lad, Ian... Well, may'en'im'er gettin' on rayte enough, too bloody rayte... but wayen gooin wom in a few dee's an'ay lives dine at one end o'th'country an ah'm at t'other as tha nowst, snag is, ay bloody wants come live wi'may, an'ah dunna know what do abite it... Ah'll tell thee... Fer th'wants o'rayte thing do, this's fost time fer a long time as ah've bin stuck... Dunna say nowt Rob... Ah's only using thee fer a synding board that's owe, sumwun talk to tha nowst... Eee, ah'll tell thee, Ian's come a long wee since that dee in'th'gardens when way wun swaypin' up th'layves. Turning point in'th'lads life was that dee... Knew ay'ad it in'im, just knew it... Aye that ah did... aye... aye... Reared three lasses... Owe on me own... an'ah reckon as ah've done an'doin'a fair enough job as'd mak me missus proud o'me... e'en if ah does say mesen. Lost th'missus ower Rita tha knowst, 'er's th'youngest lass... aye... Tell thee what, 'er's more like th'missus thun t'other two... Aye, and that's t'other problem... bloody'ell... Tha cost tell ah'm mithered costna? never thowt as ah'd bay lark this. Ah've come ower owe weird... Thowt as a walk dine'ere'd clear thowd'ead… but dust know? Ah'm buggered if not one of me lasses wus more of an'andful as that lad is..."

"I am worried Bob. It's Ian. Me and him are getting on all right, too right in fact, but we are going home in a few days, and he lives down at one end of the Country and I am at the other, as you know. The snag is, he wants to come and live with me, and I don't know what to do about it. I will say this, for the want of the right thing to do, this is the first time in a long while that I have been stuck. Don't say anything Bob, I am only using you for a sounding board, that is all. Someone to talk to you know. Now I'll tell you, Ian has come a long way since that day in the gardens, when we were sweeping up the leaves. That was the turning point in the lad's life was that day. I knew he had it in him, just

300

knew it, yes, that I did... yes...yes... I reared three girls, all on my own, and I reckon that I have done and doing a fair enough job that would make my wife proud of me, even if I do say so myself. I lost my wife over Rita you know. She's the youngest daughter... yes... I'll tell you what, she is more like my wife than my other two daughters. Yes, and that is another problem... bloody hell you can tell that I am worried, can't you? I never thought that I would be like this, I have come over all weird. I thought that a walk down here would clear my head, but do you know? I am buggered if not one of my girls was more of a handful as that lad is."

I could understand every word Jack was saying, and I also knew what he was implying as well... I could tell before, many weeks before in fact, that Ian and Rita, were something that was meant to be. I had seen them together the day before as well, the day of the concert, and they looked good together then, even better in fact. Maybe Rita's mother was looking down on them and persuading a kindly God to move a mountain or two and bring them together.

Maybe Jack's accident had happened for a purpose? Deep down at the bottom of a mine, a sliver of coal had embedded itself in Jack's right eye in a freak accident caused by a pit-prop. His eye was white and useless and wasted... Was the whole thing just a useless waste? Why did Ian's rich father buy Ian that fancy expensive sports car, and why did Ian have to go and crash that car in the way he had? Was the whole thing just a complete waste? Or was it meant to be? In the great scheme of things, did Jack and Ian have to suffer? Did they really have to suffer just so that they could be brought together years later, here at this place, at this particular fraction of time?

Jack had been quiet for a while, and so had I. I allowed some of my thoughts to translate themselves into the spoken word and broke the silence by saying.

"Why are we here? I mean, what's the purpose of all this? You know... Life, and... Life, and, and the universe, and all that? What's the meaning of it all?"
Jack looked quizzically at me but remained thoughtful for a few moments longer, and then he said, softly and in a matter-of-fact tone of voice.

"If I knew that, ah'd bay a self-righteous pompous ass. If it wus thesen as knew, they'st bay same as well, and so wud every bugger else as thowt they knew... The's only one God'o'mighty, an'ay inna sayin' nowt. That sort o'thing inna fer th'likes of us to know, an'tha shudst realise it... Tha shudst get things lark that ite o'thee mind Rob, thee'ead inna big enough tak it... Do summat useful... put yon kettle on an'mak they an'may a drink."

301

Once again, a translation, for those who might need it: -

"If I knew that, I would be a self-righteous pompous ass. If it was yourself that knew, you would be the same as well, and so would every bugger else as thought they knew... There is only one God All Mighty, and he isn't saying anything. That sort of thing isn't for the likes of us to know, and you should realise it... You should get things like that out of your mind Rob, your head isn't big enough to take it. Do something useful... put the kettle on and make you and me a drink."

We sat, quietly, side by side at the table, both of us holding steaming mugs in our hands and both of us nurturing our own thoughts. Jack was perfectly right of course. It wasn't and isn't for us mere mortals to understand the true meaning of life. Try as we might, the true meaning of life, the universe and everything, remains tantalisingly out of our reach... And that is how it should always be... If ever we found out... What then for the human race?????

I felt tired. Confused and tired... I wasn't sure what more to say… but then…

"Jack…I reckon th'best thing as 'as'appened to that lad Ian, is sitting beside me… Janet, my wife Janet, she was one of three lasses, Joan, Janet and Joyce… three girls, all with the initial J… Janet's dad was a farmer… I think he tried for a son but he got three girls… Janet's mum had rheumatoid arthritis, she had it for long while, years in fact, it must've been hard for Janet's dad to run the farm and look after his wife and three girls… But then, he got me when I married Janet… I were always more than glad to help out on the farm, and Janet's dad… Janet's dad, by 'eck 'e were a fine man… died a few weeks ago… fine man… did me proud he did Jack. Gave me the hand of his middle daughter, and I'd be nowt without her, or me two girls… As for you and Ian? Well! what have you got to lose Jack? what have you got to gain?"

I don't know from where that last bit came, but I quickly realised just how poignant it was, and thought it best to leave it there.

Just as I reached the door, Jack coughed and then his chair scraped on the floor. Reaching into his jacket pocket, he drew something out and offered it to me.

"Here Rob, this's a sycamore seed... funt it this afternoon, up in th'woods... Tak a look at it. Wun wing's bigger'n t'other, designed that way, so as t'kaype it on th'wind longer... Them's weird… Aye, and, wise words, theyst just said, Rob, for a confused beggar like theyat, anyrood… but if tha cost tell may 'ow

302

a sycamore con think on t'mak a seed like that, wi'wings, when th'bloody tree conna see in th'fost place... Well... dust'ear... Theyst bay th'smartest mon in th'world."

"Here Rob, this is a sycamore seed, found it this afternoon up in the woods. Take a look at it, one wing is bigger than the other, designed that way to keep it on the wind longer... Those are weird... yes, and, wise words you've just said Rob, for a confused beggar like you are anyroad, but if you can tell me how a sycamore can think on to make a seed like that, with wings, when the bloody tree can't see in the first place... Well... do you hear... You would be the smartest man in the world."

I've still got that seed, all these years later, but I haven't got any of the answers.

That night I climbed the stairs to my lonely room with a heavy heart. Maybe it was the brandy? The company? Ann and Cyril going home? Not for the first time did I want to go home... Life... If there aren't any answers, there is one certainty. It is far too short... There was so much I wanted to do... and I wanted to do it all with Janet, my wife. I was coming to the end of my time at the Manor. Seventeen more days, seventeen days and I will be going home to Janet and my two girls.

Reaching the top of the stairs I paused awhile. The long corridor stretched out ahead of me, dark windows on the left and white doors on the right with not another person in sight... I found myself speaking to the spirits of the place when I said. "What a day... What is it with this place and the Manor that makes me feel so, so melancholy, and so confused? That good man back there... Jack... He doesn't seem to know just what he's done or capable of doing... He is the best thing that's happened to Ian. And here I am talking to myself, again."

I must have sat for a long while, on the edge of my bed before doing something. By this time, it must have been around one o'clock in the morning and I still wasn't ready for bed. I couldn't think what to do. I had thought of going out for a walk and take the cane with me, out there in the dark, the dark I was strangely getting more and more used to every day, but I couldn't bring myself to do it... In truth I had had enough for one day.

"Come on Bob, get undressed and get in bed... Nah, I anna ready for bed... Paper! Paper? you poor tired sod, talking to yourself, why's paper come to mind? Pen and paper?"

Well, I got some paper and a pen, and sat on the edge of my bed again, with the desk in front of me. I had no idea what I was about to write. These feelings had occurred before, in this room. I had already made some notes on some of the things that had happened so far. But this time was different. The feelings were stronger... I had an urgent need, a desire to write... But to write what?

I did some almost illegible scribbling, and then some slightly more legible scribbling, and then at long last, it started to come, very fragmented, and not quite all at once... Not at first anyway... No... What I was about to embark upon in that early hour on the morning of the twenty eighth of November nineteen eighty-four, was just the beginning. I needed a starting point though. Or did I? This was hard, so hard. I had a few attempts and then gave up that particular approach... I felt like a log in a fast-flowing river full of logs and I was up front. My attempts at finding a starting point was holding the rest of the logs up. I had to let go and allow whatever it was in my mind to express itself... I wrote and I wrote and lost all sense of time. Time had no meaning. What I was writing, had little or no meaning.

After a long while I stopped and looked around. The floor was littered with white screwed up bits of paper. There were even more papers on my bed, but these weren't screwed up. Some sheets were neatly stacked, one on top of the other. I took off my glasses to rub my eyes, then I put them on again and looked at the latest scribbling's.

The folk he will take with him. A shilling's not worth a shilling if he leaves them   The rogues on the road. He needs to.

I picked up another piece of paper.

The horses are... Straining, strong and straining, reins are tight

in his hands. If a man had a If a man's

A journey is ahead of someone, me

304

I picked up another sheet of paper from the pile on the bed.

a man must hold on

If a man's got hold on while His heart is breaking A journey lies ahead

onwards,

life's end but there's no fear, he hasn't any.

There were no more words, at least not readable ones on that page. There were others, other pages, but I couldn't be bothered anymore. I gathered up all the bits and pieces and shoved them in a drawer and then got into bed.

It wasn't many seconds before my mind entered that confusing, half awake, half asleep state where the brain tries to make sense of what has happened that day... I was far too tired to do anything other than to mumble something to myself. "If I'd still been on the Post, it'd be time for me go to work about now... Ruddy hell... perish the thought..." I pulled the sheets up under my chin and lay back in the darkness of my room and knew no more.

I awoke to the sound of alarm bells and someone knocking on my door. Then Jim came in, told me it was just a fire drill and then dashed out just as quickly as he had come in. It didn't take me long to get dressed and follow all the others downstairs and out to the front of the Lodge.

Beryl had come down from the Manor. She stood in the half light of a winter's morning, wearing a dark thick woollen coat and gloves and was holding a clipboard in her impatient fingers.

We had hardly begun to assemble ourselves when she started calling out our names. I stayed on the path, and so did a lot of others. Jim was part of a smaller group who were standing on the grass a few yards away. I couldn't help noticing his bubbly personality and it puzzled me, and a few others, that someone could be like he was at that time of the morning. I looked again while Beryl worked her way through the alphabet of surnames. I didn't need to listen too intently. My name would be a while in coming. Jim was playfully taunting some of those around him. Barry was standing next to me, he looked at me and said: -

"Whatever he's on I'll have a double helping."

Having covered the alphabet as far as and beyond the letter G, for Grice... Jim and most of his group started to head back to the warmth of the Lodge. Then he noticed me and cried out.

"Hey Bob... Hiya... Hey, listen to this... You should know this one... See if you do... What spends all its life in a corner and yet goes all around the world? Come on... What spends its life in a corner and yet goes all around the world, oh, come on come on, you're not quick enough... He isn't quick enough, does anybody else know?"

"Robert Weaver." Shouted Beryl.

"Er, sorry! Yes, I'm here." I then turned to Jim and said. "I give in Jim... What is it that goes all around the world and yet spends its life in a corner?"

Beryl had finished and was on her way down the drive back to the Manor. A few of the residents followed in her wake, while the rest of us made our way back inside the Lodge to get ourselves ready for another day up at the Manor. I was heading for the Lodge entrance when Jim decided to put me and whoever else might be interested, out of our misery.

"Fancy... You being on the Post and all that. The answer is... A stamp, a stamp spends its life in the corner of an envelope, and goes around the world, well it can, I know most of them don't, but do you get it now? Good joke or what?"

Strange how I never noticed how really cold the day was, until I ventured out, about half an hour later. I was one amongst many, and we were without Jim. I pulled the collar of my jacket up around my ears, shoved the cane behind me in my belt and then, thrusting my hands deep into my trouser pockets I walked in the early morning light and followed the large talkative group ahead of me.

A surprise was in store for me, for me and a few others after arriving at the Manor.

 I was casually blending in with the usual large crowd in the main hall, while we waited for the breakfast gong to sound. So far, I had met up with Peter, and then Samantha and Denise, and I was just about to greet my silent friend, the gentle giant, when a familiar voice cried out from a few yards away. This was Jim. Someone had gone and popped his bubble. I might have been just a little bit glad that someone had, if it hadn't been for the seriousness in his voice as he pushed his way through the crowds to stand in front of me and said: -

"What a cock-up. What a bloody cock-up... The ruddy nerve of them. They've only gone and changed everything around, that's all. And I mean Everything! Where you were yesterday... Forget it... Where you thought you were today... Forget it... Same goes for me, and Royston here. And Josie... In fact. Now I come to think of it, what they've done will more than likely concern our entire intake group, huh, what's left of us that is... Have we got time? come on let's go over to the commerce building and find out proper. Oh blast, it'll have to wait... damn that breakfast gong. I'm going help Josie... Straight away after breakfast Bob... Straight away, me and you're going over there to find out exactly what's going on."

"Right, Er, right..." Was all I could manage to say. Jim melted into the crowd and then a large hand gently came to rest on the top of my head. Royston. I turned around to look up at him. He knew something was wrong. He must have been able to lip read at least some of what Jim had been saying because he had a concerned look on his face as he gestured for my hand and began signing. "WHAT ABOUT WOODWORK"

I couldn't do, or think of anything, other than to tell Royston to come to me after breakfast and we would go and find out what was going on.

With the fast diminishing crowd heading for the dining room, and us two tagging on at the tail end, we just had to leave the situation at that.

Inside the dining room I managed to temporarily forget about what lay in store for us, this was mainly because of what was happening by the time I got to my table. A few tables down, there was some consternation. Our new House Captain was trying to attract attention. A rugged, no nonsense man swept past me and said. "Shurrup and sit down Graham...leave it a bit." Graham did as he was told.

Just then, my attention was diverted towards the late arrival at our table... This was Adrian... and behind him came the dining room ladies with our breakfast.

Dog-less, and clearly disappointed at being so, Adrian checked that this was his table, then he felt for his chair and sat down beside me. Adrian didn't say much, in fact, I don't think any of us did. We just sat there and ate our meal.

307

The House Captain got his opportunity and spouted the usual dialogue and then the dining room began to heave as the residents, almost as one, got to their feet and started to leave the room.

The natural flow soon spilled out into the main hall and it was here that I noticed that Adrian had found a benefactor in the ever-obliging Jack Townley. Adrian was making quite desperate pleas, urging his guide onward towards the main entrance, he was holding onto Jack's right arm and I shouldn't need to say who was holding onto Jack's left arm... I had a good idea as to where they were going, the three men were heading for the kennels.

Meanwhile. Three more men were about to head for the Commerce building. and the shortest route would be by way of going through the Lounge.

A tall, fair haired young woman was standing by the French window, she was in her early twenties. As we approached, I recognised her to be one of a recent Intake. She had been, albeit briefly, a friend of the other young woman who couldn't take to the Manor and had gone home. I didn't know a lot about this young woman but I knew she was blind, and just like many others there at the Manor she wore dark glasses, but that wasn't all she was wearing, or not wearing as the case may be. Closer still and the anxiety in her clearly showed. I stood there like a fool and tried to take in this transformed vision before me and also had a lot of difficulty trying to compare her to how I had seen her the week previous. Although I did notice the many rings dangling from her ears. I hadn't noticed the one through her nose, until this moment. I hadn't taken her to be anything more radical than any other young woman in her early twenties. I couldn't remember what she had been wearing when first seeing her but it certainly wasn't what she was wearing now. Royston nudged me and I looked round in time to get a 'thumbs up' approval. Jim was quick, quicker than I had expected. He stepped forward and said.

"Hello Ros, remember me? Jimbo? Where're you off to all dolled up? Wow! any shorter and that red skirt would make a good belt... right material anyroad. What do they call these? Fishnet tights eh?"

I thought just then that Jim might have stepped out of line, gone overboard, or whatever... but this young woman; he had called Ros, short for Rosalyn, I think. Anyway, she could certainly fend for herself. Blind or not. Jim backed off just in time. He seemed to decide not to mention the silver studded black leather jacket Ros was wearing. Instead, he renewed his earlier approach by saying. "Can we get past you love... Or do you want to come with us?"

For the first time, I heard Ros's voice. It was a sweet Kentish accent and seemed in total contrast to her outfit, so much so that I looked her over once more, just to make sure that I wasn't seeing things… ahem…! Where was I? Oh, yes… Ros looked in the general direction of Jim's voice, then she seemed to read our minds, because she continued by saying.

"Yes, I would like some assistance, why the bloody hell do you think I'm stood here… When you have finished ogling, perhaps we can go now can we?"

With a wide grin on his face, Jim took her by the arm and we followed, me and Royston. Others followed, but we three were in the lead.

Rather strangely, I was surprised when Royston caught hold of my upper arm the moment we had stepped outside beyond the French window. This was daylight. He didn't normally need to do this sort of thing in the daylight. Even with his tunnel vision I knew he could manage reasonably well as long as it wasn't dark.

As we walked in the wake of Jim and Rosalyn I began to realise. I chanced to look up at Royston and then I followed his gaze, straight to the rear of the girl in front. I was his guiding eyes, his escort, while he looked in another direction. You can't blame him; us… we're only males. Trouble was… I was the one who had to look where we, the two of us were going.

We made our way down the concrete steps and along by the low brick wall at the base of the embankment on our left, and as soon as we turned to our right and entered through the glass doors of the commerce building the girl up front and Jim, parted company. She went one way while Jim stayed where he was and watched her departure for a second or two… Then, with that curious way of his. He turned his head towards the wall, he looked back the other way and once he was sure it was safe, he turned to us and said.

"If that girl doesn't make Steven hot under the collar then he aint no red-blooded male. Come on let's see what idiot's been messing up our week, get over here and help me Bob."

Steven came in through the glass doors while we were looking on the board. Quite a lot of residents were coming in as well. A couple of minutes later, in came Sandra… by this time we had sorted out the confusing arrangement of coloured geometrical shapes and translated their meaning into the entirely new schedule for the remainder of that week. Jim challenged Sandra and she said: -

"It has little to do with me boys... Just take it that this new schedule will help... You don't have to make a big fuss over it. If you've sorted out, on your way."

Most of the people had come through the glass doors and dispersed to the various departments by the time Jim had written three copies of the new timetable. Royston, Jim and myself were already late for the first session of the day, in the Crafts department, but there was very little enthusiasm from any of us. Royston was all for going over to Gordon's place and ignore the new timetable, until I pointed out to him that all that had happened here was that they had changed our morning around and, altered what we should be doing in the afternoon as well, but he was annoyed and also confused and he wasn't the only one. Jim looked at the piece of paper and read out what the new schedule was and I translated the relevant parts that concerned Royston, and the rest of the new schedule went like this.

Crafts. Royston, Jim, Josie, Bob, Peter.
Coffee break.
Woodwork. Royston, Jim, Bob.
Braille. Peter, Josie.
Lunch.
Typing. Jim, Bob, Josie, Peter.
Remedial's. Royston.
Tea Break.
Braille. (3 to 4pm) Royston, Jim, Josie, Bob, Peter.
Mobility. (4 to 5pm) Royston, Jim, Josie, Bob, Peter.

"Hold on Jim." I said. "What's happened to our so called, free periods?"
Just then, Sandra came around the corner from the direction of the Braille and Engineering departments. "Are you still here? She remarked as she came towards us.

"Yeh..." Said Jim in a thoughtful frame of mind, and then, more assertively he asked Sandra why these changes had had to come about, and then he picked up on what I had said and asked her why the powers that be had done away with our free periods. We didn't get much satisfaction out of Sandra. She reiterated once more that these changes had little to do with her and advised us to just get on and do it. So, we did. First stop... Crafts department.

Josie wasn't there, and neither was Peter. "Of course. They don't know do they." Shouted Jim, much to the dismay of Sally and Gerry. Jim ignored the puzzled looks of our tutors as he left the Crafts department almost as soon as we had entered, so off he went in search of our two colleagues. Five minutes later he was back with Josie as well as Peter and we finally managed to try and settle down to doing some work. Or did we?

Royston's wicker basket that he had been making didn't get much more done to it, but this was mainly because no one had bothered to wet any cane. I strongly suspected that even if there had been a bundle of wet cane ready to hand, Royston's heart wasn't really up to the task. Neither was Josie or even Jim. And as for Peter? Whoever thought of sending him to the Crafts department couldn't have realised that Peter had little or no interest in craft-work of this nature, and besides. Even if Peter could have managed to find something of interest to do while he was in there with us, it would have been very difficult for him to achieve anything of a practical purpose because he seemed to be more troubled than usual that day with a loss of sensation in his fingertips, due no doubt to his diabetes. As for me? Well. Truth be known. I didn't get all that much done either. In fact, I didn't do anything. Full credits to Gerry for trying though. He picked up on the leathercrafts that we had been doing the week previous, and he even challenged me to come up with a project design for something made out of leather. He gave me one or two ideas, such as a leather belt, embossed, or tooled, as he called it, but I couldn't come up with enough enthusiasm. The only project I wanted to get stuck into was in the woodwork machinery shop a hundred yards or so away on the far side of the Manor. Jim was standing nearby, he was like I was, wondering what else to do, but Gerry soon managed to get Jim feeling a lot keener than me, and in the end they both left me to it and went off to the other side of the room. Full of renewed vigour, Jim had suddenly decided that he wanted to make himself a belt. I was left to, either sit there by myself or help Josie with another one of her stuffed felt animals.

It was a confusing first assessment session, one way or another, but this was only just the beginning. It was Josie who first sowed the idea in my mind when, just as I was getting her another handful of Kapok, she took it from me and said.

"Sure, I've just the thing for you to do Bob... Why don't you make your wife something out of leather? There must be something you could make her, a purse or...?"

I watched as Josie stared straight ahead and away as she held the shapeless black and white mass of felt, and then she pushed some more wadding in at the base of what was slowly taking on the shape of another stuffed penguin. I mulled over this idea of hers in my mind before I ventured to give a reply, which was.

311

"Nah... I dunna think so... I know little enough about leathercrafts Josie, and nothing at all about how to make a purse... I couldn't do anything like that, it's far too ambitious..."

Sally had overheard our conversation and so had a few others as well. Sally went on to tell us about a man in a small village called Saint Marychurch, who had an established business making leather goods, particularly leather purses and handbags.

"We take some of our more enthusiastic members there to see how it's done." Said Sally. "If you could only generate a tiny spark of interest Robert, it might be worthwhile to see if we can get you on our next outing... No? still no interest, hmm? can we not persuade you? oh, well."

She dropped her shoulders and walked away muttering words of.

"I don't know what to do with him. I honestly don't."

These words hung heavy on my mind. Whether I was supposed to hear them or not, I couldn't help but reflect on Sally's disappointment. It was almost as if she had just given up on me. I watched her talking to Gerry and one or two of the senior residents and then, a few seconds later, Gerry called out my name. Sally was pushing his wheelchair towards me, then she turned around abruptly and went to help someone who wanted, and deserved to be helped. I looked down to Gerry. He lifted up his sightless eyes as he spoke and said: -

"Robert. You may go, in fact I would like you to go right now... Your presence here is not desired. I have no time for time wasters... Just one word of warning. Don't enter any other department, or leave the grounds... Off you go, and the next time you come into this department, do try and bring a little more of the right attitude with you... That's it... I could say 'Get out of my sight' but I won't. I will say though that I am disappointed with you."

I looked around me. Those that could were staring at me, and it seemed as if those that couldn't were as well. Jim crossed the room and collared me before I got to the door.

"Where are you going to go?"

Stunned by this sudden development, all I could say was. "I, I don't know."

Without looking back, I closed the door on my way out and, for the want of something better to do, I walked down the short path and stepped up towards the French window entrance to the Lounge, but the door wouldn't open. I was still feeling dazed as I walked around by the front of the Manor saying something like. "Even the Manor doesn't want me."

I had nowhere else to go, so I made my way around to the front entrance, and on my way, I came across the kennels and looked in on the dogs. Two of them. One black and the other one golden. The black one was Dollar. Adrian's dog. I called out her name but she didn't respond, she just continued lying near the wire mesh with her head resting on her front paws. The other dog was eying me warily from a safe distance. I straightened up and went on my way. There was no one else about, just me, and my thoughts, and a cold, sunny day.

The situation was slightly different when I turned the corner to enter the Porch.

Here was another renegade, Ian. Ian without Jack Townley? was this possible? Well, he was here. I thought of ignoring him as he sat on what I knew from personal experience, was a damned cold stone slab of a seat. I noticed how he picked up his head at my approach and then discounted me. His head slumped down to his chest again and a finger went up to push the dark glasses back and he seemed to be dismissing me by ignoring me. As far as I knew, Ian didn't know who I was, but then... I was wrong.

"What are you messing about at Bob?" His voice echoed off the stone walls.

Feeling flabbergasted, twice in the space of five minutes. All I could do was to stand and look incredulously at Ian. He picked his head up again and the light caught the black of his glasses. Did I see a smile on his face? It was hard to tell. Incredibly, even though I still hadn't spoken a single word, Ian seemed to know that it was me. How? he sat there and grinned up at me.

"How did I know it was you Bob? By the sound of your footsteps of course, you can go inside if you want, or you can sit down, I wouldn't recommend sitting down though, it's bloody cold on the old arse."

I should have known... While I had been in Stepping Hill Hospital under the care of Mr Gupta. My head swathed in bandages and lying flat on my back. Waiting, just waiting for the love of my life, from one visit to the next, it hadn't taken me very long to recognise the sounds of Janet's footsteps when she came to visit. I found that I could soon tell if Janet was in the first batch of visitors or not and my heart would skip a beat in my excitement when I was

313

able to pick out Janet's footsteps even amongst the many others walking onto the ward.

Yes, I had done all of that myself when I had been blind, so why I found a similar situation so incredulous I don't know... What I did say, was: -

"You're amazing Ian, do you know that? Really amazing, you sit here and confidently announce that you know who I am... Sorry to barge in on you, I've just been expelled from the Crafts department, not taking enough interest. Anyroad if you don't mind me asking, what're you doing here without Jack?"

I soon achieved results from the flippant, almost nonchalant attitude I had quickly adopted on entering the Porch. I somehow knew that I could reach a kindred spirit by this method and Ian responded by saying.

"I don't like crafts either. I've been spending a lot of my time in the typing place that's where the future lies for me, I'm sure of it. Computers are the future Bob, computers and typing, they go together. I want to find a job up North, probably in Banking. North's where Jack lives. His accent and yours are a bit alike, what part did you say you come from Bob?"

"Cheshire."

Just then, the door opened on my left and a particularly noisy group of people came out from the interior of the Manor. In amongst this group was someone I vaguely recognised. It wasn't hard to focus attention on this stout young man, this tubby lad called Simon. Only that wasn't the name these three other male residents were calling him at that moment. One of them, he could see, pulled the group to a halt and announced loudly.

"Hey I know what we can call this atheist prat... We'll call him Jumbo... That's it, Jumbo... Yeh"

Someone else came through the old oak door to join the group, this was someone tall with ginger hair and a ginger beard. Terry, the Intake tutor, he quietened their rowdiness by saying.

"Alright, alright! Let's have a bit less noise, shall we? Give you a break from the routine as it's such a nice day and this is how you behave, oh, hello Bob, Bob, and Ian... Got nowhere to go the pair of you? Come on you four... Sort yourselves out and let's be getting on our way... I said we're going to America

314

Lodge. Not the United States of America, America Lodge is a part of the centre... Come on. Raymond, you take Simon. I want you to be his escort."

A few moments later, Terry and his newest Intake group had stepped outside beyond the curved stone archway of the Porch and were busy chatting away as they went down the drive, out of sight and away from us... It was quiet for a few seconds after that, until the main door opened once more and out came Jack Townley. He acknowledged my presence with a very sudden stern look on his face, and then he turned to address his charge and said.

"Well that's sorted ite then Ian... it's owe clear fer may an'they t'goo dine tine... Get thee arse off that cowd slab'n get thee cane undone."

Ian jumped to his command, but I knew, and Ian must have known, that Jack's sudden authoritarian tone of voice was directed at me and not him.

Jack turned around to look at me, but only when he was sure of Ian. The stern look on his face had been replaced by a slightly less severe look, then he thought to enlighten me by saying.

"I were in Sandra's office just nah when Sally phooned t'say as they'n just kicked Bob Weaver ite... Come on! Shape thesen Bob, tha's only two wicks left t'goo. Shape thesen?"

They stepped outside, beyond the curved stone arch entrance. I watched them go. Then I was alone... Not a soul about. Just me and the Manor. Me and this ancient building and I was at the entrance to this beguiling place, this building which had seen many a troubled soul pass through its portals. I took a deep breath and said. "They come and they go, and I'm just the likes of a tiny speck of sand in a seaside bucketful of sand... and if I'm not careful I'll end up leaving here in a worse state than when I arrived. Why am I doing this? Why can't I concentrate and get stuck into things? What's stopping me? If only I knew…if only I knew..."

Footsteps, I could hear footsteps, and they weren't Janet's footsteps, although; given these circumstances it would be good if they were. These were a woman's footsteps all the same and they seemed vaguely familiar. Then she came into view from around the corner to my left as I looked out, and she came to an abrupt halt when she saw me... This was Shirley. She had stopped so suddenly that the front of her coat opened and her long dark red skirt wafted out and then back again. She also had to adjust the glasses on her face and compose herself before saying. "Oh, it's... it's you... I wasn't expecting to see you here... What are you doing?"

"Nothing."

"Nothing? you must be doing something, you can't be doing nothing, I mean, nothing at all... Oh, but I am sorry I really must dash... I, I'm afraid I've erm, been rather naughty... I shouldn't really be here you see... I ought to be in the braille department... but Wendy is just 'so' busy... I, I didn't think she would notice my absence... I did try to talk to her, I really did. In the end I thought it best to just slip out... terrible to deceive her like that, her being blind and all... needs must though, please excuse me won't you Bob, only I have to go to my room and then get back."

Shirley was already reaching for the door latch and within a few seconds she had gone inside. I couldn't go inside. If Sandra was in there, as I had good reason to believe she was, then I didn't particularly relish an encounter with her, with the head of the Care Staff.

Considering that they should be in one of the many departments around the place, there were quite a few residents who were not, myself included. I had already encountered that week's new Intake, and Terry, and then Ian and Jack, then Shirley. And now, the blue minibus was pulling up outside and who should get out on the driver's side but Gillian Roberts. I didn't want her to see me and for me to have to explain. Too late though, she already had seen me.

I watched as she helped three blind women down from the back of the bus and she then proceeded to guide them towards the Porch entrance. Too late for me to retreat, in they came... Gillian glanced down on me with a reproachful look. She seemed to know that I had done something wrong, again. I was feeling like a schoolboy who had just played a silly prank and had been ordered to go and sit outside the Headmasters office. Without saying anything, I watched as Gillian held the door, guided the three ladies through and at the same time, without looking back at me, she asked me to stay where I was until she came back.

I immediately thought of going off up into the woods. Over to the arbour. Anywhere, just to get away from having a ticking off, or whatever, from Gillian.

When she came back after about two or three minutes, maybe five at the most. I couldn't help feeling a wave of relief that she didn't seem to be annoyed with me, like Gerry, and Jack, and, and myself.

Gillian's initial attitude was to just quietly sit down beside me and a long half minute or so passed before she spoke, calmly and soothingly.

"I have just been having a word with Sandra... you have been in trouble with Gerry. But more so with yourself; I fear. Am I right? You know, you really must do what your heart tells you to do."

With equal calm, I found myself saying. "If I did that, I'd be back home with my wife and children."

"No... I don't mean that and you know I don't... This has been coming for a long while... You are so nearly there. I've seen this so many times, but you are different. I am not quite sure what it is about you Robert..."

I don't know if she had been looking at me during this conversation, I do know where I was looking. I was looking at the joints in the stone flags beneath my feet and nowhere else... A rustling sound made me look up towards her as she stood over me, she then handed me a piece of paper and said.

"Read this. It is in large print so you should manage... I was going to give it to you this afternoon, yes, I know it is Tuesday but you at least are going to have me this afternoon anyway, whether you like it or not. Read it will you. I want you to read it."

I adjusted my glasses and read: -

"Ahead by Roger Mc Kuen.

Who brings home the torch, the winner or the loser? Is the beginning where the race starts, or is it the anticipated ending. Just another way of saying. Stop the clock, and let's begin again. Coming out ahead... Coming out ahead sometimes. I've yet to feel that I was the winner. Unless I raced myself and passed the mark I had set before... Otherwise... otherwise. I, I've felt... felt that competition was just that, a trophy match, a rally for a ribbon... Sorry I..."

Gillian took the paper from my hands and continued reciting the verse for me.

"A trophy match, a rally for a ribbon... I don't compete. I am lesser that no man and I have found no one better. I know all creatures, beings, people, to be unalike. How can I compete, win or lose a race, with someone, other than myself... Now Robert... You read the last part... go on."

Very reluctantly I took hold of the piece of paper and: -

"Being me is hard enough... but someone other... Never."

There was a long silence between us. The sun was shining and a gentle but cold breeze was blowing a few dead leaves about inside and outside the Porch. At last, I was the one who spoke and very quietly said.

"I must have been trying to do something like this last night. It was a load of rubbish though, made a mountain of rubbish paper and little else..."

"Aha! Perfect. Where? At the lodge? your room at the lodge? This is good, better than I could have hoped for in your case. The fact that you have at least and at last done something in the way of some prose."

I looked at her, but shut my mouth and looked away. Gillian carried on: -

"You must persevere, you must... You are so close... If only you knew, but you don't... Take my advice and please persevere. What you were doing last night you must finish. You will never get anywhere until you do."

We hadn't come into what might be called, physical contact in the five or more minutes that we had been there, but now, physical contact did occur, in the way of Gillian's hand reaching out to mine, as she softly but earnestly said: -

"Sandra has asked me to tell you not to go into Gordon's place today. Shall I go and see if you can have the rest of the day off so that you can go and do some writing like I suggested?"

"No."

"Well... why don't you just try and relax, take it easy for a while until you feel in the mood once more. What else have you got today discounting woodwork that is?"

"Typing."

318

"Well, what better opportunity could you ask for? Your relationship with Pauline is alright, isn't it?"

"Yes, fine... but I don't think I could do anything like you're suggesting in Pauline's place... it'll be too busy."

"Well, if it's quiet you need, then when you finish here at three o'clock, go and do it, go to your room at the lodge and just do it... I will not pester you into a mobility lesson or anything of the like... If you really have something inside you that you want to try and get down on paper you simply have got to write it down, all of it."

She got to her feet to leave me but just before she did, she gave a swish of her clothes and a slightly melodramatic turn of her body, then she pulled the collar of her long black coat across her mouth and with dark wide eyes, she looked down on me and said: -

"Write it all down... If the place should burn down all around you, you mustn't stop. Do it... Write it tonight. Tonight... Oh! one more thing... Here. I think this might now be appropriate."

She had already given me the paper we had both read out, now she passed me another piece of paper. I glanced at it and when I looked up, she was gone... and the ancient iron latch on that ancient old oak door rattled noisily. I looked back at the paper and read: -

"While mystery is a mainstay. The lack of knowledge on a chosen subject, needs the Miner's pick, the Mason's trowel and the Astronomers strict surveyor's gaze...Wow! is this deep or what?"

It worked though. I did a lot of wandering about in the woods up until lunchtime, and then I went with Josie, Jim and Peter over to the typing section and did my best in there... More than my best in fact, if that's possible. By heck Pauline wasn't half stunned by the time I had finished, and I reckon that electric typewriter very nearly blew a fuse. Come three o'clock, and a bewildered looking Pauline, and a few others left behind me, I went in search of Royston and took him back across to the Manor and there I explained that I had to go somewhere and off I went. Straight to America Lodge and my room.

CHAPTER TWENTY EIGHT

The sun had gone down and night was drawing in as I stood by my bedroom window looking out across the rooftops of the Lodge. I had come here with such a keen passion to complete what I had started the day before and inspired by what Gillian had said to me. I had been here for around about an hour. I looked away from the darkening scene outside back to the interior of my room, it was a similar scene to the night before, only not quite as badly littered with screwed up bits of paper.

On my arrival, I had enthusiastically set about procuring pen and paper and somewhere to sit and had written something, but not a lot... The enthusiasm was still there but the inspiration of it all evaded me and that was why I was standing by the window.

Just then there was a knock on my door, I ignored it at first but whoever it was seemed persistent and there were voices out there as well, when the voices and the knocking became louder, I relented and went to open the door to whoever was out there... I was not really in a good mood for being disturbed. Barry was there, along with Jim and another man, who I didn't know... I was about to ask what they wanted when the unknown dark-haired man of heavy features brushed past me muttering.

"I don't know why I let myself get caught up in all this... I used to be a television engineer I used to be one Barry, I told you I used to be one, come on let's get this done."

He then indicated for Jim and Barry to come with him. Barry shrugged his shoulders in passing and mentioned something about a television gone wrong downstairs. Jim noticed the half dozen or so screwed up pieces of paper on my bed and being nosy he went to pick them up. I wanted to take them off him but didn't, because the man with no name was standing on tip toe and pulling himself up onto my window sill. Frustration got the better of me and caused me to cry out.

"What're you doing?"

No reply, all I could do was to watch and wonder. I was baffled, a more unlikely person than this man would be hard to imagine, for him to be in my room trying to squeeze his large bulk through my tiny window. He did it though and then he went out of sight. After about half a minute the man came back to the open window at about the same time that Jim was reading the contents of one of the pieces of paper. I wasn't standing on ceremony and I wasn't about to be ridiculed, so I snatched the paper from his hands before he got beyond the first line and suggested that he should go and assist Barry to help the other man get back inside.

The man came back, feet first and when he was standing in my room once more, he looked at Barry and declared.

"There you are... That should do it, the aerial's pointing in the right direction now... Just in time too, another few minutes and it'd be too dark to see, beginning to drizzle a bit as well."

Barry was following the man out through the door when he turned to me and said, by way of an excuse for the intrusion. "Television engineer. Used to be one, lucky to have him around. I'm glad though, Spurs are playing tonight, in an hour or so. Come on Jim... Leave Bob alone we've intruded enough... Told you Bob's room was the best one to get at it from."

Barry and the unknown man left my room but Jim wouldn't go. He wanted to stay and find out what it was that I was doing. But how could I tell him when I wasn't all that sure what it was that I was doing?

Jim picked up on the wrong vein of my frustration and frustrated me even more by just being there. Eventually, he went and left me to the project, my project, the one that Gillian knew more of than I did. Gillian had somehow inspired me, but inspired me to do what? I had very little idea. I was getting nowhere fast, even before Jim and Barry and Mr Tubby stuck their noses in.

"Now what do I do?" I mumbled to myself.

A few minutes later I was downstairs approaching the Den. The sounds of many voices was a bit disconcerting to my goals, but why should I care... I wasn't about to go in the Den... I had decided to try something totally stupid... I was going to attempt to get the spirits of this place to help me to sort out my confused brain. I was going to go and open that typing room door and see what might happen... I did... nothing happened... Or did it?

There was a woman at the other end of the corridor. She was calling out my name and coming towards me... Sandra. What's the head of care staff doing here? what does she want with me, I wondered? Removing my hand from the brass doorknob and turning to my left to look at the old brown clock nearby I noticed the time of ten past five. I glanced into the Den. There were at least twenty residents in there, perhaps we should all be up at the Manor now, getting ready for the evening meal, but today was Tuesday, and we were all veterans... So, what did it matter if we weren't up at the Manor?

"Yes?" I said, when Sandra was standing in front of me.

"Were you about to go and do some typing? After what you did in Pauline's today? You do surprise me."

"No, I er...No."

"Would you come with me please. I was on my way home but I thought. No... I must have a word with you."

She took me to the Lounge, the one room in the Lodge I had avoided ever since I had had my possessions stolen many weeks since. I realised, as I went to sit down that I was about to sit in the same high-backed red chair that I had fallen asleep in all that time ago... Then I looked up at Sandra as she brought another chair over towards mine and sat down to face me... We were all alone, there was no one else to disturb us, and then she began.

"There's more stop start in you than I don't know what... You drag your feet one minute and then you break out and go like the wind the next. I'd like to know what it is with you? You astonished Pauline and upset Gerry and Sally today. All along you have been like this...You seem to have extremely good dexterity and yet. May I ask you a question? This concerns the severe head-aches you are prone to... Is this why you behave like you do? If it is so, why don't you let us help you... We might be able to arrange a specialist doctor to see you... We are here to help you know, and I do want to help you, we all do... Come on, I think I can tell by your subdued manner that something is wrong, what is it? tell me before it is too late... I mean, before, before you go home... Come along, say something."

"Specialists won't be able to help me."

I took a deep breath and continued. "Specialists back home told me the headaches are something I've just got to learn to live with, and I try to. They come and they go... Some days are worse than others. Sometimes I think as I don't belong here. And then there's other times as I think as I do. I sometimes think that bump on me head did more damage than I know of... I get so confused... There's so much going on and it's all jumbled up in my head."

322

"Then let us help you."

"You are helping me."

With this last statement, I got to my feet, thanked her for her concerns and left her sitting there. I don't know, even now, after all this time, if it was something Sandra had said, or whether it was something I had said. Or if it was all just circumstantial and that I was just ready, at long last to write, what I was about to write that evening.

The Den, I could hear was still noisy. There were people milling about in the dimly lit hall and at the bottom of the stairs. One or two were heading for the main door and white canes were already being unfolded. I didn't hang about, especially when I heard the door opening behind me. I went up the stairs. I heard Sandra say goodnight to someone, and carried on my way.

It must have been around two or three o'clock the following morning when I looked at the mess of paper on my bedroom carpet and then looked at the single sheet of paper in my hands...

CHAPTER TWENTY NINE

I had a restless sleep. I was worried about something. I woke up and it was dark, but then, this was the time of year for dark mornings. In that half-awake, half asleep stage when your mind is telling you one thing but the body is demanding a little longer in bed, it causes confliction which can be confusing, and it was. I reached for my glasses, wearily swung my feet out of bed and trod a paper strewn carpet to put on the light. Then I looked around the room and pondered on what I had been doing the night before.

"Did I actually do some writing or was it just a wonderful relief of a dream."

I bent down to pick up a piece of paper but this set my head thumping so I decided against it. Then I remembered, or thought I remembered that I had finished it, what I had been doing was done... Hold on... Where was it? I looked around the room for that single sheet of paper, the culmination of more than just one night's work... but I couldn't find it. I looked everywhere, with a thumping head I even looked under the bed. Nothing. Not a thing. Plenty of screwed up bits of paper, but that one single sheet of paper wouldn't be screwed up and lying on the floor... If I had really done what I thought I had done, it wouldn't be on the floor... My heart was pumping more than enough blood up into my head, or at least trying to... I didn't want gravity to increase the blood flow any more. No choice though, if I wanted to find out what I had done with that piece of paper, if I really had done it and it hadn't all been just a dream? No, I had to find it. I've done it and it's here somewhere?

A tiny light of inspiration came to the assistance of my troubled head. With bare feet which wouldn't even have shamed an elderly pupil of Sir Stanley Mathews, I dribbled all those screwed up bits of paper into a pile nearer to my bed... Having done this, I sat down on the bed and timidly bent down without lowering my head too much and began picking up the papers. Then I flattened them out on the top of my bed and only when I had done them all, did I realise that I hadn't done much more than I had the previous night.

Feeling more than a bit frustrated, I filled the tiny desk drawer while I muttered to myself. "Just a dream Bob... Wishful thinking... I've never written verse or poetry in my entire life... so what makes me think I can do something like that now? Rubbish scribbling's that's all it is."

I lay back on my pillow... Desperate thoughts were running rampant in my head... Maybe it's under the pillow? in the bed? in my trousers? my jacket pocket? I forced myself to look in all of these places, but to no avail... finally, I decided that I hadn't done anything, it was all a dream, a rather nice dream, but only that. In the dream I had found relief from pent up feelings by the writing. I lay back on the pillow once more and rested for a few minutes in the hope that the headache would subside, and the mystery piece of paper would magically reappear... I must have dozed.

When I woke up once more it was to a knocking on my door. A timid knocking, almost like a scraping scratchy sort of knocking. The light was still on and my glasses were still on my face, but as I looked over towards the window, I noticed that it was still dark out there... The timid tapping sound came to my ears once more. I went to the door not knowing what to expect. I should have, but I didn't expect to see Jim standing there, all sheepish and looking hurt. I could do without this.

"What is it Jim? what do you want?" He didn't answer, so I asked him again before I started to close the door, his foot went and blocked me though. I looked down. Then he spoke at last.

"You hurt me last night. I thought we were buddies, pals, friends. Why did you treat me like that in front of those two? What is this thing you're so secretive about?"

"Come in Jim. I'm sorry about last night. Come in and I'll tell you a story, better still, what time is it?"

"Five past six, why." Said Jim in a bemused voice.

"Come in." I said as I opened the door wider. "Come on while I get a change of clothes and then we'll go down and get a drink, and I'll tell you all about it."

It was an opportune moment that Jim should turn up like he did. I needed someone to talk to instead of myself all of the time, and now... Jim was here. He had wanted to know what I was doing for a long while, probably even before I knew what I was doing, but would he still be curious after I have unburdened myself on him... I would soon find out.

The Lodge was still sleeping as we made our way downstairs, and even Ruth or whoever was on care staff duty, was nowhere to be seen, or heard, and, thankfully, along with all the rest of the people at the Lodge, that's the way it stayed for the best part of the next glorious hour while I told Jim my story.

A brown plastic beaker of milk, a couple of tablets fizzing away in a yellow beaker and I drank them both while Jim got the bread and jam out and then put the kettle on for himself. A few more minutes while things settled down, and then I was about to begin.

I looked around me at the two-tone green of the walls surrounding us and then looked up at the two yellow orbs hanging from the ceiling. "No flashing lights, so far so good." I murmured, and then quickly explained for the sake of Jim's curious look. "I get them with the onset of a migraine, okay so far, I hope."

Jim came and sat opposite me, I finished off the sandwich and took a deep breath and more or less, word for word, this is what followed.

"Jim... I've been trying to write down how frustrated I've been feeling. You know, you must have heard me say that I'm expecting compensation for the accident that happened to me a few years ago. Eighty-one it happened, thirtieth of June... Ever since then I've been torn one way and then another... people back home, friends, family... family, except Janet. and her dad, but he's dead

325

now. I think it was Janet's dad dying that's brought things to this point... That and this place and the Manor as well... It's the compensation Jim... it's a dirty word as far as I'm concerned, but I need it, I need it for the sake of my family, for Janet and my two girls... I've been blind and I don't like it... I might go blind again someday and what do I do then? who's going to look after me and my family? Frank Pepper, he's a good guy that I know. He's the post office union rep, he's picked me up many a time when I've floundered, him and the other lads on the post have helped me a lot, but Frank's done most... Four times I went back on the Post and... and four times I failed... before the first time I had to go for a medical. Had loads of them, medical's... post office, dhss. First time back on the post I tried hard to convince them I was okay. I'd just spent over twelve-month convalescing. Seven months of that were spent doing nothing, wasn't allowed to in case things went wrong. Seven months of purgatory. Three operations and trying to get used to not seeing as well as I used to... They said then that I'd be alright, they said that I wouldn't have to work, wouldn't need to when I got the compen... I tried telling them that I wanted to work... I wanted to get back on the post... Alright, maybe my driving days were over, but I could still do a walking duty. I'd had a bit of a stiff knee because of the accident but that was getting better. Anyroad, got a chance to get back. first chance I had, beginning of August it was, nineteen eighty-two... a couple of weeks before, I managed to convince the post office medics that I could do it... Didn't reckon on trying to ride a bike though, none of us did. Couldn't see over me right shoulder... So, I walked... my knee and a bad head stopped me, two days I lasted. Then there was a second and a third time, third time was when the nights were drawing in... didn't reckon on the dark. Fourth time I lasted nearly a week... bad that were Jim, don't... rather not talk about it... then the welfare woman from the post office said as they were going to medically retire me... That were bad Jim... cried like a baby in my wife's arms... I'd lost me job... my job was the only thing apart from Janet as kept be going, thoughts of getting back on the Post... It was the only job I knew, the only one I wanted to know. The hardest part was when I had to hand me uniform back... that hurt... by heck that hurt Jim... I were lost for a while... they put me on the dole... Twelve months I did, a full twelve months... supposed to sign on every second week, which I did, and I went down in between as well... A woman at the job centre kept saying. Don't worry Mr Weaver, you just keep coming in to sign on. That's all you need to do. She didn't say they couldn't help me, or more to the point, wouldn't help me. No, they wouldn't come out with it and say as they couldn't help someone with a visual problem. That's what it was like though. Why else would I spend twelve full months that I did on the dole? and nothing to show at the end of it? Dole money only ran for twelve months... That ran out on first of July this year... we spent the next couple of months living on Janet's family allowance and my small pension from the post office and that's been going on the mortgage anyway. After the dole ran out and for a bit before that, I thought as I'd try and do something for myself... I've got me own lathe so I tried a bit of wood-turning... Did alright but the motor wasn't up to it... besides, I knew a couple of blokes who did woodturning and they only got enough out of it for a paying hobby. What chance did I have? I tried writing... Janet got me going on that. Used her typewriter, a portable one... wrote a story for me girls, all about some children and their father who was an archaeologist and an expedition to the Sahara desert and the Atlas mountains. Tomb of the Spider King I called it... I killed off their dog in the story... well, spiders did... but Carol and Paula came home from school that day and read what I'd typed and played heck with me... I had to rewrite half a dozen pages to put the dog back in again. It's in a drawer back home that story is... no one wants to read my story Jim... Then some bright spark came from Warrington and told me as I'd... wait for it... slipped through the net... Ian Allwood's his name... He's the one as got me to come down here... I know you know him Jim, don't say anything yet. Let me carry on, I want to tell someone, you, before this place wakes up, get it off me chest if I can... Anyroad... here I am... before I came here though a lot of folk started telling me not to try as hard as I had been doing... There's plenty as have been telling me that all along anyroad and compensation is at the heart of it all... Even Albert tried to tell me to lay it on like he was doing. His's a compensation claim as well you know... He's back home now putting in his claim. I'm still here, still worrying about mine... All I want to do is to find a job... If I can't find a job, or I can't end up actually doing a full-time job, then I'm going to have to rely on whatever compensation I can get for the accident so that I can support my own family in the way that I always have done... That's all I want Jim... All I want to do and that's the God's honest truth and some folk still think as I'm mad for wanting to get back to work... Work is all I know... I want to work... I need to work... I have to... work... This bloody compensation business is slowly driving me round the bend."

There were a few quiet moments and then it was Jim who spoke when he said.

"You know what this is don't you... This is just like Ian only not quite as bad as he was... You're coming through what he's been through, I've been through something like this as well, do you remember a few weeks ago when I kept on going out at all hours of the night and that time when Josie was worried and you were as well and then I walked in here, do you remember that? Well that was just me trying come to terms with my eyes problem. Listen Bob... I don't think I'm supposed to tell you this, but it's something Gill said the other day. Monday... yeh late Monday afternoon. When she sent you off and me and Royston went down to the lodge and back, she said then that you were going through a hard time coming to terms with something to do with your eyesight problems, but she didn't think it was your eyesight that was the problem in coming to terms. No! I didn't understand that either, took no more notice than that... Until now... So, so, it's your accident and the compensation you're so worried about... I can see what you mean, but put yourself in my shoes though and things would be different. I'm going blind through macular degeneration... I aren't getting any compensation for that am I? No, I wish I was, but I'm not... I agree with Albert. His was a genuine accident same as yours was... and you and him and everybody else ought to get what's coming to them and then some… You deserve compensation for what that other driver put you through, don't you think so? If you don't then you are crackers... If it was me, I'd go for every penny that that bastard's insurance company will pay out. Oh, they'll try and wangle a way out of it and no doubt they'll try to find out from this place, or from Ian Allwood but I wouldn't worry if I were you, I mean... well... Put it this way... Can you go back and do your job at the Post office? No... I know that and you've just confirmed it... It's your job that counts, whether you can do the job you did before the accident or not... If not and you can't then they've got to pay out, they've got to pay out anyway. Just because you're good with your hands doesn't mean you're good with your eyes does it? Your face is scarred and your eyes are crap compared to how they must have been before your accident. You'll get your compen, don't you worry... Listen, I've known you for a long while now and for most of that time you've kept me and most everyone else at arms-length… If all this, what you've just been telling me is the reason behind it all. Then I think it's time you stopped and concentrate on the real things, the real issues... I've seen you struggle; you think you're okay; you manage... but how long did it take you to accept using a cane? that was the hardest part for me I'll tell you. Took some doing for me to accept it, but I have and it's not as bad as I was thinking it might be. I know I came with one, came with a cane. Hey that's not bad is it... Anyroad, I only played about with it before I came here, just so as to keep me wife happy, show her that I was coping... but I wasn't, not underneath it all… I was just showing off... Same when I got here if you... Anyway... So what, I know I'm going blind, it'll take a few more years yet but eventually it'll happen, but then again, I might die before then anyway, so, why should I worry about it... Get on with life that's what I say. Enjoy it while you can, and stop pissing about worrying about something that might never happen."

"That's what I've been trying to do Jim. All along I've been trying to ignore the compensation. I've been telling myself that it isn't important, but then someone always comes along and tells me that it is important. Then you come and say your bit... Then there's this place... All I want to do is get back to normal. I know I can't but that's all I want."

328

"Wouldn't we all? Besides, I don't know what you're on about... If you were going down the same track as Albert you wouldn't have lasted this long. You can't do that sort of thing anyway, no more than I could... Don't you think they know when someone's laying it on? Don't you think they'll find out one way or another? Of course they will and they do. Anyroad. I reckon you knackered any chance of you doing anything like that, just as soon as you did that thing way back in what was it? second week here, in engineering? when you did what you did on that big mechanical saw? And what about yesterday in Pauline's? phew... None of us could keep up with you there. This's what you should be doing, you can do it so do it. Do what you can. If I were you, I'd just concentrate on getting the best out of this place... It sounds like this place is waking up. Here comes the first one... Thought so... Morning Ted."

Jim leaned across the table towards me and whispered.

"Ted was in the cutlery trade. You think you've got problems, just take a close look at his face if you get a chance. I was just saying Ted... Just telling Bob here that you worked in the cutlery trade... Ted was telling me all about it last night Bob... Going finish off telling me what you were saying last night Ted?"

There was very little in the way of a reaction from the man, so Jim tried again.

"Cutlery trade? before your accident? had a bad accident didn't you Ted?"

"Yes." Came the simple response from this tired looking man. Jim didn't want to talk to me about this man with him being there, so he was trying his best to include him in with our conversation, and I think that Jim was also still trying to make a point with me as well, little did he know that he already had and what he had said to me and what I had been able to say to him had already settled my mind a great deal. Even if the writing had only been done in my dreams, for that was the way it seemed to me. If it had been just a dream, it didn't seem to matter all that much now... I would have liked to have had the physical side of it in my hands, feeling and reading what I thought I had put to paper would have been a great comfort to me, but, even so, I was beginning to relax now. I was beginning to see the light at the end of the tunnel, the remaining pieces of the jigsaw were fitting into place. This place... the Manor and me, we were beginning to win the battle.

I had seen Ted here at the Lodge and also up at the Manor, but not close up. I didn't even know his name until Jim mentioned it. Ted was just one of the many blind people at the Lodge and at the Manor. I looked up just then as something fell on the floor with a clatter. Ted was over by the cooker inside

329

the inglenook fireplace. He had his back to me and he seemed to be feeling for, or trying to do something. I had seen the blind of this place coping before now, I had helped where and when I could, now it seemed as if one more could do with some help, I didn't yet know by how much or why this man deserved special treatment. But he did, by heck he did... I was in for quite a shock.

Naturally, on seeing him flounder, I got to my feet in order to go around the tables to help him, but I wasn't quick enough. Jim was already on that side of the room anyway and he went to Ted's assistance. He brought Ted to the table to sit him opposite me and then Jim went back to sort out what had happened.

Ted hadn't protested at Jim's intervention as some might have done, and I got the distinct impression that he wanted someone to help him to make a hot drink. For the short while it took Jim to put the kettle on, I had taken these few moments as an opportunity to look across at Ted and at his features. He seemed to have both his eyes, but it also seemed that they were useless for seeing with. One, his right eye, appeared to be fixed and looking inward towards his nose, while his left eye, mostly looked upwards, but then it would drift around towards the other eye and then back upwards again, his left eye was the only one that moved. He had a good head of fair, mousy coloured hair, uncombed as yet, and there was an indentation in the skin of his forehead. His nose was disfigured and there was a heavy crescent shaped scar down the left-hand side of his face, all the way from his temple to his chin. His hands were on the table in front of him and he was fidgeting. As if the close-up appearance of this poor unfortunate man hadn't been enough to see. Now, I noticed something else... The thumb and first finger on his right hand were missing. No wonder he was allowing Jim to make him a drink... I think it must have been around the same moment in time that the kettle came to the boil that Ted opened his mouth with an obvious painful action and then, uttered the words.

"Seen enough have you?"

Jim was quick. "Don't be like that Ted, Bob's sitting across from you, he's in a bad way as well. Do you remember me telling you? Postman? head injuries? I've told you, oh yes, I have... Anyroad... sounds like some others are getting up and about time too... come on you pair, get this inside you... Here, sorry Ted, left hand left hand... sorry, not too hot is it?"

A lot of the other residents began to fill the inside of the Den to capacity, the three of us remained where we were and we had just about managed to get some form of dialogue going between us. That was, until Josie came on the scene, and Jim went to help her and her female colleague a few minutes later. I

330

watched Jim and then lost him for a moment behind a rather noisy group of four men who had just come in. Then I saw Jim helping Josie to a chair at the tables and he went on to do the same for the young woman I knew only by the name of Christine. I watched for a few seconds longer and was intrigued to see if Christine would start to do what I had seen her do previously. She was blind and had been from birth. She had a nice, almost permanent smile on her face, and short curly hair, she was about eighteen years old and about just over half that number in weight. Around ten stone, and yes, she began rocking backwards and forward in her chair. This didn't seem to bother anyone, least of all Josie, who was sitting beside her. And just then, Christine began to rattle off some sayings, just like she had done a few evenings previous, only these were new ones that I hadn't heard before.

"Josie. Did you know that men marry women hoping that they won't change but women marry men hoping that they will… And. The most important thing in communication is to hear what isn't being said… A good idea is salvation by imagination… Behind every good man there is an even better woman…"

Just then another of the residents cried out. "Where's the sodding butter?"

Christine smiled and then said. "Bad temper is its own scourge; it hurts the individual more than the victim."

"That may be so Christine, but where the sodding, bloody, hell, is the butter? oh I give up."

"The only real failure in life is to give up looking for the butter."

"It's here." Said Jim. "For goodness sake calm down before you burst a blood vessel."

Jim stayed at the already crowded worktop. I tried to ignore the pushing and shoving going on around us as I waited for him to come back.

When he did come at last, he sat beside me and leaned across the table in order to hear and be heard in order to carry on the conversation with Ted. Christine had gone silent now but she carried on rocking backwards and forwards.

"Well said Christine…" Said Jim. "Now then Ted, what was it you were saying last night? something about a theory over when and how we buy cutlery?"

The way he began moving his mouth and jaw made it seem as if Ted's face would crack wide open, but Jim seemed to ignore this and encouraged him further into talking.

"Johnstone's. Viner's own them now, but it was Johnstone's when I started. Some bright spark from Viner's told us that the future would be bright for us, all because almost everyone buys at least two sets of cutlery in their lifetime. Cocky bastard. Never liked him…"

He stopped to have a drink and this was where Jim took over.

"Most everyone does buy at least two sets of cutlery in their lifetime… apart from wedding gifts and the like… and I suppose that's where the first set comes from anyway, and do you know why we buy two sets Bob? It's because half the first set always gets lost when you have your children and they use them out in the garden and so on, and they get thrown out with the rubbish… potato peelings and the like…"

"Is this Postman across from me Jim?"

"Yes why?"

Ted didn't answer Jim. He looked across at me and said. "I got all this in an accident at work… grinding wheel accident. Blinded. Not their fault, mine… How did you get yours?"

As I have said, I hardly knew this man, but I could tell by the way that he gingerly started to massage his jaw, that Ted had talked too much, so, in spite of the seemingly many eager ears in the immediate vicinity, I threw caution to the wind and explained, in a very much condensed manner, just how I had come to be blinded and how I had got some sight back. I even went on to, again, in a brief way, to say how I had come to start here. Ted seemed to be listening intently despite the growing volume of people coming in to the Den and the accompanying increase in the noise levels.

When I had finished, I chanced to look around me and slowly realised that I didn't feel as awkward as I had expected to be, or had been on many occasions in the past. Jim was smiling… What did I do? what did I say? Why was he smiling at me? I watched as Jim got to his feet and stood over me and said.

"Come on Bob… come on, let's get out of here."

We were standing at the base of the stairs. Jim was about to go over towards the door leading on to Josie's room and I was just turning to go up the stairs, when he stopped me and said. "That writing? All them notes? do you think you really did do something last night or not? I mean, can you remember anything of it?"

I was feeling just as puzzled as I turned back and thoughtfully answered.

"I don't know Jim... I know it started with 'If.'"

"Bloody Rudyard Kipling that is. If you can keep your head when all about you are losing theirs and blaming it on you... Come on!! I mean to say... don't tell me you've written something like that Bob... Oh, now, that's, that's I don't know what. I'll tell you what though. I'll just go in here and see if Josie needs any help, she was damned quick to get out from the den... I'll just see... You go upstairs I'll follow you in a couple of minutes, we've got about a quarter of an hour before we have to be heading for the Manor... Go on up, I'll soon be with you, who knows, we might be able to piece something together from all those bits of paper that you've been doing. Go on get going."

True to his word, Jim came and knocked on my bedroom door only about a minute or two after I had arrived there, and between us we rummaged through the contents of the drawer and straightened out all the bits of paper and gathered up all the others as well. Then we stood there and we hardly knew where to begin... We had to be quick, time was running out and we would have to get going. Jim picked up a few sheets of paper and looked through them and put them down one at a time on top of the bed. "Nothing here." He declared a minute later, and then. "You haven't really written anything proper, have you? Most of this is just bits and pieces, none of it's anything like... Hey, hold on, what's this? Here we are, listen to this bit... If a man... Hey, you were right, it does start with, If. There's two or three lines here, this makes a bit of sense... Listen... If a man must hold hard with good hands to the reins... That's it! That's it... This has to be the start, but... Reins, reins? what does reins mean? As in horse reins did you mean? Hey come on Bob... You have written something here, listen here's another bit on this paper. The coach full of people he must take with him... Here's another bit, at the bottom. It goes... They will all forsake him... just for the sake of a shilling... Shilling? Compen link there... Hey Bob, I think you may have something here. Hey, this is 'Not' bad, not bad at all, here's another bit... It goes... Too long's he stopped too long has he strained with his hands on the reins... reins, there it is again. Oh, you must have done something here Bob... This is no dream. You've done

333

something here, you must have? Where is it though? what have you done with the finished piece? God! don't just stand there, don't you realise what this means? Sorry... I don't either... I'm getting carried away a bit here aren't I? getting just a bit too excited. Hey, but Bob... I mean way-hey... Bob... if you could only find it. Or, or do it... Write it all down I mean, wouldn't that be great? Hey! I'd better go... Josie will be needing me to help her get up to the Manor... I am sorry Bob... Are you coming?"

"No Jim. You go. I'm even more confused now."

The bedroom door opened, Jim went out, the door closed... I sat on my bed in a daze. Idly, I picked one of the sheets of paper up in my hand and glanced at it and read it... I didn't know what to do... Slowly, very slowly, I looked around the room... My gaze fell on the wardrobe. Something about the wardrobe was pulling me. Confused thoughts came into my head and then notched up a gear and ran rampant, racing through my mind. "No, not the suitcase. I would have remembered putting it in the suitcase..."

I got to my feet, slowly, full of trepidation and anxious not to be disappointed I went across the room and opened the wardrobe door, and lifted out my case. But I didn't open it... I didn't need to...

As I stood in front of the wardrobe, I just happened to look upwards. A flush of excitement came over me and it came on so hard and sudden, and painful, that I felt as if I had been thumped in the stomach. The adrenaline surged into my veins as I saw the white edge of a piece of paper sticking out from the top of the wardrobe, where the door had concealed it, until now. Slowly, I reached up with my right hand, while I dropped the suitcase back down inside the wardrobe with my left hand... The wardrobe door must have closed itself... I don't remember doing it... All I do remember, was standing there with a piece of paper in my hand. It wasn't typed, it was all in longhand and it was all there. A tear ran down my cheek. I couldn't see to read what I had written, I had to calm my racing heart, sit down, wipe my eyes and....

If a man must hold hard with good hands to the reins
and sit back and do not a thing,
while his mind is in turmoil with ideas and plans
and the horses are stamping and straining.

A journey lies ahead, to life's bitter end,
but no fear has this man of the journey.
Unsure he may be of the road and the rogues
but to get under way he's determined.

Too long has he halted, too long has he strained
with both of his hands to the reins.
He yearns to be free of the torment inside him
and get up and tackle the ride.

The Coach full of people he will take safely
with him, his Wife, his Family and his Friends.
All will forsake him if he climbs down to leave
them, just for the sake of a shilling.

There is fear in his heart, that before he
can start on this varied and difficult journey,
that before he can do what this man has to do
his heart... and his hands... will be shattered.

Bob Weaver 28/11/84

"Yes... It's true alright... Thank you God...thanks."

Rather hastily I realised that l would now have to get a move on, I hadn't had a wash or a shave, and by now most if not all the Lodge residents would be on their way up to the Manor, this thought was confirmed and highlighted even more as I walked along the deserted corridor towards the top of the stairs.

I had only gone about a third of the way up Middle Lincombe Road when a car pulled up beside me. Tim Dunce was the only person I knew who drove a bright yellow car. I welcomed his invite and got in.

We passed the tail end of the last of the residents to leave America Lodge just before we went through the gates to the Manor, so l wasn't late after all. Tim, shrewd psychologist that he was could not put a title to the contentment in me that must have shown while I had been in his car, and perhaps, just perhaps, it might also have shown in the more confident manner that I had set out on that walk up to the Manor that morning. I didn't tell Tim what I had done. After all? what was it but some verse, and one heck of a load off my mind.

CHAPTER THIRTY

There was a bit of a fuss going on at my table in the dining room that morning, and it was all centred around Adrian. He didn't look any the worse for his foolhardy experience, for it turned out that he had been reported missing soon after the lads who shared his room had woken up that morning. There had been a bit of a panic apparently, but they had found him, without too much trouble. Still in his pyjamas and dressing gown, around the back of the main porch, trying to get to his dog inside the kennels. How he got there, unaided, and undetected, remains a mystery. There was one more bit of sadness about it all though, and this came about when I was just forcing the last of the rubbery egg down my throat. Adrian had finished, well, he hadn't really started on his breakfast, when he spoke and said, to no one in particular. "I, I was having a bad dream. D, d Dollar, Dollar was dead, I had, I had to find out... I'm sorry."

Laurie said. "You've already said that mon, now calm ye doon, calm ye doon."

I did my bit as well, but that was all it was, a bit. It was going to take a lot more than this to really ease Adrian's mind over his beloved animal.

A minute or two later, Graham Sutton got to his feet to make the morning announcements. He spouted the usual things, like; "Will those who are terminating this week please see Sandra as soon as possible." Then Graham went on to talk about the outings arranged for the remainder of that week. He didn't, much to my surprise, mention the old perennial problem which was to do with the Gents toilets. He did mention something concerning Adrian though, and when his name was mentioned I just happened to be looking at Adrian and the look of surprised amazement on his face was a picture in itself. Graham was reminding us that the Care Staff, as dedicated as they were, couldn't do everything and be everywhere, and could those that can see, please help those who can't. Or as Graham himself put it.

"... so, in light of what I have just said about our young friend Adrian, can I ask that all of you RVs help the staff and keep an eye on your fellow residents, the totals amongst us."

Christopher said something just then which took my mind back to that very first day, when I had come to 'sample' this place. I had commented then about the peculiar descriptive used at the Manor. I had queried the use of the title, Terminating. Now, an age later. Christopher was questioning the use of the descriptive RVs. Laurie saved me the bother.

"RV, means those with residual vision mon... Will you noo let me pass, ah've a place t'goo... You'rre looking a might differrent the morning Bob. Come into some money have ye?"

I looked up, surprised, but quick enough to smile and answer.

"No Laurie... something better than money, something a whole lot better."

Gerry and Sally were already there when we arrived. One look at me and Sally turned to speak to Gerry. I should have gone in there with more of a real idea of what I wanted to do, if I was going to stand any chance of staying in there and not risk being thrown out again. I would have to think, and quickly. I went straight up to them. No use beating about the bush... Anyway, the result was, that I found myself making a tooled leather belt, under the guidance of a wheelchair bound, blind, master craftsman.

I don't think I overdid my new found enthusiasm. At least, I hope I didn't... I left the crafts department tutors a little bit bemused though, having actually made, and wearing a new belt in my trousers.

337

Our group were entering the Manor Lounge via the French windows, but I decided to make my way towards the arbour for a chance to reflect on what I had just achieved, I really wanted to be on my own but didn't mind in the slightest when both Jim and Royston followed my impulsive initiative and tagged on behind. Royston wanted a cigarette and quickly lit one up, and Jim wanted to find out a bit more about this. "Intriguing newcomer, this late arrival at the Manor." As he put it.

We three were soon sitting on the white bench within that secluded part of the Manor gardens, but two others must have had the same idea. In they came at the one and only entrance. Jack Townley and Ian. It was their footsteps on the gravel path which prompted me and Jim to go quiet as we looked in that direction and then heard Jack call out.

"What at they thray doin'in'ere? Thowt as I'd funt a place t'ave a natter an'what does way find?"

"Hey-up Jack who's in'ere anyroad." Said Ian in a curiously twisted dialect, to which I couldn't help myself but respond, in a light-hearted way, by saying.

"I reckon there's going t'be one Mum and Dad as'll hardly know their son when he gets back home... if he goes home."

"I anna, aren't, not going home, I'm not am I Jack?"

There was a thinly disguised, defeated tone to Jack's voice, to which Ian took not the slightest notice of, when Jack responded after a bit more prompting, and said.

"Ay inner gooin back wom, ay's comin wi'me come Frydee... Dunna know what th'bloody 'ell ay's gooin do... Ah just 'ope's ay knows what ay's doin'... 'cause I dunna... Anyrood, come thee on lad let's layve'em to it."

"Just a minute Jack... you've been telling me for a while now to... 'shape up. I think as I'ave, a bit. Royston can't hear us, so I'll tell him later on... but I was about to read something to Jim, it inna much, but it's a start, it's summat as I did last night, down at the lodge, it inna much as I say, but to me it's one hell of a load off me mind. Will you stay and listen Jack? and Ian if you want to."

"Aye." said Jack.

"Aye." said Ian.

"Get on with it then." Said Jim.

"Right… It's something I wrote last night, don't know how I did it but I did, so here goes… If a man must hold hard with good hands to the reins, and sit back and do not a thing, while his mind is in turmoil with ideas and plans and the horses are stamping and straining… A journey lies ahead to life's bitter end but no fear has this man of the journey, unsure he may be of the road and the rogues, but to get under way he's determined… Too long has he halted, too long has he strained, with both of his hands to the reins, he yearns to be free of the torment inside him and get up and tackle the ride… The Coach full of people he will take safely with him, his wife, his family and his friends, all will forsake him if he climbs down to leave them, just for the sake of a shilling… There is fear in his heart, that before he can start, on this varied and difficult journey, that before he can do, what this man has to do, his heart and his hands will be shattered… Rubbish or what?"

"He's got a compen claim Jack."

"Aye Jim. Ah knows… This wunna get th'compen fer thee Rob, but if it's peace of mind tha wants… well, thas got it wi'that."

With that last remark, Jack and Ian got to their feet, then disappeared out of sight and we were left with the diminishing sounds of footsteps crunching on gravel. The time it had taken us to get to this place and the few minutes we had actually been sitting there must already have added up to the length of time it would have taken for us to have our daily dose of bromide and a biscuit and then get ready for the next assessment lesson. Jim seemed to know this as well because he turned to me just then and said: -

"Well? Can I take it that you found what you were looking for?"

"Yes, Jim and thanks."

"What for?"

"For spurring me on."

"Time we were making tracks Bob, tell me more in a bit, come on Royston."

Gordon was a bit subdued in his attitude towards me, but pleasant enough in his welcoming us into his domain. Jim was at the polishing stage of his jewellery box and off he went, without any prompting, towards the opaque plastic screen. Royston was nearing the final stages of sanding his table. Gordon and I helped him uncover it and lift it out from beneath the bench. Everyone else went about their own tasks and because I was still interested in having a good look at Royston's work and missed what Gordon was saying.

"... little interest, I might have known... Here we go."

"No, we don't." I said, as quickly and as inoffensively as I could. I then apologised and walked off towards the door leading on and around to the machine shop.

Just as I was about to start, something caught my eye and it pleased me no end. There, on the bed of the lathe near to the spindle, awaiting the next workpiece, mine or the next man's, was a bright, shiny, brass washer.

I got to work, and apart from a slight interruption when Gordon came into see how I was getting on, I was left on my own to do my own thing.

I had plenty of time to finish the bowl, even though I had to stop and search for another piece of beeswax when the small piece I had found had been used up.

Only when I was satisfied, did I stop. And then, with a ridiculously easy pull, I removed the bowl and faceplate from the spindle of the lathe, and carried them still attached, through to the main workshop to show Gordon and see if he could find any fault with my work. Which he did, he had to... but I didn't mind. That bowl was good enough for me, and most men. Gordon didn't say anymore on the subject, he just went off to his office, carrying my work with him. I thought that would be the last I would see of my mahogany bowl. If it wasn't good enough for Gordon, it wasn't good enough for anybody or to go on display. Never mind... I had enjoyed making it.

Sid was nearby and asked me what I thought of the chessboard that he was making. He held it up and then offered it to me across the bench. I wasn't even going to pretend that I was an expert on judging the quality of Sid's project, never mind Gordon's tutorial skills in helping him to get this far. But even so... I had to say that I thought his chessboard was very good. Sid was in a happy mood which made me quick to leave the scene before he could do his party trick with his false eye, and made my way down to the bottom end of the shop to see how Royston was doing.

I could tell straight away that Royston was finding it a bit difficult to meet the extremely exacting standards of smoothness required before lacquering could begin. He hadn't yet reached the 'flour-paper' stage of sanding and I doubted if he would before the end of that session, but this was good as it happened. Far better to do the final sanding and the first of the lacquering within a short space of time and on the same day. I tried to ease his frustration by way of telling him this, but to show willing and talk in sign language wasn't easy to accomplish. So, having tried, I picked up a sheet of fine sandpaper and got on with helping him with the tedious but necessary job of sanding his table top.

Twenty minutes later, his table still wasn't finished but the session was over, time for lunch. I was tired and exhausted. The strain of the day and especially the night before, was all beginning to tell on me. I needed to find somewhere quiet, but first of all, lunch.

After lunch I was in the Lounge looking for a bit of quiet. The bay window area seemed the most inviting, there was a high-backed chair conveniently in the right position, facing the window, with its back to the room so I didn't delay in claiming that chair. One of the windows of the bay was partly open which let in a faint, welcoming breeze to dilute the slightly smoky air, perfect, and despite the many voices around me, I soon nodded off. Only to be rudely awakened by a tall, and agitated, man of silence. I looked up and was instantly concerned to try and ease whatever it was that was causing Royston's anxiety.

Royston had that, lost schoolboy look, on his face, and I could tell that he was worried. "Come on Bob, get your brain in gear." I mumbled to myself as I got to my feet. Then I remembered. "Typing... I've got typing and you've got Remedial's me old friend." No time to lose, I indicated for him to come with me and we set off up the length of the, now empty room, through the French window and on over to the Commerce building.

Royston didn't seem to mind when I left him at the door to the Remedials department, I was of an anxious mind though as I made my way further along the corridor towards the typing department, I was muttering to myself.

"I wonder what Pauline is going to have to say about me being late?"

This was where an unwelcome change of venue and a bit of confusion came about. I had no sooner knocked on the door and entered Pauline's domain when she gave me a curious smile and said: -

"You're supposed to be in with Wendy aren't you."

"I don't know, am I? I thought I wasn't due there until three o'clock."

"You are now... It seems you have another appointment at three o'clock. Don't ask me where that is to be, I don't know. I asked Royston to tell you to go straight to the braille department, go on."

Back down the corridor I went. Deserted now, that corridor was... I could hear the sounds of machinery coming from the Engineering department straight ahead, but there was no one in sight. I knocked on the door of the Braille room on my left, then took a deep breath, and held it. Sure enough, a thick cloud of smoke greeted me... I announced who I was and Wendy popped her head around the door and removed the cigarette from her mouth just long enough to say.

"About time too Robert, come in come in, I won't ask why you did not turn up yesterday, come in, are you in?"

I was in alright. The door closed behind me as I looked around the misty interior, at least four more people were smoking in that room... I had to breath out, I had no choice. I was imagining how sore my eyes and lungs were going to be if I had to endure this for any length of time. 'Find out what she wants and then get out of here' I thought to myself, so I asked her. I stood there in front of this attractive woman, if it wasn't for the inevitable fag in her mouth, and I asked her what it was she wanted me for. I was trying to limit my intake of air, trying not to breath too deeply, but this was having an opposite effect on me. There seemed to be very little oxygen in that room. It gave me some further cause for concern when Wendy invited me to go and sit down.

"Somewhere, and I'll come and find you in a few minutes."

Sid was there, about half way down the room, on the window side and he was one of those who were smoking, I had never seen him with a cigarette in his mouth before, not even on that Sunday a few weeks previous, when he and Royston and myself had gone on the day outing to Plymouth. I felt like commenting on this, but I didn't. Instead, I cut a swathe through the swirling grey mist and went and sat at the only available space beside a thin featured man. And I never did find out what his name was... The opportunity just didn't happen, not even there in that smoke-filled room. And I dropped myself in it straight away... All I said, by way of conversation, was: -

"How do... reminds me of something does this... I wonder what Sir Walter Raleigh would think of all this smoke if he could come back."

"What smoke". I can't see any smoke." Said the blind man as I went to sit beside him. I watched him finger a watch on his wrist and a small metallic voice said. "One fifteen" Then the man reached into his pocket and drew out a packet of cigarettes and a lighter. Dismayed, I looked at the book on the table top in front of him, the book without any writing in it.

Wendy wanted to test me, she wanted to find out how far I had got with the Braille system. Not all that far in reality, but far enough to seemingly satisfy her. By that stage in the three-month course, I had got about as far as halfway through the small book of contractions which she had given me a week or so earlier. I felt really great when she said at last, that I could go if I wanted to.

Go! I could hardly get out of the room fast enough... I had spent a good three-quarters of an hour in that room, eating tobacco smoke, the last twenty minutes of which I had had the presence of Wendy standing beside me as I ran my fingers over those dammed raised up dots and did my level best to translate Braille into the spoken word. Wendy didn't say it was good, or bad. She lit another cigarette and stood there pensive while she made up her mind about me. Then she said I could go.

Where was I supposed to be going at three o'clock? I didn't really know or care. I was near the door and the way out when Wendy called out.

"Oh Robert. I almost forgot to tell you. After the tea-break you must wait in the main hall... Gillian wants to see you there."

Over at the Manor there were two members of staff hovering about outside the care staff office and one pleasant lady in a light blue overall who was busy with a cloth on the stair rails. Apart from these three there was no one else in the main hall. A bathroom was what I needed, splash a bit of water on my face. The closest bathroom I knew of was on the first floor. Neither of the two care staff ladies challenged me as I went to climb the wide staircase and the cleaning lady started to move out of my way before realising that she didn't need to, I smiled to her and carried on up the stairs to the landing and went around the deserted balcony towards the fire door and my old stamping grounds.

When I came back out onto the balcony, I was feeling very much refreshed. There was still that acrid taste at the back of my throat though. Still... Not to worry, I had decided to let nature clear that problem, there was still time before tea-break, for me to get down the stairs and outside for a bit of fresh invigorating sea air. But...

I was near the top of the stairs when a door banged and a figure came out onto the balcony to my left, this was followed by the door banging once more and the first figure was joined by a second, more familiar figure. Terry's ginger hair and beard were not hard to place. I could hear my old Intake tutor remonstrating now, and from the sound of things it seemed that he was beginning to lose his patience, if he hadn't done so already. Nothing to do with me, I decided. With these glasses I need to look where I am going. I went down the first step towards the oblong table and the deserted hall at the bottom of the stairs.

"Robert..." I looked up. Terry called again. "Robert... will you take this young man down with you and look after him for a few minutes?"

This wasn't a request; it was an order. Terry really was annoyed. Reluctantly I backtracked. As I got closer, I heard some of the choicest of bad language coming from this young man, then Terry tried once more to calm the situation before he turned to me and said: -

"Here Robert. Simon, shut up, now listen... Listen to me! Oh, God give me strength..." "

"He isn't here..."

"Simon... Will you pleeease be quiet. Robert, Bob, I don't know why I am doing this? Do you think you could take him off my hands for at least a couple of minutes, just, just, take him downstairs and, and stay with him while I find a solution, I shall not be long so just take him down with you."

I reached out in the classical manner, so as to guide Simon's hand towards my arm and then we could get on our way. I didn't say anything, I think this was partly because I didn't particularly want him to start on me... I should be so lucky! He did start on me. The moment he felt my hand on his arm he tried to back away and shouted. "Get your hands off and leave me alone."

This lad didn't back away very far. Terry was behind and pushed him towards me. "Thanks Terry." I said as I gripped Simon's arm and headed for the stairs.

I was worried... It suddenly occurred to me that he could fall down the stairs in the angry mood this lad was in and I might end up falling down there with him. He was still resisting me and we were very near the top of the stairs when I chanced to look over my left shoulder to see where Terry was... He wasn't. There was only the sound of the Intake room door closing.

"Bloody marvellous." I said to myself as much as to Simon... Then I stopped at the top of the stairs and said. "Hey! Bloody well giveover... Stop it! we're at the top of the stairs now and you'll have us both cartwheeling down t'th' bottom if you aren't careful."

What did I say? I was stunned, momentarily stunned. Simon had instantly grabbed my upper arm at the sound of my voice and had gone deathly quiet. He was now standing perfectly calm and still and he seemed to be waiting for instructions. Incredible. I could hardly believe it... I stepped forward and went down one step ahead of him and he followed me, we did this, very slowly and deliberately on each and every one of those wide steps, all the way down to the bottom and Simon was the very essence of good behaviour, he was marvellous this was fantastic. Nothing at all to worry about.

When we stepped out from the bottom stair and arrived at the oblong table two paces further forward, I steered Simon's hand towards the yellow pine top while I looked up once more towards the balcony and was just in time to witness a figure leaning over the rail, this figure spoke and said: -

"Oh, you've landed, good." And then he disappeared, and left me to utter those words again.

"Thanks Terry." My words echoed around the otherwise deserted main hall. I turned back to Simon. This was good. We hadn't had any mishap after all... Had I made a friend here? I must have. He was still calm, as I thought, but there was an odd expression on his face. He might have been a bit worried about coming down the stairs with a stranger... I'll keep the momentum going here. I've made a breakthrough; I might even have begun to make a new friend. This was great, I was full of myself. But not for long. I started to say something but, Simon was quicker.

"Well... What are you waiting for? You can piss off now, I don't need you, I don't need you or anyone."

With an instantly deflated ego, I retaliated by saying. "Two of you aggressive idiots in just over two months is more than enough for me thank you very much... Anyway, here comes Terry so I'll leave you to it... A lad like you could do with some ruddy tranquillisers I'm off... All yours Terry."

I didn't see Sandra, head of care staff, until I nearly bumped into her. She was just inside the Lounge, nearest the door and she seemed to be waiting for someone, but not me. I wondered if she had just seen what had gone on between me and young Simon, but if she had been observing us, she didn't let on.

There was a sudden noise. The residents were coming in through the French windows at the other end of the room, I was too late for that bit of fresh air, so I just stood there and waited. Sandra seemed to pick out the person she was waiting for, I watched while she went over to a tall man, a blind man in a bright green pullover and then they came back and past me and on out into the main hall. This left me pondering on what to do... go and get a bit of fresh air after all, or go for a cup of bro, cup of tea. I didn't need much persuading... The residents in the Lounge went one way as I went in the other direction and gently closed the French window on my way out.

I came back into the Manor by the front entrance and this situation was almost the opposite to what had happened ten minutes or so earlier; the residents were now coming out as I was going in and feeling satisfyingly refreshed by the salty sea air.

I sat on the bench nearest the Mobility office door and waited as instructed... I even had the cane, folded, but minus the strip of Velcro, as it had been since the night out at the Palmer's home. The cane was the first thing Gillian looked at when she came down the stairs, she then looked wide-eyed at me and said: -

"Well?"

"Yes... I have done it. Thanks for encouraging me the way that you did."

"My pleasure... Where is it then?"

"Here, I've only the one though, just that."

Gillian took the piece of paper from me, then quietly sat down on the bench beside me and read in silence, before saying. "Oh, my!"

346

"Is it alright?"

"Let me put it this way... You 'have' used the miner's pick, and 'the mason's trowel'... And the Astronomers strict surveyors gaze... and more... here you are, I want a copy please, asap. Come on now, we have a place to go to."

She gave me the warmest smile and said no more.

About halfway between the Manor and the Lodge, Gillian stopped to pick up two more passengers on their way into Torquay. They were pleasant enough, Samantha and Denise were, but they were preoccupied with more important things than to bother to talk to me all that much. They were glad of the lift though and a few minutes later, the two inseparables were getting out of the back of the minibus where we had stopped down by the harbour. Gillian said something, and then, to the sounds of tearing Velcro, two canes unfolded. As she helped Denise down, Samantha called back and said: - "Yes, it's fine so far, very much better than the black elastic, thank you Gill, we'll make own way back, see you Bob, bye."

Saint Marychurch was where we ended up and even as I was climbing down from the back of the parked mini-bus I still had no idea what was going on. Gillian was free with her knowledge of where we were, but not where we were going, not yet, I think she wanted it to be a surprise, and it was.

The buildings were white, we were on an upward incline, the road was narrow, twisting and cobbled, and crowded. Such was the street we turned into within a couple of minutes of leaving the mini-bus. Fortunately, at least for me, there was sufficient street and shop lighting to save me the bother of using the cane, which was probably just as well, because there didn't seem enough room to use one anyway. Gillian seemed more intent on getting to where we were going, she was also directly in front of me, all I had to do was to follow in the footsteps of this dark, secretive figure. There were, as I have already mentioned, a great many people around us and I soon realised that most of them were tourists. Gillian made sure that I was still with her and then she turned to the left off the street and down a tiny alley, beneath the low arch of a tunnel and then we came out onto a very small, unevenly cobbled yard. The entire area was well lit by the glow of yellow lamps which made the white pebbledash walls surrounding us take on a different hue and reflected off the tiny windows.

347

The sky above was dark and getting darker. There was a smell of leather in the confined space of the yard where we were standing and there was a small crowd of people coming out of a low doorway that Gillian seemed to be interested in the most. She waited patiently, I had little option other than to do the same. Another small crowd, of tourists, I supposed, were coming through the archway towards us. Gillian tugged the sleeve of my coat and I followed, her in to the most fantastic leathercrafts shop I have ever seen in my life.

Leather-goods were everywhere, all sorts, shapes and sizes of handbags and belts and purses. Most of the handbags hung from their straps from the low, dark ceiling. The walls were of a dingy much faded white and to paint them whiter would have been complete and utter sacrilege. It was bad enough that the only thing spoiling the illusion of antiquity was the white fluorescent light at the far end of the shop where a figure was busy hammering away at something. There were more leather-goods in a pile on a table top nearby. There was no daylight now to come in through the tiny four paned windows; but there was a group of people trying to get in. Gill smiled at me in the dim interior and told me to shut my mouth and try and watch where I was going, while she led the way towards the leather craftsman working away at the bench beneath the white alien fluorescent light.

Gillian introduced us; she obviously knew the man, and I quickly forgot his name for I was far too intrigued with my surroundings and had to ask him again. I did remember his handshake though, now that was something; Strong and dirty, and just like his craft; Adam Fernyhough's skin was hard and tough as leather. If it hadn't been for the white fluorescent light above us, I could have easily stepped back in time, to a period where I could have belonged. This was good and I liked it, and I wanted to be a part of it but, how could I? Painful reality was about to step in and taint this mirage more than the white light and the noisy questioning tourists could do, up until now.

"This... is... brilliant." I said slowly as I tried to take in my surroundings once more. "But, why have you brought me here?"

"I was going to anyway," Said Gill. "but Gerry and Sally both thought, as you showed such an interest this morning, in the Crafts department, they suggested that I should bring you here sooner rather than later, in order to stimulate your latent emotive tendencies a little further, I agreed, and judging by the response, we were correct in our assumptions. Right. Now then... are you wearing the belt you made this morning, oh, good, let us see it then."

I removed my new belt and in between serving his customers, Mr Fernyhough took my pitiful and pathetic work and studied it embarrassingly carefully, embarrassing for me that is. I tried to move out of criticisms way and edged away from the immediate area of the white light. Then he spoke to me as well as the man who had just bought his wife a new handbag.

"I hope you like it sir. If you don't, bring it back and I'll exchange or refund, I can't say fairer than that now can I, thank you… Now then, this is what I call showing ability… part of the pattern isn't quite deep enough and other parts may be just a shade too deep, consistency, real plodding consistency, 'and' practice, lots and lots of practice. If you like leathercrafts I would say stick with it and you might get there. You like my set up? I bet you'd love the same. Where are you from?"

"Congleton, Cheshire. Up in'th'north."

"Up in, the, North." The man mocked, none too seriously. I was beginning to like this man, this man and all that he stood for. I stood back and watched as he served a few more of his customers, and then looked around for Gillian. She was over by the window. The customer that the craftsman was serving started to ask some questions, so I moved even further away and eventually ended up standing beside Gillian to ask about the object that seemed to intrigue her so much. It was a handbag, but no ordinary handbag… Nothing in that fantastic place could ever hope to be ordinary, except perhaps for the disillusionment of that one bright light, but of course, I also needed that light in order to see most of what I had seen in that ageless setting, and the man needed that light as well, and if ever I ventured into his world, his craft, I would be needing good lighting too, but, this wasn't meant to be. I nearly became a Leather-craftsman, but not quite, but of course, I digress. The facts were, that I became so engrossed by what I experienced that day in that craft workshop, that I desired nothing better than to be a leather worker.

All too soon, it was time to go. I wanted to go back there at some time in the near future, I wanted to…. I should have made some sort of arrangement there and then, this man may have taken me on as an apprentice for those last two weeks of my stay at the Manor, and then again, he might not have. Would he really, willingly take on a partially sighted man? however keen and dedicated this man might be? I didn't have the chance to find out. Soon, all too soon, I was on my way back to the Manor in the back of the bus and Gillian was in the driving seat.

That was my one and only visit to the Leathercraft workshop in Saint Marychurch. Gillian, and the others back at the Manor, they all seemed to think that I was sufficiently intrigued by what I had done that morning in the Manor Crafts building, followed by this visit to Adam Fernyhough's, to start me on the path to being some sort of a dedicated leather craftsman. But I already was a dedicated craftsman of almost anything to do with wood. It was an illusion for anyone to think otherwise, the simple fact of me not achieving more of what I knew I could achieve in Gordon's woodworking department, was that it just wasn't challenging enough for me. I didn't want someone like Gordon cutting my mitres for me on a jewellery box, or cutting the veneer squares for a chessboard, or even to the extent of showing me how to turn a wooden bowl. I could, albeit with a struggle, due to my now poor eyesight, do all of these things myself. Still, for all of that, I was in a very buoyant mood when we arrived back at the Manor with about twenty minutes to go before evening mealtime.

CHAPTER THIRTY ONE

It didn't take Jim all that long to find me. I was sitting in the main hall, enthusiastically digesting the experience of the outing to Saint Marychurch when in he came with a lot of other residents, Josie included. The first thing he wanted to know was; Where had I been. So, I told him, and explained to him, and Josie and whoever else might be interested, that I was planning to be a leather worker when I get back home. Jim seemed to want to put me down a bit when he commented on the fact that I had only made a leather belt so far, so how could that decide my future for me? So, then I had to go into more detail about the place I had been to with Gillian. This didn't seem to impress Jim either, but then, what would, I didn't know. Just then Jim changed tack, so to speak and remembered a joke he wanted to tell me. Jim's jokes always seemed to attract an audience, this was no exception, the main hall was almost full to capacity and all of us were waiting for the evening mealtime gong to sound. Jim was where he liked to be, at the centre of attention when he began with: -

"There was this sales rep, and he was lost in the Country and his car had broken down. He stood there with the bonnet up wondering what to do when he notices a horse coming towards him across a field. The man looked back at his car and the horse leaned over the fence and said "It's your distributor,

350

you've got damp in your distributor." The man was dumbfounded. A talking horse, he couldn't believe it... Anyway, he has a look, and sure enough, he dries it out and puts it back again and the car starts up first time... Anyway, by this time it's going dark. The man shouts after the horse as it's gone back across the field, he shouts... "Thanks," and then curses himself for thinking that a horse could talk to him like that. Anyroad, a bit further down the road he sees a bed and breakfast sign, and he pulls up in a farmyard... He gets out and asks if there's a bed for the night and he's told yes. Then the man says to the farmer's wife. 'My car broke down and do you know what? You'll think I'm crazy, but I swear, a horse came up and told me what he thought the problem was with my car.' 'Was it a white horse?' says the farmer's wife. 'Why yes.' says the man... 'Oh, that's alright then, because the black one knows nothing at all about cars.' "Good eh?"

Yes, well, it wasn't bad, even I had to admit that much, and so did a lot of others nearby, judging by the jostling and the handclapping. A minute or so later the much-awaited gong sounded and we all began to file through into the dining room.

It was a quiet early part to the evening following our evening meal. I was sitting in the main hall again and all the benches seemed to be occupied. There was the usual crew of people, these included Samantha and Denise. Then there was Peter and Josie and of course Jim. Royston and Sid put in an appearance and they went out together after about twenty minutes for an early evening drinking session. We were to meet up with them a bit later on. I noticed Adrian sitting nervously on a bench nearest to the main entrance, unfortunately for him, this was also directly opposite the care staff office and it was a shame that the care staff ladies, of this particular night shift, soon took offence at the presence of Dollar, Adrian's guide dog, inside the building. Jim and I went across to Adrian's assistance, he looked as if he was in need of some, but, this red haired, still wet behind the ears Care Assistant was hell bent on asserting her authority and demanded unconditionally that the dog would have to go... So, go it did... along with a lot of us as well...

Jim took charge straight away and luck was with us that night, at least, in one direction it was, as I shall explain.

We had no sooner agreed on a visit to the Hole-in-the-Wall pub when in walked Terry, our Intake tutor and he offered to drop us of at our destination on his way home.

351

It turned out to be a good outing that night did. Most of us were free of our inhibitions and just got on with having a good time and it was particularly amazing for those who were feeling of an observant nature, just how Adrian was beginning to relax. There was concern from some of our group as to how much beer Adrian could take, but we needn't have worried, Adrian knew when enough was enough. He savoured his second pint for the remainder of the evening, with his friends around him and his dog at his feet. This was all that Adrian desired. Even Denise and Samantha seemed to be relaxed and carefree.

It was about an hour after we had arrived at the Hole-in-the-Wall that Royston and Sid came in.

It was a crowded corner of the pub that night that was filled with Manor residents and, inevitably... Jim took centre stage once more and decided to tell us another of his jokes. This one was still on the same theme of his earlier joke back at the Manor. It was a joke about horses, just a shade on the crude side, but even the ever-prudent Josie didn't seem to take offence as Jim managed to get a few more people around him and then he began.

"There was this guy, owned some really big stables... Hey! What's this? thanks', that will wet the whistle nicely, now, where was I? Oh yes, this man owned a stable, he comes back one day with a Zebra and he puts it in with his other horses, but she's curious is this Zebra and says to one of the horses. What do you do? The horse turns and says. I'm a show jumper, if I do well, my master gets a trophy and I get a good bale of hay. The Zebra turns to another horse and asks it. What do you do? Oh, I'm a flat racer, if I do well, my master gets a trophy and I get a big bag of oats... Anyroad, this Zebra turns to another horse and says... And what do you do? I'm a stud, says the other horse... And what does a stud do? asks the Zebra... You just take those pyjamas off sweetheart and I'll show you says the horse... Good eh? I knew you'd like it... Oh I'm too good for this place, I am just too good."

Things started to quieten down a bit shortly after Jim had told us his latest joke. I didn't dare have too much to drink myself, because of having to get back to the Manor. This was the one thing on my mind that was really bothering me. How were we going to get back? The closer to closing time it got, the more anxious I became. Not for me, for the others! because now, as each day went by, I was getting better and better at coping with the dark, but I knew only too well that I would be worse than useless to any of my blind colleagues if we should end up walking back to the Manor. There had already been a discussion on the fact that we may all have to walk back and this didn't seem to bother a lot of them, but one more slow look around me only served to confirm the fact in my mind that there were a lot more blind in our group than there were the not so blind and I reflected once more on a thought which had occurred to me more than an hour since, which was... Out there, in the dark, to which section, of this group, did I belong? I tried encouraging Jim to put his resourceful abilities to the test once more and asked him if he would have one more try at getting someone at the Manor to come and pick us all up. While he was gone, Sid did his gruesome party trick with his false eye for a few of us and the locals. Fortunately, it was too noisy in that pub for anyone to hear him tapping his eye with a coin. The locals soon scattered and most of our group couldn't care or else couldn't see what Sid was doing, and then he surprised us when he came up with a suggestion, which was.

"Why don't we send the worst of the totals back in a taxi? They'll have to pay for themselves of course, but then the rest of us can make our own way back."

We all knew that taxis were out of the question because, where would we find three or four taxis at this time of the night? but one taxi, one taxi to take... As Sid put it... to take the worst of the totals back to the Manor. Well, yes, why not? I was still hopeful of an alternative that would get us all safely back to the Manor though, but I was still feeling reasonably cheerful over Sid's solution. Until Jim came back from the phone and said that they were busy at the Manor and we would just have to make our own way back. That's when my mood really began to change... I looked around. Fourteen people and only five who can see. Jim, Samantha, Royston, Sid, and me, and once we got out there on the streets of Torquay, they could discount me and Royston. That would leave Samantha, Sid and Jim. I could take care of myself, but could these three? Three people who hadn't got a decent pair of eyes between them? Could they take care of all the rest? No way.

"Jim?" I said "Sid's just made a suggestion... No, it's not a rude one, shut up... This is serious... Phone for a taxi to take some of the worst of us back to the Manor and the rest of us will walk it. Go on, give it a try, if you can get more than one taxi so much the better."

Well... He did try, he even came back and took some of my ten pence pieces but, our suspicions were confirmed, Jim still couldn't find more than one taxi to come for us and that would have to do. While they were deciding who should go and who shouldn't, I sat and fingered the cane in my hands and silently considered whether I should leave this group and just make my way back to the Lodge on my own. I almost managed to convince myself that I would be absolutely no use to any of these good folks once we were out there in the dark, so why shouldn't I just get up and go on my own?

353

I got to my feet and looked around me, but I couldn't leave them. Not Josie, Samantha, Denise, Royston, Adrian, and Peter. I didn't know the others well enough. I wasn't going to be much use in helping any of them, but I couldn't just leave them to it. No. Adrian had his dog, but was Adrian experienced enough yet? and did Dollar know her way back to the Manor? No... I couldn't be that irresponsible. It wasn't up to me to get them back to the Manor, but it was up to us, those of us who were classified as RVs, those of us with residual vision who had a moral duty to help those who were completely blind.

Two things happened in quick succession within the next minute or so. One was the bell ringing for last orders and the other, was a man who poked his head around the door and shouted out loud. "Taxi for the blind centre."

It was dark just outside the pub. Jim was in charge, and for this I felt glad, at least it saved me the responsibility of trying to sort something out. A few minutes later, just as the regulars were coming out of the pub behind us, I was standing with the cane in my hands as I watched the receding red tail lights of the taxi disappear down the slope in front of us and on into the darkness of night. We waited while most of the locals left the scene and then Jim took charge once more and he and Sid took the lead for the journey back.

I was aware that Samantha had taken charge of both Denise and Adrian, while Jim and Sid took on the job of escorting some of the others. I was instructed to bring up the rear... This was something I felt I could do. All I had to do was to follow the group in front. They would clear a way for me to follow almost blindly behind and if anyone should falter or fall by the wayside, I should be able to detect and do something about it.

And so it was, that this ramshackle group of blind and partially sighted people set of on that mile or so, incident strewn journey back to the Manor.

We had barely turned out from the street away from the pub down by the harbour when things started to go wrong. The first casualty was Royston. I didn't know who was acting as escort for him, I just presumed that Sid would do it and he may have, but not for long. My tall and anxious friend seemed to be causing some consternation up ahead and before I knew it, he had worked his way down through the group and was now beside me, trying to make sure who I was. I assured him as best I could, only to be rewarded by a hefty slap, intended to connect in the middle of my back no doubt, but which caught my shoulder instead. I put this down to the fact that Royston was frightened and now, I was too... Not only because of the 'Greeting' which nearly knocked me off my feet, but because it seemed that I now had the responsibility of looking after him. The group had barely begun to move off once more when someone else developed a problem, Samantha. Dollar yelped a cry of pain... Samantha immediately grew concerned and began apologising. Adrian almost went to pieces... Peter cried out. "Mind me!" The group seemed to stretch out ahead and then it shrank as Jim and Sid's voices came from out of the darkness as they made their way back towards us... There was a bit of a delay in getting going once more, but eventually we did. Adrian proved to be the hardest one to settle, which was perfectly understandable. He had enough of his wits about him though to demand that someone else should help him instead of Samantha. I was only just beginning to get an idea of how bad Samantha's good eye was when it came to her coping with the darkness of night. Anyway, we began moving once more and nothing untoward happened for at least five minutes. Royston was no good out here in the dark, I was little different. We were both using our canes, but because of the size difference between me and this gentle giant, any synchronisation between the two of us was nigh-on impossible. He was holding onto my upper right arm, while I was trying to be careful where I was walking. I hadn't wanted this, I didn't want this, this extra responsibility, I had enough troubles of my own, but Royston's nervousness was transmitted, hopefully, only one way, through this physical contact and I could tell that he was worried... Very worried. I then went on and did a daft thing, without first telling him. I decided that we were too close to the rear of the group ahead of us, in as much as there was a distinct likelihood that we might end up clipping a few ankles, so I purposely dropped back a little. Royston detected this change and with a sudden extra burst of anxiety he tried to urge me on. I knew that if we stopped long enough for me to sign to him it would only make matters worse than they were, so, against my better judgement we moved on a pace and caught up once more. Then the group stopped for a moment and we did clip a few ankles with our canes. There were a few choice words bandied about and above all this I could hear Jim suggesting that Adrian and Dollar should go in front with him because he felt she was getting too confused by all the legs around her. Then we got underway again, but this time I had quickly taken advantage of the situation to sign to Royston and tell him the reason why we ought to drop back a little. He was still full of anxiety but I think he understood my reasoning.

We had been on the uphill climb away from the harbour for about ten or fifteen minutes and all seemed to be going well for the whole group when Jim decided to make light of the situation and tell us another of his jokes, and me being me, frightened and getting more and more so, I can't even recall what the joke was about. There was something of a dry laughter response but the group as a whole kept on moving towards our goal, to which I felt gratified at least.

A few vehicles passed us going in both directions and at the top end of Higher Woodfield Road two cars came past and they must have been heading for the Manor because Jim shouted out. "Bloody miserable sods, they could have stopped to give some of us a lift, mean buggers." A few minor mishaps and a good five minutes later, we were at a stop outside the gates to America Lodge. But then... Jim and Sid seemed perfectly happy to carry on and escort the Manor residents that quarter of a mile further to their beds. Royston was ready for his bed and I was more than ready for mine, but that didn't matter. It didn't matter one bit. Royston clung even tighter to my arm and when Jim and a few more people started to move away from the street light, Royston urged me to go also... I did try to tell him but by now I think he didn't really care for me or anything else, he was going to get back to the Manor at any cost and nothing else mattered. Not even me having to go with him and then to come all the way back here to the Lodge... Briefly, I heard Josie's voice and one or two others as they made their way up the drive towards the Lodge entrance and then I was forced to move on.

I wouldn't have done what I did further that night for anyone else. The only consolation was that we were at least on fairly familiar territory now and that did make things a lot easier for us.

Like a moth to a candle, I was forcing a bit of a faster pace as we crossed the yard towards the pool of yellow light over the front Porch entrance to the Manor. Roughly about twenty seconds earlier, my confused brain had registered something that I had completely forgotten about, I had not phoned home. Janet would be wondering what had happened to me. Just to complicate things even more, we were locked out. Jim was already banging on the old oak door inside the Manor Porch.

The impatient red head was about to try our patience to the limit... When she eventually came and slid the heavy iron bolts back and the door creaked noisily open, she stood there and started to reprimand us... Jim was having none of it... He brushed past her, saying: -

"This lad and his dog are both coming in while me and Sid and Bob get these others inside. Unless of course, you do it for us... Didn't think so, come on you lot let's get you inside."

The main hall lights were off and the dim night lights were on. I thought Jim was going to brighten the place up but he was taking Adrian in the direction of the light switches in order to sit him down at one of the wooden benches, while he and Sid guided the rest of our group towards the stairs... The red-haired young woman kept her distance and just stood in the pool of light coming from the care staff office open doorway. She wasn't saying anything further and neither was her companion who had just come to join her. Just then Samantha came back to me and offered to take Royston off my hands. I admit, I did have a bit of difficulty in that half-light, but when Samantha moved into the light from the office on my right and that light momentarily lit up her face, there was no mistaking the anguish and the suffering she had gone through on the journey of that night. Could she see my face? and if she could, what would she be thinking? It didn't matter, we were back, safe and sound inside the warm and comfortable confines of the Manor.

I moved forward and ended up beside the oblong table while I watched the shadows ascending the wide staircase. Then I remembered Janet again and hurriedly made my way towards the darker area of the alcove and the phone.

Finding the phone? Finding the right holes to put my finger in on the dial? In the dark? After what we had all just gone through? No problem!

When I had finished talking to Janet and come out from the dark recess of the alcove to where it was just a shade lighter, there were voices down at the far end of the hall where the care staff office light still shone, the voices were male voices and easily recognisable. There was neither sight nor sound of the two women on duty. Jim and Adrian were on their feet and about to move away when I got there... Jim seemed momentarily startled, but then he had every reason to be when I discovered what these two were planning to do.

"Oh, Hiya Bob, we're going to the den, Sid's there brewing up for us... Ready Adrian? come on Dollar, come on girl let's go before them two sticklers for the rules book come back down. Ready? good, come on then, this way."

The Den was sacrosanct, well, at least it would be up to around midnight when the cleaning staff come in, until then, none of the staff were likely to disturb us. This didn't prevent Adrian from fretting about Dollar though. Jim had seemingly done the right thing in prolonging the time that these two could have together, but one look up at the clock over the ever-open door, told me that we only had another ten minutes to go. I was tired, my mind began to wander. I knew that Adrian was going to make a good master, the way that he looked after his guide dog spoke volumes of caring, for both now and in the future. When we had arrived in the den and Sid had placed four piping hot mugs on the table and we had all sat down, Sid had made the mistake of offering Dollar a biscuit. Almost immediately, Adrian had become alarmed and demanded that she was not to given biscuits, or anything...

"Sh, shee she will get too fat... she mustn't, you mustn't d do that..." He stammered. I could see that Sid was a bit put out by Adrian's reaction. I could have just sat there and reminisced to myself and just let them talk, or to sulk as in the case of Sid, but all of this reminded me of my childhood and of a dog that was spoiled and I wanted to share these thoughts, so I did.

"I had a dog once... She wasn't really my dog, she was the family dog, but I looked after her the most... Or thought I did...My stepfather worked for a local haulage firm, Horace Pointon's. He used to drive a big green flat backed Foden lorry... One day he came back from a trip to Wales and he had a long-haired Welsh Corgi with him... matted fur she had and it was a mess. We called her Cindy, my mum had to cut a lot of her fur out and then we set too and combed her... She used to run around in circles if anyone knocked on the door... I used to enjoy taking her for walks after school... I used to like being on me own with this dog... Mum wouldn't dream of getting Cindy canned food, all she ever had was scraps off the table and us six kids didn't leave much in the way of scraps I can tell you, but somehow, she got more than was good for her... I used to think as I was doing her a favour, because most weeks when I'd come home from school, I'd spend some of me Saturday Market job earnings, I'd go and buy some broken biscuits as Woolworths used to sell in big shiny tins... I think they were something like a tanner for a pound weight of broken biscuits, that's about two and a half pence of modern money, anyroad, I'd eat some of them biscuits on me way home, and my sister's and my brother would try and grab the rest, but I always managed to save some for Cindy and I'd feed her, sometimes I'd even manage to save her a bit of meat as well. We were always brought up to leave the meat on our plates until last, because our Aunty Madge would sometimes just walk in our house without knocking and me mum mustn't have wanted her to see our plates without meat on them... aye, meat had to be eaten last... by heck... I'd have got a right belting if me mum had ever seen me feeding Cindy any meat... Anyroad, as for Cindy, somehow, she got more food than was good for her and she ended up getting a bit fat... Then she got a sort of asthma, she had a lot of trouble breathing... she couldn't walk all that far but I didn't know no different then. I still used to feed her the wrong sorts of food... Anyway... we couldn't afford the vets or owt like that... Trouble was... If I'd taken her for longer walks in the first place then I might have done her more good, but I suppose I was no different than any other kid... In winter, especially in winter, all I used to do for walks was to go round the block and up a gully to where I could hide out of mum and dads arguing. But then, one day, mum said as Cindy would have to be put down and she'd get dad to do it when he gets home... he knew what he was doing, he'd come home late every night...   There was no way he were going to do it... Cindy was getting a lot worse and so me and me brother

358

decided to do it... we decided to take her down to the old cattle market behind the Town hall, there was an old black and white building there with a corrugated tin roof, this was where they put animals down, not like now with their drugs, they did it with electricity in them days... me and me brother watched this man put Cindy in a box that had a tin tray in the bottom with some water in it, then he put a clip on one of her ears and closed the door and flicked a switch... there was a hell of a yelp but she was soon gone... bloody cruellest way of killing anything I thought, then and now... Anyway, we went home and me stepdad was having his tea and he started crying... Me and me brother weren't crying though... I think we must have been too shocked to cry. I said as I'd never do anything like that again... What? what is it Jim? Why are you looking at me like that?"

Jim indicated for me to look at Adrian... He was crying, he was just sitting there, quietly sobbing and the tears were gently running down his cheeks. Jim leaned over to me and whispered.

"It's alright, he's okay, just leave him alone, do him good to get some of the stress out of his system... Anyroad, if I'm not too much mistaken, here comes the night shift cleaners...   Come on Adrian, give us a hand here Sid, will you? Let's go and get this lad's dog settled down for the night and then we'll get him settled down as well. It's alright Bob... You stay here till we get back... you can wash the cups while we're gone."

They must have passed the cleaners in the corridor... Two women and one man came in and they seemed a bit put out by my presence, but I stayed long enough to wash our cups and then I hung around for a good four or five minutes near the open door, before deciding that I really was in the way there in the Den. So, I left the place but I didn't turn right out in the corridor, for this was the turn which would have taken me through to the main hall. Suddenly, I didn't want to go that way...

The Porch light was the only light... The large bulk of the Manor over on my left-hand side was invisible and as dark to me as the night sky above. I knew the Manor was there, just the same as I knew that if I could see well enough there would be an ivy encrusted wall on my right, and if I could look up and behind me, and see, I would see the window of the room I had spent that very first night, here at the Manor. Tomorrow, or rather, today, today was now Thursday the 29th of November... It was a dry night, and a gentle sea breeze was blowing... It was so dark that I couldn't see a hand in front of my face and yet, as I stood there contemplating on what I had achieved that day.

The verse... The leather belt... Such a long day. More was to come though. I still had the return journey to make, a journey in the darkness of night, with nothing to help me except a few pieces of metal covered in white plastic... And this is the object which can give me so much confidence and help me to get back to America Lodge?

Feeling for the Velcro strap on the cane, I gave it a tug and let the sections fall away, the elastic between each of the four sections pulled the cane in line and I finished off by tapping the sections together on the hard ground at my feet, and then. Not without some trepidation, I set off on the final leg of the journey on that important and very eventful day.